Experiment and Evaluation in Information Retrieval Models

Experiment and Evaluation in Information Retrieval Models

K. Latha

CRC Press
Taylor & Francis Group
Boca Raton London New York

CRC Press is an imprint of the
Taylor & Francis Group, an **informa** business

A CHAPMAN & HALL BOOK

CRC Press
Taylor & Francis Group
6000 Broken Sound Parkway NW, Suite 300
Boca Raton, FL 33487-2742

© 2018 by Taylor & Francis Group, LLC
CRC Press is an imprint of Taylor & Francis Group, an Informa business

No claim to original U.S. Government works

Printed on acid-free paper

International Standard Book Number-13: 978-1-138-03231-6 (Hardback)

Library of Congress Cataloging–in–Publication Data

Names: Latha, K., author.
Title: Experiment and evaluation in information retrieval models / K. Latha.
Description: Boca Raton : CRC Press, Taylor & Francis Group, [2016] |
Includes bibliographical references and index.
Identifiers: LCCN 2017004392| ISBN 9781138032316 (hardback : alk. paper) |
ISBN 9781315392622 (ebook) | ISBN 9781315392615 (ebook) |
ISBN 9781315392608 (ebook) | ISBN 9781315392592 (ebook)
Subjects: LCSH: Data mining. | Querying (Computer science) | Big data. |
Information retrieval--Experiments. | Information storage and retrieval
systems--Evaluation.
Classification: LCC QA76.9.D343 L384 2016 | DDC 006.3/12--dc23
LC record available at https://lccn.loc.gov/2017004392

Visit the Taylor & Francis Web site at
http://www.taylorandfrancis.com

and the CRC Press Web site at
http://www.crcpress.com

Contents

Preface... xiii
Acknowledgments xvii
About the Author xix

Section I   Foundations

1 Introduction 3
   1.1   Motivation 3
         1.1.1   Web Search...4
   1.2   Evolutionary Search and IR..4
   1.3   Applications of IR 5
         1.3.1   Other Search Applications..7

Section II   Preliminaries

2 Preliminaries 11
   2.1   Information Retrieval 11
   2.2   Information Retrieval versus Data Retrieval 12
   2.3   Information Retrieval (IR) versus Information Extraction (IE)............................ 12
   2.4   Components of an Information Retrieval System... 13
         2.4.1   Document Processing... 13
         2.4.2   Query Processing.. 15
         2.4.3   Retrieval and Feedback Generation Component 15

3 Contextual and Conceptual Information Retrieval 19
   3.1   Context Search... 19
         3.1.1   Need for Contextual Search 19
         3.1.2   Graphical Representation of Context-Based Search 19
         3.1.3   Architecture of Context-Based Indexing.. 20
         3.1.4   Approaches for Context Search 22
                3.1.4.1   Searching Based on Explicitly Specifying User Context.......... 22
               3.1.4.2   Searching Based on Automatically Derived Context............... 22
         3.1.5   Traditional Method for Context-Based Search: User Profile-Based
              Context Search... 22
   3.2   Conceptual Search 23
         3.2.1   The Semantic Web 23
         3.2.2   Ontology.. 23
         3.2.3   Approaches to Conceptual Search 24
         3.2.4   Types of Conceptual Structures.. 24
         3.2.5   Features of Conceptual Structures.. 25
         3.2.6   Framework for Concept-Based Search... 25
         3.2.7   Concept Chain Graphs.. 26

4 Information Retrieval Models...27
   4.1   Boolean Model...27
   4.2   Vector Model..28
       4.2.1   The Vector Space Model..28
       4.2.2   Similarity Measures 28
            4.2.2.1   Cosine Similarity...28
            4.2.2.2   Jaccard Coefficient..29
            4.2.2.3   Dice Coefficient...29
   4.3   Fixing the Term Weights...29
       4.3.1   Term Frequency 30
       4.3.2   Inverse Document Frequency 30
       4.3.3   *tf-idf*..30
   4.4   Probabilistic Models 31
       4.4.1   Probabilistic Ranking Principle (PRP)..31
       4.4.2   Binary Independence Retrieval (BIR) Model..............................32
       4.4.3   The Probabilistic Indexing Model 33
   4.5   Language Model...33
       4.5.1   Multinomial Distributions Model 34
       4.5.2   The Query Likelihood Model 35
       4.5.3   Extended Language Modeling Approaches 36
       4.5.4   Translation Model..36
       4.5.5   Comparisons with Traditional Probabilistic IR Approaches 37

5 Evaluation of Information Retrieval Systems 39
   5.1   Ranked and Unranked Results...39
       5.1.1   Relevance 39
   5.2   Unranked Retrieval System..39
       5.2.1   Precision 39
       5.2.2   Recall...40
       5.2.3   Accuracy...40
       5.2.4   *F*-Measure 41
       5.2.5   *G*-Measure...41
       5.2.6   Prevalence 42
       5.2.7   Error Rate 42
       5.2.8   Fallout...43
       5.2.9   Miss Rate 43
   5.3   Ranked Retrieval System..43
       5.3.1   Precision and Recall Curves...43
       5.3.2   Average Precision...44
       5.3.3   Precision at *k*...44
       5.3.4   *R*-Precision 44
       5.3.5   Mean Average Precision (MAP)...45
       5.3.6   Breakeven Point...45
       5.3.7   ROC Curve..46
            5.3.7.1   Relationship between PR and ROC Curves 46

6 Fundamentals of Evolutionary Algorithms 47
   6.1   Combinatorial Optimization Problems 47
       6.1.1   Heuristics 47

   6.1.2 Metaheuristics 48
   6.1.3 Case-Based Reasoning (CBR) 48
  6.2 Evolutionary Programming 48
  6.3 Evolutionary Computation 49
   6.3.1 Single-Objective Optimization 50
   6.3.2 Multi-Objective Optimization 50
  6.4 Role of Evolutionary Algorithms in Information Retrieval...............50
  6.5 Evolutionary Algorithms 51
   6.5.1 Firefly Algorithm 51
   6.5.2 Particle Swarm Optimization 52
   6.5.3 Genetic Algorithms 52
   6.5.4 Genetic Programming..53
   6.5.5 Applications of Genetic Programming........................54
   6.5.6 Simulated Annealing 54
   6.5.7 Harmony Search 55
   6.5.8 Differential Evolution 55
   6.5.9 Tabulated Search...56

Section III Demand of Evolutionary Algorithms in IR

7 Demand of Evolutionary Algorithms in Information Retrieval 59
  7.1 Document Ranking...59
   7.1.1 Retrieval Effectiveness 59
  7.2 Relevance Feedback Approach 60
   7.2.1 Relevance Feedback in Text IR...................................61
    7.2.1.1 Query Expansion..62
   7.2.2 Relevance Feedback in Content-Based Image Retrieval 62
   7.2.3 Relevance Feedback in Region-Based Image Retrieval...............63
  7.3 Term-Weighting Approaches 64
   7.3.1 Term Frequency 65
   7.3.2 Inverse Document Frequency 65
  7.4 Document Retrieval..65
  7.5 Feature Selection Approach..66
   7.5.1 Filter Method for Feature Selection.............................67
   7.5.2 Wrapper Method for Feature Selection 67
   7.5.3 Embedded Method for Feature Selection....................67
  7.6 Image Retrieval 68
   7.6.1 Content-Based Image Retrieval 69
    7.6.1.1 Feature Extraction 71
    7.6.1.2 Color Descriptor 71
    7.6.1.3 Texture Descriptor 72
    7.6.1.4 Shape Descriptor 73
    7.6.1.5 Similarity Measure.....................................73
   7.6.2 Region-Based Image Retrieval....................................73
    7.6.2.1 Image Segmentation 74
    7.6.2.2 Similarity Measure.....................................75
   7.6.3 Image Summarization...75
    7.6.3.1 Multimodal Image Collection Summarization............76

7.6.3.2   Bag of Words 77
7.6.3.3   Dictionary Learning for Calculating Sparse Approximately ... 79
7.7   Web-Based Recommendation System 80
7.8   Web Page Classification 81
7.9   Facet Generation 83
7.10   Duplicate Detection System 84
7.11   Improvisation of Seeker Satisfaction in Community Question Answering
       Systems 86
7.12   Abstract Generation 87

Section IV   Model Formulations of Information Retrieval Techniques

8   TABU Annealing: An Efficient and Scalable Strategy for Document Retrieval 91
8.1   Simulated Annealing 91
       8.1.1   The Simulated Annealing Algorithm 92
       8.1.2   Cooling Schedules 92
8.2   TABU Annealing Algorithm 93
8.3   Empirical Results and Discussion 94

**9   Efficient Latent Semantic Indexing-Based Information Retrieval Framework
     Using Particle Swarm Optimization and Simulated Annealing 99**
9.1   Architecture of Proposed Information Retrieval System 99
9.2   Methodology and Solutions 100
       9.2.1   Text Preprocessing 100
       9.2.2   Dimensionality Reduction 101
               9.2.2.1   Dimensionality Reduction Using Latent Semantic
                          Indexing 101
               9.2.2.2   Query Conversion Using LSI 102
       9.2.3   Clustering of Dimensionally Reduced Documents 103
               9.2.3.1   Background of Particle Swarm Optimization (PSO)
                          Algorithm 103
               9.2.3.2   Background of *K*-Means 105
               9.2.3.3   Hybrid PSO + *K*-Means Algorithm 106
       9.2.4   Simulated Annealing for Document Retrieval 106
9.3   Experimental Results and Discussion 106
       9.3.1   Performance Evaluation for Clustering 106
       9.3.2   Performance Evaluation for Document Retrieval 108

**10 Music-Inspired Optimization Algorithm: Harmony-TABU for Document
     Retrieval Using Rhetorical Relations and Relevance Feedback 113**
10.1   The Basic Harmony Search Clustering Algorithm 113
       10.1.1   Basic Structure of Harmony Search Algorithm 113
       10.1.2   Representation of Documents and Queries 113
       10.1.3   Representation of Solutions 114
       10.1.4   Features of Harmony Search 114
       10.1.5   Initialize the Problem and HS Parameters 115

        10.1.6 Harmony Memory Initialization 115
        10.1.7 New Harmony Improvisation 115
        10.1.8 Hybridization 116
        10.1.9 Evaluation of Solutions 116
    10.2 Harmony-TABU Algorithm 116
    10.3 Relevance Feedback and Query Expansion in IR 118
        10.3.1 Presentation Term Selection 118
        10.3.2 Direct Term Feedback (TFB) 119
        10.3.3 Cluster Feedback (CFB) 120
        10.3.4 Term-Cluster Feedback (TCFB) 120
    10.4 Empirical Results and Discussion 121
        10.4.1 Document Collections 121
        10.4.2 Experimental Setup 121
    10.5 Rhetorical Structure 123
    10.6 Abstract Generation 123

11 **Evaluation of Light Inspired Optimization Algorithm-Based
    Image Retrieval** 125
    11.1 Query Selection and Distance Calculation 126
    11.2 Optimization Using a Stochastic Firefly Algorithm 127
        11.2.1 Agents Initialization and Fitness Evaluation 127
        11.2.2 Variation in Brightness of Firefly 127
        11.2.3 Strategy for Searching New Swarms 127
    11.3 Experimental Setup 129
    11.4 Visual Signature 129
    11.5 Performance Measures 130
    11.6 Parameter Settings of Firefly Algorithm 130
    11.7 Performance Evaluation 131

12 **An Evolutionary Approach for Optimizing Content-Based Image Retrieval
    Using Support Vector Machine** 135
    12.1 Relevance Feedback Learning via Support Vector Machine 136
    12.2 Optimization Using a Stochastic Firefly Algorithm 137
    12.3 Image Database 139
    12.4 Baselines 139
    12.5 Comparison Methods 140

13 **An Application of Firefly Algorithm to Region-Based Image Retrieval** 143
    13.1 Image Retrieval 144
        13.1.1 Image Segmentation 144
        13.1.2 Image Representation 144
        13.1.3 Similarity Measure 144
    13.2 Optimization Using a Stochastic Firefly Algorithm 146
        13.2.1 Firefly Agent's Initialization and Fitness Evaluation 146
        13.2.2 Attraction toward New Firefly 146
        13.2.3 Movement of Fireflies 147
    13.3 Image Databases 147
    13.4 Performance Evaluation 148

14 An Evolutionary Approach for Optimizing Region-Based Image Retrieval Using Support Vector Machine 151
   14.1   Region-Based Image Retrieval 151
   14.2   Behavior of Fireflies 153
   14.3   Why Is the Firefly Algorithm So Efficient? 153
   14.4   Machine Learning 154
   14.5   Support Vector Machines 155
   14.6   Optimization of SVM by PSO 155
        14.6.1 SVM-Based RF 156
   14.7   Optimization Using a Stochastic Firefly Algorithm 157
   14.8   Image Databases 157
        14.8.1 COIL Database 157
        14.8.2 The Corel Database 158
   14.9   Baselines 158
        14.9.1 The Proposed SVM: FA Approach 158
   14.10 Discussion 159
        14.10.1 Comparison of FA with PSO and GA 160

15 Optimization of Sparse Dictionary Model for Multimodal Image Summarization Using Firefly Algorithm 161
   15.1   Image Representation 162
   15.2   Problem Formulation 163
   15.3   Optimization of Dictionary Learning 165
   15.4   Sparse Coding 166
   15.5   Iterative Dictionary Selection Stage 167
   15.6   Performance Analysis 167
        15.6.1 Experiment Setup 167
        15.6.2 Experimental Specification 168
        15.6.3 Baseline Algorithms 168
        15.6.4 Mean Square Error Performance 168

Section V Algorithmic Solutions to the Problems in Advanced IR Concepts

16 A Dynamic Feature Selection Method for Document Ranking with Relevance Feedback Approach 173
   16.1   Overview 173
   16.2   Feature Selection Procedures 173
        16.2.1 Markov Random Field (MRF) Model for Feature Selection 175
        16.2.2 Correlation-Based Feature Selection 175
        16.2.3 Count Difference-Based Feature Selection 176
   16.3   Proposed Approach for Feature Selection 177
        16.3.1 Feature Generalization with Association Rule Induction 178
        16.3.2 Ranking 178
                16.3.2.1 Document Ranking Using BM25 Weighting Function 179
                16.3.2.2 Expectation Maximization for Relevance Feedback 179

16.4 Empirical Results and Discussion 179
    16.4.1 Dataset Used for Feature Selection 179
    16.4.2 *n*-Gram Generation 180
    16.4.3 Evaluation 180

17 TDCCREC: An Efficient and Scalable Web-Based Recommendation System 185
    17.1 Recommendation Methodologies 185
        17.1.1 Learning Automata (LA) 186
        17.1.2 Weighted Association Rule 187
        17.1.3 Content-Based Recommendation 188
        17.1.4 Collaborative Filtering-Based Recommendation 189
    17.2 Proposed Approach: Truth Discovery-Based Content and Collaborative
        Recommender System (TDCCREC) 190
    17.3 Empirical Results and Discussion 193

18 An Automatic Facet Generation Framework for Document Retrieval 197
    18.1 Baseline Approach 198
        18.1.1 Drawbacks 198
    18.2 Greedy Algorithm 198
        18.2.1 Drawbacks 199
    18.3 Feedback Language Model 199
    18.4 Proposed Method: Automatic Facet Generation Framework (AFGF) 200
    18.5 Empirical Results and Discussion 202

19 ASPDD: An Efficient and Scalable Framework for Duplication Detection 205
    19.1 Duplication Detection Techniques 205
        19.1.1 Prior Work 207
            19.1.1.1 Similarity Measures 207
            19.1.1.2 Shingling Techniques 207
        19.1.2 Proposed Approach (ASPDD) 208
    19.2 Empirical Results and Discussion 210

**20 Improvisation of Seeker Satisfaction in Yahoo! Community Question
Answering Using Automatic Ranking, Abstract Generation, and History
Updation** 213
    20.1 The Asker Satisfaction Problem 214
    20.2 Community Question Answering Problems 214
    20.3 Methodologies 216
    20.4 Experimental Setup 220
    20.5 Empirical Results and Discussion 225

Section VI   Findings and Summary

21 Findings and Summary of Text Information Retrieval Chapters 231
    21.1 Findings and Summary 231
    21.2 Future Directions 233

22 Findings and Summary of Image Retrieval and Assessment of Image Mining Systems Chapters 235

22.1 Experimental Setup 235

22.2 Results and Discussions...236

22.3 Findings 1: Average Precision-Recall Curves of Proposed Image Retrieval Systems for Pascal Database..237

22.4 Findings 2: Average Precision and Average Recall of Proposed Methods for Different Semantic Classes...238

22.5 Findings 3: Average Precision and Average Recall of Top-Ranked Results after the Ninth Feedback for Corel Database...240

22.6 Findings 4: Average Precision of Top-Ranked Results after the Ninth Feedback for IR with Summarization and IR without Summarization............241

22.7 Findings 5: Average Execution Time of Proposed Methods..............................242

22.8 Findings 6: Performance Analysis of Top Retrieval Results Obtained with the Proposed Image Retrieval Systems...243

22.9 Summary..245

22.10 Future Scope 246

Appendix: Abbreviations, Acronyms and Symbols...249

Bibliography..257

Index 279

Preface

The goal of this book is to provide an understanding of the contributions of concrete areas such as framework efficiency variability factors and query variability factors to overall retrieval variability. This brought together eight different information retrieval (IR) models (for text and images) and set them to improve performance effectiveness. For each designated model, a detailed analysis of each framework with its retrieved documents was done, and observations have yielded hypotheses for individual models that are tested in experiments. Algorithmic solutions to the problems in advanced IR concepts are evolved, and various real-time applications are attempted.

Content and Structure

This book is organized into 22 chapters and six sections. Section I introduces information retrieval concepts. Section II provides prerequisites for reading this book and gives necessary background information for state-of-the-art research in optimization research studies of text and image retrieval systems based on relevance feedback and multimodal image summarization systems. Section III explores the demand of evolutionary algorithms in IR, which is required for forthcoming chapters. Section IV (Chapters 8 through 15) discusses various model formulations of information retrieval techniques: Chapters 8 through 10 focusing on text information retrieval and Chapters 11 through 15 focusing on image retrieval. Chapter 8 implements TABU annealing, a heuristic approach that is a combination of TABU and simulated annealing with a clustering approach. The results of the proposed approach are superior to simulated annealing and TABU. Chapter 9 discusses a text mining framework consisting of four distinct stages: (1) text preprocessing, (2) dimensionality reduction using latent semantic indexing, (3) clustering based on a hybrid combination of particle swarm optimization and K-means algorithm, and (4) information retrieval process using simulated annealing. This framework provides more relevant documents to the user and reduces the irrelevant documents.

Chapter 10 proposes a novel clustering method based on harmony search (HS) optimization, a metaheuristic algorithm that mimics the improvisation of musicians. By modeling retrieval as an optimization problem, the harmony clustering approach was hybridized with TABU to achieve better retrieval. Experimental results reveal that the proposed algorithm can find better results when compared to HS and TABU methods. Finally, feedback language models are used to further improve the retrieved results.

Chapters 11 through 15 provide the research stimulus, the objective of the research performed, optimization of the image retrieval process, and summarization of the multimodal image collection. This elucidates the proposed work making use of five diverse approaches in an image mining system. Out of five, four approaches are based on image retrieval via employing the firefly algorithm in the relevance feedback loop of content-based image retrieval (CBIR), integrating support vector machine (SVM) with Gaussian firefly algorithm as a relevance feedback model in CBIR, making use of the Gaussian firefly algorithm in region-based image retrieval (RBIR) as a relevance feedback model, and embedding SVM with a Gaussian firefly algorithm in the relevance feedback loop of RBIR for capably retrieving most wanted images from a large database by optimizing the image retrieval performance. Only one approach for image summarization adopts the firefly algorithm to develop a summary in order to obtain a fast overview of the image set with no need for skimming through the whole database by optimizing the multimodal image collection summarization performance.

As part of the investigation, the following observations were made: (1) Ranking search results is essential for an IR and Web search; (2) Websites recommended by the search engines have no guarantee for information correctness; (3) Faceted interfaces represent a new powerful paradigm that has been proven to be a successful complement to keyword searching; (4) In newly emerging domains like comment e-rulemaking, many of the comments are "form letters" and modified copies of form letters (near duplicates), and spotting exact, near duplicates and their unique component(s) is a more challenging task; and (5) It is necessary to investigate a problem of information seeker's satisfaction in question answering communities.

Section V, the essential part of this book, spans Chapters 16 through 20 and covers more advanced IR concepts. Chapter 16 focuses on document ranking used by IR frameworks to rank matching documents according to their relevance to a given search query. We describe a 0/1 knapsack procedure for automatically selecting features to use within a generalization model for ranking. We propose an approach for relevance feedback using an expectation maximization method, and experimental results show that a feature selection algorithm produces models that are either significantly more effective than or as equally effective as models such as the Markov random field model, correlation coefficient method, and count difference method.

Chapter 17 introduces a Web recommender system called truth discovery-based content and collaborative REcommender that helps users make decisions in the complex information space and provides the user with further reading material by combining content and collaborative filtering. Along with this, a truth finder is incorporated to present trustworthy websites to users—this outperforms existing methods like learning automata and weighted association rule. Results suggest that the proposed system is better in predicting the next request of a Web user. Chapter 18 presents a domain-independent automatic facet generation framework to extract the facets for efficient document retrieval. Also discovered the efficiency-improving semantically related feature sets with Word Net that reflect the contents of the target information collection. Experiments show that the approach can effectively generate multifaceted arbitrary topics and that the approach is comparable to traditional approaches like baseline, greedy, and feedback language models. Chapter 19 deals with a framework for the duplicate document detection problem that uses a dynamic program called All Pairs Shortest Path based Duplicate Detection in the text collection to minimize the impact of duplicates on search results. And when comparing our solution to the state-of-the-art, it was found that the method has produced promising results in improving the accuracy of exact duplicate detection, and also detected partial and neighbor replica.

Chapter 20 investigates the problem of predicting information seeker satisfaction in Yahoo! question answering communities, and determining whether an asker is satisfied with the answers submitted by the community participants. This explores automatic ranking, creating an abstract from retrieved answers, and history updation for user satisfaction. Experimental results obtained from an evaluation of thousands of real questions and user ratings demonstrate the feasibility of modeling and predicting asker satisfaction.

Section VI, with Chapters 21 and 22, deals with the findings and summaries of previous chapters and presents experimental validation of the proposed work and provides discussion of the results. Conclusions and scope for future work are also elaborated.

MATLAB® is a registered trademark of The MathWorks, Inc. For product information, please contact:

The MathWorks, Inc.
3 Apple Hill Drive
Natick, MA 01760-2098 USA
Tel: 508 647 7000
Fax: 508-647-7001
E-mail: info@mathworks.com
Web: www.mathworks.com

Acknowledgments

I would like to premeditate my gratefulness and thanks to Taylor & Francis for emboldening my research and making the promulgating part of my book a gratifying one. Special thanks are extended to my family. Words cannot express how grateful I am to my parents for all the sacrifices they have done on my behalf. Their benediction made me sustain this far. I also thank all my well wishers who supported and encouraged me to endeavor towards my goal. I would also like to express my very special appreciation to my son, S. Ranjith Kumar, who patted my back whenever I felt low and gave me in-citation to consummate such a prodigious task of writing a book. He backed me in the moments when there was no one to answer my queries.

Thanks to every one to make this servitude a successful one.

About the Author

Dr. K. Latha is an assistant professor of computer science and engineering at Anna University, Tiruchirappalli, Tamil Nadu, India. She earned her BE (ECE) from Bharathidasan University, her ME (CSE) from Madurai Kamaraj University, and her PhD from Anna University Chennai. Her areas of research interest include information retrieval, data mining, text mining, Web mining, cloud computing, and network security. She has 17 years of teaching experience and has produced several doctorates in Anna University, Chennai. Published works include more than 100 papers in international journals and conferences and authored two engineering technical scientific books. Best paper awards were received for five technical papers published by IEEE. She has delivered special lectures, keynotes, and a presidential address, and acted as a resource and chairperson in many international conferences. She received a leader's charity award in academic excellence at Madurai Kamaraj University for Master of engineering in CSE. She is closely associated with IIT Kanpur. She has received grants from AICTE, TEQIP, and organized several workshops, seminars, and conferences. She has been appointed as a research advisory council member by Anna University, Chennai, and has generated over 5 lakhs in research funding that includes UGC (University Grant Commission) and TEQIP-II Sponsored Young faculty research support scheme. She is a principal investigator of a research proposals entitled, "Portal for Indian Legal System: An e-governance initiative" under UGC Minor Research Project and "Sustaining Ecosystem from Species Extinction Using Data Mining Techniques," under YFRSS. She has acted as an expert in the Constitution of Oral Examination board for the conduct of Viva-Voce in respect of the Research Scholars for PhD Programme, Anna University, Chennai, and she has been appointed as a member of the Inspection Committee for Inspection-CAI–Anna University, Chennai-Affiliation-Consideration of granting of provisional/permanent affiliation for engineering colleges. She has also been invited to peer review research articles from Springer, Elsevier, Oxford University Press, ICTACT, and IEEE etc.

She has been awarded Outstanding Scientist award for Data Mining from Venus International Foundation, Registered trust in India on 19th December 2015. She has Received Best Academic Researcher award from ASDF Global Awards 2016 and Best Young Researcher (Female) award from South Indian ASDF awards 2016 from the presenters of Association of Scientists, Developers and Faculties.

Section I

Foundations

1

Introduction

1.1 Motivation

Internet resources have rapidly increased in recent years; the problem of ordinary users has become finding desired information in such an environment. Owing to advanced technology, digital documents have become more popular for storing and broadcasting information, when compared to traditional paper documents. In particular, it is likely that the information needed by a user is scattered in a huge number of databases. Taking into consideration effectiveness of the search and the cost of searching, a convenient and efficient approach is to select a subset of databases that are most likely to provide useful results with respect to the user query.

An information retrieval system begins when a user perforates a query. Queries are formal statements, such as search strings, that distinguish a user's information need. A single document or several documents may match the query, perhaps with different degrees of relevance. The information retrieval system ranks the matching documents based on the relevance and presents them to the user. Information retrieval is an effortless technique. A user having an information requirement, rendering that into a search statement, and executing that search to find the information have become part of everyday life. The World Wide Web has become a repository of all information a person wants, swapping the library as a more convenient research tool.

The goal of an information retrieval system is to minimize user operating cost in finding valuable information. An information retrieval (IR) system retrieves relevant information by comparing query and document text. From the computer's point of view, these texts represent bags of words. The online documents are retrieved using ranking algorithms that involve measuring word overlap. When human beings retrieve information, they use background knowledge to interpret and understand the text and effectively add words that may be misplaced. Ranking algorithms exclusively based on matching the literal words that are present will fail to retrieve much relevant information.

IR has become an important area of research in past decades due to the rapid growth of information in diverse areas. Technically, an IR is defined as a system for storing, representing, indexing, retrieving, and delivering documents. The evolution of IR systems has been related to the growth of computer processing power. Earlier systems were about automating the indexing processes manually in their libraries. These systems migrate the structure and group of card catalogs into structured databases. Many universities and public libraries are using IR systems to provide access to books, journals, and documents. One of the most visible IR applications is Web search engines.

1.1.1 Web Search

IR involves several types of information access. The Web search is a significant part of this spectrum of information systems. Web search now presents an important section of Web activity. The three forms of searching the Web are as follows:

- Using search engines that index a portion of a Web document as a full-text database
- Classifying the Web documents based on subjects by using the Web directory
- Using Web searching to exploit its hyperlink structure

Generally, Web search in search engines is performed through text queries. Because of the enormous size of the Web, text alone is usually not selectively adequate to limit query results to a convenient size. Search engines for the Web are one of the most publicly visible IR technologies. Search engines are critically important to help users find relevant information on the World Wide Web.

Search engines maintain the subsequent processes in near real time:

- Web crawling
- Indexing
- Searching

Through Web crawling from site to site, a user can get information from search engines. The spider checks for the typical filename addressed to it, before sending certain information back to be indexed depending on many features, including labels, page content, JavaScript, Cascading Style Sheets (CSS), headings, as evidenced by the typical HTML markup of the informational substance, or its metadata in HTML tags.

Indexing refers to associating words and other specific tokens established on web pages to their domain names and HTML-based fields, making the associations in a public database accessible for Web search queries. A query from a user can be a single word or group of lexis. The index helps to locate information related to the query as quickly as possible. Some of the approaches for indexing and caching are trade secrets, whereas crawling is a simple process of visiting all sites on a methodical basis.

1.2 Evolutionary Search and IR

For the purpose of evolutionary search (ES), a proper encoding, representing the solution of the given problem as encoded chromosomes suitable for an evolutionary search process is essential. Locating appropriate encoding is a nontrivial problem-dependent task affecting the performance and consequences of evolutionary search while fixing the problem. The solutions can be encoded into binary strings, real vectors frequently with tree-like hierarchical structures, depending on the particular application.

The iterative stages of an evolutionary search process begin with an initial population of individuals generated randomly or implanted with possibly good solutions. An artificial evolution consists of iterative application of genetic operators, introducing the algorithm of evolutionary benefits such as inheritance, survival of the fittest, and random perturbations.

The current population of problem solutions is adapted with the aim to form a new and hopefully better population to be utilized in the next generation. An iterative evolution of problem solutions ends after satisfying the specified termination criteria, particularly the decisive factor of finding an optimal solution. After terminating the search process, an evolution winner is decoded and presented as the most optimal solution.

Evolutionary computation techniques are stochastic artificial search methods that are inspired by natural biological systems. Evolutionary algorithms figure out a separation of evolutionary computation; in general they involve techniques to implement and stimulate similar to those in *biological* evolution such as *reproduction, mutation, recombination, natural selection,* and *survival of the fittest.* A candidate solution to the optimization problem plays a significant role in individuals in a population, and the cost function decides the situation by which the solutions exist. In evolutionary computation, there are two main facts that form the root of evolutionary systems: (1) *recombination* and *mutation* make essential diversity and thereby facilitate innovation, while (2) *selection* acts as a force raising quality.

The changed pieces of information due to recombination and mutation are chosen randomly. Selection operators can be either deterministic or stochastic. Individuals with a higher fitness have a higher chance of being selected than individuals with a lower fitness. This approach is used to search for useful term-weighting schemes in traditional text-based IR. By using this evolutionary learning approach, the space of possible term-weighting schemes is searched in a guided manner.

1.3 Applications of IR

In an IR, search is the heart of the retrieval process; the field covers a wide variety of inter-related problems associated with the representation, storage, exploitation, and retrieval of human-language data. Areas where IR techniques are employed include general and domain-specific applications.

The *Selective Dissemination of Information* (SDI) is a service that consists of routing to readers, on a regular basis, news alerts related to their reader's profiles. SDI is a documentation watch tool. SDI refers to tools and resources utilized to keep a user informed of new resources on particular topics. SDI was formerly a phrase related to library and information science. These systems provide automated searches that inform the user of the availability of recent resources, meeting the user's specific keywords and search parameters. Alerts can be received in a number of ways, including email, voicemail, instant messaging, text messaging, and Rich Site Summary (RSS) feeds.

An *information filtering* system removes redundant or unnecessary information from an information stream using automated and semi-automated or computerized approaches prior to presentation to a human user. Its main goal is management of the information overload and growth of the semantic signal-to-noise ratio. To do this, compare the user's profile to some reference features. These features may originate from the information item or the user's social environment. This distinguished application was established in the field of email spam filters. On the presentation level, information filtering takes the form of user preferences-based newsfeeds, etc.

Digital libraries and other specialized IR systems support access to collections of high-quality material, typically of a proprietary nature. This may include newspaper articles, medical journals, maps, or books not positioned on a generally obtainable website due to copyright restrictions. Given the editorial quality and restricted scope of these collections, it is possible to take advantage of structural features such as authors, titles, dates, and other publication data to narrow search requests and improve retrieval effectiveness. In addition, digital libraries contain electronic-generated text by optical character recognition (OCR) systems from printed material; character recognition errors related to OCR output create yet another complication for the retrieval process.

Recommender systems are real-time information filtering systems that attempt to present to the user information items to which the user typically pays attention. Recommender systems add information items to the information flowing to the user, as opposed to taking down information items from the information stream to the user. Recommender systems typically use collaborative filtering methods or a mixture of collaborative filtering and content-based filtering approaches, though content-based recommender systems do exist.

Text clustering and categorization systems group documents according to shared properties.

The clustering and categorization stem differs from the information provided to the system. Systems are categorized with training data illustrating the various classes. Examples of sports, car, and electronics articles might be a categorization system, which would then arrange unlabeled articles into the same categories. A clustering system works without a training set. Clustering groups documents into cluster groups according to patterns it discovers itself.

Summarization systems shrink documents to a small amount of key paragraphs, sentences, or phrases describing their content. For example, the snippets of text displayed with Web search results represent summarization.

An *information extraction* system identifies named entities, such as places and dates, and combines the information into structured records that show the relevance between the entities. Creating lists of books and their authors from Web data is an example of information extraction.

Topic detection and tracking systems recognize events in streams of news articles and similar information resources, tracking these events as they change. The input to this system is a stream of stories. The stories may or may not be presegmented, and the events may or may not be known to the system. This leads to the definition of three technical tasks to be addressed in the topic detection and tracking study. These are the systems tracking of known events, the detection of unknown events, and the segmentation of a news source into stories.

Expert search systems identify members of organizations who are experts in a specified field. In this system, the user submits a query representing a topic; the search system finds the people strongly associated with the query using the document collection. It ranks the people according to the strength of association with the query and returns the ranked list. A mixture of association relationships among terms, documents, and people in different contexts in the document sets might be helpful for expert search. Relevance between terms and documents, co-occurrence between terms and people in bodies of documents, co-occurrence between terms and people within titles and authors of documents, and co-occurrence between people in documents are examples of potentially functional association information.

Question answering (QA) systems integrate information from multiple sources to provide concise answers to specific questions. This type of system often incorporates and extends other IR technologies, including search, information extraction, and summarization. QA is concerned with implementing systems that automatically answer questions posed by humans in a natural language. A QA implementation may construct its answers by querying a structured database of knowledge, typically a knowledge base. Additionally, QA systems can pull answers from an unstructured collection of natural language documents.

Multimedia information retrieval systems expand relevance ranking and other IR techniques to images, video, music, and speech. Multimedia information retrieval aims at extracting semantic information from multimedia data sources. Owing to rapid growth in technology, a vast amount of multimedia data are captured and stored in a server. The data sources are composed of directly perceivable media such as audio, image, and video, and indirectly perceivable sources such as text and biosignals. The not perceivable sources used in multimedia are bioinformation, stock prices, etc. The special characteristics and requirements are considerably dissimilar from alphanumeric data. The text document information retrieval has restricted capability to handle multimedia data effectively.

1.3.1 Other Search Applications

Desktop and file system search provides another example of a widely used IR application. A desktop search engine provides search and browsing facilities for files stored on a local hard disk and possibly on disks connected to a local network. These systems require greater awareness of file formats and creation times than do Web search engines. Since files may change rapidly, these systems must interface directly with the file system layer of the operating system and have to be engineered to hold a serious update pack.

Besides the desktop and the general Web, enterprise-level IR systems provide document management and search services across businesses and other organizations. The facts of these systems vary extensively. Some are essentially Web search engines applied to the corporate intranet, crawled web pages perceptible only inside the organization and provided a search interface analogous to that of a typical search engine. In many industries, these systems help satisfy regulatory requirements concerning the maintenance of email and additional business interactions.

An *image retrieval* system is a computer system for searching and retrieving images from a vast amount of digital image databases. Most traditional and universal approaches to image retrieval use some method of adding metadata such as captioning, keywords, or descriptions to the images, so that retrieval can be executed over the annotation terms. Manual image annotation is time-consuming, laborious, and expensive. To tackle this, there has been a huge amount of research done on automatic image annotation. Additionally, growth in social Web applications and the semantic Web have stimulated the improvement of several Web-based image annotation tools.

An image search is a specific data search utilized to invent images. When searching for images, a user may enter query terms such as image file/link or keyword, or may click on some image. Then the system will show images related to the query. The relevance used for search criteria could be meta tags, color distribution in images, region/shape attributes, etc.

Music information retrieval (MIR) is the interdisciplinary work of retrieving information from music. MIR is a tiny but emerging area of research with many real-time applications. MIR is being utilized by businesses and academics to sort out, operate, and even create music.

A *3D content retrieval* system is a tool for surfing the Internet, searching, and retrieving three-dimensional digital content from a large database of digital images, for example, computer-aided design (CAD) and cultural heritage 3D scenes. Conducting 3D content retrieval utilizes techniques to add annotation text to 3D content files such as the file name, link text, and the web page title so that the related 3D content can be found through the text retrieval system. Owing to the inefficiency of manual annotation of 3D files, researchers have investigated different ways to computerize the annotation process and define a unified standard to create text descriptions for 3D contents. In addition, the increase in 3D content has demanded and stirred superior ways to retrieve 3D information. The shape-matching approaches for 3D content retrieval have become more popular. Shape-matching retrieval is a technique that compares and distinguishes similarities between 3D models.

A *news search*, for example, might use a routing scheme to split the day's news into sections such as "economy," "sports," and "weather," or to send headlines of interest to particular subscribers.

Federated search is an information retrieval technology that allows the instantaneous search of various searchable resources. The user makes a particular query distributed to the search engines, databases, or other query engines involved in the federation. The federated search then integrates the results received from the search engines to the user for representation. This is often a technique to integrate disparate information resources on the Web.

Blog search was the foremost search engine to present full-blown blog and feed search capabilities. The blog search is similar to Google search by typing search terms in the field and considering the most relevant results interrelated to the topic. Blog search looked at diverse applications in the world of blogs like Blogger, Live Journal, and Weblog. Users can Google to access and search the blog database by themselves by formatting the URL in browser's address bar.

Mobile search is an evolving branch of IR service centered on the union of mobile platforms and phones, or used to communicate information with other mobile devices. The search engine can find mobile content on websites available to mobile devices on mobile networks. Mobile content has shown a media shift toward mobile multimedia information. Simply, mobile search is not a spatial shift of PC Web search to mobile equipment. It is like a tree branching into specialized parts of mobile broadband and content, both of which show a fast-paced evolution.

Social search is retrieving and searching on a social searching engine that mostly searches for user-generated content such as news, videos, and images. They search content on social media like Facebook, Twitter, Instagram, LinkedIn, and Flickr. Social search is an enhanced version of Web search that integrates traditional algorithms. An idea behind social search is that instead of a machine deciding to retrieve web pages for a specific query based on an impersonal algorithm outcome, web pages retrieved by the human network of the searcher might be more appropriate to that particular user's requirements.

Section II

Preliminaries

2

Preliminaries

2.1 Information Retrieval

As stated by science and technology, information retrieval (IR) is the technique and process of searching, recovering, and manipulating information from huge amounts of stored data. *Britannica Concise Encyclopedia* says information retrieval is recovery of information, particularly in a database stored in a computer. Mooers (1950) defined IR as follows: Information retrieval is the name of the process or method whereby a prospective user of information is able to convert his or her need for information into an actual list of citations to documents in storage containing information useful to the user. Modern retrieval is the most usual method of information access, mostly due to the increasing widespread use of the World Wide Web. IR systems are posed a user information need, generally in the form of a query, and they must return the location of pieces of information related to this query, usually in the form of documents.

In this context, IR deals with the problem of identifying and presenting documents of unstructured data that fulfill the information need from within collections of documents. Unstructured data refers to data that have a semantically random structure that can be conveyed explicitly to a computer, as contrasting to a relational database. The term *document* refers to the granularity of the information obtained by the user. The document can represent abstracts, articles, web pages, chapters, sentences, snippets, emails, and so on. Moreover, the term *document* is not limited to textual information; there may be interest in retrieving and accessing multimedia data, like images, audio, or video.

A user information requirement also referred to as a query must be translated in order for the retrieval system to process it and retrieve information related to a query. This translation is usually made by extracting keywords that summarize the description of the information needed. Finally, the information must be presented in such a way that the user is able to find the wanted documents. A good IR system must support the browsing and filtering of documents to facilitate a user's retrieval experience. Central to a typical IR scenario is the notion of relevance. The most difficult part of the retrieval process is deciding which documents are associated to or satisfy a certain query. Documents should be preferably ranked in decreasing order of relevance. A retrieval system achieves its maximum retrieval effectiveness when the relevant documents with respect to the query are ranked higher, whereas the nonrelevant are ranked lower.

A perfect retrieval system would retrieve only the relevant documents. This system does not exist and will not exist, because search statements are necessarily deficient, and relevance depends on the subjective opinion of the user. More than one user may pose the same query to an IR system, resulting in different relations on the retrieved documents.

2.2 Information Retrieval versus Data Retrieval

The IR system and data retrieval system differ in that IR deals with unstructured/semi-structured data, while a data retrieval system (a database management system [DBMS]) deals with structured data with distinct semantics. The other differences between the data and the information are discussed as follows.

Data retrieval is the background of an IR system. It is the process of obtaining data from a database management system. In this case, it is considered that the data are represented in an ordered way, and there is no uncertainty in data. In order to retrieve the desired data, the user presents a set of criteria by a query. The DBMS software is used for managing databases, and it selects the demanded data from the database. The retrieved object or data may be stored in a file or be printed or viewed on the monitor. A query language, such as Structured Query Language (SQL), is used to prepare the queries. Each DBMS may have its own language, but most relational.

The two primary forms of the retrieved data from a database are reports and queries. There are some overlaps between the reports and queries, but queries generally select a small portion of the database in a whole database. The retrieved report shows huge amounts of data. Queries also present the data in a typical format and usually display it on the monitor, but the reports allow formatting of the output as the user needs and is normally printed. Reports are intended using a report generator built into the DBMS.

Data retrieving systems can be found in the operating system search. The best example for the data retrieval system is a Windows search—you would have to specify the exact name of the file that you desire. Information retrieval systems are like Web search engines. Google is the best-known Web search engine. It processes the natural language and provides the output in the entire set of documents matching the query. To decrease the computation time of the IR system, documents with the frequent terms are scanned, which are measured as relevant to the document. The output displayed sends feedback as an input for the subsequent queries. The performance of the system with every query is increased in this method. There are more information retrieving systems to reduce the time of searching a document, and this is done with the help of indexing.

2.3 Information Retrieval (IR) versus Information Extraction (IE)

Information retrieval is the task of identifying an unstructured nature that satisfies a user's information need from within a huge amount of information resources. The searches can be based on metadata or on full-text indexing. An information extraction (IE) is the process of automatically extracting structured information from an unstructured or semi-structured machine-readable document. In most cases this activity is known as processing human language texts by means of natural language processing. Activities in multimedia document processing, like content extraction and automatic annotation of images or audio or video, could be seen as information extraction.

Information extraction aims at identifying a particular class of data from domain-specific document collections. An extraction processes the documents in order to find the specific objects and the relationships between the predefined objects, filling a structured template with the extracted information. The two processes associated with information extraction are determination of facts that go into structured fields in a database and the extracted text that could be used to summarize an item. The process of extracting facts is called *automatic file build*. Information extraction analyzes unrestricted text in order to extract information about entities, prespecified events, and relationships.

The first automated information retrieval systems were introduced in the 1950s and 1960s. Information extraction should not be confused with the well-established technology of information retrieval, which given a user query selects a subset of related documents from a huge collection of resources. The user then browses the selected documents in order to satisfy the information need. Depending on the IR system, the user may be further assisted by the chosen documents being relevance ranked or having searched terms highlighted in the text to facilitate identifying passages of specific attention. The difference between the aims of IE and IR systems can be summed up as follows: IR retrieves documents relevant to query from collections; and IE extracts pertinent information from documents. The two techniques are opposite to each other, and their use in combination has the potential to create powerful new tools in text processing.

2.4 Components of an Information Retrieval System

Information retrieval has three major components: document processing, query processing, and retrieval feedback. The document-processing stage is composed of two tasks. First, the documents are preprocessed to construct a unified document representation and then get a general representation of all different document formats. Then the query-processing component performs a mapping from the information need to a system query. Finally, the retrieved results are evaluated by using the retrieval and feedback component. The architectural components of the retrieval process are visualized in Figure 2.1.

2.4.1 Document Processing

Document parsing is the initial state of preprocessing. Documents appear in all sorts of languages, character sets, and formats; frequently, the same document may contain multiple languages or formats, for example, French email with Portuguese PDF attachments. Document parsing deals with the recognition and breaking down of the document structure into an individual component. In this stage, unit documents are formed; for example, emails with attachments are split into one document indicating the email and the other the number of documents that are attachments to the mail.

After parsing, a document is tokenized by using *lexical analysis*, seen as an input stream into words. Some of the issues related to lexical analysis comprise the correct identification of abbreviations, dates, cases, and accents. The complexity of this operation depends on the language: for instance, the English language has neither diacritics nor cases, French has diacritics but no cases, and German has both diacritics and cases. The identification of abbreviations, in particular, time expressions would require more discussion than can be presented in this chapter due to the complexity and extensive literature in the field.

A subsequent step optionally applied to the results of the lexical analysis is *stop-word removal*. The list of stop words considered in a user query includes articles (a, the), prepositions (in, over), interjections (oh, but), conjunctions (and, but), pronouns (he, it), and forms of the verb (is, are). To remove stop words, an algorithm compares index term candidates

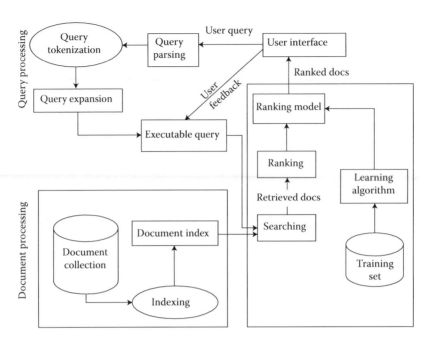

FIGURE 2.1
Information retrieval architecture.

in the documents beside a list of stop words and rejects certain terms from inclusion in the index for searching. The subsequent phases take the full-text structure resulting from the primary phases of parsing and lexical analysis and process the text document, in order to find the relevant keywords to serve as index terms.

Phrase detection, in this stage, it captures text meaning away from what is possible with pure bag-of-word approaches. Phrase detection is performed in multiple ways, including rules and morphological analysis. For example, scanning the sentence *"search engines are the most observable information retrieval applications"* would result in the noun phrases of possible outcomes being *search engines* and *information retrieval*. A common approach to phrase detection relies on the use of thesauri, that the classification schemes contain words and phrases, recurrent in the expression of ideas in written text. Thesauri consist of synonyms and antonyms and may be composed of various approaches.

In order to normalize the word, *stemming and lemmatization* aims at stripping down word suffixes. In particular, stemming *chops off* the ends of words. Stemming removes word suffixes after the removal of stop words from the document processing. The process has two goals: first, in terms of efficiency, stemming reduces the distinctive words in the index, in which it decreases the storage space required for the index. An effectiveness of retrieval stemming improves recall by dropping all forms of the word to a stemmed form. The well-structured stemming algorithm will cut off inflectional suffixes and derivational suffixes, but using pathetic stemming algorithm will cut off only the inflectional suffixes. According to the Porter stemmer, the sentence *"Search engines are the most observable information retrieval applications"* would result in the following after stemming: *"Search engine are the most visible inform retrieve applic."*

Lemmatization is the process of grouping the various inflected forms of a word so they can be analyzed as a single item. It determines the lemma for a given word. *Lemmatization* may involve complex tasks such as context understanding and identification of part of speech of a word in a sentence. In many languages, words appear in a number of *inflected* forms. For example, in English, the verb *to walk* may appear as *walk, walks, walking, walked*. The base form, *walk* that one might find in a dictionary, is called the *lemma* for the word. The grouping of the base form with the part of speech is often called the *lexeme* of the word. *Lemmatization* is very much related to *stemming*. The difference is that a stemmer operates on a single term *without* the knowledge of context, and therefore cannot distinguish between words that have different meanings depending on part of speech.

Term weighting is the next phase of the document processing. The words in a text have different descriptive power. The index terms can be weighted in different ways to account for their significance within a document or a document collection. The search engines assign a binary weight 1 for presence and 0 for absence of the specific term. Measuring the frequency of occurrence of a term in the document creates more sophisticated weighting.

The *index* or *inverted file* is the data structure that stores the index information. The index information will be searched for all individual queries. An inverted file starts from a listing of alphanumeric strings in a set of documents and being indexed with the whole number of the documents identified. The string sequence occurs in a more linguistically complex list of entries. The *term frequency* (*tf*) and *inverse document frequency* (*idf*) weights point to each document in which the term occurs in a document repository.

2.4.2 Query Processing

Query processing has several steps, but a system can slash these steps and proceed to match the query to the inverted file at several places throughout processing. Document processing shares many steps with query processing. The conventional IR system used for analyzing a search query is *parsing*. As soon as a user inputs a query, the search engine must *tokenize* the query stream, whether a keyword-based or a natural language processing (NLP) system (i.e., smash it into comprehensible segments). Usually, a token is defined as an alphanumeric string that occurs between whitespace and punctuation. Combined with the Boolean retrieval model, logical operators could be used to specify the search query. The named entities, single terms, and phrases are recognized by the NLP system.

Query expansion of search engines usually includes only a single statement of a user's information desires in a query. It becomes extremely plausible that the information needed may be expressed using synonyms, relatively the accurate query terms in the documents that the search engine searches. *Query term weighting* involves computing weights for the terms in the query in query processing. The user can control this process by indicating either the weight of each term or simply which term or concept in the query is more significant and appears in all retrieved documents to ensure relevance.

2.4.3 Retrieval and Feedback Generation Component

Retrieval is the process of retrieving the documents of information required by a user through a query in to a document collection. Queries will be indexed in the same way as a document and compared with a document index to determine if a document is likely to be relevant to a query. The retrieved documents are presented either as a list (best match) or a set (exact match). The relevance assessments are the list of documents assessed as being relevant for each query. The idea behind *relevance feedback* is to obtain the results that are primarily returned from a given query and to use information about whether or not those results are appropriate to carry out a new query. The feedback can be distinguished into three types: explicit feedback, implicit feedback, and pseudo feedback.

The success of relevance feedback depends largely on two components: the user's evidence as to what constitutes relevant material and the quality of the relevance feedback algorithm. The information given by the user is vitally important in helping the relevance feedback algorithm make good query modification decisions.

Minka and Picard proposed an interactive learning system that takes the relevance feedback approach toward image data. Their system splits the initial image feature groupings according to both negative and positive feedback given by the user. In an image database system, this learned division would act as complex, refined queries, much like the queries in textual systems.

The theory behind *PicHunter* is incorporating the responses from the user and a probabilistic model of that user. First, PicHunter represents an example of a general Bayesian framework that uses relevance feedback to direct a search. PicHunter uses Bayes's rule to predict the target of a user's need, given his or her actions. This is done through a probability distribution over probable image targets, rather than by refining a query. Second, an entropy-minimizing algorithm is described that attempts to maximize the information obtained from a user of the search. Third, PicHunter makes use of hidden annotation rather than a possibly inaccurate or inconsistent annotation structure that the user must learn to make queries. *PicHunter* refines its answers in reply to user feedback, rather than refining any query.

Harman suggests two possible methods for implementing relevance feedback on Boolean systems. The first is to present the user with a list of possible new query terms. These can be chosen, for example, by the term distribution in the relevant documents. This means selecting those terms that appear more frequently in the relevant than in the nonrelevant documents and which would be useful to include in a new query. Another approach is for the system to automatically modify the Boolean queries.

Spink looked at the various types of feedback in mediated Boolean information-seeking sessions. Based on her study of searches, she proposed a classification of five types of feedback. These are not all types of relevance feedback; they also include query modification actions that are intended to modify the search in some other way. Her classification of feedback types is as follows:

- *Content relevance feedback* is the second most common type of feedback. In all the searches studied, the user and intermediary used the content of documents to make a relevance decision. The decision could be either negative or positive. This was the only type of feedback where the user's decisions were more common than the intermediary's decisions. Based on content relevance feedback, searchers could modify their query to perform a search again with modified query.

- *Term relevance feedback* was the identification of new search terms by the user or intermediary from the relevant material. This was used fairly evenly across searches—that is, intermediaries and users employed it in approximately the same number of searches, but intermediaries tended to use the technique more often within a search. This type of feedback was used far less often than content or magnitude feedback.

- *Magnitude feedback* refers to feedback based on the size of the retrieved set of documents. Decisions were that the retrieved set was too large, too small, or just about right. This type of feedback was the most commonly observed feedback type. Intermediaries used this type of feedback in all searches; users initiated magnitude feedback in around three-quarters of the searches.

- *Tactical review feedback* was based on search strategies. This feedback specifically involved the intermediary examining the search history to make a decision about how to proceed with the search, for example, to avoid repeating a previous search. This may not be an operation that is likely to be performed by an inexperienced user of the system.
- *Terminology review* corresponds to around 1% of feedback instances. It involves the intermediary or user making a strategic decision by looking at terms in an inverted file. For example, the intermediary may search for alternative spellings of query terms.

Typically, the user marks the documents he or she finds relevant, either based on the title and brief description shown in the initial list or by essentially reviewing the full document, which the user can link to from the results page. The algorithm applied for user-based relevance feedback is normally identical to that for automatic relevance feedback. The system then again does the search with the revised query, and the optimistically enhanced query produces a revised ranked list of documents. The loop of the relevance feedback is iterative and can be performed many times until the user is satisfied.

3

Contextual and Conceptual Information Retrieval

3.1 Context Search

Traditional retrieval models presuppose that the user's information need is completely represented by the user's query. When the same query is submitted by different users, a typical search engine returns the same result regardless of who gave the query. This may not be appropriate for users with different informations needs. In order to address this problem, personalized information retrieval (IR) is an active area that aims at enhancing an IR process with the user's context such as distinct taste and interests in order to deliver accurate results in response to a user query. Because users may have different characteristics, the idea is to present differently the contents for each user when users submit the same query. The goal is to automate this adaptation in order to reduce the cognitive overload of the user when he or she queries the search engine for documents.

3.1.1 Need for Contextual Search

Some keywords have multiple contextual senses or meanings known as *polysemy*. For example, in English "mouse" is a pointing device in computing and rodent in other uses. Polysemy can also be classified as noun-polysemy and verb-polysemy, and so on—the keyword "mouse" is an example of noun-polysemy. There are numerous words that when used as noun, verb, and so on, lead to different meanings. For example, "fly" if used as a noun refers to an insect, and if used as a verb refers to "the act of moving in the air." These different meanings are also called different contextual perceptions of words.

Whenever any such keyword is given to a search engine, it fails to capture the actual context of the keyword that a user desires before processing the query. As a result, documents are evaluated for multiple contextual senses, and consequently, large numbers of documents are returned in response to a user query having the same keyword but in different senses. To avoid this problem, contextual search is needed.

3.1.2 Graphical Representation of Context-Based Search

Figure 3.1 depicts a graphical understanding of the context-based search engine. In this figure, a user is searching the keyword "palm" on the search engine. The word "palm" could mean various things, such as a type of tree, a part of the human hand, or even a popular handheld device. Here the user's expectation is to get pages related to handheld devices, but actually the keyword-based search engine returns the pages related to tree, human, handheld devices, and so on. The context-based search provides the user with pages of handheld devices, which is the user's expected result from a search engine.

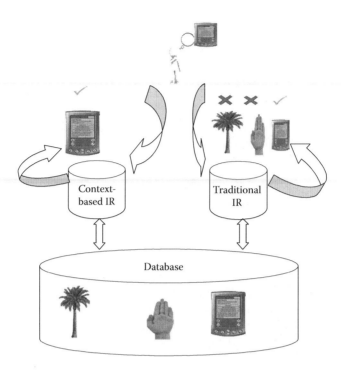

FIGURE 3.1
Context-based search.

3.1.3 Architecture of Context-Based Indexing

The architecture of context-based indexing is depicted in Figure 3.2. The web pages are gathered by a crawler and are stored in the massive store. Each web page document is identified by its document ID.

Various components of context-based architecture are as follows:

- *Crawler:* This is an Internet boat that systematically browses the Web, for the aim of Web indexing.

- *Crawled web page repository:* This is the group of web documents that have been collected by the crawler from the World Wide Web.

- *Indexer:* It keeps an index of the documents that are being gathered by the crawler, which is in the form of attaching lists that contain the term as well the document identifiers of the documents which hold the given term.

- *Document preprocessing:* This stage performs stemming as well as removal of stop words. A stop word does not have any semantic content. Familiar stop words are prepositions and articles, as well as a high occurrence of words in documents that do not help in the retrieval process.

- *Thesaurus:* It is a dictionary of words available on the World Wide Web from thesaurus.com, which holds the words as well as their multiple meanings.

- *Word-Net:* This is a lexical database for the English language. It categorizes English words into sets of synonyms called SynSets, each expressing distinct concept.

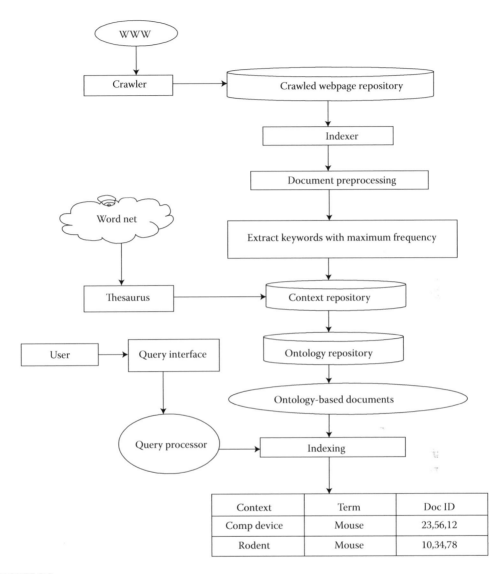

FIGURE 3.2
General architecture of context-based indexing.

- *Context repository:* This is a database that holds the various contexts, and new contexts derived from a thesaurus are stored in this repository. The context repository maintains a database of several types of context data.
- *Ontology repository:* This is a database of ontologies that holds the various relationships between objects in different domains. An ontology repository contains various concepts with their relationships.
- *Ontology-based context of the document:* This indicates the semantic or theme of the document that has been extracted using context repository, thesaurus, and ontology repository.

- *Indexing:* After gathering the context of the document on the basis of ontology, this is a final index that is being created. Rather than being formed on the term basis, the index is created based on context with context as the first field, term as the second field, and finally the document identifiers of the pertinent documents.
- *Query interface:* This is the component of the search engine that accepts user queries.
- *Query processor:* This module searches the result in the index and provides the pertinent result to the user.

3.1.4 Approaches for Context Search

There are two generic approaches for searching based on the user's context level. They are

- Searching based on explicitly specifying user context
- Searching based on automatically derived context

3.1.4.1 Searching Based on Explicitly Specifying User Context

This method requires the user to specify the context information manually as metadata for the search engine throughout the search process in order to increase the precision level of returned results. Inquirus 2 is a meta search engine that behaves as a mediator between the user query and other search engines. When searching on Inquirus 2, the user has to enter a query and specify constraints such as the information need category, maximum number of hits, and display formats. For example, a user looking for research papers can specify documents with "references" or "abstracts" to be rated higher.

3.1.4.2 Searching Based on Automatically Derived Context

This method requires deriving the context information based on the content of other documents users already view—that is, the previous search history of users. Enrich the given user query with the derived context information in order to improve the precision of search results. For example, the objective of IBM's Watson Project is to create a cognitive technology that dynamically learns as it processes user queries. When introduced with a query, Watson creates a hypothesis that is evaluated against its present bank of knowledge based on previous questions. As associated terms and relevant documents are matched against the query, Watson's hypothesis is modified to show the new information provided through unstructured data based on information it has obtained in previous situations. Watson's ability to build off previous knowledge allows queries to be automatically filtered for similar contexts in order to supply accurate results.

3.1.5 Traditional Method for Context-Based Search: User Profile-Based Context Search

Corinne Amel Zayani proposed the method of context-based search based on users interests derived from their profile document. The objective of this method is to reduce the cognitive overload of the user when he or she queries semi-structured documents. Here individual characteristics of users are modeled in user profiles. The characteristics correspond to information connecting to an individual, such as personal information (name, age, etc.), interests, and preferences. This method works in the following steps:

1. Select the user's interests to use for query enhancement. This part gathers user's interests from the user profile.

2. Sort the selected user's interests in diminishing order of frequencies (degrees) and in combining them into a Boolean combination of enriched queries.

3. Return the search results based on enriched queries.

4. Update the user profile from the query. This update consists of adding new interests (conditions of the initial query) to the profile or increasing frequencies for existing ones.

3.2 Conceptual Search

Conceptual search is a technique that provides words that are similar in concept to a query word. A concept search will return documents that associate to the same concept as the query word, regardless of whether the query word exists in the search results documents. It is an automated IR method that is used to search electronically saved unstructured text for information that is conceptually similar to the information provided in a search query. Most search technology in use today is traditional keyword search that requires the search term to appear in the retrieved documents. Many of these traditional search engines have mimicked conceptual search through the use of synonym lists and other human-maintained query expansion approaches.

Conceptual search allows you to locate information about a topic by understanding what words mean in a given context. Concept-based IR represents both documents and queries using semantic concepts, alternative to keywords, and performs retrieval in that concept space. The advantage of using concepts is that different terms with identical meanings are mapped to the same concept (e.g., the terms "automobile" and "vehicle" map the same concept in concept-based IR). Using high-level concepts makes the retrieval model less reliant on the particular terms being used.

3.2.1 The Semantic Web

Semantics is the research of the meanings of signs, such as terms or words. Depending on the approaches, models used to add semantics to terms, separate degrees of semantics can be achieved. Semantic Web is the new generation Web that tries to state information such that it can be used by machines, not just for display purposes, but for automation, concatenation, and reuse beyond applications. Semantic Web is about explicitly declaring the knowledge embedded in many Web-related applications, integrating information in an intelligent way, providing semantic-based access to the Internet, and gathering information from texts.

3.2.2 Ontology

Ontology consists of a finite list of terms and the associations between the terms. The terms denote essential concepts (classes of objects) of the domain. For example, in a university setting, staff members, students, courses, modules, lecture theaters, and schools are some important concepts. In the context of the Web, ontology provides a shared understanding of a domain. Such a shared understanding is necessary to overcome the difference in terminology. Ontologies are useful for improving the accuracy of Web searches by exploiting generalization/specialization information. That is, if a query fails to find a relevant document, the search engine may recommend to the user a more general query. If too many answers are retrieved, the search engine may suggest to the user some specializations. In concept-based information retrieval systems, ontology can serve as a resource specification and can be used for query formulation.

Typical components of ontologies include the following:

- *Terms*: Important concepts (classes of objects) of the domain (e.g., professors, staff, students, courses, departments)
- *Relationships*: Links between these terms: typically class hierarchies a class C to be a subclass of another class C' if every object in C is also included in C' (e.g., all professors are staff members)
- *Properties*: Features, characteristics, or parameters that objects (and classes) can have (e.g., X teaches Y)
- *Restrictions*: Formally stated descriptions of what must be true in order for some assertion to be accepted as input (e.g., only faculty members can teach courses)
- *Axioms*: Coherency description between concepts/properties/relations via logical expressions; assertions (including rules) in a logical form that together comprise the overall theory that the ontology describes in its domain of application
- *Events*: The state of changing the values of attributes or relations among the concepts

3.2.3 Approaches to Conceptual Search

There are two basic approaches to conceptual search:

1. *Statistical methods*: Statistical methods usually learn from text and do not require any pre-built language models. Statistical methods examine how terms are used within the document collection to be searched. The statistical method determines the underlying structure of the language based on the documents in the collection.
2. *Linguistic methods*: This method includes natural language processing (NLP) and syntactic approaches and requires models of language that are created and maintained by humans. These models are based on insight into the language and content, or from a training set of related text in order to find universal properties of language and to account for the language's development.

3.2.4 Types of Conceptual Structures

The main types of conceptual structures used in concept-based information retrieval systems are described below.

- *Conceptual taxonomy*: Conceptual taxonomy is a hierarchical organization of concept descriptions according to a generalization relationship. Each concept in taxonomy has a link to its most specific subsumes ("parents" or super concepts) and links to its most general subsumes ("children" or subconcepts) in a taxonomy.
- *Formal or domain ontology*: Ontology is a conceptual representation of the entities, events, and their relationships that compose a specific domain. Two primary relationships are abstraction and composition ("part-of" relationship).

- *Thesaurus*: Thesaurus is a collection of words or phrases mapped through a set of relationships including synonym, antonym, and "isa" relationship. It provides automatic semantic term expansion of queries in IR systems.
- *Predictive model*: Predictive models like neural networks can be used for concept-based IR.

3.2.5 Features of Conceptual Structures

Conceptual structures used for concept-based IR are characterized by the following features:

- *Type of conceptual structure*: Concept taxonomy, domain ontology, top ontology, linguistic ontology, semantic linguistic network, predictive model, thesaurus, and dictionary
- *Form of representation of a conceptual structure*: Tree, semantic network, context vectors, conceptual graphs, rule-based language, logic language, etc.
- *Relationships supported by a conceptual structure*: Subsumption, a kind-of, a part-of, associations, relations, etc.
- *Way of creation of a conceptual structure*: Manual creation, automatic learning, and NLP

3.2.6 Framework for Concept-Based Search

Figure 3.3 shows general steps in a concept-based IR system.

Initially, information resources and user query are represented based on concepts. Second, discover concepts in information resources and user queries. Because words can be ambiguous, so that one word may represent many concepts, there is a need to disambiguate them. This process is known as word sense disambiguation (WSD). Finally, do conceptual matching among the extracted concepts. At this step it is simple to find precise concept matching, but the important part is to match the remaining relevant concepts with the use of a knowledge repository.

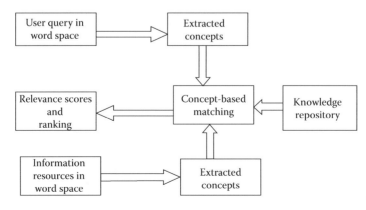

FIGURE 3.3
General framework of concept-based IR.

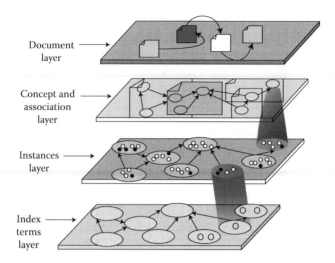

FIGURE 3.4
Concept Chain Graph layers.

The knowledge repository gives information about concepts and their association with other concepts. At this point, which relationships to choose to go to relevant concepts is a problem. So this step needs a knowledge repository that does not miss any concepts and any associations in the application domain. Developing such a knowledge base is a challenge for concept-based access.

3.2.7 Concept Chain Graphs

Rohini K. Srihari proposed the Concept Chain Graphs (CCGs), which are a new content representation for the IR model and are conducive to text mining. Here, the concepts and associations are represented as a graph. CCG is a hypergraph $G(E, V)$ with E edges and V nodes representing a set of documents D with the following properties:

- Each node V represents a term, a concept, or a document.
- Each edge E represents an association between two concepts or a membership link.

A CCG is a hierarchical relationship of index terms, concepts, associations, and documents using directed as well as undirected links and can be viewed as of four layers as shown in Figure 3.4.

- *Document layer*: Contains documents and links (e.g., hyperlinks) between them
- *Concepts and associations layer*: Consists of concepts and associations coming from corpus or ontology mapping
- *Instances layer*: Tracks instances of concepts and associations detected in the corpus back to documents; also maintains instance-specific information of last offsets and type
- *Index terms layer*: Consists of index terms and hits

4

Information Retrieval Models

4.1 Boolean Model

The Boolean information retrieval model is a classical information retrieval (IR) model and, at the same time, the first model of IR probably used by many IR systems. The Boolean model is based on set theory and Boolean logic. The documents are regarded as sets of terms. A document is relevant to a query if the document makes the query formula true. In this model, queries and the corresponding documents are combined by using the operators of George Boole's mathematical logic, such as the conjunctive (AND), disjunctive (OR), or negation (NOT) operators. The Boolean retrieval model is an exact-match model. The model retrieves documents that exactly match the user's query.

Combining terms with the AND operator will be a document set that is smaller than or equal to the document sets of any of the single terms. For example, for the query *"information* AND *retrieval* AND *system"* the system will return all documents that have the three query terms. Combining the terms with the OR operator will be a document set that is larger than or identical to the document sets of any of the single terms. For instance, the query *"information* OR (*retrieval* AND *system*)" retrieves all the documents in a corpus that contains the word *"information"* and the documents that contain the words *"retrieval"* and *"system"* together in a document.

The advantages of this model are that the concept of a set is quite intuitive. The Boolean retrieval model offers a framework that is easy to understand by a common user of an IR system. Its main drawback is that it does not assign ranks to retrieved documents. Retrieval strategy is based on a binary decision criterion without any notion of a grading scale, which causes the worst retrieval performance. It is complex to translate an information need into a Boolean expression. Most users find it difficult and awkward to express their query in terms of expressions.

Nevertheless, the Boolean model remains popular with users because of the unambiguous control that is offered by the systems to the user. The Boolean model serves as a starting point of many of the retrieval models; it is firmly grounded in mathematics, and its perception of document sets offers a prevailing method of reasoning about information retrieval. In this way, the Boolean retrieval model is "a model of models" and serves as a reference point for other retrieval models.

4.2 Vector Model

Peter Luhn was the first to introduce a statistical model for IR, based on the notion of similarity to search information. The vector model recognizes that the use of binary weights is too limiting and proposes a framework for partial matching of query and documents. This is accomplished by assigning nonbinary weights to index terms in queries and terms in documents. The assigned term weights are ultimately used to compute the degree of similarity between each document and the user query. By organizing the retrieved documents in decreasing order of this degree of similarity, this model considers the documents matching the query terms partially.

4.2.1 The Vector Space Model

Gerard Salton and his colleagues base the vector space model on Luhn's similarity criterion that has a stronger theoretical motivation suggested. The similarity measure is usually the cosine of the angle that divides the two vectors $\vec{d}_j$ and $\vec{q}$. If the cosine of an angle is $0°$, then the value is 1; if an angle is 0, then the vectors are orthogonal in the multidimensional space. The cosine formula is given by

$$\cos(\vec{d}_j, \vec{q}) = \frac{\sum_{i=1}^{t} w_{ij} \times w_{iq}}{\sqrt{\sum_{i=1}^{t}(w_{ij})^2} \cdot \sqrt{\sum_{i=1}^{t}(w_{iq})^2}} \tag{4.1}$$

The metaphor of angles between vectors in a multidimensional space makes it simple to describe to the common user. Up to three dimensions, one can easily visualize the document and query vectors. The intuitive geometric interpretation makes it relatively easy to apply the model to new IR problems. If index representations and queries are properly normalized, then the vector product measure of Equation 4.1 does have a strong theoretical motivation. Then the formula becomes normalized:

$$\text{Score}(\vec{d}_j, \vec{q}) = \sum_{i=1}^{t} n(d_j) \cdot n(q) \tag{4.2}$$

4.2.2 Similarity Measures

4.2.2.1 Cosine Similarity

The cosine similarity of two documents on the vector space is a measure that calculates the cosine of the angle between the two documents. This metric is a measurement of orientation and not magnitude. The comparison between documents takes place on a normalized space, because it does not take into consideration the magnitude of all word counts of each document.

The cosine of two vectors can be derived by using the Euclidean dot product formula:

$$\vec{x}.\vec{y} = \|\vec{x}\| \|\vec{y}\| \cos\theta$$

The two vectors of attributes, x and y, and the cosine similarity $\cos(\theta)$, is represented using a dot product and magnitude as

$$\text{Similarity} = \cos(\vec{x}, \vec{y}) = \frac{\vec{x} \cdot \vec{y}}{|\vec{x}| \, |\vec{y}|} \qquad (4.3)$$

$$= \frac{\sum_{i=1}^{n} x_i \times y_i}{\sqrt{\sum_{i=1}^{n} x_i^2} \times \sqrt{\sum_{i=1}^{n} y_i^2}}$$

4.2.2.2 Jaccard Coefficient

The Jaccard coefficient measures similarity between collected sample sets, and the definition is as follows: the size of the intersection divided by the size of the union of the sample sets:

$$\text{Jaccard}(x, y) = \frac{|x \cap y|}{|x \cup y|} \qquad (4.4)$$

4.2.2.3 Dice Coefficient

The Dice index (dice coefficient) is a statistic applied to compare the similarity of two samples. The Dice coefficient method is applied to find the presence or absence of data, and is

$$QS = \frac{2|x \cap y|}{|x| + |y|} \qquad (4.5)$$

where $|x|$ and $|y|$ are the two samples. QS is known as the quotient of similarity and ranges between 0 and 1. When taken as a string similarity measure, the coefficient may be calculated for two strings, x and y, using bigrams as follows:

$$s = \frac{2n_t}{n_x + n_y} \qquad (4.6)$$

where n_t is the number of character bigrams found in both strings, n_x is the amount of bigrams in string x, and n_y is the number of bigrams in string y. This coefficient is not very different from the Jaccard index. However, it does not satisfy the triangle inequality; it can be considered a symmetric version of the Jaccard index.

4.3 Fixing the Term Weights

The document and query term weights of the vector represent the importance of the term for expressing the meaning of the document and query. There are two widely used products of two statistics for calculating term weights; namely, *tf* (term frequency) and *idf* (inverse document frequency). The term frequency and inverse document frequency values become greater proportionally to the number of times a word appears in the document.

Variations of the *tf-idf* weighting scheme are utilized by search engines as a central tool in scoring and ranking a document's relevance given a user query. *tf-idf* can be used for stop-words filtering in a variety of fields including text summarization and classification. The ranking is computed by summing the *tf-idf* for each query term; many more sophisticated ranking functions are variants of this simple model.

4.3.1 Term Frequency

The term frequency ($tf_{t,d}$) of term t in a document d is defined as the number of times that t occurs in d. The *tf* of a term t is indexed by the maximum term frequency of term t in the document d to bring the range 0–1. The raw frequency of t by $f_{t,d}$, then the simple *tf* scheme is $tf_{(t,d)} = f_{t,d}$. Mathematically, the term frequency of a term t in document d is given by ratio of the frequency of the occurrence specific term and the term with the maximun frequency of occurrence in the corpus.

$$tf_{t,d} = \frac{freq_{t,d}}{\max_l(freq_{l,d})} \tag{4.7}$$

where $freq_{t,d}$ represents the sum of the term t appearing in document d.

4.3.2 Inverse Document Frequency

The *inverse document frequency* is a measure of information the word provides—that is, the term t is common or rare across all documents d. It is the logarithmically scaled inverse division of the documents that contain the word, obtained by dividing the total number of documents by the number of documents that have the term t, and then taking the logarithm of that quotient. The inverse document frequency (*idf*) of a term is given by

$$idf_i = \log \frac{N}{n_i} \tag{4.8}$$

where n_i is the number of documents in which the term i occurs, and N is the total number of documents. The expression of *idf* comes from the information theory perspective. If the term i occurs in n_i number of documents among a total of N documents, then the term will occur in a randomly picked document with probability (n_i/N). Therefore, the fraction of information carried by the statement "A document d contains the term i" is given by

$$-\log \frac{n_i}{N} = \log \frac{N}{n_i} \tag{4.9}$$

4.3.3 *tf-idf*

The *tf-idf* weight of a term is the product of its *tf* weight and its *idf* weight. Then *tf-idf* is calculated as

$$tf - idf(t,d,N) = tf(t,d) \cdot idf(t,N) \tag{4.10}$$

A high weight in *tf-idf* is reached by a high term frequency *tf* and a low document frequency of the term in the collection of documents.

4.4 Probabilistic Models

Maron and Kuhns formulated a classic retrieval method, with a criterion that implicitly goes against Luhn's idea to use the measure of similarity between index representations and query. The retrieval system should rank the documents, judging the probability of the document as being relevant to a specific query.

Robertson and Van Rijsbergen found that documents and queries are also viewed as vectors, but the vector space similarity measure is replaced by a probabilistic function (Robertson et al. 1981; Robertson 1997). The probabilistic model is based on estimating the probability that a document will be relevant to a particular query. The higher this estimated probability, the more likely the document is to be relevant to the user. The probabilistic retrieval model also refers to the binary independence retrieval model. The idea behind the probabilistic retrieval model is the probabilistic ranking principle.

4.4.1 Probabilistic Ranking Principle (PRP)

The retrieval system needs to deal with uncertainty; it is better to use probability and give users the retrieval result according to the probability of relevance. This is the beginning of the probabilistic ranking principle, formulated by Robertson. The reference retrieval system's response to each request is a ranking of the documents in the set, according to decreasing probability of usefulness to the user. The probabilities are estimated as accurately as possible based on whatever data are made available to the system. Then the overall effectiveness of the system to its users will be obtained based on that data.

Robertson justified the PRP optimal retrieval procedure through decision theory. If the cost of reading a nonrelevant document is a_1 and the cost of missing a relevant document is a_2, then the minimal cost of retrieving a document d will be

$$a_2 \cdot P(r|d) > a_1 \cdot P(\bar{r}|d) \tag{4.11}$$

or

$$a_2 \cdot P(r|d) > a_1 \cdot (1 - P(r|d)) \tag{4.12}$$

then

$$P(r|d) > \frac{a_1}{a_1 + a_2} \tag{4.13}$$

where $P(r|d)$ represents the probability of relevant documents, $P(\bar{r}|d)$ denotes the probability of nonrelevant documents, and $a_1/(a_1 + a_2)$ is the cut-off of the probability ranking list. In order to develop a PRP for interactive IR, fulfill the following requirements:

Judge the whole interaction process: The new approach should cover all of the interactions of a user with an IR system, instead of focusing on document ranking.

Allow for diverse costs and benefits of different activities: The types of activities in interactive IR require different efforts. Vice versa, the benefit resulting from an action may also vary, as modifying a query will often have a bigger effect than declaring a document to be relevant.

Allow for changes of the information need: Ultimately, the model should be more active than the classical ranking principle. In this model, any positive information a user finds during a search may change his or her information need.

4.4.2 Binary Independence Retrieval (BIR) Model

The probabilistic model of IR is a generic model that allows many interpretations. The binary independence model is a probabilistic IR technique to make the estimation of document and query similarity probability feasible, based on some assumptions. The BIR model assumption is that documents are binary vectors. The presence or absence of terms in documents is recorded. Terms are independently distributed in the collection of relevant documents, and they are independently distributed in the collection of irrelevant documents. The representation is an ordered set of Boolean variables. The representation of a document or query is a vector with one Boolean element for each term.

More specifically, a document is represented by a vector $d = (x_1, ..., x_m)$, where $x_t = 1$ if term t is present in the document d, and $x_t = 0$ if it is not. Many documents can have the same vector representation with this simplification. Queries are also represented in a similar way. Independence signifies that terms in the document are considered individually from each other, and no relation between the terms is modeled. This assumption is very limiting, but it provides better results for many situations. This assumption allows the representation to be treated as an instance of a vector space model by taking into account each term as a value of 0 or 1 along a dimension orthogonal to the dimensions used for the other terms.

The probability $P(R|d,q)$ of a document is relevant, and derives from the probability of relevance of the terms vector of that document $P(R|x,q)$. By using the Bayes rule,

$$P(R|x,q) = \frac{P(x|R,q) * P(R|q)}{P(x|q)}$$

(4.14)

where $P(x|R = 1, q)$ and $P(x|R = 0, q)$ are the probabilities of retrieving relevant documents, respectively. If so, then that document's representation is x. The exact probabilities are not known beforehand, so estimates from statistics about the collection of documents must be used. $P(R = 1|q)$ and $P(R = 0|q)$ specify the prior probability of retrieving a relevant or nonrelevant document, respectively, for a query q:

$$P(R = 1|x,q) + P(R = 0|x,q) = 1$$

(4.15)

Robertson and Sparck Jones were interested in the binary independence model and its use in relevance feedback. In the relevance feedback, a user enters a query to a search engine, which produces an initial ranking of its document collection based on some measure. The user examines the top-ranked documents and gives feedback to the system on which are relevant to their interest and which are nonrelevant. The shortcoming of BIR is that by taking into account only the presence or absence of terms, the BIR ignores information inherent in the frequencies of terms. For instance, all things being equal, we would expect that if one occurrence of a word is a good clue that a document belongs to a class, then five occurrences should be even more predictive.

4.4.3 The Probabilistic Indexing Model

In the past, most of the probabilistic models investigated were based on a rather simple document representation, namely binary indexing. The probabilistic indexing model shows that significant improvements in retrieval effectiveness can be achieved when binary indexing is replaced by weighted probabilistic indexing. Bill Maron and Larry Kuhns introduce the probabilistic indexing model in 1960. Unlike Luhn, they do not focus on automatic indexing by IR systems. Manual indexing was still guiding the field, so they suggested an indexer, who runs through the various index terms T that possibly apply to a document D, and assigns a probability $P(T|D)$ to a term given a document instead of making a decision for each term. So, every document ends up with a set of index terms, weights are calculated by $P(T|D)$, where $P(T|D)$ is the probability that if a user wants information of the kind contained in document D, they will formulate a query by using T.

By using Bayes' rule,

$$P(D|T) = \frac{P(T|D)P(D)}{P(T)} \tag{4.16}$$

They suggest to rank the documents by $P(D|T)$—that is, the probability of the document D is relevant to the user entering a query by utilizing the term T. Note that $P(T)$ in the denominator of the right-hand side is constant for an entered query term T, and therefore the documents are ranked by $P(T|D)P(D)$, which is a quantity proportional to the value of $P(D|T)$.

In Bayes theorem,

- $P(D)$ is the a priori probability of document D.
- $P(T|D)$ is defined by a manual indexer.

4.5 Language Model

Statistical language modeling (LM) refers to the task of estimating the likelihood that a query will result in finding a document generated by the same language model of the query. Documents are ranked based on the probability of the query Q in the document's language model. The probabilistic retrieval models and language models for IR share the theoretical foundations underlying the general probabilistic IR work. The most used application of language modeling is speech recognition and IR. However, estimating the probabilities of word sequences is more costly, since sentences can be arbitrarily long and the size of a corpus need to be very large. *N*-gram models often approximate the statistical language model:

Unigram model: $P(w_{1,n}) = P(w_1)P(w_2) \ldots P(w_n)$

Bigram model: $P(w_{1,n}) = P(w_1)P(w_2|w_1) \ldots P(w_n|w_{n-1})$

Trigram model: $P(w_{1,n}) = P(w_1)P(w_2|w_1) \, P(w_3|w_{1,2}) \ldots P(w_n|w_{n-2,n-1})$

The models are described above. Each word unigram model occurs independently; consequently, the probability of a word sequence or sentence becomes the product of the probabilities of the individual words. The bigram and trigram models consider the local context: for a bigram, the probability of a new word depends on the probability of the previous word; for trigram, the probability of a word depends on the probabilities of the previous two words. The speech recognition or machine translation applications word order is important, and higher-order (trigram) models are used. In information retrieval, the role of word order is less clear, and unigram models have been used widely.

To establish the *n*-gram language model, the probability estimation is normally derived from frequencies of *n*-gram patterns in the training set. More frequently, many possible word *n*-gram patterns do not appear in the actual information used for assessment, even if the size of the data set is huge and the value of *n* is small. Therefore, for rare or hidden events, the likelihood estimates are directly based on counts becomes challenging. This is referred to as the data sparseness problem. The problem is addressed, and smoothing has been used to resolve this in any language model.

4.5.1 Multinomial Distributions Model

For the unigram language model the sequence of words is inappropriate, and so such models are often called *bag of words* models, even though there is no constraint on the earlier context. However, the multinomial model provides the probability of a particular ordering of terms. Nevertheless, any other set sequence of the bag of terms will have the same probability. From this perspective, the formulas represented above do not represent the multinomial probability of a bag of words, because they do not sum each potential ordering of those words, as is done by the multinomial coefficient in the standard presentation of a multinomial model:

$$P(d) = \frac{L_d!}{tf_{t1,d}!, tf_{t2,d}!, \ldots, tf_{tM,d}!} P(t_1)^{tf_{t1,d}} P(t_2)^{tf_{t2,d}} \ldots P(t_M)^{tf_{tM,d}} \tag{4.17}$$

Here, $L_d = \sum_{1 \le i \le M} tf_{ti,d}$ is the length of document *d*, *M* is the size of the term vocabulary, and the products are the terms in the vocabulary. The fundamental problem in designing language models is that we do not know what exactly should be used as the model M_d. However, in general, random samples of text that is representative of that model are used. This problem makes a lot of sense in the unique key utilization of language models. In speech recognition, those have a training sample of (spoken) text. But, in the future, the user definitely uses the various words in diverse sequences, which were not observed before, and so the model has to simplify ahead of the pragmatic data to allow mysterious words and sequences.

Then the interpretation is overcast in an IR, where a document is finite and fixed. The strategy to adopt in IR is as follows: the user thinks that the document *d* is only a representative sample of text drawn from a model distribution, treating it like a fine-grained topic. Then a language model is estimated from this sample, and that model is used to compute the probability of observing word sequence and rank the documents according to their probability of generating the query.

4.5.2 The Query Likelihood Model

The basic approach for using language models for IR assumes that the user has a rational idea of the terms that are probably to appear in the model document that can satisfy the information they require, and that the query terms the user chooses can distinguish the ideal document from the remaining collection set. The query is thus generated as the piece of text representative of the ideal document. The task of the system is then to estimate, for each of the documents in the collection, which is most probably the document. That is, computed by using Bayes rule,

$$P(d|q) = P(q|d)P(d)/P(q) \tag{4.18}$$

$P(q)$ is the same for all documents, and so can be ignored. The prior probability of a document $P(d)$ is frequently common in all the documents d, so it can be ignored. But, given these simplifications, it returns results ranked by simply $P(q|d)$ the probability of the query q in the LM derived from d. In other words, a probability distribution over words for each document is estimated, and the probability that the query is a sample from that distribution is calculated. Documents are ranked according to this probability. This is generally referred to as the *query-likelihood* retrieval model and was first proposed by Ponte and Croft. They represent a query as a vector of binary attributes, one for each unique term in the vocabulary, indicating the presence or absence of terms in the query. The number of times that each term occurs in the query is not captured. There are a couple of assumptions behind this approach: (1) the *binary* assumption: all attributes are binary. If a term occurs in the query, the attribute representing the term takes the value of 1. Otherwise, it takes the value of 0; and (2) the *independence* assumption: terms occur independently of one another in a document. These assumptions are the same as those that underlie the *binary independence* model proposed in earlier probabilistic IR work. The most frequent way to do this is to use the multinomial unigram model; the model is equivalent to a multinomial Naive Bayes model, where the documents are the classes, each considered in the estimation, as a separate language. In this model,

$$P(q|M_d) = K_q \prod_{t \in V} P(t|M_d)^{tf_{t,d}} \tag{4.19}$$

where again $K_q = L_d!/tf_{t1,d}!, tf_{t2,d}!, \ldots, tf_{tM,d}!$ is the multinomial coefficient for the query q, which will henceforth be ignored, because it is a constant for a specific query. The generation of queries is a random process in the language model retrieval. The method is to

- Infer a language model for each document.
- Estimate the $P(q|M_{d_i})$, the probability of generating the query according to each of these document models.
- Rank the documents based on the probability.

The intuition of the basic model is that the user has a document need in his or her mind and generates a query based on the words that appear in the particular document. The users have a sensible idea of terms that are probably to occur in a document of their interest. Then, they will decide the query terms that differentiate these documents from others in the collection set. The document collection statistics are an essential element of LM, rather than used heuristically as in different approaches.

4.5.3 Extended Language Modeling Approaches

In this section, a few processes that extend the fundamental LM approach are briefly discussed. Rather than looking at the probability of a document in language model M_d, the query language model M_q is generated for the probability of a document. The important motivation that doing things in this direction and creating a *document likelihood model* is less appealing. However, it is simple to incorporate relevance feedback into a model. The user can develop the query with terms from the relevant documents in the typical way and then update the language model M_d.

Rather than directly generating in either direction, a language model should be made from both the document and query. For instance, one way to model the risk of returning a document d as relevant to a query q is to utilize the *Kullback–Leibler (KL) divergence* among their respective language models:

$$R(d;q) = KL(M_d \| M_q) = \sum_{t \in V} P(t | M_q) \log \frac{P(t | M_q)}{P(t | M_d)} \tag{4.20}$$

K-L divergence is an asymmetric divergence measure originating in information theory, which measures how bad the probability distribution M_q is at modeling M_d. One disadvantage of using K-L divergence as a ranking function is that the scores are not analogous across queries. Kraaij and Spitters suggest an alternative proposal, which models similarity as a normalized log-likelihood ratio. Basic LMs do not address the issues of alternate expression, which is synonymy or any variation in the use of language among the documents and queries. Berger and Lafferty introduce translation models to bridge this query-document gap.

4.5.4 Translation Model

A *translation model* generates the query words not in a document by translation to alternate terms with related semantics. Taking a different angle, Berger and Lafferty view a query as a distillation or translation from a document. The query generation process is described in terms of a noisy channel model. To determine the relevance of a document to a query, their model estimates the probability that the query would have been generated as a translation of that document. Documents are then ranked according to these probabilities. The translation model also provides a basis for performing cross-language IR. It assumes that the translation model can be represented by a conditional probability distribution $T(\cdot|\cdot)$ between vocabulary terms. The form of the translation query model is then

$$P(q|M_d) = \prod_{t \in q} \sum_{v \in V} P(v|M_d) T(t|v) \tag{4.21}$$

The term $P(v|M_d)$ is the basic document language model, and the term $T(t|v)$ performs translation. A notable feature of this model is an inherent query expansion component and its capability to handle the issues of synonymy and polysemy. However, as the translation models are context independent, their ability to handle the ambiguity of word senses is only limited. While significant improvements over the baseline language model through the use of translation models are reported, this approach is not without its weaknesses: the need of a large collection of training data for estimating translation probabilities, and inefficiency for ranking documents. This model is clearly more computationally intensive, and it needs to build a translation model. The translation model is built using separate resources but can be built using the document collection if there are pieces of text that naturally interpret or summarize other pieces of text. In general, translation models, relevance feedback models, and model comparison approaches are demonstrated to improve performance over the basic query likelihood LM.

4.5.5 Comparisons with Traditional Probabilistic IR Approaches

The language modeling (LM) approach has introduced a new method of probabilistic models. A number of researchers attempted to relate the LM approach to the traditional probabilistic retrieval approaches and evaluate their dissimilarities. Sparck and Robertson inspect the concept of relevance in the traditional probabilistic approach (PM) and the new language modeling approach. They have identified the two differences between the two models. The first difference between the models is in both approaches, a matching on index keys between a document and a query implies relevance. The relevance figures explicitly in PM but is never stated in LM. Then the next more significant distinction is that the fundamental principle of LM is to recognize the ideal document that generates the query rather than a list of relevant documents. Once the ideal document is recovered, retrieval becomes the end. Because of this, they argue that the difficulties are in describing significant processes such as relevance feedback in the existing LM approaches.

Zhai and Lafferty (2001), Lavrenko and Croft (2001) address these issues directly and suggest new forms of the LM approach to retrieval that are closely related to the traditional probabilistic approach. Zhai and Lafferty argue that in the traditional probabilistic approach proposed by Robertson and Sparck Jones, a document could be thought of as generated from a query using a binary latent variable that indicates whether the document is relevant to the query. They show through mathematical derivations that the probabilistic approach and language modeling approach are on equal footing in terms of the relevance ranking and analysis of the ranking process, while a similar binary latent variable is introduced to LM.

However, this does not represent that the PM and LM are just a deterioration of both model. They point out that the length normalization of documents is the significant issue in PM, but it is not so in LM. Another difference is that in LM there is a larger amount of data for estimating a statistical model than in PM which is the advantage of *turning the problem*. Zhai and Lafferty suggested the risk-minimization framework for both models, and the relevance model suggested by Lavrenko and Croft (2001) moves away from estimating the probability of generating query text to estimating the probability of generating document text or comparing query and document language models directly.

Zhai and Lafferty point out that traditional IR models rely heavily on ad hoc parameter tuning to achieve satisfactory performance, whereas in LM, statistical estimation methods are used to set parameters automatically. Hiemstra (2001) relates LM to traditional approaches by comparing Hiemstra's model with the *tf-idf* term weighting and the relevance weighting combined together in the BM25 algorithm. In information retrieval, BM25 (Best Matching) is a ranking function used by search engines to rank matching documents according to their relevance to a given search query. It is based on the probabilistic retrieval framework. They conclude that LM and PM have important similarities. Probabilistic interpretation and justification of the *tf-idf* weighting are provided in LM. Fuhr (1992) shows the relation between the LM approach and other probabilistic retrieval models in the framework of uncertain inference.

5

Evaluation of Information Retrieval Systems

This chapter discusses various evaluation techniques available for information retrieval (IR) systems. The efficiency of an IR technique is measured with the help of test collections. The details of test collections are discussed later in this chapter. The IR system produces results in ranked and unranked manners for each result set; this chapter discusses the formal evaluation methods.

There are many factors involved in evaluating a technique. Retrieving results alone will not justify a technique as the best one. The other factors of performance are speed, accuracy, cost, and so on.

5.1 Ranked and Unranked Results

The results produced by various IR techniques can be classified into two types: ranked and unranked. Few IR techniques produce results in an orderly manner, which is considered as ranked results. Other techniques produce results in an unordered manner, which is considered as unranked results. There are evaluation schemes available for both sets of techniques.

5.1.1 Relevance

The basic methodology in evaluating an IR system is binary classification, which groups the result either in relevant or nonrelevant classes.

5.2 Unranked Retrieval System

The basic evaluation technique in this classification is precision and recall. The general form is expressed in contingency matrix form, which represents the general raw count of the documents in each corresponding section (Table 5.1).

5.2.1 Precision

Precision denotes the fraction of relevant instances in the retrieved results. Precision is also known as positive predictive value. Precision and recall evaluation metrics are used in Boolean retrieval or top-k retrieval techniques.

TABLE 5.1

2×2 Contingency Matrixes

	Relevant Documents	Nonrelevant Documents
Documents retrieved	True positive	False positive
Documents not retrieved	False negative	True negative

$$Precision = \frac{|\text{relevant documents} \cap \text{reterived documents}|}{|\text{reterived documents}|} \tag{5.1}$$

Notation expressed using the contingency matrix is as follows:

$$Precision = \frac{(true\ positive)}{(true\ positive + false\ positive)} \tag{5.2}$$

$$Precision\ \% = \frac{true\ positive}{true\ positive + false\ positive} * 100\% \tag{5.3}$$

In Equations 5.1 through 5.3, the *true positive* is the number of relevant documents retrieved, and *false positive* is the number of irrelevant documents. The objective is to maximize the precision value.

5.2.2 Recall

The most frequently used method for evaluating IR is precision and recall. Recall denotes the fraction of relevant instances that are retrieved. Recall is also known as sensitivity. In other words, recall can be defined as the number of true positives divided by the total number of elements that actually belong to the positive class (i.e., the sum of true positives and false negatives, which are the items that were not labeled as belonging to the positive class but should have been):

$$Recall = \frac{|\text{relevant documents} \cap \text{reterived documents}|}{|\text{relevant documents}|} \tag{5.4}$$

Notation expressed using the contingency matrix is as follows:

$$Recall = \frac{(true\ positive)}{(true\ positive + false\ negative)} \tag{5.5}$$

Recall is the ratio of relevant retrieved documents to the total relevant documents.

5.2.3 Accuracy

Accuracy is used to find the proportion of true results among the total number of documents. Accuracy is commonly used to evaluate machine learning classification work and is calculated using the contingency matrix:

$$\text{Accuracy} = \frac{(\text{true positive} + \text{true negative})}{(\text{true positive} + \text{false positive} + \text{false negative} + \text{true negative})} \quad (5.6)$$

In Equation 5.6 accuracy is the ratio of relevant retrieved documents and irrelevant documents not retrieved to the entire document set.

Issues in Precision and Recall

- Measuring recall is difficult when the number of relevant records that exist in a dataset is unknown.
- Determining whether a record is relevant or irrelevant can be problematic. Some records can be marginally relevant and to some extent irrelevant.
- Human relevance assessments are necessary.
- Assessments have to be binary.

5.2.4 *F*-Measure

The *F*-measure combines both precision and recall values. This is the weighted harmonic mean of both values. This is also known as the balanced F_1 score. The best value of the F_1 score is 1, and the worst value is 0. Recall and precision are evenly weighted. Mandl says precision, recall, and *F*-measure are set-oriented measures and thus cannot adequately be used in ranked results systems.

$$F_1 = 2 * \frac{\text{precision} * \text{recall}}{\text{precision} + \text{recall}} \quad (5.7)$$

The general formula for the *F*-score or *F*-measure is

$$F_\beta = (1 + \beta^2) * \frac{\text{precision} * \text{recall}}{(\beta^2 \cdot \text{precision} + \text{recall})} \quad (5.8)$$

In Equation 5.8, F_β measures the effectiveness of the retrieval with respect to a user for β times as much importance to precision and recall (Table 5.2).

5.2.5 *G*-Measure

G-measure is the geometric mean of precision and recall. Geometric mean is often used when comparing different items. This is also known as the Fowlkes–Mallows (FM) index.

TABLE 5.2

F-Measure β Values

β Value	Description
0.5	$F_{0.5}$ gives more weight to precision than recall
2	F_2 weights higher recall than precision

In general, the geometric mean is defined as the nth root of the product of n numbers—that is, for a set of numbers $a_1, a_2, \ldots, a_n$, the geometric mean is defined as

$$\left(\prod_{i=1}^{n} a_i \right)^{1/n} = \sqrt[n]{a_1 a_2 a_3 \ldots a_n} \tag{5.9}$$

In G-measure, $a_1, a_2 \ldots$ are numbers, and when applying precision and recall we get

$$FM = \sqrt{\text{precision} * \text{recall}} \tag{5.10}$$

This can be rewritten as

$$FM = \sqrt{\frac{\text{true positive}}{\text{true positive} + \text{false positive}} + \frac{\text{true positive}}{\text{true positive} + \text{false negative}}} \tag{5.11}$$

The FM index can be defined as the number of points that are common or uncommon in the two-hierarchical clustering, C_1, C_2. If we define

True positive: The number of points that are present in the same cluster in both C_1 and C_2

False positive: The number of points that are present in the same cluster in C_1 but not in C_2.

False negative: The number of points that are present in the same cluster in C_2 but not in C_1

True negative: The number of points that are in different clusters in both C_1 and C_2

5.2.6 Prevalence

Alex Hartemink says that, " prevalence measures the proportion of cases that are positive and is thus independent of the classifier"; the prevalence of negative cases could also be defined analogously. Using the contingency matrix, prevalence is stated as follows:

$$\text{Prevalence} = \frac{\text{true positive} + \text{false negative}}{\text{true positive} + \text{false positive} + \text{false negative} + \text{true negative}} \tag{5.12}$$

5.2.7 Error Rate

Error rate is the percentage of false results (relevant not retrieved and irrelevant retrieved) among the total number of documents:

$$\text{Error Rate} = \frac{\text{false negative} + \text{false positive}}{\text{true positive} + \text{false positive} + \text{false negative} + \text{true negative}} \tag{5.13}$$

TABLE 5.3

Unranked Results Evaluation Measures and Their Applications

S. No	Evaluation Method	Application
1	Precision	Used in a collection of documents for multiple users query
2	Recall	
3	*F*-Measure	
4	*G*-Measure	
5	Prevalence	Used in government dataset, healthcare domain, etc.
6	Error rate	Used in multimedia-based applications such as images, speech recognition, etc.
7	Fall out	
8	Miss rate	

5.2.8 Fallout

The false positive rate is the percentage of irrelevant documents retrieved among the total number of documents. Gerald says that, "fallout can be viewed as the inverse of recall and will never encounter the situation of 0/0 unless all the items in the database are relevant to the search." It is the probability that a retrieved item is nonrelevant. Recall can be viewed as the probability that a retrieved item is relevant. From a system perspective, the ideal system demonstrates maximum recall and minimum fallout. This implicitly has maximum precision:

$$\text{Fall out} = \frac{\text{false positive}}{\text{false positive} + \text{true negative}} * 100\% \tag{5.14}$$

5.2.9 Miss Rate

Miss rate or false negative rate is the proportion of real positive that are retrieved as negative (false-drops) (Table 5.3):

$$\text{Miss Rate} = \frac{\text{false negative}}{\text{true positive} + \text{false negative}} * 100\% \tag{5.15}$$

5.3 Ranked Retrieval System

This section discusses the evaluation techniques relating to the ranked retrieval system.

5.3.1 Precision and Recall Curves

In 1998, Lee and Fox quoted that the general problem with a Boolean search is the observation of AND versus OR, which gives opposite extremes in a precision/recall trade-off, but not the middle ground.

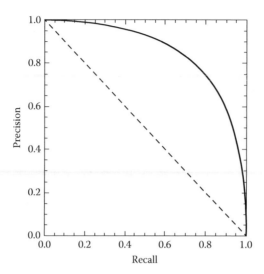

FIGURE 5.1
Sample PR-curve.

Precision and recall are inversely related. When the precision value increases, the recall value falls, and vice versa. PR curves are used to balance between these. A PR curve is obtained from ranked results (Figure 5.1).

The dashed lines denote the bad set of retrieved documents. The continuous line represents that the PR graph is constructed using the obtained PR values. PR values represent two axis in the graph. The scale of these values ranges from 0.0 to 1.0. Based on these values the PR curve is obtained.

In a ranked result, each element contains a top-k value out of k retrieved documents. For such a set, the precision and recall values are plotted on a graph to obtain the PR curve. If the obtained results are relevant, then both precision and recall will increase, and the curve moves toward the top right. If the retrieved document is nonrelevant, then the recall value will be high but the precision value will be low.

5.3.2 Average Precision

The average precision value for the query is calculated by finding the average for each relevant document in the ranked list.

5.3.3 Precision at *k*

In Web search applications, the user requires the relevant links in the first page or within the first 30 results. Hence there is a need to compute the precision at low levels of ranked retrieved results.

5.3.4 *R*-Precision

An alternative to precision at k is R-precision. Initially, we require a collection of relevant documents. This collection is termed as *Rel*. This *Rel* set is a subset of the returned ranked

TABLE 5.4

Precision at k

Retrieved Documents	1	2	3	4	5	6	7	8	9	10
Relevant documents	Y	Y	Y	Y	Y	N	Y	Y	N	Y
Precision at each rank	1/1	2/2	3/3	4/4	5/5	5/6	6/7	7/8	7/9	8/10

documents. In this method each retrieved element is assigned a value 1 for the relevant element among the top-k values. For example, see Table 5.4.

The precision at rank 10 is $8/10 = 0.8$—that is, 80%.

5.3.5 Mean Average Precision (MAP)

Among various evaluation techniques, the mean average precision (MAP) has good stability. Turpin says MAP is the average precision across multiple queries. It is the most commonly used measure in research papers. It assumes that the user is interested in finding many documents for a set of the query. In a dataset multiple queries are executed and for each query the average precision is calculated separately. Then the average is found for these computed values.

5.3.6 Breakeven Point

This evaluation technique also uses a PR curve. A single point in the PR curve is chosen as the breakeven point or the best point in the curve, whereas the point at K and R-precision all other points are considered for computation.

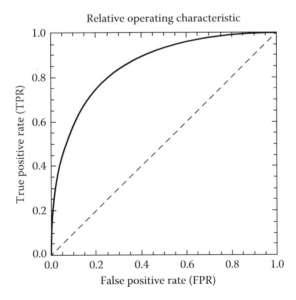

FIGURE 5.2
Sample ROC curve.

TABLE 5.5

Ranked Results Evaluation Measures and Their Applications

S. No	Evaluation Method	Application
1	Precision at k	Web search
2	R-precision	Algorithm evaluation
3	Average precision	Related document retrieval
4	Mean average precision	Effectiveness in queries

5.3.7 ROC Curve

Receiver operating characteristics (ROC) curve is for demonstrating the performance of the binary classification system. The curve is plotted on a graph consisting of two axis: true positive rate (TPR) and false positive rate (FPR). Both axis have a range of values from 0 to 1. The ROC curve is plotted using a cumulative distribution function. Selecting optimal models and discarding suboptimal models can be done easily (Figure 5.2).

In Figure 5.2, the dashed lines denote a bad set of documents. The continuous curved line represents the best result set—it contains more relevant documents.

5.3.7.1 Relationship between PR and ROC Curves

The performance of machine learning algorithms is evaluated using PR and ROC curves on a given dataset. Usually a dataset contains a fixed number of positive and negative examples. For any dataset there exists a one-to-one correspondence between the PR curve and the ROC curve, such that the curves will contain equal numbers of elements in a contingency matrix, such that all recall values are not equal to zero (Table 5.5).

6

Fundamentals of Evolutionary Algorithms

6.1 Combinatorial Optimization Problems

Combinatorial optimization is an approach to find the finest solution out of a very large set of possible solutions. When the set is so large, and it is unfeasible to search through all of them, various methods can be used to narrow down the set or speed up the search. The following examples explain combinatorial optimization problem concepts.

Packing problems can be viewed as complementary to cutting problems in that the aim is to fill a larger space with specified smaller shapes in the most profitable way. There are geometric packing problems in one dimension, two dimensions, and even three dimensions, such as those that arise in filling trucks or shipping containers. The determined size is not always length or width; it may be weight, for example.

In applied mathematics and theoretical computer science, combinatorial optimization is a subject that consists of locating an optimal object from a limited set of objects. This is an area of optimization, where the set of possible solutions is distinct or can be reduced to a distinct one, and the goal is to find the most excellent probable solution. To work with problems of combinatorial optimization, the aim is to discover the finest solution, one that reduces a known cost function.

There are some methods to resolve problems that are not composite, such as branch and cut or branch and bound. As the search space difficulty grows, the cost of those algorithms can enlarge exponentially, creating the search of a solution not possible. An additional way to undertake these problems is to discover a suboptimal explanation but in a reasonable time. In a few cases you may even locate the optimal solution to the problem. Such a method can be separated into two main groups: heuristics and metaheuristics. A new promising technology called *case-based reasoning* (CBR) can be used to crack combinatorial optimization problems in addition to these groups.

6.1.1 Heuristics

Heuristic algorithms consign to the use of systematic actions that typically trade off the excellence of a solution for processing speed. A lot of heuristics are derived from comparatively easy, rational ideas for finding answers to problems, but which will not essentially produce a favorable solution. In a few instances, heuristics create provably optimal solutions. Heuristics are distinct by a set of legitimate moves or transformations of a present solution. High-quality solutions to composite combinatorial problems can be found by developing the knowledge of the application field. Heuristic algorithms are easy to implement and good solutions can be found with relatively small computational effort; however, resign to find the global optimum solution of a problem. In huge problems, a heuristic algorithm rarely finds the best solution.

6.1.2 Metaheuristics

The word *metaheuristic* was initially coined by Glover (1986). It is currently used to refer to the growth of heuristic thoughts that go beyond local search actions as a means of looking for a global optimum, classically by analogy with natural processes. These algorithms are commonly used algorithms that are not based on the problem and offer good results but usually not "the best solution." Examples of metaheuristics include TABU search, simulated annealing, ANT systems, and genetic algorithms.

6.1.3 Case-Based Reasoning (CBR)

CBR is based on the knowledge that new problems are frequently related to previously encountered problems, so that past explanation may be of use in the present state. CBR typically applies retrieval algorithms and identical algorithms to a case based on past problem-solution pairs. At the maximum level of generalization, a general CBR cycle may be explained by the following processes:

- *Retrieve* the most related cases.
- *Reuse* the information case to solve the problem.
- *Revise* the proposed solution.
- *Retain* the parts of this experience likely to be useful for future problem solving.

6.2 Evolutionary Programming

This is a global optimization algorithm and is an instance of an evolutionary algorithm beginning the field of evolutionary computation. The strategy is a sibling of other evolutionary algorithms such as learning classifier systems and genetic algorithms. It is occasionally confused with genetic programming due to the resemblance in name, and more recently it illustrates a strong functional resemblance to evolution strategies. This programming is one of the main evolutionary algorithm paradigms. It is related to genetic programming, but the formation of the program to be optimized is fixed, while its numerical parameters are authorized to evolve.

It was initially used by Lawrence and J. Fogel in the United States in 1960 in order to use simulated evolution as a learning process aspiring to produce artificial intelligence. J. Fogel exercised finite-state machines as predictors and developed them. Presently evolutionary programming is a broad evolutionary computing dialect with no fixed representation, dissimilar to some of the other dialects. It is harder to discriminate from evolutionary strategies.

Evolutionary programming was presented by Dr. Lawrence J. Fogel while serving at the National Science Foundation in 1960. He had been tasked to present a report to the U.S. Congress. At the occasion, artificial intelligence was inadequate for two main avenues of study: modeling the human brain or "neural networks," and modeling the problem-solving behavior of a human specialist or "heuristic programming." The earlier addressed making a mathematical representation of neurons and their connectivity, but little was really known then about how the brain actually operates. The current approach was originally conducted through search-based approaches and later linked by knowledge-based approaches. The heuristic approach necessitates knowledge about the problem domain and some form of proficiency. Both are determined on emulating humans as the most advanced intelligent organisms fashioned by evolution.

The different application areas of evolutionary programming are

- Traffic routing and planning
- Signal processing
- Military planning
- System identification
- Learning in games
- Pharmaceutical design
- Epidemiology
- Cancer detection
- Control systems

6.3 Evolutionary Computation

In computer discipline, evolutionary computation is a subfield of artificial intelligence that can be distinguished by the kinds of algorithms it uses. These algorithms, called evolutionary algorithms, are based on accepting Darwinian philosophy, hence the name. Precisely they belong to the family of trial-and-error problem solvers and can be considered global optimization techniques with a metaheuristic or stochastic optimization nature, illustrated by the use of a population of candidate solutions. They are mostly functional for black box problems, frequently in the context of expensive optimization.

Evolutionary computation utilizes iterative development, such as enlargement or growth in a population. This population is then certain in a guided random search with parallel processing to attain the desired end. Such actions are often stimulated by biological mechanisms of evolution. As evolution can create highly optimized processes and networks, it has many applications in computer science.

A wide variety of problems in engineering, industry, and many other fields, involve the concurrent optimization of several objectives. Many real-world decision-making problems need to attain several objectives: reduce the risks, maximize the consistency, minimize deviations from desired levels, minimize cost, and so on. In many cases, the objectives are distinct in incomparable units, and they present some degree of conflict among them. These problems are called multi-objective optimization problems (MOPs). Let us consider, for example, a shipping company that is interested in minimizing the total duration of its routes to improve customer service. The company also needs to minimize the number of trucks used in order to decrease operating costs. Clearly, these objectives are in conflict because adding more trucks reduces the duration of the routes but increases operation costs. In addition, the objectives of this problem are expressed in different measurement units.

6.3.1 Single-Objective Optimization

Single-objective optimization holds one single objective that desires to be optimized. Many real-world decision-making problems require achieving several objectives: reduce the risks, increase the reliability, minimize deviations from desired levels, minimize cost, and so on. The chief objective of single-objective (SO) optimization is to discover the "best" solution, which corresponds to the minimum or maximum value of a single-objective function that lumps all dissimilar objectives into one. This kind of optimization is useful as a tool that should give decision makers insights into the nature of the problem, but typically cannot provide a set of alternative solutions that trade different objectives beside each other.

6.3.2 Multi-Objective Optimization

Multi-objective optimization algorithms allow for optimizations that get into account multiple objectives concurrently. Every objective can be a minimization or a maximization of an output. It is an area of multiple criteria decision making that is concerned with mathematical optimization problems involving more than one objective function to be optimized concurrently. Multi-objective optimization has been applied in many fields of science, including engineering, economics, and logistics where most favorable decisions require to be taken in the presence of trade-offs between two or more conflicting objectives.

6.4 Role of Evolutionary Algorithms in Information Retrieval

Information retrieval (IR) systems are used to store items of information that need to be processed, searched, and retrieved corresponding to a user's query. Generally information retrieval is performed based on the keywords. The system initially extracts keywords from documents and then assigns weights to the keywords by using different approaches. This system has two problems. One is how to extract keywords accurately, and the other is how to decide the weight of each keyword.

There has been an increasing interest in the application of artificial intelligence tools to IR in the last few years. Evolutionary algorithms (EAs) are not specifically learning algorithms, but they offer a powerful and domain-independent search ability that can be used in many learning tasks, since learning and self-organization can be considered as optimization problems in many cases. Owing to this reason, the application of EAs to IR has increased in the last decade. Among others, EAs have been applied to solve the following IR problems: automatic document indexing, document and term clustering, query definition, matching function learning, image retrieval, design of user profiles for IR on the Internet, web page classification, and design of agents for Internet searching.

Several works have been published in the spot of IR and search query optimization as this theme becomes more and more demanding. The use of different evolutionary algorithms was anticipated at multiple stages of the IR process.

Simulated annealing (Jin-kao Hao and Jerome Pannier) provides high precision and recall rate for document retrieval, to find a set of superior solutions (set of more relevant documents). It is used for finding relevant documents from a huge corpus where linear searching is virtually impossible.

Geem et al. used harmonic search optimization techniques that deal with document clustering. Harmony clustering is hybridized with Tabulated search (TABU) to improve retrieval. A relevance feedback method such as term feedback, cluster feedback, and term-cluster feedback are used to improve the retrieved results.

Athraa Jasim Mohammed et al. used EAs for document clustering. Document clustering is widely used in IR. The existing clustering techniques suffer from a local optima problem in determining the k number of clusters. Various efforts have been made to address such a drawback, and this includes the utilization of swarm-based algorithms such as particle swarm optimization and ant colony optimization.

Fan et al. (2004) bring in a genetic ranking function discovery framework, and Nyongesa et al. used evolutionary interactive learning for user modeling. Quite a few contributions toward evolutionary optimization of search queries were introduced. Many researchers used genetic programming to optimize Boolean search queries over a documentary database with an emphasis on the comparison of several IR effectiveness measures as objective functions.

D.T. Pham et al. presented a new clustering method based on the bees algorithm. This method employs the bees algorithm to search for the set of cluster centers that minimize a given clustering metric. One of the merits of the proposed method is that it does not become trapped at locally optimal solutions. This is due to the ability of the bees algorithm to perform local and global searches simultaneously.

Danushka Bollegala et al. proposed a differential evolution-based rank learning method for IR. This method (named as RankDE) directly optimizes the mean average precision (MAP) over a set of queries, without requiring any convex approximations as required by most of the previously proposed rank learning algorithms for information retrieval.

Different types and techniques of evolutionary algorithms are described in the following sections.

6.5 Evolutionary Algorithms

6.5.1 Firefly Algorithm

The firefly algorithm (FA) is a metaheuristic algorithm, enthused by the flashing actions of fireflies. The key reason for a firefly's flash is to act as a signal system to attract other fireflies. In the firefly algorithm, the objective function of a known optimization problem is based on differences in light intensity. It helps the fireflies to travel towards brighter and better-looking locations in order to find optimal solutions. All fireflies are considered by their light intensity associated with the objective function. Each firefly is changing its position iteratively. The firefly algorithm has three rules:

1. All fireflies are unisexual, so that one firefly will be paying attention to all other fireflies;
2. Attractiveness is proportional to their brightness, and for any two fireflies, the less bright one will be paying attention by (and thus move to) the brighter one; however, the brightness can decrease as their distance increases;
3. If any fireflies brighter than a given firefly, it will move randomly.

The intensity should be linked with the objective function. Firefly algorithm is a nature-inspired meta-heuristic optimization algorithm. The intensity of a firefly is determined by the value of the objective function. For maximization problems, the brightness is relative to the value of the objective function.

The latest, complete review showed that the firefly algorithm and its variants have been used in just about all areas of discipline. The firefly algorithm has attracted much attention and has been functional to many applications: digital image compression and image processing, nano-electronic integrated circuit and system design, and so on.

6.5.2 Particle Swarm Optimization

Particle swarm optimization (PSO) was developed by Dr. Eberhart and Dr. Kennedy in 1995, stimulated by the flocking and schooling patterns of birds and fish. Over a number of iterations, variables in a group have their values attuned closer to the member whose value is adjoining the target at any given moment. The aspiration of the algorithm is to have all the particles position the optima in a multidimensional hypervolume. This is achieved by handing over initially arbitrary positions to all particles in the space with small initial random velocities.

There are similarities between PSO and the evolutionary computation method such as genetic algorithms (GAs). The method is initialized with a population of arbitrary solutions and searches for optima by updating invention. However, in dissimilarity between GAs among PSO, the PSO has no evolution operators such as mutation and crossover. In PSO, the probable solutions, called particles, fly throughout the problem space by subsequent current optimum particles.

Every particle maintains the track of its coordinates in the problem space, which are related to the best result it has achieved so far. This value is called *pbest*. An additional "best" value that is tracked by the particle swarm optimizer is the finest value, obtained so far by any neighboring particle. This position is called *lbest*. When a particle obtains all the population as its topological neighbors, the finest value is a global best and is called *gbest*.

Each particle's movement is prejudiced by its local best-known position but is also guided toward the best recognized positions in the search space, which are modernized as better positions found by other particles. This is predictable to move the swarm toward the best solutions. When improved positions are being revealed, these will then come to guide the movements of the swarm. The particle swarm algorithm is initiated by making the initial particles, and assigning them preliminary velocities. It evaluates the target function at each particle location, and decides the best function value and the best location. It chooses new velocities, based on the present velocity, the particle's individual best locations, and the best locations of their neighbors. It then iteratively keeps informed the particle spot (the new location is the old one plus the velocity, modified to keep particles within bounds), velocities and neighbors.

6.5.3 Genetic Algorithms

GAs are adaptive heuristic search algorithms based on the evolutionary information of natural selection and genetics. As such they symbolize an intelligent utilization of a random search used to respond to optimization problems. Even if randomized, GAs are by no means random, as an alternative they exploit historical information to head the search straight into the region of enhanced performance within the search space. The essential techniques of the GAs are intended to simulate processes in natural systems needed for evolution—particularly those follow the main beliefs first laid down by Charles Darwin of "survival of the fittest." In nature, competition between individuals for scanty resources results in the fittest folks dominating over the weaker ones. It is improved over conventional artificial intelligence (AI) in that it is healthier. Unlike older AI systems, they do not smash easily even if the inputs are somewhat distorted, or in the presence of sensible noise. Also, in penetrating a large state space, multimodal state space, or n-dimensional surface, a GA may offer significant benefits over a more typical optimization method.

GAs simulate the continued existence of the fittest among individuals over a successive generation for solving a problem. Each generation consists of a population of character strings that are like the chromosomes that we observe in our DNA. Each character signifies a point in a search space and a probable solution. GA is based on a similarity between the genetic arrangement and performance of chromosomes within a population of individuals using the below foundations:

- Individuals in a population compete for resources and mates.
- Those individuals most victorious in each "competition" will make more offspring than those individuals who are weak.
- Genes from "good" individuals spread throughout the population so that two high-quality parents will sometimes produce offspring that are enhanced than either parent.
- Thus each consecutive generation will be more suited to their environment.

6.5.4 Genetic Programming

Genetic programming (GP) is an automatic technique for making a working computer program from an advanced statement of a problem. Genetic programming initiates from a high-level statement of "what wants to be prepared" and automatically generates a computer program to solve the problem.

In AI, GP is a method whereby computer programs are prearranged as a set of genes that are then modified by an evolutionary algorithm. The result is a computer program gifted to carry out well in a predefined task. Often confused to be a type of genetic algorithm, GP can certainly be seen as an application of genetic algorithms to problems where each entity is a computer program. The processes used to encode a computer program in an artificial chromosome and to appraise its fitness with respect to the predefined job are central in the GP method and still the subject of active study.

Genetic programming can be viewed as an addition of the genetic algorithm, a model for testing and selecting the best option among a set of results, each represented by a string. GP goes a step farther and builds the program or "function"—the part that is tested. Two approaches are used to select the victorious program: cross-breeding and the tournament or contest approach. A tricky part of using genetic programming is determining the fitness function, the level to which a program is helping to arrive at the desired goal.

Genetic programming is a form of programming that uses biological evolution to handle a composite problem. The most efficient programs survive and compete or cross-breed with other programs to continually approach the needed solution. Genetic programming is an approach that seems most suitable for problems in which there are a large number of fluctuating variables such as those connected to artificial intelligence. The genetic programming model is predominantly used with the LISP and scheme programming. It can also be used with C and other programming languages.

6.5.5 Applications of Genetic Programming

There are many applications of genetic programming, including

- "Black art" problems, such as the computerized synthesis of analog electrical circuits, controllers, antennas, networks of chemical reactions, and other parts of design.
- "Programming the unprogrammable" (PTU) relating to the automatic formation of computer programs for unconventional computing devices such as cellular automata, multi-agent systems, parallel systems, etc.
- "Commercially usable new invention" (CUNI) involving the use of genetic programming as a computerized "invention machine" for creating commercially usable new creations.

6.5.6 Simulated Annealing

Simulated annealing (SA) is a technique for finding a high-quality solution to an optimization problem. If you are in a position where you want to maximize or minimize something, your problem can possibly be tackled with simulated annealing. SA is a probabilistic practice for resembling the global optimum of a given method. Distinctively, it is a metaheuristic to approximate global optimization in a large search space, and also it is a comparable method for optimization.

It is characteristically described in terms of thermodynamics. It is habitually used when the search space is discrete. For problems where finding the accurate global optimum is less important than finding a satisfactory local optimum in a fixed amount of time, SA may be a preferable substitution for a brute-force search or gradient. Simulated annealing interprets slow cooling as a slow reduction in the likelihood of accepting inferior solutions as it explores the solution space. Accepting inferior solutions is an essential property of metaheuristics because it allows for a more widespread search for the optimal solution.

Simulated annealing is a system for finding a good solution to an optimization problem and injects just the right amount of arbitrariness into things to escape local maxima early in the process without attainment off course late in the game, when a solution is close by.

This makes it fine at tracking behind a decent response, no matter its starting point. Annealing is a process in metallurgy where metals are slowly cooled to a state of low power where they are very strong. The arbitrary movement corresponds to high temperature; at low temperature, there is little randomness. SA is a process where the temperature is reduced gradually, starting from a random search at high temperature and ultimately becoming dropping as it approaches zero temperature. The arbitrariness should tend to jump out of local minima and find regions that have low heuristic values; a steep fall will guide to local minima. At high temperatures, a gradual decline in steps is more likely than at lower temperatures.

SA upholds a current assignment of values to variables. At each step, it picks a variable and a value at random. If assigning that value to the variable is the progress or does not boost the number of hits, the algorithm allows the assignment and there is a new current assignment. Otherwise, it accepts the assignment with some likelihood, based on the temperature and how much worse it is than the current assignment. If the change is not accepted, the current assignment is unbothered.

6.5.7 Harmony Search

In computer science and operations research, harmony search (HS) is a phenomenon-mimicking algorithm stimulated by the improvisation method of musicians, planned by Zong Woo Geem et al. in 2005. In the HS algorithm, each instrumentalist (= decision variable) plays (= generates) a note (= a value) for finding a best harmony (= global optimum) all as one. Harmony search does not need discrepancy gradients; thus it can believe discontinuous functions as well as unremitting functions. It can handle discrete variables as well as continuous variables and does not necessitate an initial value setting for the variables. HS is free from deviation and may escape local optima. HS may conquer the drawback of the GA building block theory that works well only if the association among variables in a chromosome is cautiously considered. If neighbor variables in a chromosome have weaker relationships than remote variables, the building block theory may not work well because of crossover operation. However, HS openly considers the relationship using an ensemble operation. It has a novel stochastic derivative applied to discrete variables, which uses musician's experiences as the searching direction. Certain HS variants do not need algorithm parameters such as harmony memory considering rate (HMCR) and pitch-adjusting rate (PAR); thus, novice users can simply use the algorithm.

6.5.8 Differential Evolution

In evolutionary computation, differential evolution (DE) is a method that optimizes a difficulty by iteratively trying to get a better candidate solution with consideration of a given measure of quality. Such methods are usually known as metaheuristics as they build few or no assumptions about the problem being optimized and can hunt very large spaces of candidate solutions. However, metaheuristics such as DE do not assure an optimal solution is ever found.

DE is used as a multidimensional real-valued method but does not use the gradient of the problem being optimized, which means DE does not need the optimization problem to be differentiable as is necessary by typical optimization methods such as gradient descent and quasi-Newton methods. DE can consequently also be used on optimization problems that are not even continuous, are noisy, change over time, and so on.

Global optimization is necessary in fields such as engineering, statistics, and finance. But many realistic problems have objective functions that are nondifferentiable, noncontinuous, nonlinear, loud, flat, multidimensional, or have a lot of local minima and constraints. DE can be used to find fairly accurate solutions to such problems. DE is an evolutionary algorithm. This class also includes genetic algorithms, evolutionary schemes, and evolutionary programming. DE optimizes a problem by maintaining a population of key candidates and creating new candidates by combining existing ones according to its simple formulae, and then keeping whichever candidate solution has the most excellent score or fitness on the optimization problem at hand. In this method the optimization problem is treated as a black box that simply provides a measure of quality for the candidate solution, and the gradient is therefore not essential. DE is used in different applications such as design of digital filters, optimization of strategies for checkers, improvisation of profit in a model of a beef property, and optimization of fermentation of alcohol.

6.5.9 Tabulated Search

TABU search (TS) was formed by Fred W. Glover in 1986 and formalized in 1989. It is a metaheuristic search method employing a local search technique used for mathematical optimization. Local searches obtain a latent solution to a problem and check immediate neighbors in the hope of finding an enhanced solution. Local search techniques have a propensity to develop into suboptimal regions or on plateaus where many answers are equally fit. This search improves the performance of local searches by applying its basic rule. First, at each step worsening moves can be accepted if no recovering move is obtainable. The prohibitions are introduced to discourage the search from coming back to previously visited solutions. The execution of TABU search utilizes memory structures that explain the visited solutions or user-provided sets of rules. The word *tabu* comes from Tongan, a language of Polynesia, used by the aborigines of Tonga to point out things that cannot be touched because they are sacred. It is a metaheuristic algorithm that can be used for solving combinatorial optimization problems. Current applications of TS span the areas of resource planning, very-large-scale integration (VLSI) design, molecular engineering, flexible manufacturing, waste management, mineral exploration, biomedical analysis, environmental conservation, logistics, pattern classification, and so on. There are three main strategies of TABU search: forbidding strategy, freeing strategy, and short-term strategy. The TABU search memory structures can roughly be divided into three categories: short term, intermediate term, and long term.

Section III

Demand of Evolutionary Algorithms in IR

7

Demand of Evolutionary Algorithms in Information Retrieval

7.1 Document Ranking

In information retrieval (IR), ranking is a central part of many IR problems, such as collaborative filtering, document retrieval sentiment analysis, and advertising. The ranking of query results is one of the primary problems in IR, the scientific/engineering regulation behind search engines. With the known query q and a collection D of documents that match the query, the complexity is to rank—that is, sort—the documents in D according to some criterion so that the "most excellent" results emerge early in the result list exhibit to the user. Naturally, ranking criteria are phrased in terms of relevance of documents with respect to an information requirement expressed in the query.

Ranking is frequently reduced to the calculation of numeric scores on query/document pairs; a baseline score function for this reason is the cosine resemblance between *tf-idf* vectors representing the query and the document in a vector-space model, BM25 scores, or probabilities in a probabilistic IR representation. A ranking can then be calculated by sorting documents by descending score. An approach is to describe a score function on pairs of documents d_1, d_2 that is positive if and only if d_1 is more relevant to the query than d_2, and use this information to sort.

Ranking functions are appraised by a range of means. One of the simplest is by determining the precision of the initial k top-ranked results for some fixed k; for example, the quantity of the top 10 results that are pertinent, on average, over many queries. Habitually, computation of ranking functions can be simplified by taking benefit of the examination that only the comparative order of scores matters, not their absolute value; therefore, the terms or factors that are independent of the document may be detached, and terms or factors that are independent of the query may be precomputed and stored with the document.

7.1.1 Retrieval Effectiveness

The conservative way to measure the excellence of the results returned by a system in answer to a query is to use precision and recall. Precision is the number of relevant documents retrieved separated by the total number of documents retrieved. Recall is the number of relevant documents retrieved divided by the total number of relevant documents. Preferably, recall and precision should both be equal to one, meaning that the system returns all pertinent documents without introducing any irrelevant documents in the result set. Unfortunately, this is impossible to attain in practice. If we try to increase the recall score (by adding more disjunctive terms to the query, for example), precision suffers;

similarly, we can only increase the precision score at the expense of recall. In adding, there is lot of trade-off among retrieval effectiveness and computing cost. As the technology travels from keyword matching to statistical ranking to natural-language processing, computing costs rise exponentially.

7.2 Relevance Feedback Approach

Relevance feedback is one of the conventional ways of refining search engine rankings. It works as follows: the search engine produces an initial set of rankings. Users choose the relevant documents within this ranking. Based on the information in these documents, a more suitable ranking is obtainable. In some situations, users do not have sufficient domain knowledge to form excellent queries. But they can choose relevant documents from a list of documents once the documents are exposed to them. For example, when the user shoots a query "matrix," here both movie and "maths" contents are retrieved. Then say the user chooses the "maths" documents as relevant. This feedback can be used to refine the search and retrieve more documents from the mathematics field. We can distinguish among three types of feedback: explicit feedback, implicit feedback, and blind or "pseudo" feedback.

A user who is explicit provides feedback to help the system get better. Top k decisions are taken as relevant. This type of feedback is distinct as explicit only when the assessors know that the feedback provided is interpreted as relevance decisions. Users may specify relevance explicitly using a binary or graded relevance system. Binary relevance feedback shows that a document is either relevant or irrelevant for a specified query. The graded relevance feedback demonstrates the significance of a document to a query on a range using numbers, letters, or descriptions.

Implicit feedback is inferred from user activities, such as noting which documents they do and do not select for viewing, the duration of time spent viewing a document, or page browsing or scrolling actions. There are a lot of signals during the search process that one can use for implicit feedback and the kind of information to provide in response.

The major differences of implicit relevance feedback from that of explicit include

1. The user is not assessing relevance for the use of the IR system, but only satisfying his or her needs.

2. The user is not necessarily knowledgeable that his or her behavior will be used as relevance feedback.

Pseudo-relevance feedback, also known as blind relevance feedback, gives a method for automatic local studies. It automates the manual part of relevance feedback, so that the user gets enhanced retrieval performance without a comprehensive interaction. The method is to do normal retrieval to discover an initial set of most relevant documents, to then assume that the top k ranked documents are relevant, and last to do relevance feedback as below this assumption. The procedure is as follows:

1. Obtain the results returned by initial query as relevant results.

2. Select the top 20–30 terms from these documents using, for instance, *tf-idf* weights.

3. Do query expansion, insert these top terms to query, and then compare the returned documents for this query and finally return the most relevant documents.

Issues with relevance feedback include the following:

- The user must have sufficient knowledge to form the initial query.
- This does not work too well in cases like misspellings, cross-lingual IR (content-based image retrieval [CBIR]), and mismatch in user's and document's vocabulary (Burma versus Myanmar).
- Relevant documents have to be similar to each other (they need to cluster), but there should be little similarity between relevant and nonrelevant documents. That is why this technique does not work too well for inherently disjunctive queries (pop stars who once worked at Burger King) or generic topics (tigers) that often appear as disjunctions of more specific concepts.
- Long queries generated may cause long response times.
- Users are often reluctant to participate in explicit feedback.

7.2.1 Relevance Feedback in Text IR

Relevance feedback is the retrieval chore where the system specifies not only a user query but also user feedback on several of the top ranked results. Feedback provides the retrieval system an opportunity to develop its results by exploiting the extra information through more detailed techniques. This can be useful in cases where the users want as many relevant results as possible.

The plan of relevance feedback is to engage the user in the retrieval process so as to progress the final result set. The user provides feedback on the relevance of documents in a primary set of results. The basic procedure is as follows:

- The user concerns a simple query.
- The system precedes an initial set of retrieval results.
- The user marks some returned documents as relevant or nonrelevant.
- The system calculates a better representation of the information needed depending on user feedback.
- The system displays a modified set of retrieval results.

Relevance feedback can go through one or more iterations of this sort. The process utilizes the idea that it may be tricky to formulate an excellent query when you do not know the collection well, but it is simple to review particular documents, and so it makes sense to engage in iterative query enhancement of this sort. In such a situation, relevance feedback can also be efficient in tracking a user's evolving information need: seeing some documents may guide users to process their understanding of the information they are seeking.

In the majority of collections, a similar idea may be referred to using different words. This problem, known as synonymy, affects the recall of most IR systems. For example, you would desire a search for "aircraft" to match "plane," and for exploration on "thermodynamics" to match references to "heat" in appropriate discussions. Users frequently attempt to address this problem themselves by physically refining a query.

The techniques for handling this problem are classified into two main classes: global methods and local methods. Global methods are techniques for increasing or reformulating query terms independent of the question and results returned from it, so that changes in the query wording will cause the latest query to match other semantically similar terms. Global methods include

- Query expansion/reformulation with a lexicon
- Query expansion via automatic lexicon generation
- Techniques like spelling correction

Local methods regulate a query relative to the documents that primarily appear to match the query. The basic methods here are

- Relevance feedback
- Pseudo-relevance feedback, also recognized as blind relevance feedback
- Indirect relevance feedback

7.2.1.1 Query Expansion

In relevance feedback, users provide extra input on documents, and this input is used to reweight the terms in the query for documents. In query expansion, on the other hand, users provide added input on query words or phrases, perhaps suggesting additional query terms. Various search engines recommend related queries in response to a query; the users then opt to utilize one of these alternative query suggestions. The essential question in this form of query expansion is how to make alternative or prolonged queries for the user. The most regular form of query expansion is global investigation, using some form of vocabulary.

The *Rocchio algorithm* is based on a technique of relevance feedback established in IR systems which stemmed from the SMART Information Retrieval System around the year 1970. Similar to many other retrieval systems, the Rocchio feedback approach was created using the vector-space model. This algorithm is founded on the assumption that most users have a general conception of which documents should be denoted as relevant or nonrelevant. Consequently, the user's search query is revised to include an arbitrary gain of relevant and nonrelevant documents as a means of increasing the search engine's recall, and perhaps the precision as well.

7.2.2 Relevance Feedback in Content-Based Image Retrieval

Content-based image retrieval (CBIR) is a method to discover images related in visual content to a known query from an image database. It is generally performed based on an evaluation of low-level features, such as texture, color, or shape features, extracted from the images themselves. While there is much research addressing content-based image retrieval, research concerning the performance of content-based image retrieval techniques are still limited, particularly in the two aspects of retrieval accuracy and response time. Retrieval accuracy is inadequate because of the big gap among semantic concepts and low-level image features, which is the major problem in content-based image retrieval.

For instance, for dissimilar queries, diverse types of features have different significance; an issue is how to derive a weighting scheme to balance the relative significance of different feature types, and there is no general formula for all queries. The relevance feedback method can be used to bridge the gap. Relevance feedback, initially developed for IR, is a supervised learning technique used to enhance the effectiveness of IR systems.

The main thought of relevance feedback is using positive and negative instances provided by the user to better the system's performance. For a certain query, the system initially retrieves a list of ranked images according to predefined similarity metrics, which are regularly defined as the distance between feature vectors of images. Then, the user chooses a set of positive and/or negative examples from the retrieved images, and the system subsequently refines the query and retrieves a new list of images. The important issue is how to integrate positive and negative examples to process the query and how to adjust the relationship measure according to the feedback. The original relevance feedback technique, in which the vector model is used for document retrieval, can be demonstrated by Rocchio's formula.

Relevance feedback is a best query modification method in the area of content-based image retrieval. The important problem in relevance feedback is how to efficiently exploit the feedback information to get better retrieval performance.

Content-based image retrieval systems extract visual features from any images automatically. Resemblances between two pictures are calculated in terms of the differences among the corresponding features. To take into account the subjectivity of human observation and connect the gap between the high-level concepts and the low-level features, relevance feedback has been projected to improve retrieval performance. Throughout the progression of image retrieval, the user indicates the relevance of the retrieved objects, and the system will then process the query results by learning from this information.

There have been several studies on enhancing retrieval efficiency in CBIR systems based on relevance feedback (RF) methods mostly implemented from the IR area. RF methods assume two-class relevance feedback: relevant and nonrelevant classes. For example, support vector machines (SVMs) have been used to distinguish between relevant and nonrelevant images.

7.2.3 Relevance Feedback in Region-Based Image Retrieval

Region-based image retrieval (RBIR) was newly projected as an extension of CBIR. An RBIR technique automatically fragments images into a variable number of regions, and extracts for every region a set of features. Then, difference functions decide the distance between a database image and a set of reference regions. Unluckily, the huge evaluation costs of the dissimilarity function are restricting RBIR to relatively tiny databases.

An increasing number of applications need complicated image search facilities. The most famous ones are remote sensing, Internet, news, medical imagery, and media. Conventionally, these applications mostly organize keyword-based search operations. Newer search engines as well integrate content descriptors derived from the pixel value of the picture into their retrieval algorithms. Habitually, one refers to this approach as CBIR. RBIR is a promising addition of the classical CBIR: rather than deploying global features over the complete content, RBIR systems separate an image into a number of homogenous regions and extract local features for each region.

Apart from the classical relationship search, RBIR gives a novel query category: the search for images containing related parts of a reference image, for instance, "discover pictures of this brown dog in an arbitrary environment." Searching with a single reference region is an easy extension of CBIR.

The very first attempts for image retrieval were based on exploiting existing image captions to categorize images into prearranged classes or to make a restricted vocabulary. Although relatively easy and computationally efficient, this method has several restrictions mostly deriving from the use of a limited vocabulary that neither allows for surprising queries nor can be extended without reevaluating the probable association between each image in the database and each new addition to the vocabulary. As well, such keyword-based techniques assume either the preexistence of textual image annotations or that annotations using the prearranged vocabulary are executed manually. In the latter case, contradiction of the keyword assignments between dissimilar indexers can also hamper performance.

To defeat the limitations of the keyword-based technique, the use of the image visual contents has been proposed. This type of approach utilizes visual content by extracting low-level indexing features for each image or image segment (region).

The relevant images are retrieved by comparing the low-level features of each item in the record with those of a user-supplied sketch or, more often, a key image that is either selected from a restricted image set or is supplied by the user. One of the initial attempts to realize this scheme is the query by image content system.

A region-based approach to image retrieval has been approved; thus, the process of inserting an image into the database starts by applying a color image segmentation algorithm to it, so as to break it down to an amount of regions. The segmentation algorithm working for the analysis of images to regions is based on a variant of the *k*-means with connectivity constraint algorithm, a member of the popular *k*-means family.

RBIR is an image retrieval approach that centers on content from regions of images, not the content from the whole image in early CBIR. For RBIR, it primarily segments images into a number of regions and takes out the set of features that are recognized as local features from a segmented region.

A relationship measure determining the similarity among target regions in the query and the set of segmented regions from the other image is used later to determine relevant images to the query based on the local region features. The inspiration of RBIR approaches is based on the fact that a high-level semantic understanding of images can be improved depending on local types of images, rather than global features.

7.3 Term-Weighting Approaches

In real-world IR systems, the fundamental document collection is not often stable or definite. For example, in private systems, such as records or emails stored in a computer, documents are regularly added, removed, or edited. Likewise, in venture and public environments, the endurance of public repositories of information is a standard situation, resulting in active collections of documents that are constantly updated.

Term weighting is a core mission in IR settings with direct impact in many higher-level responsibilities, such as automatic summarization, index construction, or topic detection and keyword extraction.

In IR, *tf-idf* (term frequency-inverse document frequency) is a numerical statistic that is designed to reflect how significant a word is to documenting a collection or corpus. It is regularly used as a weighting aspect in IR and text mining. The *tf-idf* range increases proportionally to the number of times a word appears in the document; however, the frequency of the word in the corpus is offset, which helps to account for the fact that some words appear more frequently in common.

Variations of the *tf-idf* weighting scheme are regularly used by search engines as a central tool in scoring and ranking a document's relevance known by a user query. Then *tf-idf* can be successfully used for stop-words filtering in different subject fields as well as text summarization and classification. One of the simplest ranking functions is calculated by summing the *tf-idf* for each query term; many more complicated ranking functions are variants of this simple model.

7.3.1 Term Frequency

Assume we have a collection of English text documents and desire to decide which document is most associated to the query "the brown cow." A simple method to start is to eliminate documents that do not include all terms "the," "brown," and "cow," but this still leaves many documents. To additionally discriminate them, we may count the amount of times each term occurs in every document and sum them all together; the amount of times a term is present in a document is called its term frequency.

7.3.2 Inverse Document Frequency

Because the term "the" is so general, term frequency will be predisposed to incorrectly emphasize documents that use the word "the" more habitually, without giving sufficient weight to the more significant keywords "brown" and "cow." The term "the" is not a high-quality keyword to differentiate relevant and nonrelevant documents and terms. Therefore, an inverse document frequency factor is included, which diminishes the weight of terms that occur very regularly in the document set and boost the weight of terms that occur rarely.

Characteristically, the *tf-idf* weight is collected by two terms: the first calculates the standardized term frequency (*tf*), the number of times a word appears in a document, divided by the total amount of words in that document; the next term is the inverse document frequency (*idf*), calculated as the logarithm of the amount of the documents in the database divided by the number of documents where the specific term appears.

TF: Term Frequency, which shows how frequently a word occurs in a document. Because every document is dissimilar in length, it is achievable that a term would emerge many more times in long documents than in shorter ones. Thus, the term frequency is habitually divided by the document length as a way of normalization:

$$\text{TF}(t) = \frac{(\text{Number of times term } t \text{ appears in a document})}{(\text{Total number of terms in the document})} \tag{7.1}$$

IDF: Inverse Document Frequency, which measures how important a term is. While computing TF, all terms are considered equally important. However, it is known that certain terms, such as "is," "of," and "that," may appear a lot of times but have little importance. Thus, we need to weigh down the frequent terms while scaling up the rare ones, by computing the following:

$$\text{IDF}(t) = \log\_e\left(\frac{\text{Total number of documents}}{\text{Number of documents with term } t \text{ in it}}\right) \tag{7.2}$$

7.4 Document Retrieval

Document retrieval is the automatic process of creating a list of documents that are relevant to a query demand by comparing the user's demand to an automatically formed index of the textual content of documents in the system. These documents can then be right of entry for use within the same system.

Document retrieval is distinct as the matching of some stated user query beside a set of free-text records. These records might be any unstructured text, such as real estate records, newspaper articles, or paragraphs in a guidebook. Document retrieval is referred to as a subdivision of text retrieval. Text retrieval is under the concept of IR. Normally the information is stored primarily in the form of text. Text retrieval is a vital area of study today, because it is essential to all Internet search engines.

This document retrieval system gets information from certain criteria by matching text records alongside client queries, as different than expert systems that answer questions by inferring above a logical knowledge database. A document retrieval method consists of a database of documents, a classification algorithm to construct a full-text index, and a user edge to access the database.

A document retrieval system has two major responsibilities:

- Discover relevant documents to user queries.
- Calculate the matching results and sort them according to importance, using algorithms such as PageRank.

Internet search engines are conventional applications of document retrieval. The majority of retrieval systems presently in use vary from simple Boolean systems through to statistical or natural language processing systems. There are two major classes of indexing schemata for a document retrieval scheme: form-based or word-based, and content-based indexing.

Form-based document retrieval tackles the exact syntactic possessions of a text, comparable to substring matching in string searches. The text is usually unstructured and not essentially in a natural language; the system could, for example, be used to process huge sets of chemical representations in molecular biology. A suffix tree algorithm is an instance for form-based indexing. The content-based approach developed semantic connections among documents and parts. Most content-based document retrieval systems exploit an inverted index algorithm.

A signature file is a method that generates quick and dirty filters, for example, Bloom filters, that will maintain all the documents that match the query and optimistically a few ones that do not. The way this is done is by generating for each file a signature, characteristically a hash coded version. One technique is superimposed coding. A postprocessing step is completed to discard the false alarms. Since in most cases this structure is substandard to inverted files in conditions of speed, size, and functionality, it is not used extensively; however, with proper constraints it can beat the inverted files in certain environments.

7.5 Feature Selection Approach

In machine learning and statistics, feature selection, also known as variable selection, variable subset selection, or attribute selection, is the method of selecting a subset of relevant features to utilize in model construction. Feature selection methods are used for three reasons:

- Simplification of models to build them easier to interpret by researchers/users
- Very tiny training times
- Improved generalization by reducing overfitting

The important principle when using a feature selection method is that the data hold many features that are redundant or irrelevant, and can thus be detached without incurring much loss of information. Redundant or irrelevant features are two distinct ideas, because one relevant feature may be redundant in the occurrence of another relevant feature with which it is strongly associated.

Feature selection methods should be distinguished from feature extraction. Feature extraction generates new features from functions of the original features, whereas feature selection precedes a subset of the features. Feature selection methods are frequently used in domains where there are many features and relatively few samples. The feature selection methods are usually handy in three classes based on how they combine the selection algorithm and the model building.

7.5.1 Filter Method for Feature Selection

Filter-based feature selection has become vital in many classification settings, particularly object recognition, recently faced with the feature learning approach that creates thousands of cues. Filter methods examine basic properties of data, ignoring the classifier. Most of these techniques can execute two operations, ranking and subset selection: in the existing, the significance of each individual feature is evaluated, habitually by neglecting probable interactions among the elements of the joint set; in the latter, the final subset of features to be selected is offered. In some cases, these two operations are carried out successively; in other cases, only the selection is carried out. Filter methods hold back the least interesting variables. These techniques are particularly efficient in computation time and robust to overfitting. Nevertheless, filter methods tend to select redundant variables because they do not consider the associations among variables. Therefore, they are mostly used as a preprocess method.

7.5.2 Wrapper Method for Feature Selection

Wrapper methods assess subsets of variables that permit, unlike filter approaches, the sensing of possible interactions between variables. The two main drawbacks of these methods are as follows:

- Increased overfitting risk when the number of observations is inadequate
- Major computation time when the number of variables is large

7.5.3 Embedded Method for Feature Selection

Recently, embedded methods have been proposed to decrease the classification of learning. They try to merge the merits of both previous methods. The learning algorithm takes advantage of its own variable selection algorithm. So, it needs to know preliminarily what a good selection is, which limits their utilization.

7.6 Image Retrieval

Image retrieval could use metadata or content. Most familiar methods of image retrieval employed for image searching use related metadata such as text or keywords. Metadata-based image retrieval can be made easy by applying traditional IR technologies. Nevertheless, such image retrieval may go through several serious problems. Inability to upgrade with the ever-growing, rapidly changing, and unimpeded image databases such as the Internet exists as the major problem. Hence, human input is required for image annotation, proving expensive. Moreover, the second problem is that such annotations are subjective and the process of encoding the entire meta-information about images for image retrieval in any predictable or unpredictable situation is cumbersome. The user's view of resemblance between images varies with the database content, the background, and the application, and consequently, annotations cannot match the user's conception. Thus, these troubles aggravate the exploration of content-based image retrieval.

One of the hopeful approaches to circumvent the issues in metadata-based image retrieval is the content-based retrieval. Content-based image retrieval is composed of whichever technology aids in sorting out digital picture archives based on their visual content. CBIR started becoming popular in the year 1992, and a great deal of interest in research on content-based image retrieval has been observed over the last 20 years. Hence, enormous novel techniques and systems and support for such systems has started emerging. Content-based image retrieval denotes a set of techniques to retrieve semantically related images from an image database based on automatically derived image features (Long et al. 2003). A primary work for CBIR systems is comparison of similarities, extraction of features of each image based on its pixel values, and description of the rules for comparison of images. The extracted features are useful for image representation for determining similarity with other images in the database. Images are compared by measuring the discrepancy of the feature components to other image representations.

One of the limitations in the performance of content-based image retrieval systems includes the gap between low-level features and high-level semantic concepts. Region-based features for the expression of views of the user on image content and comprehension of the user's intentions using RF are the two ways being used to minimize the semantic gap. Global feature extraction was used previously by CBIR methods to acquire the image descriptors. A variety of features of images including color, texture, and shape are extracted by query by image content (QBIC) (Flickner 1995), formulated at the IBM Almaden Research Center. Worldwide, color histograms are utilized for extracting color features, texture data are gathered based on coarseness, contrast, and direction; and shape features deal with the curvature, moments invariants, circularity, and eccentricity. Likewise, the Photobook system (Pentland et al. 1997), Virage (Gupta and Jain 1997), and VisualSeek (Smith and Chang 1997) make use of global features to denote image semantics.

The global strategies are insufficient to support searching of images where particular objects in an image with specific colors and/or texture are there, and shift/scale similar queries, where the location and/or the facet of the query objects may not be related. For example, if there are two flowers in an image with dissimilar colors, red and yellow, then the global features depict the image as the global average color, orange. This revelation is certainly not the representation of the semantic meaning of the image. Thus, the limitation of global features is obvious.

Region-based retrieval systems endeavor to prevail over the drawbacks in global-based retrieval systems by signifying images as collections of regions corresponding to objects such as flowers, trees, sky, and mountains. A key prerequisite for a high-quality region-based image retrieval system is a strong segmentation algorithm (Deng and Manjunath 2001). A segmentation algorithm picks an input image and groups pixels that look alike regarding certain feature (e.g., color, texture, or shape). The result of this clustering part is segregation of an image into regions, which match physical objects (flowers, people, trees, cars) if done well. Regardless of the extracting global image, the feature descriptors are extracted on each entity. Color, texture, and shape features are retrieved on each pixel that pertains to the object, and every object is illustrated by the average value of these pixel features. The main objective of exploiting regional features is to augment the capability of both capturing and demonstrating the user's acuity of image content.

Relevance feedback, an online learning technique that actually came into existence for the purpose of IR (Rocchio 1971), concentrates on improving the effectiveness of IR. The central part of relevance feedback is to allow the user to pilot the system. For this reason, the approach allows user-system interactions, and the user can judge and rate the retrieved data in view of that. Besides, the system dynamically reads the user's intent and gradually delivers better results. Right from its introduction in the mid-1990s, content-based image retrieval has captured wide attention, and it is known to afford striking performance enhancement (Zhou and Huang 2003). RF strategies to date demonstrate a few unsolved critical problems. The chief issue is that user interaction is long and difficult, making it a challenge to keep the number of iterations to convergence minimal. The job becomes hard for only a small number of images (possibly none) is being retrieved during the first RF steps, so that positive examples are not accessible for succeeding retrieval (Huang et al. 2008). Therefore, another approach must be framed to search the solution space.

One more vital problem takes into account the possibility of stagnation, in which a suboptimal local solution may be acquired, which makes further searching of the image space impossible. During an increase in the size of the database, this issue becomes much more prominent. This also raises the need for further means to broaden the exploration. The present work brings about the formulation of the image retrieval problem as an optimization problem to be solved using a firefly algorithm. The interaction of the user with the machine is utilized as an iterative supervision of the classification. The feedback of the user aids in achieving the objective of minimizing a fitness function that considers the characteristics of the appropriate and inappropriate images, as points of attraction and repulsion. The recommended systems offer a better investigation of the search space as well as evade the pooling of local minima. The firefly algorithm (Yang 2008) was chosen for this work, not only as a potent optimization tool, but also an efficient space searching mechanism. The overall target of the planned systems is to enhance the performance of CBIR systems and create an adaptive CBIR framework.

7.6.1 Content-Based Image Retrieval

Content-based image retrieval is a dynamic approach involved in the active area of research concerned with the search for similar images in large databases. Images are usually represented by approximations of their contents in such systems. Representative approximations include statistics and Fourier or wavelet transformations of the raw image content. Feature extraction thus targets extracting semantically meaningful information but requires a trivial amount of storage (Datta et al. 2008). A comprehensive account of a few feature extraction techniques is presented in Section 7.6.1.1. The similarity between two images is typically measured using the information acquired by feature extraction. Images are illustrated by points in the high dimensional feature space. Each point of the

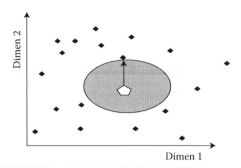

FIGURE 7.1
Two dimensions nearest neighbor.

feature illustrates one dimension in the feature space. A metric is defined to compute the real similarity between two of these points. An outline of common metrics is provided in Section 7.6.1.5. In the basic model displayed in Figure 7.1 (Han and Kambr 2006), the exploration for images similar to a query image q ends up in the discovery of the k nearest neighbors of q. The model can also back up more intricate queries that can involve more than one query image and more than one feature type.

Content-based retrieval employs the image data to signify and access the images. The content-based retrieval system involves offline feature extraction and online image retrieval. A theoretical framework for content-based image retrieval is exemplified in Figure 7.2 (Long et al. 2003). In the offline stage, the system spontaneously extracts visual attributes (color, shape, and texture information) of an image in the database based on the pixel values, and the collected data are stored in another database within the system referred to as a feature database. The feature data, otherwise known as visual signature for the visual attributes of each image, are trivial in size compared to the image data; hence, the feature database entails a compact form of the images. Thus, one of the key advantages of visual signatures despite original pixels is the substantial abstraction of image illustration. Yet, the primary purpose of application of signature is achieving an enhanced correlation between image representation and visual semantics (Long et al. 2003).

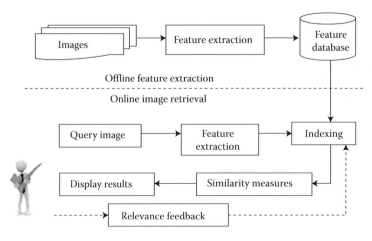

FIGURE 7.2
Principle of content-based image retrieval.

Online image retrieval allows the user to present a query example with a feature vector to the system. Consequently, the system will measure and compare the distances in terms of similarities between the feature vectors of the query example and of the media in the feature database and rank accordingly. Eventually, the search results will be ranked, and the results that are most similar to the query examples will be returned. In case of noncompliance with the search results, the user can offer a relevance feedback to the retrieval system with the provision to learn the information needs of the user.

7.6.1.1 Feature Extraction

Feature extraction involves acquisition of abstract but semantically meaningful data from images to be used as visual signatures for the image. Hence, the signatures should be similar for similar images. While representing images, due attention is required for features and approaches that could efficiently code the visual attributes and best represent the images. As feature extraction of the image is in general performed offline, computation is not laborious. This section discusses three features: texture, shape, and color, the most often used in feature extraction.

7.6.1.2 Color Descriptor

Color is the significant feature of visual recognition by humans. We usually differentiate images based on color features. Color simplifies object identification, and this is the reason behind the widespread use of powerful color descriptors in CBIR. For effective extraction of the color features from an image, an apt color space and a significant color descriptor have to be defined.

Color space is determined to enable the specification of colors. In the color space, each color is denoted in a coordinate system by a single point. Various color spaces, such as RGB (red, green, blue), HSL (hue, saturation, and lightness) or HSV (hue, saturation, and value), International Commission on Illumination (CIE) CIE LAB, CIE UWV, and CIE LUV, have been created for several purposes (Gonzales and Woods 2002). No particular color space has been identified as the best for CBIR, but a proper color system is needed to confirm perceptual uniformity. This makes the RGB color space, a commonly used system for illustrating color images, unsuitable for CBIR as it cannot assure perceptual uniformity and is also device dependent (Gevers and Smeulders 2000). Color representations are mostly converted from the RGB color space to the HSV or HSL, CIE LAB, CIE UWV, or CIE LUV color spaces with perceptual uniformity. We adopted the HSV color space in the current work for its ease of transformation from the RGB color space. The HSV color space is generated to deliver an instinctive representation of color and to estimate the means of perception and manipulation of color by humans. RGB to HSV is a nonlinear but reversible transformation. The hue (H) denotes the central spectral component (pure color), as in red, blue, or yellow. The addition of white to the pure color changes it: the less white, the color is more saturated, corresponding to the saturation (S). The value (V) relates to the brightness of color. The CIE LAB, CIE UWV, or CIE LUV color spaces confirm perceptual uniformity, which facilitates color comparison by use of similarity metrics (Haeghen et al. 2000).

Besides selection of a color space, it is necessary to develop an efficient color descriptor for local and global color representation. Various color descriptors, such as color histograms (Ouyang and Tan 2002), color moments (Yu et al. 2002), color edge (Gevers and Stokman 2003), color texture (Guan and Wada 2002), and color correlograms (Moghaddam et al. 2003) have been developed. The present work exploits the use of color histogram and color moment technique for color feature extraction in the proposed system of image retrieval.

7.6.1.2.1 Color Histogram

Color histogram is the popular method to characterize color features of an image. Color histogram is a kind of bar graph in which the height of each bar denotes the amount of a particular color of the color space being used in the image (Gonzales and Woods 2002). The bars in a color histogram signifying the *X*-axis are called bins. The number of bins varies with the number of colors in an image. The *Y*-axis displays the number of pixels in each bin, which are of a particular color. The color histogram represents the global and regional distribution of colors in an image while still and not dependent on rotation about the view axis.

In color histograms, the number of bins can be minimized by placing similar colors in the same bin, and the process is termed *quantization*. Simultaneously, the space needed for storing the histogram data and time for comparison of histograms are greatly reduced. Apparently, quantization decreases image information and is a trade-off between space, processing time, and accuracy in the results (Lew et al. 2006).

7.6.1.2.2 Color Moments

The drawbacks of quantization imposed by using histograms can be overcome by color moments for the estimation of probability distributions (Stricker and Orengo 1995). These moments are robust to noise and completely describe the underlying probability distribution and are thus preferred over histograms. Nevertheless, most color descriptors are restricted to the first (mean), second (variance), and third (skewness) central moments due to computational problems emerging while estimating higher-order moments. The distance function for comparing these moments is largely based on the weighted Euclidian distance.

7.6.1.3 Texture Descriptor

Texture indicates recurrent patterns of pixels over a spatial domain. Textures will be displayed as random and unstructured on repetitive addition of noise to the patterns. Texture properties are homogenous visual patterns in an image but are not due to the presence of only a single color or intensity. Several texture properties as viewed by the human eye are, for instance, regularity, directionality, smoothness, and coarseness. Several methods for assessing texture features are being practiced due to the lack of a proper mathematical definition for texture. Regrettably, no single method is best for all types of textures. Manjunath and Ma (1996) have reported that the popular methods for texture feature description are statistical, model-based, and transform-based methods. Each description has been utilized for specific purposes.

The word *transform* implies the mathematical representation of an image. Discrete Fourier transform, discrete wavelet transforms, and Gabor wavelets are some of the texture classifications brought about using transform domain features. The features of texture are defined by frequency analysis of the image content by transform methods. Fourier analysis encompasses splitting up a signal into sine waves of different frequencies. Wavelet analysis splits a signal into shifted and scaled versions of the original wavelet (mother wavelet). In other words, it implies the decomposition of a signal into a family of basis functions obtained through translation and dilation of a special function. Moments of wavelet coefficients in various frequency bands have been shown to be effective for representing texture (Datta et al. 2008). Wavelet transform computation involves recursive filtering and subsampling, and it disintegrates a two-dimensional (2D) signal into four subbands at each level, which are termed as LL, LH, HL, and HH (L = Low, H = High) as per their frequency characteristics (Chang and Jay Kuo 1993).

The most commonly used descriptor is the edge histogram, which detects various kinds of edges in the image and reports their corresponding frequencies of occurrence. The underlying hypothesis is that edges will be common for similar images. The edge histogram descriptor demonstrates the spatial distribution of edges and can retrieve images with similar semantic meaning. Hence, it mainly looks for matching image-to-image, exclusively for ordinary images with nonuniform edge distribution. Wavelet transform and edge histogram are also employed in the present work of image retrieval systems.

7.6.1.4 Shape Descriptor

Shape is another widely used feature in CBIR systems. The shape of an object is the typical surface configuration indicated by the outline or contour. Shape recognition is vital in CBIR for the reason that it relates to regions of interest in images. Shape feature representations are boundary based and region based (Datta et al. 2008). In our proposed system, we have not taken shape features into account during similarity distance computation. Our future work will include the shape feature in the proposed system.

7.6.1.5 Similarity Measure

Similarity measure implies the similarity between two images as denoted by their feature values. Choice of similarity metrics is the vital part of CBIR as it directly affects its performance. The type of measurement depends on the type of feature vectors chosen to compare similarity (Long et al. 2003). If the features extracted from the images are offered as multidimensional points, the distances between consequent multidimensional points can be measured. Euclidean distance is the typical metric applied to calculate the distance between two points in multidimensional space (Qian et al. 2004).

Euclidean distance may not be a perfect similarity measure for other features such as color histograms or may not fit the human view of similarity. Swain and Bllard (1991) proposed histogram intersections to identify known objects within images using color histograms. Numerous other metrics, such as Mahalanobis distance, Minkowski distance, Earth Mover's distance, Kullback–Leibler divergence, and proportional transportation distance have been put forth for particular tasks.

7.6.2 Region-Based Image Retrieval

In traditional CBIR, we acquire the signature for the whole image and are recognized as global features. Indeed, global features do not contain spatial information about images, making images with even similar global features to appear as perceptually dissimilar. The simplest manner by which the extraction of local image features can be done is by decomposing images into fixed blocks and then extracting features block by block (Rahman et al. 2006). One more approach to extract local features is by image segmentation by partitioning the image into visually homogeneous regions that can explain the semantic meaning of the image.

7.6.2.1 Image Segmentation

The aim of segmentation is to streamline and/or modify the representation of an image into a more meaningful and easier to evaluate form (Shapiro and Stockman 2001). Image segmentation finds objects and boundaries (lines, curves, etc.) in images. In other words, it can be defined as the process of allocating a label to every pixel in an image such that pixels with the same label share some visual properties. Image segmentation produces a set of segments that totally represent the entire image, or a set of contours extracted from the image. Pixels in a particular region are alike with respect to certain characteristics or computed features, such as color, intensity, or texture. The difference between adjacent regions with respect to the same characteristic(s) is remarkable (Shapiro and Stockman 2001).

Various methods of image segmentation have been used in region-based tasks for several purposes, for example, image retrieval, image annotation, and object recognition despite low performance levels. The clustering approach of image segmentation (Pappas 1992; Wang et al. 2001) groups image pixels into clusters. Each cluster creates an object and is used to extract the local features. Spectral clustering is a type of clustering that includes eigenvectors of the data in the clustering process. Normalized cuts (Shi and Malik 2000) is another solution for image segmentation, and it is employed in our work. This approach is closely related to graph theory, and in it, the nodes of the graph are the points in feature space, and edge develops between pairs of nodes.

Normalized graph cuts are a category of spectral clustering meant specifically for image segmentation. Here, the pixels of the image create the nodes of a graph whose weighted edges imply similarity (in gray tone, color, or other attributes) between pixels, and the algorithm *cuts* the graph into two subgraphs. $G = (V, E)$ is a graph whose nodes are points in measurement space and whose edges each have a weight $w(i, j)$ indicating the similarity between nodes i and j. The objective in segmentation is to discover a divider of the vertices into disjoint sets $V_1, V_2, \ldots, V_m$ such that the similarity within the sets is high and among varied sets is low. The graph can be divided into two disjoint graphs with node sets X and Y by discarding any edges that join nodes in X with nodes in Y. The degree of dissimilarity between the two sets X and Y can be calculated as the sum of the weights of the edges that have been disposed; this total weight is known as a *cut*:

$$cut(X,Y) = \sum_{u \in X, v \in Y} w(u,v) \tag{7.3}$$

The segmentation problem can be formulated to find the *minimum cut* in the graph, and the same can be repeated until the regions are adequately uniform. Nonetheless, the minimum cut approach prefers cutting small sets of isolated nodes; thereby, large uniform color/texture regions cannot be found. The *normalized cut* (Ncut) is defined in terms of *cut* (X, Y), and the *association* between X and the full vertex set V is given by

$$asso(X,V) = \sum_{u \in X, t \in V} w(u,t) \tag{7.4}$$

The definition of normalized cut is then

$$\mathrm{N}cut(X,Y) = \frac{cut(X,Y)}{asso(X,V)} + \frac{cut(X,Y)}{asso(Y,V)} \tag{7.5}$$

From this definition, it can be interpreted that the *cut*, which separates small isolated nodes, will not have small Ncut values, and only divisions with small Ncut values will be helpful in image segmentation.

Various other image segmentation criteria include edge detection (Ma and Manjunath 1997), region growing (Deng and Manjunath 2001), mean-shift (Wu et al. 2006), genetic algorithms (Liu et al. 2006), watershed (Chiang et al. 2005), spectral clustering (Jiang et al. 2005), and max-flow/min-cut (Guan and Qiu 2007). The image is partitioned into overlapping or nonoverlapping tiles (Shyu et al. 2003), or important properties of images are focused by some other approaches (Ko et al. 2004; Nguyen and Worring 2005). Unluckily, no single generic method exists for all types of images.

The feature descriptors discussed in Section 7.6.1.1 can be extracted from each object instead of a global image. Color and texture features are extracted from each pixel pertaining to the region as each region is defined by the average value of these pixels in our work.

7.6.2.2 Similarity Measure

In region-based extraction, different images may have different numbers of segmented regions. This creates a difference in the total number of features extracted from different images contrary to the same number of features extracted from each region. Hence, Euclidean distance cannot be useful for associating region-based images. In region-based image retrieval, similarity is computed as a weighted sum of the similarity between the given regions. The distances between regions must be measured to identify a match.

The distance between two images is computed using the Earth Mover's distance (EMD) based on the abstract representation of images (Rubner et al. 1998). The EMD calculates the minimum cost required to convert one distribution into another. It considers the transportation problem (Hitchcock 1941), and linear optimization algorithms can address this issue efficiently. EMD assures perceptual similarity and can work on variable-length representations of the distributions. Hence, EMD is apt for a region-based image similarity metric and is employed in our work. The ground distance is an equally weighted Euclidean distance between the features of two code words. As Euclidean distance is a metric and the total weight of each signature is limited to be 1, the distance is a real metric, reported by Rubner et al. (1998). EMD includes the features of all the segmented regions to utilize the information about an image completely. EMD is free of inaccurate segmentation by permitting a many-to-many relationship of the regions to be effective.

Otherwise, integrated region matching (IRM) (Wang et al. 2001), a simplified form of EMD, can be applied as the measure of image similarity. IRM makes use of a greedy algorithm to attain approximation while solving a linear programming problem. Subsequently, IRM is not a metric, making most of the traditional indexing techniques infeasible.

7.6.3 Image Summarization

Content sharing and social networking media together with swift progress in the digital multimedia data have urged the application of vital tools for much better browsing and retrieval through effective representation, analysis, and summarization of data. Summarization techniques serve to deliver a condensed representation of an individual multimedia data collection. Depending on the application domain and the type of data, summaries may be composed of images, text, video segments, or a mixture of these.

This focus on summarization of the image collection (Kennedy and Naaman 2008) implies the practice of selecting a typical portion of images from a larger group of images.

Methods based on clustering (Morana et al. 2009), similarity pyramids methods (Chen et al. 2000), graph methods (Jing et al. 2007), neural networks methods (Deng 2007), and formal concept analysis (Nobuhara 2007) are among those being employed to create summaries of image collection. These strategies apply visual features such as color, shape, and texture for the illustration of images. Further, in real time, many images have user-annotated text tags (Tseng et al. 2007, 2008), which facilitate better understanding of the images. Nevertheless, the majority of previous works have not made use of these tags during the summarization process. A combination of images and texts by multiple kernel learning has been performed in a recent work (Guillaumin et al. 2010), and it has become apparent that text tags could enhance the image classification performance.

The overlying facts persuade us to look upon textual content for image summarization based on sparse dictionary model rather than mere image content. Sparse representation involves approximation of an input signal with a linear combination of a few dictionary atoms (Wright et al. 2009) and has grabbed the attention of various researchers while being successfully utilized in robust face recognition, visual tracking (Mei and Ling 2011), and transient acoustic signal classification (Zhang et al. 2012). Joint sparse representation has bestowed a substantial improvement of performance in a variety of multitask learning applications including target classification, biometric recognitions, and multiview face recognition (Zhang et al. 2012) when compared to several other proposed sparsity constraints (priors). However, the performance of joint sparse representation declines with a large set of training samples like sparse representation, though results obtained were noteworthy (Yuan et al. 2012). This limitation becomes even worse with multiple training matrices, which makes the solution complex. Therefore, Shafiee et al. (2014a,b) suggest integrating dictionary learning in joint sparse representation to circumvent this problem and illustrated improved results on face recognition. These facts motivate us to consider leveraging the dictionary learning for the joint sparse representation model to construct the summary and to represent the image. Specifically the image summarization problem is reformulated into a dictionary learning problem by choosing the bases that can be sparsely united to signify the original image and attain a minimum global reconstruction error, such as MSE, which is described as the NP-hard problem.

Existing sparse coding and dictionary learning techniques such as PCA, the MOD (Engan et al. 1999), and K-SVD (Aharon et al. 2005) utilize machine learning techniques to acquire more condensed representations. The MOD algorithm stems from the GLA (Gersho 1992), and both MOD and K-SVD algorithms update the bases iteratively. Code words are updated as the centroids from a nearest neighbor clustering result in the MOD algorithm and in the K-SVD algorithm a new basis is evolved directly from the calculated result. Since all these existing sparse coding and dictionary learning techniques result in local optimum, the current work has adopted the firefly algorithm for dictionary learning to achieve a global optimum with a high probability by diminishing the optimization function while undergoing adequate search steps.

Thus the problem of image summarization is formulated as the issue of dictionary learning under multimodality, sparsity, and diversity constrictions, and the firefly algorithm is adopted to train the dictionary by resolving the optimization function efficiently.

7.6.3.1 *Multimodal Image Collection Summarization*

There is always an increasing growth in the quantity of images existing on the World Wide Web and in electronic collections, and particularly due to the large size of the image collections, navigation or exploration through the bulk set becomes automatically difficult. This increases the need for an effectual image summarization system that could lead users to get a summary of a photo collection automatically. The summarization system will choose the representative photos from a corpus, thus constructing an informative summary. The image collections mostly include supplementary nonvisual content such as text descriptions, comments, user ratings, and tags. These multimodality data will supply a semantic meaning to the visual data in the images, thereby increasing the performance of various image content analysis jobs.

The assimilation of text and image features comprises a latent mixing phase to position the text and image features onto a lower-dimensional space, and a multimodal similarity evaluation phase for combining both channels linearly either at the feature or at the scoring level (Hare et al. 2006). The inputs for this multimodal fusion—that is, the text and image matrices—are taken from a data preprocessing phase. In the latter phase, text/image processing techniques are exploited to process text corpus and labeled image data for exemplifying target words as separate text- and image-based feature vectors, stored in target-by-feature matrices.

A latent semantic space is created by latent multimodal mixing using both data modalities with the intent to identify a group of latent factors, which describe the link between multimodal features. To serve this purpose, row normalization and concatenation of the text and image matrices are performed that result in a single matrix whose row vectors are projected onto a lower dimensionality space by singular value decomposition, and then projected back to acquire a concatenated matrix with the original features but of lower rank.

In multimodal similarity evaluation for pairs of target words, data in the text- and vision-based (sub)matrices is assimilated in two ways both at the feature and the scoring levels. In the first approach, the integrated text- and image-based feature vectors of words are applied as their single representation, and these multimodal representations are compared to assess the similarity of pairs. Under the second strategy, similarity is estimated in text and image space independently, and the two scores are combined to offer the finalized amount of similarity of a pair. In the present work of multimodal image summarization, feature-level fusion is piloted.

7.6.3.2 Bag of Words

Text domains involve a comprehensive study of retrieval of documents. The bag-of-words (BoW) method is an early and eminent approach for the exploration of text domains. BoW is classified into the following categories: text preprocessing, vocabulary selection, and stemming. Selected vocabulary is used to tag the document by inverted file index and retrieval is done using term frequency-inverse document frequency (*tf-idf*).

The text preprocessing step consists of breaking a text document into words, discarding all punctuation marks, and using single white spaces to replace tabs and other nontext characters to be used for further processing. The dictionary or vocabulary of a document collection is nothing but the set of various words derived by integrating all text documents of a collection. The size of the vocabulary is then minimized by filtering and stemming. Initial filtering is by means of rejecting stop-words such as articles, prepositions, conjunctions, and so on. Words of most frequent occurrence bear little information to differentiate between documents. But words occurring rarely will be statistically irrelevant and can also be omitted from the vocabulary. This step is followed by mapping verb forms to the infinite tense and nouns to the singular form. In stemming, the basic forms of words will be built—that is, stripping the plurals from nouns, the "-ing" from verbs, or other affixes, for instance "read," "reading," and so on, are allocated same stem "read." A stem refers to a natural group of words with equal (or similar) meaning, and every word is denoted by its stem once the stemming process is completed.

After finalizing the vocabulary, a vector with integer entries of length V is used to represent each document. If this vector is u then its jth component u_j indicates the number of appearances of word j in the document. The length of the document is $n = \sum_{j=1}^{N} u_j$. For documents, n is much smaller than N and $u_j = 0$ for most words j, thus providing a meager representation of a certain document. Then, document indexing using fixed vocabulary is performed by inverted file index, the most well-known and effective way to index these vectors. Inverted file index encompasses entry for all words, and each word is related to all the documents containing it and its frequency is stored. In the retrieval stage, the query words are searched in an index, and all documents in which those words are present are retrieved. These retrieved documents are ranked using *tf-idf*, defined as follows:

$$W_{ij} = f_{ij} \times (\log V - \log d_j) \tag{7.6}$$

where, W_{ij} is the weight of term j in document i, f_{ij} is frequency of term j in document i, V is the number of documents in the collection, and d_j is the number of documents containing the term j. Thus, the weight W_{ij} measures the degree of relevance of the document for a particular word. Relevant documents generally own high *tf-idf* weights compared to other documents.

The BoW model serves best for visual analytic tasks, such as object categorization. Hence, the BoW model will be applicable for generalization of primary visual content in a collection, using the summarization problem. The selection of a local descriptor in a BoW model is dependent on application: the application of both texton descriptors (Battiato et al. 2010) and scale invariant feature transform (SIFT) (Lowe 2004) descriptors (Sivic and Zisserman 2003) is prominent. The texton descriptors are apt for scene image categorization, whereas SIFT descriptors have a broad range of application. Hence, we have chosen the SIFT descriptor as the feature to construct the BoW model. SIFT is a prevalent feature extraction and clarification algorithm. It does not endow an overall representation of the image in contrast to color histogram or local binary pattern like a descriptor. Instead, it extracts desired points such as blobs and corner and defines with a scale, illumination and rotational invariant descriptors and provides an array of point descriptors as outputs.

Similar to the use of traditional BoW strategy for text retrieval, the visual content can also be illustrated using a bag-of-features (Csurka et al. 2004) approach, which exploits a predefined dictionary of visual patterns to generate an order-less distribution of image features. This dictionary is constructed from the image collection and is responsible for the presence of all visual patterns in the images. The training set of images is decomposed into sub-blocks of $n*n$ pixels to build the bag of features. The relevant visual patterns are represented using rotation invariant characteristics after extraction of visual features for each sub-block. All the extracted blocks are then assembled to get k centroids, to be used as the reference dictionary of visual patterns. Ultimately, a histogram is built with the presence of visual patterns occurring in the image. This system is common in computer vision tasks, such as image categorization and object recognition (Bosch et al. 2007).

The text related to images can be indexed by adopting a vector-space model (VSM) (Salton et al. 1975), which focuses on vector representation, where each vector component represents the frequency of a word (term) in the document. A document is in general expressed as a *tf-idf* weight of the visual words involved in the creation of the relevant vector. The similarity between the images can then be estimated by measuring the cosine similarity of the weighted vectors, achieving a normalized value in the range [0, 1]. These bags of features and text indexing in the VSM are used in our work.

7.6.3.3 Dictionary Learning for Calculating Sparse Approximately

Sparse coding is an essential tool in designing dictionaries. Sparse coding involves computation of the representation coefficients y, based on the given signal x and the dictionary D. This is also known as "atom decomposition," which needs solving:

$$(P_0) \quad \min_{y} \| y \|_0 \quad \text{subject to } x = Dy \tag{7.7}$$

or

$$(P_0, \in) \quad \min_{y} \| y \|_0 \quad \text{subject to } \| x - Dy \|_2 \leq \in \tag{7.8}$$

and is usually performed by a "pursuit algorithm" that arrives at an approximate solution, as precise estimation of sparsest representations, which is an NP-hard problem (Davis et al. 1997). Hence, approximate solutions are being aimed and numerous successful pursuit algorithms have been suggested so far in the last two decades. Among them, the simplest are the matching pursuit (MP) (Mallat and Zhang 1993) and the orthogonal matching pursuit (OMP) algorithms (Tropp 2004), which are greedy algorithms choosing the dictionary atoms in sequence. These methods are composed of the calculation of inner products between the signal and dictionary columns, and perhaps setting up certain least squares solvers. Both Equations 7.3 and 7.4 are overcome easily by varying the stopping rule of the algorithm. Another renowned pursuit method is the basis pursuit (BP) (Chen et al. 2001), which recommends a convexification of the problems put forth in Equations 7.3 and 7.4 by substituting the l_1-norm with an l_0-norm similar to that of the focal underdetermined system solver (FOCUSS) (Rao et al. 2003). The similarity to the accurate sparsity value is better, yet the overall problem turns out to be nonconvex, ending up in local minima that may deceive in the hunt for solutions. Lagrange multipliers transform the limitation into a penalty term, and an iterative method is formulated based on the notion of iterated reweighed least squares that treats the l_p-norm as an l_2 weighted norm.

BP and the FOCUSS can be inspired based on maximum *a posteriori* estimation, and undeniably numerous works have made use of this perceptive directly (Lewicki and Sejnowski 2000). The maximum *a posteriori* evaluates the coefficients as random variables by maximizing the posterior $P(y|x, D) \, \alpha P(x|D, y) \, P(y)$. The prior distribution on the coefficient vector y is presumed to be a super-Gaussian (i.i.d.) distribution that prefers sparsity. For the Laplace distribution, this method is comparable to BP (Lewicki and Olshausen 1999). In recent years, widespread learning of these algorithms has recognized that these practices can recover it well if the solution y is sparse enough (Fuchs 2004). The dictionary poses restrictions on the sparsity of the coefficient vector, and as a result it is successfully assessed.

Considering the training of dictionaries based on a set of examples $X = \{x_i\}_{i=1}^{N}$, it is presumed that a dictionary D providing the given signal examples via sparse combinations is present; hence, solving each example x_k yields a sparse representation. Dictionary learning for sparse representation y_k, at large, is expressed as minimizing the following optimization problem:

$$D^* = \arg \min_{D \in d} \left\{ \min_y \| X - DY \|_F^2 + \lambda J(Y) \right\} \tag{7.9}$$

The dictionary learning methods for sparse approximations usually begin with some early dictionary and discover the sparse estimates of a set of training signals, without changing the dictionary. The next step involves keeping the sparse coefficients fixed while optimizing the dictionary. This interchanging minimization method lasts for a few iterations or until a preferred approximation error is attained. It is quite handy in cases of the objective being based on both parameters, Y and D.

The dictionary design methods attempted to date follow the two-step process mentioned above. The first step is referred to as "sparse coding," where the coefficients are found, given the dictionary. The dictionary is then updated assuming known and fixed coefficients. The update of the dictionary columns is carried out in parallel with an update of the relevant sparse representation coefficients, leading to a faster convergence. This is the same concept we used in multimodal image summarization for dictionary learning for sparse representation. The various algorithms that have been proposed in this work differ in the methods used for the calculation of coefficients and in the procedure used for modifying the dictionary.

7.7 Web-Based Recommendation System

With rising popularity of the Web-based systems that are functional in many different areas, they tend to deliver personalized information for their users by means of exploitation of the recommendation technique. Recommendation systems are a subclass of the information filtering method that look to predict the "rating" or "preference" that a user would provide to an item.

Recommender systems have become increasingly common in recent years, and are exploited in a diversity of areas: Some popular applications comprise movies, music, news, books, research articles, social tags, search queries, and products in common. Conversely, there are also recommender systems for experts, collaborator jokes, financial services, life insurance, online dating, restaurants, and Twitter pages. Generally three basic recommendation approaches are demographic, content based, and collaborative.

The collaborative recommendations are able to bring recommendations based on the relevance feedback from other related users. Its main merits over the content-based architecture are the following: the community of users can send subjective data about items together with their ratings, and it is able to present completely new items to the particular user. Collaborative filtering approaches structure a model from a user's past behavior as well as related decisions prepared by other users. This model is then used to predict items in which the user may have an interest.

Content-based recommendations obtain descriptions of the content of the formerly evaluated items to learn the relationship among a single user and the description of the new items. In this technique a user is supposed to like a new item if the item is related to other items that are liked by the user. The content-based filtering method utilizes discrete distinctiveness of an item in order to recommend additional items with related properties. These approaches are regularly combined. The personality-based approach gets product and service preferences from a user's personality.

The demographic approach utilizes stereotype reasoning, which is mostly a classification problem, in its recommendations and is based on the information stored in the user profile that contains essentially different demographic characteristics to make initial predictions about the user. The differences between collaborative and content-based filtering can be established by comparing two popular music recommender systems—last.fm and Pandora Internet Radio:

- Last.fm generates a "station" of recommended songs by observing what bands and individual tracks the user has listened to on a regular basis and comparing those against the listening behavior of other users. Last.fm will play tracks that do not show in the user's library but are frequently played by other users with related interests. As this approach leverages the behavior of users, it is an instance of a collaborative filtering method.

- Pandora uses the properties of a song or artist in order to seed a "station" that plays music with related properties. User feedback is used to process the station's results, deemphasizing definite attributes when a user "dislikes" a particular song and emphasizing other attributes when a user "likes" a song. This is an instance of a content-based approach.

Each type of system has its hold strengths and weaknesses. In the previous instance, last.fm requires a large amount of information on a user in order to construct accurate recommendations. This is an instance of the cold start problem and is common in collaborative filtering systems. Recommender methods are useful other search algorithms because they help users discover objects they might not have established by themselves. Interestingly enough, recommender systems are regularly applied using search engines indexing nontraditional data.

7.8 Web Page Classification

Classification performs a very important role in many information management and retrieval tasks. On the Web, classification of page content is necessary to focused crawling, to the assisted development of Web directories, to topic-specific Web link investigation, to contextual advertising, and to the analysis of the topical structure of the Web. Web page classification can also help better the quality of the Web search.

Classification of Web content is dissimilar in some aspects as compared with text classification. The uncontrolled nature of Web content presents extra challenges to web page classification as matching traditional text classification. Web content is semi-structured and contains some structure information in the form of HTML tags. A web page consists of hyperlinks to point to other pages. This interconnected nature of web pages gives features that can be of greater help in classification. Initially all HTML tags are detached from the web pages with punctuation marks.

The next step is to eliminate stop-words as they are common to all documents and do not give much benefit in searching. In most cases a stemming algorithm is applied to decrease words to their basic stems. One such regularly used stemmer is Porter's stemming algorithm. Each text document obtained by the application of procedures discussed is represented as a frequency vector. Machine learning algorithms are then functional on such vectors for the purpose of training the respective classifier.

The classification mechanism of the algorithm is utilized to test an unlabeled sample document against the learnt data. A neatly developed home page of a website is treated as an entrance point for the entire website. It signifies the abstract of the rest of the website. Many URLs link to the next-level pages telling more about the nature of the organization.

The information contained the title, meta keyword, and meta description and in the labels of the A HREF (anchor) tags are very important sources of rich features. In order to score high in the search engine outcome, site promoters pump in several relevant keywords. This extra information can also be exploited. Most of the home pages are designed to fit in a single screen. The factors discussed contribute to the expression power of the home page to recognize the nature of the organization.

Two basic approaches to web page classifications are in the area of machine learning, where learning is over web pages. Using the machine learning method on text databases is referring to as text learning, which has been well studied during the last two decades. Machine learning on web pages is similar to text learning because web pages can be treated as text documents. Nevertheless, it is obvious that learning over web pages has new characteristics.

Initially, web pages are semi-structured text documents that are typically written in HTML. Next, web pages are connected to each other forming direct graphs via hyperlinks. Web pages are often short, and the text in those web pages may be inadequate to analyze them. Finally, the sources of web pages are numerous, not homogeneous, distributed, and dynamically varying.

In order to categorize such large and heterogeneous Web domain, two basic classification approaches are used: subject-based classification and genre-based classification. In subject-based classification, web pages are classified based on their contents or subjects.

The subject-based classification can be functional to construct topic hierarchies of web pages, and consequently to perform context-based investigations for web pages relating to precise subjects.

Genre-based classification is also called style-based classification, and web pages are classified depending on functional or genre-related factors. In a broad sense, the word "genre" is used here merely as a literary substitute for "a kind of text." A few instance of web page genres are online shopping, product catalog, call for paper, frequently asked questions, home page, advertisement, and bulletin board.

Representations for subject-based classification believe the text source represents the content of a web page. In order to retrieve significant textual features, web pages are first preprocessed to discard the less important data. Preprocessing consists of the following steps:

- *Removing HTML tags:* HTML tags indicate the formats of web pages. For instance, the code within and pair is the name of a web page; the content enclosed by a pair is a table format. These HTML tags may specify the significance of their enclosed content, and they can thus help weight their enclosed content. The tags themselves are detached after weighting their enclosed content.

- *Removing stop-words:* Stop-words are frequent words that get little information, such as prepositions, pronouns, and conjunctions. They are detached by comparing the input text with a "stop list" of words.

- *Removing rare words:* Low-frequency words are also detached based on Luhn's thought that rare words do not contribute considerably to the content of a text. This is to be done by eliminating words whose numbers of incidence in the text are less than a predefined threshold.

- *Performing word stemming:* This is done by clustering words that have the same stem or root, such as computer, compute, and computing. The Porter stemmer is a famous algorithm for performing this job. The common problem of the web page classification can be separated into multiple subproblems such as subject classification, functional classification, and other kinds of classification.

Subject classification: Subject classification is concerned with the subject or topic of the web page. For example, categories of online newspapers (finance, technology, sports) are instances of subject classification.

Functional classification: This is concerned with the function or type of web page. For example, determining a page is a "personal home page" is an example of a functional classification.

Based on the number of classes that can be assigned to an instance, the classification can be separated into single-label classification and multilabel classification: In single-label classification, only one class label is to be allocated to every instance, while in multilabel classification, more than one class can be allocated to an instance. When a problem is multiclass, for example, four-class classification, it means four classes are implicated: business, sports, arts, and computers. It can be single label, precisely where one class label can be allocated to an instance. In multilabel classification, an instance can relate to any one, two, or all of the classes.

Based on the type of class assignment, the classification can be separated into hard classification and soft classification. In hard classification, a request can either be or not be in a particular type of class, exclusive of an intermediate state; while in soft classification, a request can be predicted to be in some class with some possibility.

Based on the organization of types, the web page classification can also be separated into flat classification and hierarchical classification. In the flat classification, types are considered as parallel—that is, one category does not replace another. But in hierarchical classification types are prepared in a hierarchical tree-like structure, in which each type may have a number of subcategories. Classification of Web content is dissimilar in some aspects as compared with text classification. The unrestrained nature of Web content presents extra challenges to web page classification as compared to conventional text classification.

7.9 Facet Generation

Faceted search permits users to navigate a multifaceted information space by combining text search with drill-down selections in each facet. For instance, when searching "computer monitor" in an e-commerce site, users can pick a brand name and monitor the category from the provided facets: {Samsung, Dell, Acer,} and {LET-Lit, LCD, OLED}.

This method has been used effectively for many vertical applications, including e-commerce and digital libraries. Conversely, faceted search has not been explored much for general Web searches, even though it holds great potential for supporting multifaceted queries and examining search. The challenges stem from the large and heterogeneous nature of the Web, which makes it difficult to generate and recommend facets.

Some recent work extracts facets for a query from the top-ranked search results, providing what appears to be a promising direction for solving the problem. Changing from a global model that generates facets in advance for an entire corpus to a query-based approach that generates facets from the top-ranked documents, these methods not only make the generation problem easier, but also address the facet recommendation problem.

A faceted Web search (FWS) system will offer facets when a user issues a Web search query. The user can choose some terms from the facets, which will be used by the FWS system to regulate the search results to again address the user's information need. For instance, suppose a user is preparing for an international flight and wants to find baggage allowance information. When the user explores "baggage allowance" in an FWS system, the system may offer a facet for different airlines, {Delta, JetBlue, AA,}, a facet for different flight categories {domestic, international}, and a facet for different classes {first, business, economy}. When the user chooses terms such as "Delta," "international," and "economy" in these facets, the system can ideally help to bring Web documents that provide baggage allowance information for the economy class of Delta international flights to the top of the search results.

A faceted search considers automatic facet generation and facets recommendations for a query. Most of the effort is based on obtainable facet metadata or taxonomies, and extending a faceted search to the common Web is still an unsolved problem. The challenges stem from the huge and varied nature of the Web. A faceted search in the context of Web retrieval is a relatively novel field. Most proposals give solutions for at least one of the following problems:

- Extract facets and facet conditions that reflect the content of the search result documents.
- Rank facets and present facets that are suitable for the query and the user.
- Provide feedback of user-selected facet terms to the search engine.
- Two dissimilar strategies exist to solve the first problem:
  - Precompute document-precise facets and facet terms.
  - Dynamically extract the facets from the search result documents.

There is an extended history of using user-explicit feedback to get better retrieval performance. In relevance feedback, documents are obtainable to users for judgment, later than which terms are extracted from the judged relevant document, and supplementary into the retrieval model. Here, where true relevance judgment is engaged, top documents are unspecified to be relevant, which is called pseudo-relevance feedback.

7.10 Duplicate Detection System

The World Wide Web is a popular and interactive medium that circulates information today. The Web is enormous, varied, and active and thus raises the scalability, multimedia data, and temporal issues correspondingly. Owing to these circumstances, we are currently drowning in information and facing information overload. In addition to this, the occurrence of duplicate and near-duplicate Web documents has created additional overhead for the search engines, decisively distressing their performance.

In standard IR systems, all documents are centrally managed and indexed on a single server. An alternative that has advantages when the data are physically dispersed is to utilize distributed information retrieval (DIR). In DIR, multiple separate servers, potentially at separate geographic locations, all give a search service to a subset of the overall collection; the user interacts with a single interface recognized as the broker, which sends the query to the servers and combines the results.

DIR methods are usually classified as cooperative or uncooperative. In cooperative environments, distributed servers give the broker information about their contents that the broker can then use to select servers and interpret results. In uncooperative systems, the broker must obtain information from the servers by searching for and downloading answers.

For duplicates in DIR, the broker in a DIR system must perform two major tasks. The primary task is server selection: because it is expensive to search all servers for each query, brokers require selection of a limited amount of servers to search. A server selection algorithm is used to recognize the servers that are most likely to hold relevant documents.

Many different server selection techniques have been proposed; once the broker has proposed the query to each of the chosen subsets of servers and composed the returned results, it must execute result merging: based on returned information about the servers and each return query result, the broker must combine the results into a distinct list for presentation to the user.

Management of duplication across groups can be managed at either or both of the server-selection and result-merger phases. At the server-selection stage, the broker can avoid selecting servers that have a high level of collection overlapping with a server that has already been selected. For such a method to be efficient, the rate of overlap among the underlying pairs of servers must be precisely estimated in advance; tiny evaluation errors may lead to the loss of many relevant documents placed in the ignored servers.

The demand for integrating data from different sources leads to the problem of near duplicate web pages. Near duplicate data bear high similarity to each other, yet they are not bitwise identical but strikingly similar. They are pages with minute differences and are not considered as exactly related pages. Two documents that are equal in content may diverge in small parts of the document such as announcement, counters, and timestamps.

These differences are irrelevant for Web searches. So if a newly crawled page duplicate is deemed a near-duplicate of an already-crawled page *P*, the crawl engine should ignore duplicates and its complete outgoing links. Near-duplicate web pages from dissimilar mirrored sites may only vary in the header or footnote regions that denote the site URL and update time.

Duplicates and near-duplicate web pages are difficult for web search engines because they boost the space needed to store the index, either slowing down or increasing the expense of saving results and annoying users. Elimination of near-duplicates saves network bandwidth, decreases storage expenses, and improves the quality of search indexes. It also decreases the load on the remote host that is serving such web pages.

Determination of the near-duplicate web pages aids the focused crawling, improves quality and variety of the query results, and improves recognition of spam. The near-duplicate and duplicate web page detection facilitates actions in Web mining applications, for instance, community mining, plagiarism detection, document clustering, collaborative filtering, detection of replicated Web collections, and discovering large dense graphs. Near-duplicate detection (NDD) removal is essential in digital libraries, cleaning, integration, and electronically published collections of news archives.

Broder et al. defined two ideas, resemblance and containment, to measure the relationship range of two documents. He used word sequences to capably discover near-duplicate web pages. The dimensionality reduction method developed by Charikar's Simhash is to recognize near-replicate documents and plot high-dimensional vectors to tiny-sized fingerprints. They developed an approach based on random projections of the words in a document.

In lexical methods, like I-Match, a large text corpus is used for generating the lexicon. The terms that appear in the lexicon signify the document. When the lexicon is created, the words with the lowest and highest frequencies are removed. I-Match generates a signature and a hash code of the document. If two documents obtain the same hash code, it is likely that the resemblance measures of these documents are equal as well. I-Match is occasionally unstable to modify in texts.

Plagiarism detection is a method of locating instances of plagiarism within a work or document. The extensive use of computers and the beginning of the Internet have made it simple to plagiarize the efforts of others. The majority of cases of plagiarism originate in academia, where documents are characteristically essays or reports. However, plagiarism can be initiated in virtually any field, including scientific papers, art designs, and source code.

Detection of plagiarism can be either guidebook or software assisted. Manual detection requires substantial endeavor and brilliant memory and is unrealistic in cases where too many documents must be evaluated, or where original documents are not available for comparison. Software-assisted detection allows vast collections of documents to be compared to each other, making successful detection much more likely.

Systems for text-plagiarism detection realize one of two generic detection approaches, one being external, the other being intrinsic. External detection systems evaluate a suspicious document with a reference collection, which is a set of documents implicit to be genuine. Based on a selected document model and predefined likeness criteria, the detection task is to retrieve all documents that hold text that is related to a degree above a chosen threshold to text in the suspicious document.

An intrinsic plagiarism detection system (PDS) solely examines the text to be evaluated without performing comparisons to external documents. This method aims to identify changes in the unique writing style of an author as an indicator for potential plagiarism. PDSs are not proficient at reliably identifying plagiarism without human judgment. Relationship is computed with the help of predefined document models and might characterize false positives.

7.11 Improvisation of Seeker Satisfaction in Community Question Answering Systems

Question answering (QA) is a type of information retrieval. From the collection of documents, the QA system should be able to retrieve answers to questions created in natural language. QA is regarded as necessitating a more complex natural language processing (NLP) system than other types of IR such as document retrieval, and it is sometimes considered as the next step beyond search engines.

The QA research challenge deals with an extensive range of question types including definition, fact, list how, why, hypothetical, and cross-lingual questions. Search gathering varies from small local document collections to internal organization documents to news wire reports on the World Wide Web.

QA systems are classified into two major areas: open domain QA systems and closed domain QA systems. Open domain question answering contracts with questions about almost everything and can only rely on universal ontology and world knowledge. It deals with questions about nearly anything, and can only rely on general ontologies and world knowledge. But these systems usually have much more data obtainable and presented from which to extract the answer.

Closed-domain question answering deals with questions under a specific domain and can be seen as an easier task because NLP systems can develop domain-specific knowledge frequently formalized in ontologies. Alternatively, "closed domain" might refer to a situation where only a limited type of questions are accepted, such as questions asking for descriptive rather than procedural information.

Many searches have been done for expanding English-language QA systems. Also some other works have been done on Arabic, Chinese, and Spanish QA systems. The aim of QA systems is to find exact and correct answers for user's questions. In addition to user interaction, various QA systems contain at least three of the following parts: question processing, document processing, and answer processing.

To increase the reliability and ability of designed QA systems and to find correct and exact answers, we use a dynamic pattern with semantic relations among words, verbs, keywords, and also co-occurrence keywords. In the question processing module, at first the question is classified regarding linguistic theories and bases of answering questions.

Then the question's structure and keywords are specified by classification and sent to a document processing module to retrieve documents that may have proper answers. In the answer processing module, candidate answers received from the search engine will be filtered by co-occurrence patterns and ordered based on analyzing the system. Then the answers are sent to the user to validate the candidates. Finally, the system will present the exact answer.

Different types of QA systems are divided into two major groups based on the methods used by them. The first group of QA system belongs to simple NLP and IR methods. QA research attempts to deal with a wide range of question types including fact, list, definition, how, why, hypothetical, semantically constrained, and cross-lingual questions.

7.12 Abstract Generation

The amount of information on the Internet is massive, and this amount is ever growing. This builds search engines an essential tool for finding information. Since approximately every query gives more results than the user would be able to read, it is necessary that the most relevant documents are revealed first. But the majority of the time these documents hold only a small amount of relevant information for the user. This means the user frequently has to take a look at the whole document for only a distinct snippet of information, which is very time consuming. So search engines generate snippets to provide the user a "sneak preview" of the document's content.

Snippets assist the user to assess the importance of the document without the right to use it. The making of snippets is mostly based on the query terms and less on the context of the document. Regrettably this is only adequate for making relevance decisions, which is the purpose of search engines. However when the user is unknown with the topic or seeks background information, context has shown to be more important. This means different kinds of snippets are useful for dissimilar goals.

The major motivation for users to search is to "find out about" their search topic. Snippets should be based on the framework of the document. Such an objective is known as undirected information search. Generating snippets means extracting snippets from the documents and weighing these snippets according to their relevance. A snippet is relevant when it holds one or more different atomic facts than the user would use for writing an editorial. Generating these snippets necessitates a technique to extract snippets, a ranking method, and a relationship measurement to avoid redundancy.

Automatic document summarization can be separated in single and multidocument summarization. There are two most important dissimilarities among single and multi-document summarization. First, sentence extraction is a meticulous approach for single document summarization. It is rather tricky to use this approach for multidocument summarization because data content is stored in multiple documents, perhaps with overlap. Second, most single-document summarization systems use the monolithic structure of the document.

A document outline can be abstracts or extracts. An extract summary consists of sentences extracted from a document, while an abstract summary may hold words and phrases that do not exist in the original document. Snippet generation is a special kind of extractive document summarization.

One of the major uses for snippets is to permit a user to select those documents from a ranked list that best suit their information requirements. Snippets recompense for the intrinsic problems with IR systems, as if a system were ideal a user would have no need for snippets because the initial document would always perfectly satisfy their need. Consequently, a good snippet should help users distinguish the information content with respect to the query terms of one document from that of other returned documents.

The most basic way to get a good snippet is to locate a set of adjacent words that hold many query terms. By returning snippets that hold query terms, we are able to show them in context. While there may be an improved set of words to help discriminate two documents from one another, we make the supposition that a user will be more concerned with the differences between two documents in terms of query term context than other contexts.

Section IV

Model Formulations of Information Retrieval Techniques

8

TABU Annealing: An Efficient and Scalable Strategy for Document Retrieval*

This chapter presents a new method, TABU annealing, which reduces the limitations of TABU and simulated annealing (SA) and shows the results of some comparative studies that evaluated the relative performance of different optimization techniques on the same problem.

8.1 Simulated Annealing

Simulated annealing allows moves in less good goal directions once in a while to escape local minima. Annealing is the process of cooling material in a heat bath. If the solid material is heated past its melting point and then cooled down in a solid state, the structural properties of the cooled solid depend on the rate of cooling. Slow cooling leads to strong, large crystals. Fast cooling results in imperfections.

We have a problem with maximization over a set of feasible solutions and a relevancy function f calculated for all feasible solutions. The optimal solution could be calculated by exhaustively searching the space, calculating $f(s)$, and selecting the maximum. In practice, the feasible solution space is often too large for this to be practical. Local optimization solves this by searching only a small subset of the solution space. This can be achieved by defining a neighborhood structure on the space and searching only the neighborhood of the current solution for an improvement. If there is no improvement, the current solution is an approximate optimal solution. If there is an improvement, the current solution is replaced by the improvement, and then the process is repeated. In simulated annealing, the neighborhood is searched in a random way. Accept a neighbor whose relevancy is worse than the current solution depending on a control parameter called a temperature.

Metropolis Monte Carlo et al. (1953) first proposed the standard simulated annealing approach. Metropolis proposed the equation of state calculations by fast computing machines. Then the Metropolis Monte Carlo integration algorithm was generalized by the algorithm of Kirkpatrick et al. (1982) to include a temperature schedule for efficient searching. It is reported that SA is very useful for several types of combinatorial optimization to reduce the computation time. The minimum temperature is generally determined by the acceptance ratio during the SA process—that is, the temperature is decreased until the system freezes. Jonathan Rose et al. (1990) proposed a new method for estimating the maximum temperature by using equilibrium dynamics, and Romeo et al. proposed an efficient cooling method, but these methods use experimental parameters, and tuning of these parameters is necessary.

* Source of publication: doi:10.1504/IJIIDS.2009.027690; http://dl.acm.org/citation.cfm?id=1810817. Original material available in *International Journal of Intelligent Information and Database Systems*, 3(3), 326–337, August 2009.

An annealing algorithm needs four basic components:

1. *Configurations*: A model of what a legal selection (configuration) is. These represent the possible problem solutions over which we will search for a good answer.

2. *Move set*: A set of allowable moves that will permit us to reach all feasible patterns and one that is easy to compute. These moves are the computations we must perform to move from pattern to pattern as annealing proceeds.

3. *Fitness function*: To measure how well any given pattern is.

4. *Cooling schedule*: To anneal the problem from a random solution to a good, frozen placement; specifically, we need a starting hot temperature (or a heuristic for determining a starting temperature for the current problem) and rules to determine when the current temperature is low, by how much to decrease the temperature to low, and when annealing should be terminated.

8.1.1 The Simulated Annealing Algorithm

1. Select an initial temperature t_0 (a large number).
2. Select an initial solution (partition) s_0.
3. Select a relevancy function f.
4. Select a neighborhood structure for the solution space.
5. Select a temperature reduction function alpha (t).
6. Repeat.
    a. Repeat
        Randomly select s in $N(s_0)$ diff $= f(s) - f(s_0)$
        if diff > 0 then $s_0 = s$
        else generate random x in $(0, 1)$ and if $x < \exp(-\text{diff}/t)$ then $s_0 = s$
    b. Until iteration count $=$max_number_iteration
    c. $t = \text{alpha}(t)$
7. Until stopping condition

s_0 is the approximation solution. To apply simulated annealing to a problem, make several decisions: choosing t_0, alpha(t), the stopping condition, the neighborhood structure, and the relevancy function.

8.1.2 Cooling Schedules

1. alpha$(t) = a^*t$ with a between 0.8 and 0.99
2. alpha$(t) = t/(1 + b^*t)$, with b small (around 0)
3. alpha $(t) = c/\log(1 + k)$, where c is a constant at least as deep as the deepest local minimum and k the number of iterations. This cooling schedule guarantees convergence to the optimal solution.

8.2 TABU Annealing Algorithm

In a straightforward descent method we would generally take $V^* = N(i)$. However, this may often be too time consuming; an appropriate choice of V^* may often be a substantial improvement. The opposite case would be to take $|V^*| = 1$; this would drop the phase of choice of a best j. Simulated annealing could be integrated within such a framework. A solution j would be accepted if $f(j) \leq f(i)$; otherwise it would be accepted with a certain probability depending on the values of f at i and j as well as upon a parameter called temperature. There is no temperature in Tabulated search (TS); however, the choice of V^* will be crucial; to define it at each step one will use systematic memory to exploit knowledge extending beyond the function f and the neighborhood $N(i)$.

Any iterative exploration process in some instances accepts also nonimproving moves from i to j in V^* (i.e., with $f(j) > f(i)$) if one would like to escape from a local minimum. Simulated annealing does this also, but it does not guide the choice of j; TS in contrast chooses a best j in V^*.

The *K*-means algorithm consistently finds an optimal solution with less function evaluations and is fast in convergence, but it traps by the local optimum value, whereas the TABU search approach avoids the cycling condition, and thereby avoids remaining in local optimum. The simulated annealing approach is guaranteed for fast convergence, but the algorithm performance depends critically on the cooling schedule used.

Inspired by the concept of global optimization in TABU and fast convergence in simulated annealing, this section introduces a new method for retrieving documents that is significant for characterizing and predicting better results. This framework differs fundamentally from the approaches mentioned above. Instead of retrieving documents directly from the corpus, the method applies a clustering approach for the convergence, which matches the specific goal of the problem. This is accomplished by a *K*-means clustering algorithm. Then a simulated annealing algorithm is used to search for patterns in the space that are predictive of the events of interest. The resulting patterns from the SA are the initial seeds for the TABU module and apply for refining and generating the final results.

A brief outline of the method is presented below:

Step 1. Initialize each cluster C_i to contain k different document vectors from the document collection as the initial cluster centroid vectors.

Step 2. For each cluster in the solution space,

1. Assign each document vector in the document set to the closest centroid vector. Recalculate the cluster centroid.

2. Compute the fitness of the cluster based on the user's interest by the following equation:

$$F_i = \frac{1}{n_i} \sum_{d_k=1}^{n} \sum_{j=1}^{m} W_{jk} \tag{8.1}$$

where d_k denotes the document vectors, n_i is the number of document vectors belonging to the cluster C_i, W_{jk} is the weight of the kth document for the jth keyword, and m denotes the number of terms in the document vector.

Step 3. Initialize the TABU list as empty.

Step 4. The set of clusters C_i is given as input and retrieves the best clusters by the simulated annealing approach and given to TABU.

Step 5. TABU has a certain size, and when the length reaches that size, it is free from being TABU, and the process continues until the termination criteria are met.

8.3 Empirical Results and Discussion

To check the proposed method ability, it is evaluated and tested with the predefined algorithms on several performance measures, by comparing the retrieval effectiveness of documents using different document sets.

Section 8.2 explains the proposed algorithm and is tested on three real document sets, namely, cancer, AIDS, and tuberculosis, to get an intuitive idea of its qualitative behavior.

Algorithms compared: The performance and quality of the proposed projected method with *K*-means with TS (KTS) and *K*-means with SA (KSA) using the above-mentioned input dimensionality from PubMed open access initiative publications are compared. The parameters used for the test solutions are number of training patterns (documents) T, initial temperature t_0, alpha(t) based on the constraints, TABU conditions, aspiration level threshold value $A(i,m)$, and the several iterations.

Performance measures: To check the retrieval effectiveness, use three important strategies such as precision, recall, and *F*-measure.

Precision: This describes the percentage of the retrieved documents that are relevant to the query. It is formally defined as

$$\text{Precision} = \frac{|\{\text{relevant}\}| \cap |\{\text{retrieved}\}|}{|\{\text{retrieved}\}|} \qquad (8.2)$$

Recall: This is the percentage of the documents that are relevant to the query and were retrieved. It is formally defined as

$$\text{Recall} = \frac{|\{\text{relevant}\}| \cap |\{\text{retrieved}\}|}{|\{\text{relevant}\}|} \qquad (8.3)$$

F-Measure: This is defined as the harmonic mean of recall and precision:

$$F_{\text{score}} = \frac{2(\text{Recall} \times \text{Precision})}{(\text{Recall} + \text{Precision})} \qquad (8.4)$$

The harmonic mean discourages a system that sacrifices one measure for another too drastically. To measure retrieved document's quality, compute *F*-measure at different precision and recall levels.

Table 8.1 illustrates the retrieval measures such as precision, recall, and *F*-measure at the interval of 10 documents for the PubMed cancer dataset. Queries used for testing the

TABLE 8.1

Performance Evaluations on PubMed-Cancer

Document Range	KSA			KTS			Proposed		
	P	R	F	P	R	F	P	R	F
AT 10 Docs	1.00	0.33	0.59	1.00	0.33	0.596	1.00	0.33	0.59
AT 20 Docs	0.66	0.57	0.62	0.75	0.42	0.594	0.80	0.57	0.70
AT 30 Docs	0.58	0.77	0.63	0.62	0.55	0.599	0.75	0.66	0.71
AT 40 Docs	0.50	0.81	0.67	0.50	0.72	0.631	0.61	0.72	0.68
AT 50 Docs	0.35	0.84	0.57	0.31	0.84	0.54	0.39	0.84	0.61

Note: P, precision; R, recall; *F*-Measure.

cancer domain are "predicting cancer involvement of genes," "multiple malignancies," and "breast cancer." We see that the results are superior; this indicates that the proposed approach quality is quite robust.

Table 8.2 describes the mean fitness of various retrieval methodologies and compares the proposed method with the other two. In Table 8.2, the total number of relevant documents for the cancer domain in the corpus (mixture of 250 documents from different domain) is only 60. The mean fitness values for KSA and KTS are 91% and 97.5%. The proposed method is able to retrieve more relevant documents compared to the other two, and the average fitness value is 98.05%. The proposed method yields better fitness values for all domains. Here use the above-mentioned queries for the cancer domain; while the results for AIDS are from the queries AIDS treatment, AIDS mortality, and HIV and AIDS. Finally, derive the results for tuberculosis from the queries "tuberculosis treatment," "diabetes and tuberculosis," and "tuberculosis pathogenesis."

Table 8.3 presents the analysis of Retrieval strategies performances, with clustering and without clustering, in terms of convergence and time complexity. It is clearly shown that KSA, KTS and proposed override the results of SA and TS.

Evaluation of graph: The precision-recall ratio (Davis and Goadrich 2006) is presented for different input dimensionality for the approaches here. Figure 8.1 illustrates the average results over five points in the solution space to smooth the curve. The nature

TABLE 8.2

Mean Fitness of Retrieval Methods

Methods	Dataset	Relevant Documents			Mean Fitness		
		250 Docs	750 Docs	1000 Docs	250 Docs	750 Docs	1000 Docs
	PubMed-Cancer	60	180	240	91.00	89.16	83.80
KSA	PubMed-AIDS	40	120	160	90.58	85.42	82.06
	PubMed-Tuberculosis	46	138	184	91.07	84.64	82.58
	PubMed-Cancer	60	180	240	97.50	92.73	85.63
KTS	PubMed-AIDS	40	120	160	92.86	88.75	84.04
	PubMed-Tuberculosis	46	138	184	93.13	88.67	86.82
	PubMed-Cancer	60	180	240	98.05	94.39	89.93
Proposed	PubMed-AIDS	40	120	160	95.29	90.67	86.87
	PubMed-Tuberculosis	46	138	184	96.11	91.16	90.06

TABLE 8.3

Comparison of Retrieval Strategies with/without Clustering for 250 PubMed-Cancer Dataset

Methods		Documents to be Retrieved	Time Complexity
Retrieval with clustering	KSA	72	Theta($n$log$n$)
	KTS	72	Theta($n$log$n$)
	Proposed	37	Theta($n$log$n$)
Retrieval without clustering	SA	250	Theta(n^3)
	TS	250	Theta(n^3)

Source of publication: doi:10.1504/IJIIDS.2009.027690; http://dl.acm.org/citation.cfm?id=1810817. Original material available in *International Journal of Intelligent Information and Database Systems*, 3(3), 326–337, August 2009.

of the curve indicates that projected precision is inversely proportional with the recall. The curve closest to the upper left-hand corner of the graph indicates better accuracy of the retrieved documents. The delineating curve in the lower-right half of the graph shows that recall becomes 100%, but precision will fall below 100%. In the upper-left half of the graph, precision is 100%, and recall will always be below 100%. Restrict the precision and recall values to the line $p = r$ in the precision-recall curve. An IR system needs to trade-off recall for precision or vice versa. Figures 8.2 and 8.3 demonstrate that as the number of documents increases, recall increases but precision decreases.

The computed F-measure values in Figure 8.4 show that the proposed approach ranks better than the predefined algorithms for different sets of user queries. For the first two points the $F_{0.5}$ measure is computed because precision weights twice as much as recall, and

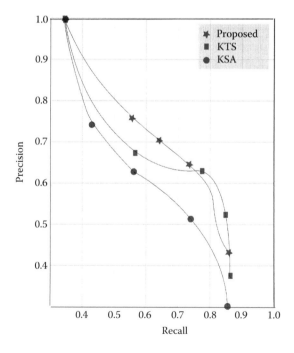

FIGURE 8.1

Performance measures of retrieval strategies for PubMed-Cancer dataset.

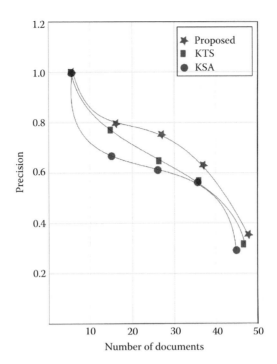

FIGURE 8.2
Comparison of precision for five document sets of cancer.

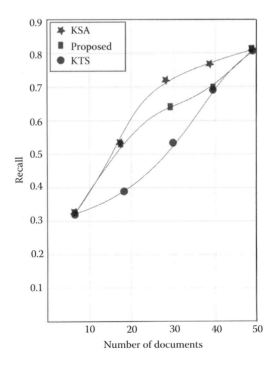

FIGURE 8.3
Comparison of recall for five document sets of cancer.

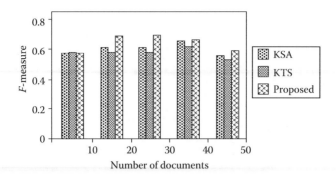

FIGURE 8.4
Evaluation of *F*-measure for retrieval methodologies on PubMed-Cancer dataset.

for the rest of the points the F_2 measure is calculated where recall weights twice as much as precision.

The general formula for a non-negative real α is

$$F_\alpha = \frac{(1+\alpha) \cdot (\text{precision} \cdot \text{recall})}{(\alpha \cdot \text{precision} + \text{recall})} \qquad (8.5)$$

9

Efficient Latent Semantic Indexing-Based Information Retrieval Framework Using Particle Swarm Optimization and Simulated Annealing[*]

In this chapter a significant amount of work has been done on information retrieval (IR) from huge corpus using various evolutionary techniques. User query modeling has been an active research area in IR. Feedback language modeling techniques are used for query reformulation. Researchers address the problem of dimensions in the solution space by using various dimensionality reduction techniques such as feature transformation (Jaimes et al. 2008) and feature selection techniques. This section uses latent semantic indexing (LSI) (Dumais 1994) for dimensionality reduction. Fast and high-quality document clustering algorithms play an important role in effective navigating, summarizing, and organizing of information. Recent studies have shown that partitioned clustering algorithms are more suitable for clustering large datasets. Here particle swarm optimization (PSO) document clustering is proposed for globalized search in the entire solution space. Finally, the simulated annealing (SA) method retrieves the documents.

9.1 Architecture of Proposed Information Retrieval System

An IR system consists of text preprocessing, clustering, and retrieval of documents based on user query. Figure 9.1 shows the proposed IR system layout.

In this framework, documents collection is an input to the text preprocessing stage. These documents are then filtered by removing punctuation and tokens, cleaned by eliminating stop-words, stemmed, and finally pruned and mapped as a term-document matrix and given to a dimensionality reduction stage. In this stage, divide the term-document matrix into a concept-document matrix and a term-concept matrix. The concept-document matrix is given as input to the clustering stage, and the term-concept matrix is given to the document retrieval stage to map the query into a concept space. Modules in the clustering stages are PSO and K-means. Then the clustered concept-document matrix is passed to the document retrieval stage. The query given by the user is then converted into a concept vector in the document retrieval stage. Simulated annealing is then used to retrieve relevant documents.

---

[*] Source of Publication: doi:10.1109/ADCOM.2008.4760433; ieeexplore.ieee.org/xpls/abs_all.jsp?arnumber =4760433. Original material available in IEEE Xplore Digital Library, *ADCOM 2008. 16th International Conference on Advanced Computing and Communications, 2008.* December 14–17. New York, IEEE.

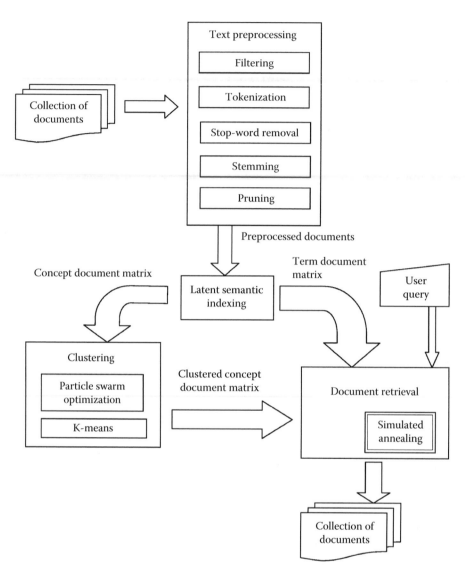

FIGURE 9.1
Architecture of proposed information retrieval system.

9.2 Methodology and Solutions

9.2.1 Text Preprocessing

Preprocessing consists of steps that take a plain text document as input and a set of tokens in the document vector as output. This method indicates the frequency of every term in the document collection. The datasets for preprocessing are from TREC, PubMed, and 7-Sectors dataset collections. The TREC (TREC 2006) dataset is a proceedings collection from the Text Retrieval conference. The PubMed dataset (PubMed Central Open Access

Initiative 2004) has documents from medical publications. The 7-Sectors dataset is a web pages collection from various domains. The goal of text preprocessing is to optimize the coming stages performance. Text preprocessing typically consists of

- Filtering
- Tokenization
- Stop-word removal
- Stemming
- Pruning

9.2.2 Dimensionality Reduction

Documents for analysis may contain hundreds of terms; many are irrelevant to the mining task or are redundant. Dimensionality reduction reduces the document size by removing such terms (dimensions) from the document. A dimensionality reduction technique takes a set of objects that exist in a high-dimensional space and represents them in a low-dimensional space. Retrieval (and clustering) in a reduced concept space might be superior to retrieval in the high-dimensional space of index terms. Unrelated documents may be retrieved simply because terms occur accidentally in them, and related documents may be missed because no term in the document occurs in the query (consider synonyms, there exists a study that different people use the same keywords for expressing the same concepts only 20% of the time). Thus, it would be an interesting idea to see whether the retrieval could be based on concepts and not on terms, by mapping terms to a "concept space" (and queries as well) followed by clustering and then setting up the ranking with respect to similarity within the concept space.

9.2.2.1 Dimensionality Reduction Using Latent Semantic Indexing

Latent semantic indexing (Deerwester et al. 1990) is a technique that projects queries and documents into a space with "latent" semantic dimensions. In the latent semantic space, a query and a document can have high cosine similarity even if they do not share any terms, as long as their terms are semantically similar. The latent semantic space (Hofmann 1999) that we project into has fewer dimensions than the original space (which has as many dimensions as terms). LSI is thus a method for dimensionality reduction.

In lexical matching methods, information is retrieved by literally matching terms in documents with those in a query. However, these methods are inaccurate when matched with a user's query. Since there are usually many ways to express a given concept (synonymy), the literal terms in a user's query may not match those of a relevant document. In addition, most words have multiple meanings (polysemy), so terms in a user's query will literally match terms in irrelevant documents. A better approach would allow users to retrieve information on the basis of a conceptual topic or meaning of a document.

LSI (Tang et al. 2004) tries to overcome the problems of lexical matching by using statistically derived conceptual indices instead of words for retrieval. LSI assumes that there is some underlying or latent structure in word usage that is partially obscured by variability in word choice. Use truncated singular value decomposition (SVD) to estimate the structure in word usage across documents. Retrieval is then performed using the database of singular values and vectors obtained from the truncated SVD. Performance results show that these statistically derived vectors are more robust indicators of meaning than each term. SVD (and hence LSI) is a least-squares method. SVD takes a matrix A (a word-by-document matrix) and represents it as $\hat{A}$ in a lower-dimensional space such that the "distance" is minimized between the two matrices as measured by 2-norm:

$$\Delta = \left\| A - \hat{A}_2 \right\| \tag{9.1}$$

The 2-norm for matrices is the Euclidean distance for vectors. Compute the SVD projection by decomposing the document by term matrix A_{txd} into the product of three matrices $T_{txn} \cdot S_{nxn} \cdot (D_{dxn})T$:

$$A_{txd} = T_{txn} S_{nxn} (D_{dxn})^T \tag{9.2}$$

where t is the number of terms; d is the number of documents; $n = \min(t,d)$, T and D have ortho-normal columns—that is, $TT^T = D^T D = I$; rank$(A) = r$; and $S = \text{diag}(\sigma_1, \sigma_2, \sigma_3 \ldots \sigma_n)$, $\sigma_1 > 0$ for $1 \leq i \leq r$.

By restricting the matrices T, S, and D to their first $k < n$ rows, one obtains the matrices $T_{txn} \cdot S_{nxn} \cdot (D_{dxn})^T$. Their product $\hat{A}$

$$\hat{A}_{tXk} S_{kXk} (D_{dXk})^k \tag{9.3}$$

is the best square approximation of A by a matrix of rank k defined in Equation 9.1.

SVD projects an n-dimensional space onto a k-dimensional space where $n \gg k$. In this application (word-document matrices), n is some word types in the collection. Values of k that are frequently chosen are 100 and 150. The projection transforms a document's vector in n-dimensional word space into a vector in the k-dimensional reduced space. Choosing the number of dimensions (k) is an interesting problem. While a reduction in k can remove much of the noise, keeping too few dimensions or factors may lose important information. LSI works well with a relatively small (compared to the number of unique terms) number of dimensions k. It shows that these dimensions are capturing a major part of the meaningful structure.

9.2.2.2 Query Conversion Using LSI

For information retrieval, represent a user's query as a vector in k-dimensional space and compare with documents. A query is a set of terms. The representation of the user query is by

$$q = q^T T_{tXk} S_{kXk}^{-1} \tag{9.4}$$

The vector of words in the user's query multiplied by the appropriate term weight is q. The sum of these k-dimensional terms vectors is $q^T T_{tXk}$ in the above equation, and the right multiplication by S_{kXk}^{-1} differentially weights the separate dimensions. Thus, the query vector is at the weighted product of its constituent term vectors. The query vector can then be compared to all existing document vectors, and the documents can be ranked by their similarity (nearness) to the query.

Advantages of this method are as follows:

- *True (latent) dimensions*: The assumption in LSI is that the new dimensions are a better representation of documents and queries. The metaphor underlying the term "latent" is that these new dimensions are the true representation. This true representation was then obscured by a generation process that expressed a particular dimension with one set of words in some documents and a different set of words in another document. LSI analysis recovers the original semantic structure of the space and its original dimensions. Deerwester et al. describe the major advantages of using the LSI representation with the following labels: synonymy and polysemy.

- *Synonymy*: Synonymy refers to the fact that describes the same underlying concept using different terms. Traditional retrieval strategies have trouble discovering documents on the same topic that use a different vocabulary. In LSI, the concept in question as well as all related documents to it are all likely represented by a similar weighted combination of indexing variables.

- *Polysemy*: Polysemy, a common property of language, describes words that have more than one meaning. Large numbers of polysemous words in the query reduce the search precision significantly. Using a reduced representation in LSI helps to remove "noise" from the data and describe rare and less important usages of certain terms.

9.2.3 Clustering of Dimensionally Reduced Documents

Document clustering is a fundamental operation used in unsupervised document organization, automatic topic extraction, and information retrieval. Clustering involves dividing a set of objects into a specified number of clusters (Zhao and Karypis 2004). The motivation behind clustering a set of document is to find inherent structure in the document and expose this structure as a set of groups. The document vector within each group exhibits a large degree of similarity, while the similarity among different clusters is minimized.

9.2.3.1 Background of Particle Swarm Optimization (PSO) Algorithm

This methodology is one principle of social psychology. This mimics the collective intelligent behavior of "unintelligent" creatures. It was developed in 1995 by James Kennedy and Russell Eberhart. It has been applied (Kennedy et al. 2001) successfully to a variety of search and optimization problems. In PSO, a swarm of n individuals communicate either directly or indirectly with one another in each search direction.

A particle (individual) is composed of three vectors:

The *x-vector* records the current position (location) of the particle in the search space, the *p-vector* records the location of the best solution found so far by the particle, and the *v-vector* has a gradient in which the particle will travel if undisturbed. Two fitness values are *x-fitness* and *p-fitness*. The *x-fitness* records the fitness of the *x*-vector, and the *p-fitness* records the fitness of the *p*-vector.

The swarm represents a number of candidate clustering solutions for the document collection. Each particle maintains a matrix $X_i = (C_1, C_2, \ldots, C_i, \ldots, C_k)$, where C_i represents the ith cluster centroid vector and k is the cluster number.

In a PSO system, at each iteration, particles *fly* around in a multidimensional search space. During flight, each particle adjusts its position according to its own experience, and according to a *neighboring* particle, makes use of the best position encountered by itself and its neighbor.

The fitness value is the average distance between a cluster centroid and a document to evaluate the solution represented by each particle. The fitness value equation is

$$f = \frac{\sum_{i=1}^{N_{ci}} \left\{ \left(\sum_{j=1}^{P_i} d(o_i, m_{ij}) \right) / P_i \right\}}{N_c}$$ (9.5)

where m_{ij} denotes the jth document vector, which belongs to cluster i; o_i is the centroid vector of the ith cluster; $d(o_i, m_{ij})$ is the distance between document m_{ij} and the cluster centroid o_i; p_i stands for the number of documents, which belongs to cluster C_i; and N_c stands for the number of clusters.

For every generation, compute the particle's new location by adding the particle's current velocity, *V*-vector, to its location, *X*-vector. In a multidimensional problem space, the ith particle changes its velocity and location according to the following equations:

$$v_{id} = w * v_{id} + c_1 * rand_i * (P_{id} - x_{id}) + c_2 * rand_2 * (P_{gd} - x_{id})$$ (9.6)

$$x_{id} = x_{id} + v_{id}$$ (9.7)

where
  x_{id} = current value of the dimension "d" of the individual "i"
  v_{id} = current velocity of the dimension "d" of the individual "i"
  P_{id} = optimal value of the dimension "d" of the individual "i" so far
  P_{gd} = current optimal value of the dimension "d" of the swarm
  c_1, c_2 = acceleration coefficients
  w = inertia weight factor

The inertia weight factor w provides the necessary diversity to the swarm by changing the momentum of particles to avoid particle stagnation at the local optima. Equations 9.6 and 9.7 require each particle to record its current coordinate x_{id}, its velocity v_{id} that indicates the speed of its movement along the dimensions in a problem space, and the coordinates P_{id} and P_{gd} where the best fitness values were computed. Update the best fitness values at each generation, based on Equation 9.8:

$$P_i(t+1) = \begin{cases} P_i(t), f(X_i(t+1)) \le j(X_i(t)) \\ X_i(t+1), f(X_i(t+1)) > f(X_i(t)) \end{cases}$$ (9.8)

where the symbol f denotes the fitness function; $p_i(t)$ stands for the best fitness values and the coordination where the value was calculated; and t denotes the generation step. It is possible to view the clustering problem as an optimization problem that locates the optimal centroids of the clusters, not finding an optimal partition. This view offers a chance to apply the optimal PSO algorithm (Cui and Potok 2005) on the clustering solution.

The whole clustering behavior of the PSO clustering algorithm is classed into two stages: a global searching stage and a local refining stage. At the initial iterations, based on the PSO algorithm's particle velocity, the particle's initial velocity v_{id}, the two randomly generated values (*rand$_1$*, *rand$_2$*) at each generation and the inertia weight factor w provide the necessary diversity to the particle swarm by changing the momentum of particles to avoid particle stagnation at the local optima. Multiple particles parallel searching, using multiple different solutions at a time, can explore more area in the problem space. Classify initial iterations as the global searching stage. After several iterations, the particle's velocity will gradually reduce and the particle's exploration area will shrink while the particle approaches the optimal solution. The global searching stage gradually changes to the local refining stage. By selecting different parameters in the PSO algorithm, we can control the shift time from the global searching stage to the local refining stage, increasing the possibility that it can find the global optimal solution. Contrary to the localized searching in the *K*-means algorithm, the PSO clustering algorithm performs a globalized search in the entire solution space and could generate more compact clustering results from the document datasets. However, to cluster the large document datasets, PSO requires many more iterations (generally more than 500 iterations) to converge to the optima than the *K*-mean algorithm does. In terms of execution time, the *K*-means algorithm is the most efficient for the large dataset. The *K*-means algorithm tends to converge faster than the PSO, but it usually only finds the local maximum.

The summarization of PSO algorithm is as follows:

1. At the initial stage, each particle randomly chooses k different document vectors from the document collection as the initial cluster centroid vectors.
2. For each particle,
    a. Assign each document vector in the document set to the closest centroid vector.
    b. Calculate the fitness value based on Equation 9.5.
    c. Use the velocity and particle position to update Equations 9.6 through 9.8 and to generate the next solutions.
3. Repeat step (2) until one of the following termination conditions is satisfied:
    a. The maximum number of iterations exceeds a predefined value.
    b. The average change in centroid vectors is less than a predefined value.

9.2.3.2 Background of K-Means

The *K*-means algorithm (Selim and Ismail 1984) is simple, straightforward, and on the firm foundation analysis of variances. The *K*-means algorithm clusters a group of document vectors into a predefined number of clusters. It starts with a random initial cluster center and keeps reassigning the data objects in the dataset to cluster centers based on the similarity between the document vector and the cluster center. The reassignment procedure will not stop until a convergence criterion is met.

The main drawback of the *K*-means algorithm is that the cluster result is sensitive to the initial cluster centroids selection and may converge to the local optima. Therefore, the initial selection of the cluster centroids decides the main processing of *K*-means and the partition result of the dataset as well. The same initial cluster centroids in a dataset will always generate the same cluster results. However, if good initial clustering centroids can be obtained using any of the other techniques, the *K*-means would work well in refining the clustering centroids to find the optimal clustering centers. It is necessary to employ some other global optimal searching algorithm for generating these initial cluster centroids.

9.2.3.3 Hybrid PSO + K-Means Algorithm

In the hybrid PSO + *K*-means algorithm (Cui and Potok 2005), the multidimensional document vector space is a problem space. Each term in the document dataset represents one dimension of the problem space. In the hybrid approach, the globalized searching ability of the PSO algorithm and the fast convergence of the *K*-means algorithm are combined. This performs fast clustering and can avoid trapping in a local optimum solution. The PSO algorithm is at the initial stage to help discover the vicinity of the optimal solution by a global search. The result from PSO is the initial seed of the *K*-means algorithm is for refining and generating the final result. The results from the experiments indicate that the PSO + *K*-means algorithm can generate the best results in just 50 iterations in comparison with the *K*-means algorithm and the PSO algorithm.

This is summarized as follows:

1. Start the PSO clustering process until the maximum number of iterations is exceeded.
2. Inherit clustering results from PSO as the initial centroid vectors of *K*-means module.
3. Start the *K*-means process until the maximum number of iterations is reached.

9.2.4 Simulated Annealing for Document Retrieval

By analogy with this physical process, each step of the SA algorithm (Kirkpatrick et al. 1983) chooses a random "nearby" solution, chosen with a probability that depends on the difference between the corresponding function values and on a global parameter T (called the temperature), that is gradually decreased during the process. The dependency is such that the current solution changes almost randomly when T is large, but increasingly goes "downhill" as T goes to zero. The allowance for "uphill" moves saves the method from becoming stuck at local minima—which are the bane of greedier methods.

SA (Hao and Pannier 1998) provides high precision and recall rate for document retrieval, to find a set of better solutions (set of more relevant documents). It is for finding relevant documents from a huge corpus where linear searching is virtually impossible. This methodology utilizes the perturbation function and the evaluation function. The perturbation function is used to randomly choose documents from a document collection. The evaluation function determines document relevancy with the user query based on the cosine similarity. Section 8.1 explained an annealing algorithm and its basic components.

9.3 Experimental Results and Discussion

9.3.1 Performance Evaluation for Clustering

For evaluating a clustering scheme validity, the system proposes the CS-measure (Anderberg 1973):

Cohesion: Patterns in one cluster are as similar to each other as possible. The fitness variance of the patterns in a cluster indicates the cluster's compactness.

Separation: Clusters are well separated. A distance measure among the cluster centers indicates cluster separation. The lower the value of this function, the better is the partitioning of the given dataset. Denote the distance metric between any two documents X_i and X_q as $d(X_i, X_q)$. Then define the CS-measure as

$$CS(K) = \frac{\sum_{i=1}^{k}\left[(1/N)\sum_{X_i \in C_i} \max_{X_q \in C_i}\{d(X_i, X_q)\}\right]}{\sum_{i=1}^{k}[\min_{j \in k, j=i}\{d(Cent_i, Cent_j)\}]} \tag{9.9}$$

Table 9.1 shows the maximization of this function actually means the index minimization. Figure 9.2 depicts the CS-measure/fitness evaluation for the PubMed dataset
Entropy (Koskela et al. 2004) is also used as a measure of quality of the clusters.

Shannon entropy or information entropy is a measure of uncertainty associated with a cluster. It quantifies a document contained in the cluster and measures the final partitioning quality. Uncertainty is maximal when all possible events are equi-probable. The reduced uncertainty is quantified in lower entropy. This measure is a probability of choosing the documents in the cluster. Attain the minimal entropy by maximizing the probability values.

Let CS be a clustering solution. For each cluster, calculate the distance between the document and the cluster centroid. For cluster j compute P_{ij}, the "probability" that document i

TABLE 9.1

CS-Measure Evaluation Using Inter-/Intracluster Similarity

Dataset	Number of Documents	Intracluster Similarity	Intercluster Similarity	CS-Measure	Fitness
	50	3.048336	1.468776	0.481828	2.074568
	100	2.665524	1.358398	0.509617	1.961488
7-Sectors	200	2.279126	1.221526	0.535962	1.865107
	300	2.317956	1.567618	0.676293	1.478211
	400	2.348737	1.902891	0.810176	1.233995
	300	2.317956	1.567618	0.676293	1.478211
	400	2.348737	1.902891	0.810176	1.233995
	50	2.667690	2.268275	0.850276	1.175812
PubMed	100	2.711492	2.334868	0.861101	1.161034
	200	3.561974	3.112963	0.873943	1.143977
	300	3.343254	3.050461	0.912422	1.095743
	400	3.259135	3.025359	0.928270	1.077040
	50	3.405556	2.220836	0.652121	1.532987
TREC	100	3.534234	2.478277	0.701220	1.425678
	200	2.983243	2.303998	0.772313	1.294476
	300	2.748156	2.227130	0.810408	1.233641
	400	3.745689	3.112506	0.830956	1.203143

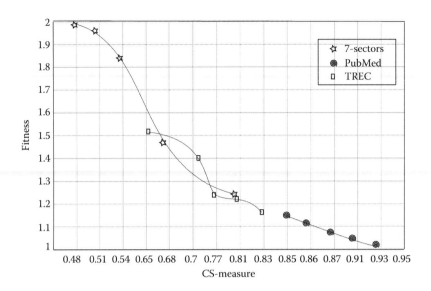

FIGURE 9.2
CS-measure/fitness evaluation for PubMed dataset.

belongs to cluster *j*. Calculate P_{ij} by taking the inverse of the distance between cluster centroid and document.

For each cluster *j*, compute probability P_{ij}, entropy E_j is given by

$$E_i = \sum_i P_{ij} \log(P_{ij}) \tag{9.10}$$

Calculate the total entropy for a set of clusters (Tan et al. 2005) as the sum of entropies of each cluster weighted by the size of each cluster.

$$E_{cs} = \sum_{j=1}^{m} \frac{n_j * E_j}{n} \tag{9.11}$$

where n_j is the size of cluster *j*, *m* is the number of clusters, and *n* is the total number of documents. The entropy values based on inter- and intracluster distances are tabulated in Table 9.2. Figure 9.3 demonstrates the entropy/fitness evaluation for the PubMed dataset.

9.3.2 Performance Evaluation for Document Retrieval

This section analyzes document retrieval performance by precision, recall, and *F*-measure. Queries generally are less than perfect in two respects: (1) they retrieve some irrelevant documents, and (2) they do not retrieve all the relevant documents. Precision and recall rate are the two measures usually used to evaluate the effectiveness of a retrieval method. If searchers want to increase precision, then they have to narrow their queries. If searchers want to increase recall, then they broaden their queries. In general,

TABLE 9.2

Entropy Evaluation Using Inter-/Intracluster Distance

Dataset	Number of Documents	Intracluster Distance	Intercluster Distance	Entropy	Fitness
	50	5.317900	26.940252	0.342681	2.074568
	100	7.114092	29.931113	0.400148	1.961488
7-Sectors	200	8.199910	36.894977	0.422243	1.865107
	300	13.65511	48.856958	0.573514	1.478211
	400	15.06305	74.863809	0.628610	1.233995
	50	25.66784	98.868382	0.084414	1.175812
	100	37.66805	103.79303	0.089903	1.161034
PubMed	200	65.93350	123.13309	0.171203	1.143977
	300	71.53097	157.84821	0.174565	1.095743
	400	81.43432	173.90272	0.189429	1.077040
	50	28.15014	107.62878	0.230331	1.532987
	100	48.11015	128.67898	0.137438	1.425678
TREC	200	66.39384	142.51082	0.151232	1.294476
	300	67.82619	171.04488	0.168031	1.233641
	400	83.67621	195.82167	0.258103	1.203143

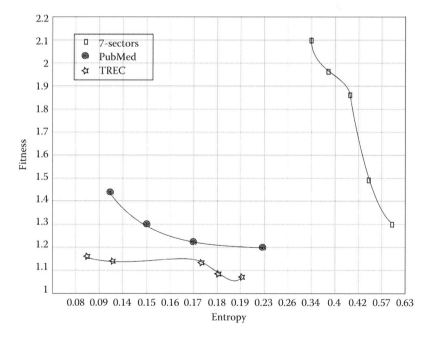

FIGURE 9.3

Entropy/fitness evaluations for PubMed dataset.

TABLE 9.3

Performance Evaluation of PubMed Dataset for Document Retrieval

Rank of Document	Precision	Recall	*F*-Measure
1	1.000000	0.003571	0.007117
5	0.833333	0.017857	0.034965
10	0.555556	0.035714	0.067114
25	0.511111	0.082143	0.141538
50	0.480769	0.178571	0.260417
75	0.443787	0.267857	0.334076
100	0.469484	0.357143	0.405680
125	0.431034	0.446429	0.438596
150	0.429379	0.542857	0.479495
175	0.422727	0.664286	0.516667
200	0.415800	0.714286	0.525624
225	0.407609	0.803571	0.540865
250	0.405844	0.892857	0.558036

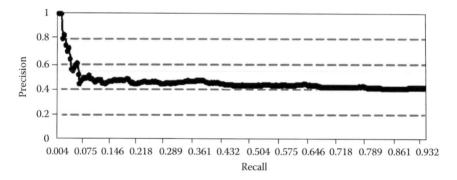

FIGURE 9.4
Precision/recall graph of PubMed dataset for proposed IR system.

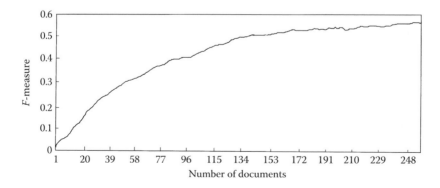

FIGURE 9.5
F-measure for PubMed dataset.

there is an inverse relationship between precision and recall. Users need help to become knowledgeable in how to manage the precision and recall trade-off for their particular information need.

The values of precision, recall, and *F*-measure are tabulated in Table 9.3. One of the two measures of recall and precision can always be optimized. Figure 9.3 illustrates the precision/recall trade-off (Davis and Goadrich 2006) for the PubMed dataset. Chapter 5 explored precision, recall, and *F*-measure and trade-off. Figures 9.4 and 9.5 demonstrate that the higher is the *F*-measure, the better is the solution.

10

Music-Inspired Optimization Algorithm: Harmony-TABU for Document Retrieval Using Rhetorical Relations and Relevance Feedback

This chapter proposes the novel clustering algorithm based on the harmony search (HS) optimization method that deals with document clustering. Harmony clustering is then hybridized with TABU to achieve better retrieval. Relevance feedback mechanisms are used, such as term feedback, cluster feedback, and term-cluster feedback, to further improve the retrieved results.

10.1 The Basic Harmony Search Clustering Algorithm

In order to cluster documents using the harmony (Geem et al. 2005) search algorithm, we must first model the clustering problem as an optimization problem that locates the optimal centroids of the clusters and not to find an optimal partition.

10.1.1 Basic Structure of Harmony Search Algorithm

The HS algorithm was originally inspired by the improvisation process of jazz musicians. Figure 10.1 shows the analogy between improvisation and optimization: each musician corresponds to each decision variable; each musical instrument's pitch range corresponds to a decision variable's value range; musical harmony at a certain time corresponds to a solution vector at a certain iteration; and the audience's aesthetics corresponds to objective function. The solution vector improves iteration by iteration and there the music harmony improves time after time.

Each music player (saxophonist, double bassist, and guitarist) can correspond to each decision variable (x_1, x_2, and x_3), and the range of each music instrument (saxophone = {Do, Re, Mi}; double bass = {Mi, Fa, Sol}; and guitar = {Sol, La, Si}) corresponds to the range of each variable value (x_1 = {100, 200, 300}; x_2 = {300, 400, 500}; and x_3 = {500, 600, 700}). If the saxophonist toots the note Do, the double bassist plucks Mi, and the guitarist plucks Sol, and their notes together make a new harmony (Do, Mi, Sol). If this new harmony is better than the existing harmony, the new harmony is kept. Likewise, the new solution vector (100, 300, 500) generated in the optimization process is kept if it is better than the existing harmony in terms of the objective function value. Just as the harmony quality enhances practice after practice, the solution quality enhances iteration by iteration.

10.1.2 Representation of Documents and Queries

For our clustering algorithms, the document is represented using the latent semantic indexing (LSI) model (Ding 1999). This is a technique that projects queries and documents

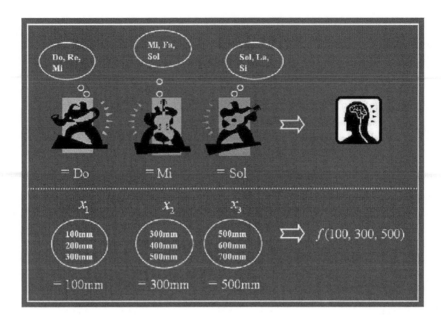

FIGURE 10.1
Analogies between improvisation and optimization.

into a space with "latent" semantic dimensions. In the latent semantic space, a query and a document can have high cosine similarity even if they do not share any terms, as long as their terms are semantically similar. This LS space that we project into has fewer dimensions than the original space (which has as many dimensions as terms). Choose the projection into the latent semantic space such that the representations in the original space change as little as possible when measured by the sum of the squares of the differences. LSI is explored in Section 9.2.2.

10.1.3 Representation of Solutions

Consider each cluster centroid as a decision variable; so each row of harmony memory, which contains K decision variables, represents one possible solution for clustering. In this case, each solution contains K vectors and corresponds to a set of K centroids $(C_1, C_2, \ldots, C_i, \ldots, C_k)$, where C_i is the ith cluster centroid vector, and K is the number of clusters. In this encoding, each element corresponds to a cluster and its value represents the candidate centroid for that cluster.

10.1.4 Features of Harmony Search

1. The HS algorithm imposes fewer mathematical requirements and does not require initial value settings for decision variables.

2. As the HS algorithm uses stochastic random searches, derivative information is also unnecessary.

3. The HS algorithm generates a new vector, after considering all the existing vectors, where methods like genetic algorithm (GA) only consider the two parent vectors.

4. HS does not need to encode and decode the decision variables into binary strings.

5. HS treats continuous variables without any loss of precision.

10.1.5 Initialize the Problem and HS Parameters

Specify the parameters of the HS in this step. These are the harmony memory size (HMS), or the number of solution vectors in the harmony memory; harmony memory considering rate (HMCR); pitch-adjusting rate (PAR); and the number of improvisations (NI), or stopping criterion. The harmony memory (HM) is a memory location where all the solution vectors (sets of decision variables) are stored. This HM is similar to the genetic pool in the GA. The HMCR, which varies between 0 and 1, is the rate of choosing one value from the historical values stored in the HM, while (1-HMCR) is the rate of randomly selecting one value from the possible range of values.

10.1.6 Harmony Memory Initialization

The algorithm maintains a store of solution vectors known as harmony memory (HM) that is updated during the optimization process. Harmony memory is the HMS $\times$ $(N + 1)$ augmented matrix:

$$\text{HM} = \begin{Bmatrix} x_1^1 & x_2^1 & \dots & x_N^1 f(x^1) \\ x_1^2 & x_2^2 & \dots & x_N^2 f(x^2) \\ x_1^{\text{HMS}} & x_2^{\text{HMS}} & \dots & x_N^{\text{HMS}} f(x^{\text{HMS}}) \end{Bmatrix} \quad (10.1)$$

HM consists of the decision variables only, with the objective function values stored separately. The initial harmony memory is generated from a uniform distribution in the ranges [LB_i, UB_i], where $1 \leq i \leq N$. Initialize the harmony memory with randomly generated feasible solutions. Each row of harmony memory corresponds to a specific centroid of clustering of documents as follows: First assign [n/k] randomly chosen documents to each cluster and the rest of documents to randomly chosen clusters. Then for each cluster, compute the centroid vector. Insert the computed centroids to the HM.

10.1.7 New Harmony Improvisation

A new harmony vector, $x' = (x_1', x_2', \dots, x_N')$ is improvised by the following three rules: (1) random selection, (2) HM consideration, and (3) pitch adjustment. In this step, we need a technique that generates one solution vector from all HMS solution vectors that exist in HM. The new generated harmony vector must inherit as much information as possible from the solution vectors that are in the HM. If the newly generated harmony vector, which corresponds to a new clustering, consists mostly or entirely of assignments found in the vectors in HM, it provides good heritability. Select each value from HM with probability HMCR and with probability (1-HMCR) that is randomly selected from set {$d_1, d_2, d_3, \dots, d_i, \dots, d_n$}. After generating the new solution, apply the PAR process. PAR is originally the rate of allocating a different cluster to a document. To apply the PAR process to document d_i, replace the current cluster of d_i with a new cluster chosen randomly.

10.1.8 Hybridization

The algorithm with the above processes performs a globalized search for solutions, where the *K*-means clustering procedure performs a localized search that uses the randomly generated seeds as the initial cluster's centroids and refines the centroid's position at each iteration. The refining process of the *K*-means algorithm indicates that the algorithm only explores the very narrow proximity surrounding the initial randomly generated centroids, and its final solution depends on these initially selected centroids. So the proposed algorithm is good at finding promising areas of the search space, but not as good as *K*-means at fine-tuning within those areas, so this may take more time to converge. It seems a hybrid algorithm that combines two ideas can result in an algorithm that can outperform either one individually. For this reason, a hybrid HS approach that uses the *K*-means algorithm may replace the refining stage in the HS algorithm.

To improve the algorithm, a one-step *K*-means algorithm is introduced. After that a new clustering solution is generated by applying harmony operations and applying the following process on the new solution. First, calculate the cluster centroids for a new solution. Then reassign each document to the cluster with the nearest centroid. The resulting assignment may represent an illegal partitioning. The illegal assignments are converted to a legal one by placing them in an empty cluster.

10.1.9 Evaluation of Solutions

Each row in HM corresponds to a clustering with assignment matrix A. Let $C = (C_1, C_2, \ldots, C_i, \ldots, C_k)$ be K centroids set for assignment matrix A. The centroid of the Kth cluster is $C_k = (C_{k1}, C_{k2}, \ldots, C_{kt})$, where t is the number of terms in all documents. The fitness value of each row is determined by the average distance of documents to the cluster centroid (ADDC) represented by that row measured by

$$f = \frac{\sum_{i=1}^{k} \left\{ \left(\sum_{j=1}^{n_j} D(C_j, d_{ij}) \right) / n_i \right\}}{K} \tag{10.2}$$

where K is the number of clusters, n_i is the numbers of documents in cluster i, D is the distance function, and d_{ij} is the jth document of cluster i. Replace the new generated solution with a row in HM, if the locally optimized vector has a better fitness value than those in HM.

10.2 Harmony-TABU Algorithm

Traditionally, efficient enumeration methods are used for supporting optimal decisions. However, their computational disadvantages such as requiring a huge amount of computation and memory made people rely on another type of methodology—that is, evolutionary or metaheuristic algorithms. The HS algorithm has been recently developed analogous to the music improvisation process where musicians in an ensemble continue to polish their pitches to obtain better harmony. The HS algorithm has been successfully applied to various real-world combinatorial optimization problems. Use the HS algorithm where optimization requires finding an optimal solution out of a huge amount of combinatorial solutions. Because an exact method may take a very long time to obtain the optimal solution, people have turned to evolutionary or metaheuristic algorithms that do not necessarily find the optimal solution, but tend to find good solutions within a reasonable amount of time. The HS model also found a better solution in terms of number of runs to reach the global optimum, average cost out of multiple runs, and computing time.

These algorithms are also modified and hybridized to reduce processing time and improve solution quality. In this section, we present a novel hybrid HS-TS algorithm and HS method that tries to find a global minimum of optimization problems. The HS-TS is a simple, direct search technique that has been widely used in various unconstrained optimization scenarios. One of the advantages of HS-TS is that it is easy to carry out in practice and does not require the derivatives of the function under exploration. It is often important because gradient information is not always available. HS, mimicking the improvisation process of music players, has been recently proved as a successful approach to solving complex optimization problems. Since the HS uses stochastic random searches, derivative information is not necessary. HS also needs fewer parameters and does not require crossover and mutation between two parent vectors.

The K-means (Selim and Ismail 1984) algorithm consistently finds an optimal solution with less function evaluations and is fast in convergence, but it traps by the local optimum value, where the TABU search approach avoids cycling conditions, thereby avoiding remaining in local optimum. The harmony approach (Mahdavi et al. 2007) is guaranteed for fast convergence. Inspired by the concept of global optimization in TABU and fast convergence in harmony, this section introduces a new method for retrieving documents that is significant for characterizing and predicting better results. Instead of retrieving documents directly from the corpus, the method applies a clustering approach for the convergence, which matches the specific goal of the problem. This is accomplished by the K-means clustering algorithm. The harmony algorithm is then used to search for patterns in the space that are predictive of the events of interest. The resulting patterns from the harmony are the initial seeds for the TABU (Gendreau et al. 2002) module that is applied for refining and generating the final results.

A brief outline of the method is presented below:

Step 1. Initialize each cluster C_i to contain K different document vectors as the initial cluster centroid vectors from the document collection.

Step 2. For each cluster in the solution space,

    1. Assign each of the document vectors in the document set to the closest centroid vector. Recalculate the cluster centroid $Cent_i$.

    2. Compute the fitness of the cluster based on the user's interest.

Step 3. Initialize the TABU list as empty.

Step 4. The set of clusters C_i is given as input, and the best clusters are retrieved by the harmony approach and are given to TABU.

Step 5. TABU has a certain size, and when the length reaches that size, it is free from being TABU and the process continues until it meets the termination criteria.

10.3 Relevance Feedback and Query Expansion in IR

The idea behind relevance feedback (Zhai and Lafferty 2001) is to take the results that are initially returned from a given query and to use information about whether those results are relevant to perform a new query. *Query expansion* (Ruthven 2003) describes the set of techniques for modifying a query to satisfy an information need. Generally, the relevance feedback has the disadvantage that irrelevant terms, which occur along with relevant ones in the judged content, are erroneously used for query expansion, causing undesired effects. An *interactive query expansion* (IQE) technique is used when the user has some interaction with the system that encompasses relevance feedback in an effective manner.

10.3.1 Presentation Term Selection

The proper selection of terms presented to the user for judgment is crucial to the success of term feedback. If the terms are poorly chosen (i.e., few relevant ones), the user will have a hard time looking for useful terms to help clarify his or her information need. If the relevant terms are plentiful, but all concentrate on a single aspect of the query topic, then we will only be able to get feedback on that aspect and miss others, resulting in a loss in retrieved results. Therefore, it is important to carefully select presentation terms to maximize expected gain from user feedback—that is, those that can potentially reveal the most evidence of the user's information need. This is like *active feedback*, which suggests that a retrieval system should actively probe the user's information need, and in the case of relevance feedback, the feedback documents are chosen to maximize learning benefits (e.g., diversely to increase coverage). The top N documents from an initial retrieval using the original query form the source of feedback terms: Consider all terms that appear in them are candidates to present to the user. These documents serve as pseudo-feedback, because they provide a much richer context than the original query (usually very short), while the user is not asked to judge their relevance. Owing to the latter reason, it is possible to make N quite large to increase its coverage of different aspects in the topic. The simplest way of selecting feedback terms is to choose the most frequent M terms from the N documents. This method, however, has two drawbacks.

First, a lot of common noisy terms are selected due to their high frequencies in the document collection, unless a stop-word list is for filtering. Second, the presentation list is filled by terms from major aspects of the topic; those from a minor aspect are likely missed due to their relatively low frequencies. We solve the above problems by two corresponding measures. First, we introduce a background model B that is estimated from collection statistics and explains the common terms, so that they are much less likely to appear in the presentation list. Second, we select the terms from multiple clusters in the pseudo-feedback documents to ensure sufficient representation of different aspects of the topic.

From each of the K estimated clusters, we choose the $L = M/K$ terms with highest probabilities to form a total of M presentation terms. If a term happens in top L in multiple clusters, assign it to the cluster where it has the highest probability and let the other clusters take one more term as compensation. Filter out terms in the original query text because of relevancy when the query is short. The selected terms are then presented to the user for judgment. Figure 10.2 shows a sample (completed) feedback form. Here this work only deals with binary judgment: a presented term is by default unchecked, and a user may check it to indicate relevance. The negative feedback is not exploited (i.e., penalizing irrelevant terms), because with binary feedback an unchecked term is not necessarily irrelevant

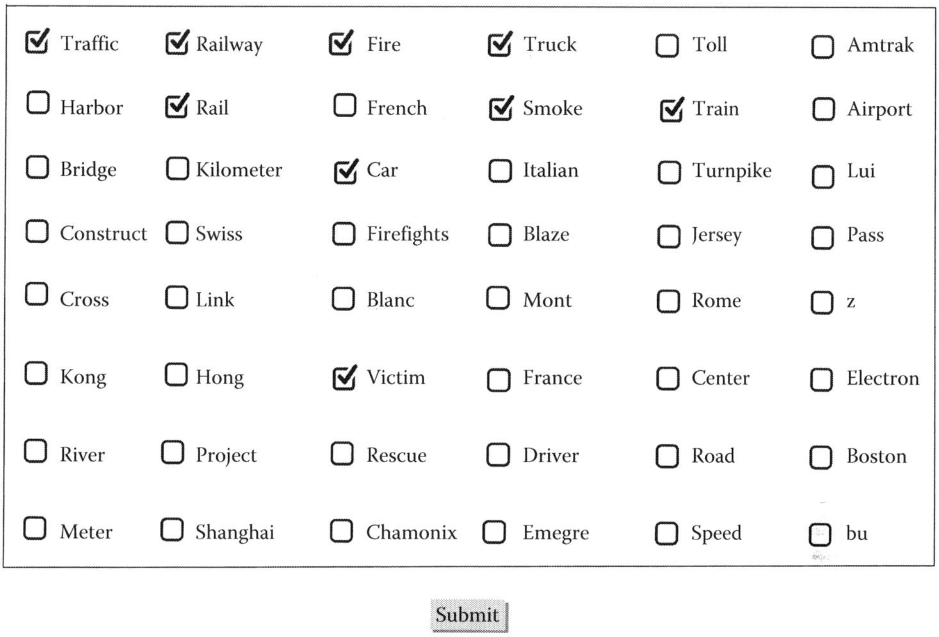

☑ Traffic	☑ Railway	☑ Fire	☑ Truck	☐ Toll	☐ Amtrak
☐ Harbor	☑ Rail	☐ French	☑ Smoke	☑ Train	☐ Airport
☐ Bridge	☐ Kilometer	☑ Car	☐ Italian	☐ Turnpike	☐ Lui
☐ Construct	☐ Swiss	☐ Firefights	☐ Blaze	☐ Jersey	☐ Pass
☐ Cross	☐ Link	☐ Blanc	☐ Mont	☐ Rome	☐ z
☐ Kong	☐ Hong	☑ Victim	☐ France	☐ Center	☐ Electron
☐ River	☐ Project	☐ Rescue	☐ Driver	☐ Road	☐ Boston
☐ Meter	☐ Shanghai	☐ Chamonix	☐ Emegre	☐ Speed	☐ bu

Submit

FIGURE 10.2
Filled clarification form for the topic transportation tunnel disasters.

(maybe the user is unsure about its relevance). We could ask the user for finer judgment (e.g., choosing from *highly relevant, somewhat relevant, do not know, somewhat irrelevant*, and *highly irrelevant*), but binary feedback is more compact, taking less space to display and less user effort to make judgment.

10.3.2 Direct Term Feedback (TFB)

This is a straightforward form of term feedback that does not involve any secondary structure. Term feedback takes less time to judge than a document's full text or summary. TFB (Spink 1994) assigns nonzero probabilities to the presented terms marked relevant, but completely ignores (a lot more) others, which are left unchecked due to the user's ignorance. Give a weight of 1 to terms judged relevant by the user, a weight of μ to query terms, zero weight to other terms, and then apply normalization: Call this method direct term feedback (TFB). If we let $\mu = 1$, this approach is equivalent to appending the relevant terms after the original query, which is what standard query expansion (without term re-weighing) does. If we set $\mu > 1$, we are putting more emphasis on the query terms than the checked ones. Note that the result model will be more biased toward θ_q if the original query is long or the user feedback is weak, which makes sense, as we can trust more on the original query in either case.

Drawbacks of this method are as follows:

1. Most of the time the presentation list may not include all the important terms.
2. TFB completely ignores the terms that are not selected in the presentation list, which is left unchecked due to the user's ignorance.

3. The user may not have in-depth knowledge about the term presented in the presentation list.

4. Sometimes a relevant term is left out because its connection to the query topic is not obvious to the user.

5. Other times a dubious term is included but turns out to be irrelevant.

10.3.3 Cluster Feedback (CFB)

Here we exploit the cluster structure that played an important role when we selected the presentation terms. The clusters represent different aspects of the query topic, each of which is relevant or irrelevant. If we can find the relevant clusters, we can combine them to generate a query model that is good at discovering documents belonging to these clusters (instead of the irrelevant ones). We could ask the user to directly judge cluster relevance after viewing representative terms in that cluster, but this would sometimes be a difficult task for the user, who has to guess the semantics of a cluster via its set of terms, which is not well-connected to one another due to a lack of context. Therefore, we propose to learn cluster feedback *indirectly*, inferring a cluster relevance through its feedback term's relevance. Because each cluster has an equal number of terms presented to the user, the simplest measure of a cluster's relevance is the number of terms that are judged relevant in it. Intuitively, the more terms marked relevant in a cluster, the closer the cluster is to the query topic, and the more the cluster should participate in query modification. If we combine the cluster models using weights determined this way and then interpolate with the original query model, for query updating, we call this cluster feedback (CFB).

Drawbacks of this method are as follows:

1. It gives equal weight to all the terms in the selected cluster.
2. It does not distinguish which terms in a cluster are presented or judged.
3. It ignores the terms that are important, but not included in the selected cluster.
4. When there are more clusters, each of them gets fewer terms to present, which can hurt a major relevant cluster that has many relevant terms.

10.3.4 Term-Cluster Feedback (TCFB)

TFB and CFB both have their drawbacks. TFB assigns nonzero probabilities to the presented terms marked relevant, but completely ignores others, which are left unchecked due to the user's ignorance, or simply not included in the presentation list, but we are able to infer their relevance from the checked ones. For example, in Figure 10.2, since as many as five terms in the middle cluster (the third and fourth columns) are checked, we should have high confidence on the relevancy of other terms in that cluster. CFB remedies TFB's problem by treating the terms in a cluster collectively, so that unchecked (not presented) terms receive weights when presented terms in their clusters are relevant, but it does not distinguish which terms in a cluster are presented or judged. Intuitively, the judged relevant terms should receive larger weights because they are explicitly indicated as relevant by the user. Therefore, we try to combine the two methods, by interpolating the TFB model with the CFB model, and call it TCFB.

10.4 Empirical Results and Discussion

10.4.1 Document Collections

Here consider the OHSUMED (Hersh et al. 1994) dataset, which was used in many experiments in information retrieval, including the TREC-9 filtering track. OHSUMED is a bibliographical document collection, developed by Hersh et al. at the Oregon Health Sciences University. It is a subset of the MEDLINE database. There are in total 16,140 query-document pairs upon which two levels of relevance judgments are made: "definitely relevant" or "not relevant."

10.4.2 Experimental Setup

Here, apply the K-means and harmony on the above-mentioned dataset. In the harmony–K-means, it first executes the harmony algorithm for more total iterations and uses the harmony result as the initial seed for the K-means module, and the K-means module executes for remaining iterations to generate the final result. In a ranked list, we can measure the precision at each recall point. Recall increases when a relevant document is retrieved. The mean average precision expresses the average precision for each query. In Table 10.1 we can see that the results obtained by a hybrid proposed approach are significantly comparable to results obtained by harmony and TABU individually. This is due to the high-quality clusters of the harmony algorithm and the local optimization of the TABU.

We discuss and compare term feedback to relevance feedback and show that it has its particular advantage. Participants submit custom-designed clarification forms to solicit feedback from human assessors provided by OHSUMED. Design three sets of clarification forms for term feedback: 1×30, a big cluster with 30 terms; 3×10, 3 clusters with 10 terms each; and 5×6, and 5 clusters with 6 terms each. The total number of presented terms (M) is 30. The clarification form is a simple and compact interface in which the user can check relevant terms. After receiving user feedback, run the feedback algorithms (TFB, CFB, or TCFB) to estimate updated query models, which are then used for a second iteration of retrieval. The evaluation metrics adopted include mean average precision (MAP)

TABLE 10.1

Comparison of the Performance Measure of Algorithms Considering Precision (P), Recall (R), and Mean Average Precision (MAP)

Methods	Metric	@10	@20	@30
Hybrid	P	0.6	0.5	0.46
	R	0.23	0.38	0.53
	MAP	0.59	0.5830	0.563
Harmonic	P	0.3	0.25	0.23
	R	0.115	0.1923	0.269
	MAP	0.3871	0.3656	0.3368
TABU	P	0.4	0.3	0.26
	R	0.15	0.23	0.34
	MAP	0.5332	0.4816	0.4321

TABLE 10.2

Retrieval Performance for Feedback Methods and Cluster Feedback Types

	TFB 1C	TFB 3C	TFB 5C	CFB 3C	CFB 5C	TCFB 1C	TCFB 3C	TCFB 5C
MAP	0.793	0.750	0.736	0.806	0.776	0.853	0.834	0.809
P@30	0.817	0.769	0.751	0.817	0.794	0.874	0.848	0.825

Note: CFB, cluster feedback; TCFB, term-cluster feedback; TFB, term feedback.

and precision at top 30, and the suffixes (1C, 3C, 6C) after TFB, CFB, and TCFB stand for the number of clusters (K).

In Table 10.2, TCFB3C achieved the highest results improvement in MAP, indicating a significant contribution of term feedback for clarification of the user's information need. For TFB, the performance is almost equal on the 1×30 and 3×10 clarification forms in terms of MAP and a little worse on the 5×6 ones. Both CFB3C and CFB5C perform better than their TFB, suggesting that feedback on a secondary cluster structure is beneficial. In CFB1C, it cannot adjust the weight of its (single) cluster from term feedback, and it is merely pseudo feedback. Although TCFB is just a simple mixture of TFB and CFB by interpolation, it is able to outperform both. This supports our speculation that TCFB overcomes the drawbacks of TFB and CFB. Table 10.3 shows various algorithms performance as the number of presentation terms ranges from 5 to 30. We find that TFB performance is more susceptible to presentation term reduction than that of CFB or TCFB. Also, the 3×10 clarification forms seem more robust than the 5×6 ones. This is natural, as for a large cluster number, it is easier to get into the situation where each cluster gets too few presentation terms to make topic diversification useful. Hence, the algorithms are able to perform reasonably well when the number of presentation terms is small.

Table 10.4 shows the number of checked terms, relevant terms, and relevant checked terms, as well as the precision/recall of user term judgment. Note that when the clarification forms contain more clusters, fewer terms are checked: 11 for 1×30, 9 for 3×10, and 8 for 5×6. A similar pattern holds for relevant terms and relevant checked terms. There seems to be a trade-off between increasing topic diversity by clustering and losing extra relevant terms.

Therefore, it is not always helpful to have more clusters. We see that TFB gets big improvement that checks all relevant terms, while CFB meets a bottleneck since all it does is adjust cluster weights, and when the learned weights are close to being accurate, it cannot benefit more from term feedback. TCFB outperforms TFB and also CFB.

TABLE 10.3

Mean Average Precision Variation with the Number of Presented Terms (TFB and CFB)

#Terms	TFB 1C	TFB 3C	TFB 5C	CFB 3C	CFB 5C	TCFB 1C	TCFB 3C	TCFB 5C
5	0.744	0.720	0.685	0.785	0.745	0.831	0.806	0.759
10	0.751	0.726	0.692	0.788	0.749	0.834	0.817	0.762
15	0.766	0.733	0.699	0.792	0.754	0.838	0.825	0.789
20	0.780	0.743	0.725	0.798	0.760	0.846	0.829	0.791
25	0.788	0.745	0.729	0.801	0.768	0.851	0.831	0.803
30	0.793	0.750	0.736	0.806	0.776	0.853	0.834	0.809

Note: CFB, cluster feedback; TCFB, term-cluster feedback; TFB, term feedback.

TABLE 10.4

Term Selection Statistics

Clarification Form Type	1×30	3×10	5×6
#Checked terms	11	9	8
#Relevant terms	13	12	12
#Checked relevant terms	7	6	5
Precision	0.63	0.66	0.62
Recall	0.53	0.5	0.41

10.5 Rhetorical Structure

A rhetorical structure analysis determines logical relations between sentences based on linguistic clues, such as connectives, anaphoric expressions, and idiomatic expressions in the input text, and then recognizes an argumentative chunk of sentences.

Rhetorical structure extraction consists of the following major subprocesses:

1. *Sentence analysis* accomplishes morphological and syntactic analysis for each sentence.

2. *Rhetorical relation extraction* detects rhetorical relations and constructs the sequence of sentence identifiers and relations.

3. *Segmentation* detects rhetorical expressions between distant sentences which define rhetorical structure. They are added onto the sequence produced in step 2, and form restrictions for generating structures in step 4. For example, expressions like "…3 reasons. First,…Second,…Third,…," and "…Of course,…But,…" are extracted, and the structural constraint is added onto the sequence so as to form a chunk between the expressions.

4. *Candidate generation* generates all possible rhetorical structures described by binary trees that do not violate segmentation restrictions.

5. *Preference judgment* selects the structure candidate with the lowest penalty score, and a value is determined based on preference rules on every two neighboring relations in the candidate.

10.6 Abstract Generation

The process consists of the following two stages:

1. Sentence evaluation

2. Structure reduction

In the sentence evaluation stage, the system calculates the importance of each sentence in the original text based on the relative importance of rhetorical relations. They are categorized into three types as shown in Table 10.5. For the relations categorized into the

TABLE 10.5

Relative Importance of Rhetorical Relations

Relation Type	Relation	Important
Right nucleus	Serial, summarization, negative	Right node
Left nucleus	Example, reason, especial	Left node
Both	Parallel, extension, rephrase	Both nodes

TABLE 10.6

Key Sentence Coverage of the Abstracts

Original	Abstract	Length Ratio	Key Sentence	Most Important Sentence
135.0	77.0	57.03%	25.0%	50.0%

right nucleus, the right node is more important. In the case of the left nucleus relations, the situation is reversed. And both nodes of the both-nucleus relations are equivalent in their importance. In order to determine important text segments, the system imposes penalties on both nodes for each rhetorical relation according to its relative importance. Then, in the structure reduction stage, the system recursively cuts out the nodes, from the terminal nodes, which are imposed the highest penalty. The list of terminal nodes of the final structure becomes an abstract for the original document. For experimental purposes, The TREC 2006 track was chosen and the generated abstract was evaluated from the point of key sentence coverage and then compared with the selected key sentences. Table 10.6 shows the average correspondence rates of the key sentence and the most important key sentence in addition to the length ratio (abstract/original).

11

Evaluation of Light Inspired Optimization Algorithm-Based Image Retrieval[*]

In this chapter, we introduce the first part of our proposed approach, which represents an image retrieval system based on the firefly algorithm, which converts the relevance feedback (RF) into an optimization algorithm, thus opening a new perspective for the development of more efficient and computationally effective RF approaches. Relevance feedback or learning to rank tasks is in general viewed as an optimization problem—to arrive at the best model as per the representation to prioritize items. Relevance feedback employs a search method led by certain objective function ranking. Objective function ranking is evaluated with a basis on supervised queries or user relevance feedback. The objective function assesses models or adjustments based on the efficacy of the ranking generated. In this regard, most researchers have exploited evolutionary algorithms (EAs). The EA flexibility facilitates the design of rank learning in numerous ways, such as through ranking function discovery (Fan et al. 2004; Torres et al. 2009; Ferreira et al. 2011), weight and parameter learning (Lopez-Pujalte et al. 2002, 2003a,b; Stejic et al. 2003a; Silva et al. 2007), among others.

As such, we introduced an image retrieval system that utilizes a firefly algorithm as a relevance feedback process that significantly improves the classification performance of the image retrieval process and better captures the user's intention. The methodology of this section is explained as follows. The process of computing features is online for query image and offline for database image. When the user submits the query image, the distances between the input image and all database images are measured based on criteria of minimum distance. The M_{FB} nearest images are then presented, and the first feedback from the user is requested. The user describes the feedback images as relevant and irrelevant in binary by mapping one for relevant and zero for irrelevant images. The relevant and irrelevant images are progressively populated across iterations. During the relevance feedback iterations, the firefly algorithm is employed as a search strategy for identifying an optimal feature subset by iteratively updating the firefly. Ultimately, the system calculates the new ranking with the updated weights based on the criteria of minimum distance and then the user is again faced with the M_{FB} nearest images for collecting the latest feedback. Until the convergence, the process is repeatedly iterated. The flashing behavior of fireflies is formulated to form an objective function that can aid in optimizing the performance of image retrieval.

By the firefly algorithm, it was recognized that the higher the number of comparisons between the fireflies to locate the best location in the swarm, the better the results can be. This comparison is based on the light intensities of the fireflies, with which they radiate. This concept makes use of the fact that a firefly agent with lower flash intensity gets easily attracted in the direction of other fireflies with higher flash intensity in which the light intensity diminishes as the distance increases. Therefore, the smaller the distance, the better is the attraction and the better is the scope of finding the best position in the pool of fireflies, which correspondingly gives the best optimal value. In particular,

---

[*] Source of publication: doi:10.4028/www.scientific.net/AMM.573.529; http://www.scientific.net/AMM.573.529. Original material available in *Applied Mechanics and Materials*, 573, 529–536, 2014.

the firefly algorithm serves as an efficient optimization engine and explores the search space effectively. The details of the proposed system are described as follows.

11.1 Query Selection and Distance Calculation

With S as a set of database images, every image C within the database is defined by three features, namely, color information, texture, and shape of the object:

$C = \{color, shape, texture\}$

Among these, the features of color and texture are taken into account. The first operation is to express the images in terms of features.

The feature computation process is online for query image and offline for database image. From that point on, every image is entirely described by its visual signature, or equivalently by a point C_S in D-dimensional space. After the selection of the query and its mapping C_Q in the feature space, the system shows the user the most similar M_{FB} images in the entire database by calculating the weighted Euclidean distance calculated between a pair of feature vectors according to the following equation (Rocchio 1971):

$$Dist(C_Q; C_S) = WMSE\left(c_q^{ch}; c_S^{ch}\right) + WMSE\left(c_q^{cm}; c_S^{cm}\right)$$

$$+ WMSE\left(c_q^{edh}; c_S^{edh}\right) + \text{WMSE}\left(c_q^{wt}; c_S^{wt}\right) \tag{11.1}$$

where c_q^{ch} and c_S^{ch} are the query and database image color histogram, respectively; c_q^{cm} and c_S^{cm} is the query and database image color moments, respectively; c_q^{edh} and c_S^{edh} are the query and database image edge direction histogram, respectively; c_q^{wt} and c_S^{wt} are the query and database image texture wavelet feature values, respectively; and $WMSE$ is the weighted Euclidean distance calculated between a pair of feature vectors as defined by Equation 11.2:

$$WMSE(c_q; c_S) = \frac{1}{N} \sum_{r=1}^{N} (c_{qr} - c_{sr})^2 w_r^k \tag{11.2}$$

where w_r^k; $r = 1, \ldots, N$; is a vector of weights related to the features; k is the iteration number; and N is equal to M_{ch} or M_{cm} or M_{edh} or M_{wt}, where M_{ch} is the dimension of the color histogram, M_{cm} is the dimension of color moments c_p^{cm}, M_{edh} is the dimension of edge direction histogram, and M_{wt} is the dimension of texture wavelet feature values. The feature vector dimension $D = M_{ch} + M_{cm} + M_{edh} + M_{wt}$ provides the overall description of the image.

After computing $Dist(C_Q; C_S)$; C_S; $S = 1, \ldots, M_{DB}$, where M_{DB} is the number of database images, the system ranks the entire database based on the distance from the query and sorts the results. After that, the first M_{FB} nearest images are shown to the user to collect the relevance feedback. In particular, the user is asked to mark the M_{FB} presented images as relevant or irrelevant based on his or her mental idea of query. Two image subsets are then created, namely, relevant and irrelevant sets. From this point on, the two image sets are maintained and updated in all the iterations of the retrieval process.

11.2 Optimization Using a Stochastic Firefly Algorithm

11.2.1 Agents Initialization and Fitness Evaluation

In this work, the image retrieval is formulated as a process of optimization. The firefly algorithm is therefore considered for the retrieval problem. For this purpose, the swarm of agents x_n; $n = 1,..., X$ or a swarm of fireflies is defined as points inside the solution space—that is, as D-dimensional feature vectors in the solution space. In this application, the decision variables of firefly algorithm are the feature vectors of the database that match the feature vector of the query image. Now, each firefly A_n is associated with relevant and irrelevant image subsets in order to initialize the swarm. Then the light intensity and the attractiveness of each firefly are calculated to initialize the stochastic optimization.

One of the most vital points in an optimization process is the description of the target function or fitness function to be maximized or minimized, which is also referred to as fitness. This fitness value must specify the effectiveness of the position reached by fireflies. When relevant and irrelevant images are taken into account, the weighted cost function $\phi^k(A_n)$ is defined (Broilo and De Natale 2010) by Equation 11.3 that expresses the fitness associated to the solution space found by the swarm of firefly A_n:

$$\phi^k(A_n) = \frac{1}{R_{rel}^k} \sum_{r=1}^{R_{rel}^k} Dist\left(A_n^k; C_r^k\right) + \frac{1}{\left(1/R_{irr}^k\right) \sum_{i=1}^{R_{irr}^k} Dist\left(A_n^k; C_i^k\right)} \tag{11.3}$$

where k is the iteration number, C_r^k; $r = 1,..., R_{rel}^k$ and C_i^k; $i = 1,..., R_{irr}^k$ are the images in the relevant and irrelevant image subsets, respectively. With the growth of firefly's distance from the irrelevant images, the fitness associated with the solution space depends only on relevant images. The computation of $Dist(.)$ is the same as that computed in the previous step as defined by Equations 11.1 and 11.2. It is to be observed that the cost function $\phi^k(A_n)$ produces a lower fitness value, when the firefly is close to relevant images and far from the irrelevant images. Thus, the lower the fitness value, the better are the positions achieved by the firefly toward the relevant image zone. Based on the value of fitness, it is feasible to re-order the firefly to obtain new ranking.

11.2.2 Variation in Brightness of Firefly

Each feature vector A_n is characterized by its respective attractiveness and the light intensity it emits. Each firefly A_n explores a new population in its neighborhood within the specified search space. The brightness or the light intensity of a firefly is correlated to the objective values. Having an N number of fireflies, x_n signifies a solution for a firefly n, and $f(x)$ indicates its fitness value. Here the brightness I of a firefly is selected to reflect its current position X of its fitness value $f(x)$:

$$I_n = f(x_n) = \phi^k(A_n) \tag{11.4}$$

11.2.3 Strategy for Searching New Swarms

The attractiveness of the firefly depends on the light intensity of adjacent fireflies. Every firefly has its unique attractiveness, which means how strongly it attracts other fireflies.

Yet the attractiveness is relative; it will differ with the distance between the nth and an arbitrarily chosen Sth feature vector:

$$r_{nS}^k = \|x_n - x_S\| = Dist(A_n; C_S), \quad n = 1, \ldots, N$$
$$S = 1, \ldots, M_{DB}$$

(11.5)

The attractiveness function $\beta(r)$ of the firefly is described by

$$\beta^k(r) = \beta_0 e^{(-\gamma(r_{nS}^k)^2)}$$

(11.6)

where β_0 is the attractiveness with distance $r = 0$, and γ stands for the light absorption coefficient. The attractiveness is based on distance between fireflies as determined by Equation 11.5. The movement of firefly n located at A_n is attracted to another more attractive firefly S located at C_S—that is, nth firefly changes its position if there exists any C_S such that $I_S < I_n$ is determined by

$$x_n^k(t+1) = x_n^k(t) + \beta_0 e^{(-\gamma(r_{nS}^k)^2)}(x_S - x_n) + \alpha\varepsilon_n$$

(11.7)

In Equation 11.7, the first expression denotes the present location of a firefly, the second expression is because of attractiveness, and the third expression represents randomization with a vector of random variable ε_n being drawn from the Gaussian distribution (Yang 2009) and $\alpha \in [0,1]$.

The movement of the firefly agent's swarm-like query points will explore the D-dimensional solutions space made of the image features, with its light intensity and attraction. It is useful to point out that the images of the database represent a discrete and fixed set of points, while the particles can move in a continuous way inside the features space. Thus, movement of each firefly is made on the continuous space, and its attractiveness term is updated considering the real position vector. The real position of firefly i is updated only after all movements toward brighter fireflies have been carried out. We note that the fitness evaluation of each firefly, for firefly ranking, is always based on the real position.

After the two phases of the firefly algorithm at the first iteration, an updating process is carried out at every further iteration. The value of the objective function, attractiveness, and movement of firefly toward other fireflies as defined by Equations 11.4, 11.6, and 11.7, respectively, are recalculated if new relevant images are tagged by the user. As a result, after every user feedback, the firefly moves toward new areas in the solution space where other relevant images may be found.

An additional operation is required to finish a single iteration: to correlate to fireflies placed in a "fine position" (the lesser the fittest, the superior the position of the firefly), the nearest images in the database analogous to Equation 11.1. Indeed, the fireflies swing randomly in a continuous space, whereas the database images are in discrete positions. Subsequently, the first fireflies of the swarm ranked corresponding to Equation 11.3 are related to their nearest image. As a result a new set of images is obtained, which is then shown to the user. If a firefly points to an image that is already classified as irrelevant or more than one firefly points to the same image, the analogous image is discarded and the next nearest images are considered until a different M_{FB} set of images is collected from the user.

After the user feedback, the above said process of firefly swarm updating is iterated. The process ends when the user verifies one of the following conditions: (1) the result of the search satisfies the user, (2) the relevant number of images targeted is achieved, or (3) the predefined number of iterations is reached. All the relevant images are presented to the user after the process ends. Thus, based on swarm intelligence, the FA finds the global optima of the objective function by investigating the foraging behavior of fireflies.

11.3 Experimental Setup

For each image database in our experiments, we simulated the presence of users by using each image as an initial query point. For a query image, 10 iterations of user-and-system interaction were carried out. At each iteration, the system examined the top 18 images, and images from the same (different) category of the query image were considered equally relevant (irrelevant) images.

11.4 Visual Signature

As usual, the feature computation process is online for query image and offline for database image. The feature components of database images are stored in a database for run-time access. The visual signature of each image is composed of four different feature vectors: the first is a 32-bin color histogram calculated in the hue, saturation, and value (HSV) color space; the second is a 9-bin color moment extracted from the HSV color space; the third is an 8-bin edge direction histogram (Wu and Zhang 2002) obtained from the edge map of an image; and the fourth is 18-wavelet texture energy values (Deselaers and Keysers 2008).

A color histogram represents the distribution of colors in the image, through a set of bins. Each bin in the color histogram corresponds to the same color in the quantized color space in which the value of each bin gives the number of pixels of the same corresponding color.

The color moments include first-, second-, and third-order central moments of each color channel in the HSV color space. The first-order central moment is the average pixels of each color channel, the second-order central moment is the standard deviation, and the third-order central moment is the skewness of each color channel. In sum, a 9-bin color moment is adopted from three color channels.

The edge map of an image is obtained by converting a color image into a grayscale image and then convolving with eight Sobel edge detectors. The eight convolved images are then put to their thresholds in all eight directions. The 8-bin edge direction indicates the number of edge pixels in eight main directions. Finally, the 18-wavelet texture features represent the three levels of wavelet characteristics of coarse, middle, and fine level frequency content of the image, where each level has six texture descriptors. Hence, the size of the feature vector was set to 67.

11.5 Performance Measures

To evaluate the effectiveness of the proposed approach, we use precision and recall as a performance measure as defined in Equations 11.8 and 11.9:

$$\text{Precision} = \frac{N_{P(Q)}}{N_{R(Q)}} \tag{11.8}$$

$$\text{Recall} = \frac{N_{P(Q)}}{N_{T(Q)}} \tag{11.9}$$

where $N_{P(Q)}$ represents the number of retrieved relevant images, $N_{R(Q)}$ denotes the total number of retrieved images for a given query Q, and $N_{T(Q)}$ indicates the total number of relevant images available in the database for a given query Q. Since the FA, particle swarm optimization (PSO) stochastic nature, all precision and recall values are calculated by averaging five consecutive runs for every query image.

11.6 Parameter Settings of Firefly Algorithm

In the FA algorithm, the brightness or light intensity of a firefly is affected or determined by the landscape of the objective function to be optimized. Attractiveness is proportional to their brightness; thus, for any two flashing fireflies, the less bright one will move toward the brighter one. The attractiveness is proportional to the brightness, and they both decrease as their distance increases. If no one is brighter than a particular firefly, it moves randomly; a firefly particle moves toward another firefly particle, which has a better objective function value (fitness).

Intrinsically, the parameter γ describes the variation of the attractiveness, and its value is critically important in finding the speed of the convergence and how the firefly algorithm behavior changes. Theoretically, γ varies from 0 to ∞; however, practically it is found by the mean length of the system to be optimized. On one end, if γ tends to 0, the attractiveness is constant $\beta_0 = 0$. This means that the attractiveness does not diminish in an idealized sky. Consequently, a flashing firefly can be seen anywhere in the domain. Thus, a global (generally single) optimum can easily be attained. This corresponds to a special case of PSO. On the other end, when γ is ∞, the attractiveness is β (r), which is a Dirac delta function. This is equivalent to the case that the flash intensity is moreover zero in the view of other fireflies. This is equivalent to saying where the fireflies move in a very foggy region randomly. No other fireflies can be seen, and each firefly roams in a completely random way. Thus, this refers to an absolutely random search method. Accordingly, the parameter γ partly controls the algorithm behavior. The attractiveness function β varies from 0 to 1.

In order to investigate the appropriate setting of FA parameters, designs of experiments (DOEs) were conducted on the proposed approaches. Owing to various parameters and levels of FA, full, fractional experimental design requires high computational resources

TABLE 11.1

Firefly Algorithm's Parameters and Its Level Considered

Factors	Levels		
	Low	Medium	High
Light absorption coefficient (γ)	0.1	5	10
Randomization parameter (α)	0	0.5	1
Attractiveness (β_0)	0	0.5	1

and is time consuming because of the large number of experimental runs of each replication. Therefore, one-third fractional factorial experimental design (3^{k-1}) was adopted in this work. The FA factors and its levels are summarized in Table 11.1. Those factors are the combination of number of fireflies (F), light absorption coefficient (γ), attractiveness (β_0), and number of generations (I). Generally, the combination factor (FI) determines the amount of search (candidate solutions) in the solution space conducted by the FA. This factor is proportional to the size of population considered. The higher the value of this combination usually means an increase in the probability of getting the best solution but requires a longer computational time and resources. In this work, the computational limitations are practically imposed; this computational (FI) are therefore fixed at 1980 in order to accommodate the computational search within the time limit. The γ factor was varied from 0 to 10, while the range of α and β_0 were set between 0 and 1 as described in Equation 11.7.

The proposed algorithm is tested with different types of parameter settings. After tuning procedures, the FA parameters are set to the optimal settings: number of fireflies (F) = 18, light absorption coefficient (γ) = 1, attractiveness (β_0) = 1, and number of generations (I) = 110.

11.7 Performance Evaluation

This section implements an image retrieval system on the subset of a Corel image database (Wang 2004) and a Caltech image database (Caltech-101). In order to evaluate the effectiveness and efficiency of the proposed method, performance comparisons are made with PSO (Chandramouli and Izquierdo 2008) and genetic algorithm (Lai and Chen 2011) in terms of top matches, precision, and recall for a particular class. The parameters used in each

TABLE 11.2

Parameters Used in Each Relevance Feedback Algorithm

Technique	Parameters
Firefly algorithm	$\beta = 1, \gamma = 1$
Particle swarm optimization	$w_1 = 0.7, c_1 = 2, c_2 = 2$
Genetic algoritm	Tournament selection method
	Probability of crossover 0.8
	Probability of mutation 0.2

algorithm were set as shown in Table 11.2. The population size is 18 agents (fireflies, particles, and population size for FA, PSO, and GA, respectively) and 110 maximum numbers of iterations.

The calculation of fitness measure in the cases of PSO and GA are computed based on the similarity between all training set images and the query pattern.

Calculate the retrieval performance of each class with the proposed and the two existing methods on the subset of Corel and Caltech databases. From the Corel subset 10 classes of images are considered for experiment. The classes are dinosaur, bus, vintage cars, sunflower, waterfall, elephant, penguin, pigeon, roses, and horses. Each class consists of 100 images. The precision of the image retrieval process as defined by Equation 11.8 for all 10 classes is computed by considering each image in the class as a query image, and the percentage of retrieval is obtained for the top 20, 40, 60, and 80 images, which gives the overall retrieval performance of the proposed and existing methods for the subset of the Corel database.

The proposed method gives the average precision rate of 90.5% for the top 20 images, whereas the PSO yields an average precision rate of 84.7%, and GA yields an average precision rate of 80.6% for the top 20 images. Similarly, average retrieval performance is tested on the Caltech database with 10 classes. The 10 classes are airplanes, bonsai, butterfly, faces, ibis, kangaroo, ketch, leopards, Buddha, and car side. Each class contains a maximum of 450 and a minimum of 95 images. The retrieved results are shown in Figures 11.1 and 11.2. From the experiment, it is observed that the proposed color, texture feature, and texture edge have good discriminative capability and get better retrieval results for the images having a texture background.

As can be perceived from Figures 11.1 and 11.2 for Corel and Caltech databases, respectively, the average precision values are high for a small number of retrieved images, and as the number of retrieved image increases the average precision values decrease, demonstrating that the system gives a better ranking for the retrieved images. This occurs because the precision values are based on the ratio of the number of retrieved relevant

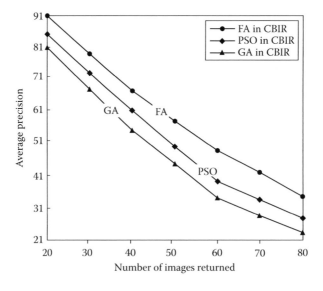

FIGURE 11.1
Average precision of top-ranked results after the ninth feedback (average precision percentage) for Corel database.

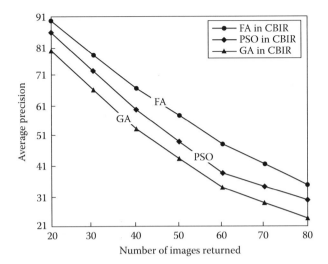

FIGURE 11.2
Average precision of top-ranked results after the ninth feedback (average precision percentage) for Caltech database.

images to the total number of retrieved images; accordingly as the number of retrieved images increases, precision started to decrease naturally.

Corel archives typically perform better, in particular for some image classes commonly used in the literature. On the other side, the Caltech database contains some particularly difficult categories, where the performance drops dramatically, mainly due to the fact that the automatic mechanism used for feedback and match analysis requires a very well-defined classification of the database, which is not the case for some Caltech database classes. In the second experiment, we compare different algorithms in terms of the computation time. The average execution time presented refers to the average time required by each RF approach to learn the user's needs and to select images to be shown on each iteration.

Although the time varies with the type of image, the average time shows the FA ranks fastest (28.70 ms), followed by PSO (43.05 ms) and GA (1.0844 s).

Thus, the experiment on Corel and Caltech database images compared with PSO and GA shows that the proposed image retrieval system based on the firefly algorithm has enhanced performance in a minimal computation time. In the next part, we investigate the possibility of integrating a RF process such as support vector machine (SVM) into a stochastic optimization engine called a Gaussian firefly algorithm so as to improve the optimization process, thereby enhancing the precision of the image retrieval process.

12

An Evolutionary Approach for Optimizing Content-Based Image Retrieval Using Support Vector Machine

In recent years, various relevance feedback methods have evolved for the image retrieval problem. The conventional method can be grouped as query point movement, query reweighting, and query expansion (Porkaew and Chakrabarti 1999). But as these methods do not absolutely make use of the information present in the feedback images, their performance is usually far from satisfactory. And thus, a number of machine learning techniques have been applied to the problem of relevance feedback in image retrieval. Some of them are Bayesian learning (Vasconcelos and Lippman 1999), boosting techniques (Tieu and Viola 2000), discriminant analysis (Zhou and Huang 2001), dimension reduction (Tao and Tang 2004), ensemble learning (Hoi and Lyu 2004), and decision tree (MacArthur et al. 2000). In addition to these, unsupervised learning methods, like expectation maximum algorithms (Wu et al. 2000) and self-organizing features maps (SOMs) (Laaksonen et al. 1999) were also discovered in the literature. Recently, support vector machines (Vapnik 1998) have been investigated in machine learning as their performance in real-world applications is relatively higher in pattern classification. Many works have related the support vector machine (SVM) to RF in image retrieval (Hong et al. 2000; Chen et al. 2001; Zhang et al. 2001; Guo et al. 2002; Hoi et al. 2004; Li et al. 2006; Tao et al. 2007).

Nevertheless, most of the SVM-based RF approaches do not regard the underlying difference between relevant and irrelevant feedback images—that is, unlike the relevant feedback images that have a similar notion for all the pictures, the irrelevant feedback images have several notions in different styles in each picture. As reported, conventional SVM-based relevance feedback learning (Hong et al. 2000; Guo et al. 2002; Li et al. 2006; Tao et al. 2007) treats relevant and irrelevant feedback images equally. Directly utilizing the SVM learning as an RF method degrades the efficiency of content-based image retrieval (CBIR) systems due to facts such as "dissimilar semantic model reside in different subspaces and every image can reside in various different subspaces" (Zhou and Huang 2001) and the purpose of relevance feedback is to point out "which one," and also due to disproportion in labeling the feedback images, where there are less relevant feedback images than irrelevant feedback images.

In addition, despite the fact that the SVM generally furnishes reasonable accuracy, the training data have frequently not been linearly separable, and SVM introduces the concept of "kernel influenced feature space," which maps the data into a higher-dimensional space where the data are separable into two classes. Normally, such a mapping space would create problems computationally. This leads to long iteration problems and stagnation in local optimal solutions. These drawbacks play a vital role in lessening the performance of SVM-based RF for CBIR. Nevertheless, the results of SVM can be made more robust by tuning the internal parameters, such that they reduce the error—that is, the misclassification effect.

To explore solutions to these problems, the process of SVM learning is embedded into a strong, well-structured, metaheuristic algorithm, called a Gaussian firefly algorithm, to increase the performing efficiency of the content-based image retrieval process. The use of the firefly algorithm finds optimum parameters for SVM and accordingly achieves more relevant feedback images. This brought in diversity so as to expand the exploration and to converge toward global optima rather than local optima when optimizing the performance of the SVM classifier which improves the retrieval efficiency. Therefore, the degrading performance of the SVM classifier is enhanced by the assistance of the firefly algorithm and therefore optimizes the relevance feedback process. Additionally, for the improvement of retrieval accuracy, random walk concepts based on Gaussian distribution are applied at the end of each iteration in a standard firefly algorithm so that all the fireflies have moved into the global best position and movements are stabilized. Many research works have coupled SVM with evolutionary algorithms (Ilhan and Tezel 2013; Kazem et al. 2013; Sudheer et al. 2014). The capability of overcoming the shortcomings of individual algorithms without losing their advantage makes the hybrid techniques superior to the stand-alone ones.

The methodology is the same as that of the above part, except that the SVM learning process has to be conducted in addition to the firefly swarm iteration process. During the relevance feedback iterations, the SVM finds the optimum hyperplane that separates relevant and irrelevant images, and it is adapted along the iteration by the Gaussian firefly algorithm. Throughout this procedure, each firefly is compared to every other firefly in the swarm, and founded on the brightness, one best location is selected. The best location so obtained represents the optimized values of the parameters of SVM, which are provided as an input to the classifier for pair wise classification. Finally, the system computes the new ranking with the updated weights based on the criteria of minimum distance. Until the convergence, the process is repeatedly iterated. The details of the proposed system are described in the following sections.

12.1 Relevance Feedback Learning via Support Vector Machine

The query selection and distance calculation were carried out as we discussed in Section 11.1, then the SVM iteration process is carried out. The SVM works on the fact that the Vapnik-Chervonenkis dimensions minimum is the structural risk (Vapnik 1995). The basic performance of SVM is as follows. Initially the input vectors are mapped into a higher-dimensional feature space, then a hyperplane is constructed that can distinguish the two categories within this feature space. A mapping function involves comparatively low-dimensional vectors within the input sample space and dot product within the feature space. The mapping of input vectors into the feature space is carried out by a kernel function.

During the relevance feedback process, the user labels each retrieved image C_f, as relevant ($y_f = 1$) and irrelevant ($y_f = 0$) according to the input query image. The two image subsets—namely, relevant and irrelevant—are now created, and they are updated in all the iterations. To perform a classification fairly well with the created relevant and irrelevant image subsets, SVM as a binary classifier is significant, which conbines the query concept of separating the relevant images from the irrelevant images using a hyperplane in the nonlinearly transformed feature space. We exploit the set of collective retrievals $R = \{(C_f, y_f) \mid f = 1, \ldots, l\}$, where $y_f \in \{1, 0\}$, as training data in the following standard SVM with generalized Gaussian kernel in order to compute SVM (to optimize the hyperplane):

$$\min_{\alpha \in R^l} \frac{1}{2} \sum_{f=1}^{l} \sum_{g=1}^{l} \alpha_f \alpha_g y_f y_g K_R(c_f, c_g) - \sum_{f=1}^{l} \alpha_f \tag{12.1}$$

$$\text{Subject to } \sum_{f=1}^{l} \alpha_f y_f = 0, \quad 0 \leq \alpha_f \leq Z$$

where α_f are known as Lagrange multipliers, and the parameter Z controls the separation error. The term $K_R(C_f, C_g)$ denotes the radial basis function kernel or nonlinear similarity measure between two feature vectors, with σ being standard deviation:

$$K_R(C_f, C_g) = \exp\left(\frac{-\|C_f - C_g\|^2}{2\sigma^2}\right) \tag{12.2}$$

Then the score $F(C)$ for each database image C is calculated using the following SVM decision function, and the images are sorted based on this score:

$$F(C_S) = \sum_{f=1}^{|R|} \alpha_f y_f K_R(C_S, C_f) + b; \quad C_S; \ S = 1, \ldots, M_{DB} \tag{12.3}$$

where b is the biases, and R is the number of support vectors. To summarize the classification process of the proposed system, the feature vectors in lower dimension space are cast into higher dimension space by using the kernel function as described by Equation 12.2. Then the classification is done as per Equation 12.1, and then the N highest score images as calculated by Equation 12.3 are fed to a Gaussian firefly algorithm for stochastic optimization. Previous studies show that selecting the parameters of SVM Z and σ plays an important role in determining the accuracy of the image retrieval process, so in this work the Gaussian firefly algorithm is employed to optimize the parameter of SVM and thereby to improve the retrieval precision of the image retrieval process.

12.2 Optimization Using a Stochastic Firefly Algorithm

In the proposed system, each firefly or agent is a parameter set of the SVM learning process and can be represented as $A_n = \langle Z, \sigma \rangle$. A set of agents or fireflies is described as a population or swarm, and the image retrieval process is formulated as a process of optimization. The optimized images from the Gaussian firefly algorithm are then fed back to the SVM at each iteration; thereby, the optimum parameters are selected for the SVM.

The characteristics analysis of optimization using a stochastic firefly algorithm is carried out as we discussed in Section 11.2. The parameter α defined in Equation 11.7 defines the fixed length movement of a firefly in a random step that is constant throughout the iteration. This fixed length movement causes the firefly to miss its better local search ability and sometimes traps it into several local optimum solutions. So it would be better if the parameter α adapts by time in order to enhance the algorithm performance. Thus, the following coefficient is defined for α whose value is always less than one, and it relies on maximum iteration number $iter_{max}$ and present iteration number $iter$ (Yazdani and Meybodi 2010):

$$W_{iter} = A + \frac{(iter_{max} - iter)^m}{(iter_{max})^m} + (A - B)$$

(12.4)

where $m \geq 1$. In Equation 12.4, $A = 0$ and $B = 1$ since $\alpha \in [0, 1]$. W_{iter} is between A and B, and its value reduces by the time. m would be a nonlinear coefficient, and it relies on the dimension of each firefly. Its value is influenced by

$$m = 10^{(-dimension)}$$

(12.5)

If the dimension is high, the value of m is low, which means the algorithm converges more accurately. This strategy changes the step length of time. Thus, it makes the firefly search the solution space globally in the initial stage, and in the end of the iterative process, the firefly exploits the solution space locally to obtain better solutions. Hence the movements of the firefly are stabilized.

If the firefly's adaptive step length follows a Gaussian distribution, then the random walk movement becomes the Brownian motion (Yang 2009), which is nothing but a social behavior of the firefly. At the end of each iteration of the standard firefly algorithm, normal Gaussian distribution is introduced in order to move all the fireflies to the global best position and is expressed in Equation 12.6:

$$p = f(x \mid \mu, \sigma^2) = \frac{1}{\sqrt{2\Pi\sigma^2}} e^{[(-|x-\mu|^2)/2\sigma^2]}$$

(12.6)

where μ and σ are its mean and variance, whereas x is the error between the best solution and fitness value of firefly m:

$$x = f(b_{best}) - f(x_n)$$

(12.7)

As standard normal distribution is employed, the value of μ is set to 0 and σ is set to 1. Then from this Gaussian distribution, a random number is drawn such that it is tied into each firefly probability (p). The behavior of the firefly is then introduced by Farahani et al. (2011):

$$x_n(t+1) = x_n(t) + \alpha \times (1-p) \times U(x,z)$$

(12.8)

where $U(x, z)$ is a random number between 0 and 1. The new solutions are evaluated and then the light intensities are updated. After evaluation, if the new position $x_n(t + 1)$ of a firefly shows a better cost, then it will move toward that new position.

Thus to summarize the process, the parameter α is adapted by time, by calculating the coefficient as described in Equation 12.4, which is influenced by a nonlinear coefficient as defined in Equation 12.5, and the normal Gaussian distribution introduced by Equation 12.6 at the end of each iteration of the standard firefly moves all the fireflies to the global best position. Equation 12.7 measures the error between the best solution and fitness value of the firefly. Then if the new position of a firefly shows a better cost after evaluation, it will move toward the new position as described by Equation 12.8.

After the two phases of the firefly algorithm at the first iteration, an updating process is carried out at every further iteration. The significance of the objective function, attractiveness, and movement of the firefly toward other fireflies are again determined if new relevant images are labeled by the user. As a consequence, after subsequent user feedback, the fireflies travel toward new locales in the search space where other new relevant images may be found. Then, the above said process of SVM learning and firefly swarm updating is iterated. An additional operation required to finish a single iteration should also be carried out. The process ends when the user is satisfied with the retrieved results.

Thus, the proposed system suitably influences the optimum parameter for SVM using the Gaussian firefly algorithm, and consequently, the number of positive feedback images increases such that it tunes the feedback learning process and improves the precision of an image retrieval system.

12.3 Image Database

In this experiment, we used Corel photo galleries (Wang 2004) covering a wide range of semantic categories of natural scenes with artificial objects. The dataset is partitioned into 25 categories, including butterfly, buildings, hills, flowers, earth, sky, trees, boats, birds, statue, horses, elephants, and so on, and each category is represented by 100 images, for a total of 2500 images. In these experiments, 600 images are randomly taken out of the whole dataset as test queries. Visual features in Section 11.4 are used here.

12.4 Baselines

Three relevance feedback methods: PSO+SVM in CBIR (Lianze et al. 2011), GA+SVM in CBIR (Seo 2007), and SVM in CBIR (Tong and Chang 2001) are compared with the proposed method. The firefly algorithm is compared with PSO and genetic algorithm for content-based image retrieval along with SVM since these two methods are in the same category of population-based optimization techniques. We choose the third one as SVM in content-based image retrieval as it is based on machine learning techniques. Altogether the three comparable methods make use of relevant and irrelevant images.

12.5 Comparison Methods

The performance of this experiment is evaluated using average precision versus recall curve ($P_{avg} \times R_{avg}$) and aims to verify whether the proposed method is significantly different from all the other baselines or comparing methods. Figure 12.1 shows the experimental results of $P_{avg} \times R_{avg}$ by varying the number of iterations from 3 to 10. These curves demonstrate that the performance of the proposed method is improved (the higher the $P_{avg} \times R_{avg}$ curve, the better is its performance) with the number of iterations. Figures 12.2 through

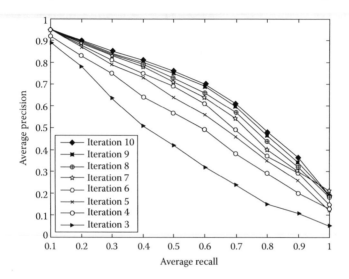

FIGURE 12.1
Average precision-recall curves CBIR based on SVM and Gaussian firefly algorithm, iterations 3–10.

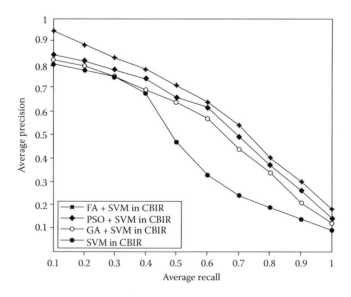

FIGURE 12.2
Average precision-recall curves CBIR based on SVM and Gaussian firefly algorithm during iteration 5.

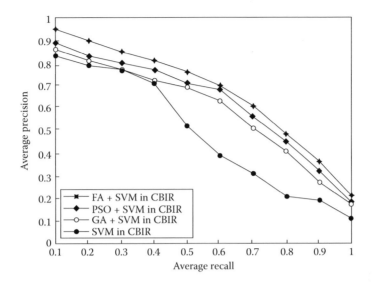

FIGURE 12.3
Average precision-recall curves CBIR based on SVM and Gaussian firefly algorithm during iteration 7.

12.4 show the experimental results of $P_{avg} \times R_{avg}$ for 5, 7, and 10 iterations of the relevance feedback process, respectively. The higher the precision-recall curve, the better is the performance. As can be observed from Figures 12.2 through 12.4, the proposed method consistently outperforms all other baselines.

The algorithm itself has better performance than the other two algorithms. In the firefly algorithm, the distance is only necessary for the movement, whereas in PSO, each particle will move a distance according to its personal best and the global best, and the GA-based retrieval method is significantly slower than PSO and firefly algorithm, as it does not directly use the information about the relevant and irrelevant images (i.e., their features),

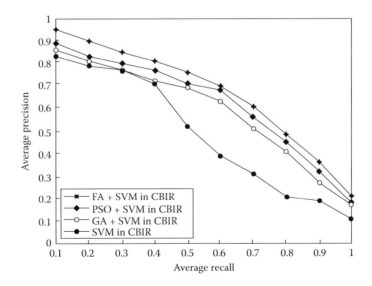

FIGURE 12.4
Average precision-recall curves CBIR based on SVM and Gaussian firefly algorithm during iteration 10.

which makes it less responsive to the user's discrepancy during the relevance feedback process. The proposed method also outperforms the SVM-based method due to the fact that the SVM could not possess the capability to benefit from the diminished number of relevant images (18) for each query image.

Thus, the performance of the proposed image retrieval system based on SVM and the Gaussian firefly algorithm outperforms for all iterations, and as the iteration increases, the average precision is also increasing in comparison with the baseline algorithms. Also, the precision-recall curve shows improvement as the number of iterations increases. In the next part, the Gaussian firefly algorithm is introduced for region-based image retrieval through optimized iterative learning that computes features of the segmented region at the object level, and the similarity comparisons are performed at the granularity of the region and thus results in more accurately retrieved results.

13

An Application of Firefly Algorithm to Region-Based Image Retrieval

The previously described systems perform retrieval primarily based on global properties of an image. Nevertheless, global features cannot sufficiently capture the important properties of individual objects and thus are incapable to reflect the user's ideal query. The understanding mechanism of the human visual system reveals that in order to estimate human perception, image similarity must be able to discriminate the region feature's properties.

The growing popularity of region-based image retrieval (RBIR) (Wang et al. 2001; Ko and Byun 2002) has tended many proposals for integrating the region-based features into relevance feedback, even though the application of relevance feedback (RF) from image level to region level is not an insignificant task. Stejic et al. (2003a) made use of the similarity of the region features for retrieval of images. They put forth a relevance feedback method from the genetic algorithm platform. A novel method for image similarity computation called the local similarity pattern (LSP) was also suggested. LSP is composed of R and F_R in which R is a set with $N \times N$ regions retrieved from image uniform partitioning, and F_R is a collection of image features obtained from each region for computation of similarity. The characteristic that most describes each LSP region is influenced by both genetic algorithm and relevance feedback. Also, Stejic et al. (2003b) presented a region and feature saliency pattern (RFSP) and defined it as a construction similar to LSP. The RFSP method uses a weight corresponding to each region and the genetic algorithm to determine the best weights for all region features, rather than using a genetic algorithm (GA) for a further determination that best describes each image part as an LSP. Consequently, the Gaussian firefly algorithm is introduced for region-based image retrieval in order to capture a user's semantics via an optimized iterative learning approach.

The Gaussian firefly algorithm based on region representations is employed as a search strategy for identifying an optimal feature subset to the image regions in order to narrow the gap between the retrieval results and user's expectations. It is intended to be close to the perception of the human visual system which better enhances the ability of capturing as well as representing the focus of the user's perception of image content. A further added worth of the proposed approach is that it establishes a stochastic component to the process, consequently permitting exploration of the search space in different ways, thus making it possible to escape from local minima and to converge to a best solution irrespective of the starting point. Besides, the resulting retrieval is highly customized and adapted to the query location as our relevance estimate is on a regional level.

The methodology of this section is expressed as follows. Initially, each image of the database is segmented using the normalized cut segmentation algorithm into regions by clustering the pixel features. The feature components are then computed from segmented regions. The process is online for a query image and offline for a database image. When the user inputs a query image, it is segmented, and the features are extracted from each region. Then the distances between the input image and all database images are measured based on Earth Mover's distance criteria. The M_{FB} nearest images are then presented, and the first feedback from the user is requested. The user describes the feedback images as relevant and irrelevant in binary by mapping one for relevant and zero for irrelevant images. The relevant and irrelevant images are progressively populated across iterations. Initially, the weights of the features are set to one. During the relevance feedback iterations, the Gaussian firefly algorithm based on region representations updates its swarm constantly to converge into the image clusters that contain the best solution and finds out approximate optimized weights for similarities with respect to the features. Ultimately, the system calculates the new ranking with the updated weights based on Earth Mover's distance, and then the user is again faced with the M_{FB} nearest images for collecting the latest feedback. Until the convergence, the process is repeatedly iterated. The details of the proposed system are described in the following sections.

13.1 Image Retrieval

13.1.1 Image Segmentation

Initially, the images are segmented using a normalized cut segmentation algorithm (Shi and Malik 2000). This algorithm works out using the technique of graph partitioning. The graph is segmented with the help of normalized cut value. The collection of points in the sample space is denoted as a weighed undirected graph, where the points in the sample space are the graphical nodes. An edge is created for every pair of nodes. The similarity between two nodes is measured by the weight along every edge.

The graph with the least cut value is the most efficient partition. This least cut partitions the tiny sets into a small cluster which becomes a less efficient segmentation. Thus, the normalized cut (uncut) criterion is useful in manipulating the cut cost as a part of all edge connections to all the nodes in the graph. The total similarity within the sets and total dissimilarity between the sets is computed using the normalized cut.

13.1.2 Image Representation

After segmentation, each image is signified by its set of regions. In particular, an image C that contains n regions is represented by

$$C = \{(c_1, w_1), \ldots, (c_n, w_n)\}$$

where c_n and w_n are the nth region features and weight, respectively. The feature components are then computed from each region. The region features extracted from a query image are computed online and those of the image stored in the database are computed offline.

13.1.3 Similarity Measure

When the user selects the query image, it is segmented, and the features are extracted from the regions. With the available region features, it is now necessary to calculate the distance between query image and database image. The Earth Mover's distance (Rubner et al. 1998) is best suited for a region-based image similarity measure, since it demonstrates perceptual similarity well and can operate on variable length representations of the distributions. Let the input query image C_Q with m regions be represented by $C_Q = \{(c_{qi}, w_{qi}) | i = 1, \ldots, m\}$, and the desired database image C_S with n regions be represented by $C_S = \{(c_{sj}, w_{sj}) | j = 1, \ldots, n\}$, where c_{qi} is the ith region feature of the input query image, and c_{sj} is the jth region feature of the desired database image. The terms w_{qi} and w_{sj} signify the ith and jth region weights query and database image, respectively—that is,

$$w_{qi} = \frac{t_{qi}}{\sum_v t_{qv}} \tag{13.1}$$

$$w_{sj} = \frac{t_{sj}}{\sum_v t_{sv}} \tag{13.2}$$

where t_{qi} and t_{sj} are the ith and the jth region size of input query image and the desired image, respectively; and t_{qv} is the total regions in an image. Then the *EMD* distance between C_Q and C_S is given by

$$EMD(C_Q,C_S) = \frac{\sum_{i=1}^{m} \sum_{j=1}^{n} h_{ij} d_{ij}}{\sum_{i=1}^{m} \sum_{j=1}^{n} h_{ij}} \tag{13.3}$$

where d_{ij} is the ground distance between the regions of c_{qi} and c_{sj}

$$
\begin{aligned}
d_{ij} &= Dist(c_{qi};c_{sj}) \\
&= WMSE(c_{qi}^{ch};c_{sj}^{ch}) + WMSE(c_{qi}^{cm};c_{sj}^{cm}) \\
&\quad + WMSE(c_{qi}^{edh};c_{sj}^{edh}) + WMSE(c_{qi}^{wt};c_{sj}^{wt})
\end{aligned}
\tag{13.4}
$$

WMSE is the weighted Euclidean distance calculated between a pair of feature vectors:

$$WMSE(c_{qi};c_{sj}) = \frac{1}{N} \sum_{i=1}^{m} \sum_{j=1}^{n} \sum_{r=1}^{N} (c_{qir} - c_{sjr})^2 w_r^k \tag{13.5}$$

where, w_r^k is the weight vectors related to the features, k is the iteration number, and N is equal to M_{ch} or M_{cm} or M_{edh} or M_{wt}. All features are evenly important at the first iteration ($k=1$)—that is, $w_r^k = 1$; $r = 1,\ldots,N$; h_{ij} is the best possible flow from c_{qi} to c_{sj} which reduces $EMD(C_Q,C_S)$ value with respect to the following constraints:

$$h_{ij} \geq 0, \quad 1 \leq i \leq m, \; 1 \leq j \leq n$$

$$\sum_{j=1}^{n} h_{ij} \leq w_{qi}, \quad 1 \leq i \leq m;$$

$$\sum_{i=1}^{m} h_{ij} \leq w_{sj}, \quad 1 \leq j \leq n; \tag{13.6}$$

$$\sum_{i=1}^{m} \sum_{j=1}^{n} h_{ij} = \min\left(\sum_{i=1}^{m} w_{qi}, \sum_{j=1}^{n} w_{sj}, \right)$$

After computing $EMD(C_Q, C_S)$; C_S; $S = 1, \dots, M_{DB}$, the system ranks the entire database based on the distance from the query and sorts the results. The first feedback is then requested from the user by presenting the M_{FB} nearest images.

13.2 Optimization Using a Stochastic Firefly Algorithm

13.2.1 Firefly Agent's Initialization and Fitness Evaluation

In our work, the image retrieval is formulated as a problem of optimization. The firefly algorithm is therefore considered for the retrieval problem. For this purpose, the swarm of agents A_n; $n = 1, \dots, N$ or a swarm of fireflies is defined as points inside the solution space—that is, as D-dimensional feature vectors in the solution space. Each swarm agent is signified by the set of its region, and each region is interpreted in terms of its feature and region weights. In this application, the decision variables of the firefly algorithm are the features and region weights. Now, each firefly is associated with N highest score images in order to initialize the swarm. Then the light intensity and the attractiveness of each firefly are calculated to initialize the stochastic optimization.

In an optimization procedure, specifying the role that has to be maximized or minimized, which is also referred to as fitness, is a significant point. This fitness value must specify the effectiveness of the position reached by fireflies. When irrelevant and relevant images are taken into account, the weight cost function $\phi^k(A_n)$ defined (Broilo and De Natale 2010) by Equation 13.7 expresses the fitness associated to the solution space found by the swarm of firefly A_n:

$$\phi^k(A_n) = \frac{1}{R_{rel}^k} \sum_{r=1}^{R_{rel}^k} EMD(A_n^k; C_r^k)$$
$$+ \frac{1}{(1/R_{irr}^k)\sum_{i=1}^{R_{irr}^k} EMD(A_n^k; C_i^k)} \tag{13.7}$$

where k is the iteration number, C_r^k; $r = 1, \dots, R_{rel}^k$ and C_i^k; $i = 1, \dots, R_{irr}^k$ are the relevant and irrelevant image subsets, respectively. With the growth of a firefly's distance from the irrelevant images, the fitness associated with the solution space depends only on relevant images. The computation of EMD is the same as that computed in the previous step as defined by Equations 13.3 through 13.6, and the region weights of query and database image are computed from Equations 13.1 and 13.2, respectively. It is to be observed that the cost function $\phi^k(A_n)$ produces a lower fitness value, when the firefly is close to relevant images and far from the irrelevant images. Thus, the lower the fitness value, the better are the positions achieved by the firefly toward the relevant one. Based on the value of fitness, it is feasible to reorder the firefly to obtain a new ranking. There are two stages of firefly algorithm that are described as follows (Yang 2008).

13.2.2 Attraction toward New Firefly

The attractiveness function $\beta(r)$ of the firefly that is described by a set of regions is described by

$$\beta^k(r) = \beta_0 e^{\left(-\gamma\left(r_{ns}^k\right)^2\right)} \tag{13.8}$$

where β_0 is the attractiveness with distance $r = 0$, and γ stands for the light absorption coefficient. A firefly attractiveness β depends on the light intensity of adjacent fireflies. The brightness I of a firefly is equivalent to its fitness value $f(x)$:

$$I_n = f(x_n) = \phi^k(A_n) \tag{13.9}$$

Thus, an agent with high/low light intensity will attract another firefly of high/low light intensity. Each firefly has its unique attractiveness, which means how strong it attracts other fireflies. Yet the attractiveness is relative; it will differ with the distance between two fireflies n and S located at positions x_n and x_S, respectively, and it is given as

$$r_{ns}^k = \|x_n - x_S\| = EMD(A_n, C_S), \quad n = 1, \ldots, N \\ S = 1, \ldots, M_{DB} \tag{13.10}$$

13.2.3 Movement of Fireflies

Firefly n located at x_n is attracted to another more attractive firefly S located at x_S. The nth firefly changes its position if there exists any x_S such that $I_S < I_n$ is determined by

$$x_n^k(g+1) = x_n^k(g) + \beta_0 e^{\left(-\gamma\left(r_{ns}^k\right)^2\right)}(x_S - x_n) + \alpha\varepsilon_n \tag{13.11}$$

Based on the movement of fireflies, it is possible to rank the N fireflies and find the current best solution. As discussed in Section 13.2, Gaussian distribution is introduced at the end of each iteration of the standard firefly algorithm. The use of Gaussian distribution in the firefly algorithm stabilizes the movement of a firefly by moving all the fireflies to their global best in each iteration, thus enhancing the convergence speed of the firefly algorithm.

After the two phases of the firefly algorithm at the first iteration, an updating process is carried out at every further iteration. The values of the attractiveness, objective function, and movement of firefly toward another firefly as defined by Equations 13.8, 13.9, and 13.11, respectively, are recalculated if new relevant images are tagged by the user and the attractiveness is based on distance between fireflies as determined by Equation 13.10. As a result, after every user feedback, the firefly moves toward new areas in the search space where other relevant images may be found. The process ends when the user is satisfied with the retrieved results.

13.3 Image Databases

Subsets employed from two heterogeneous image databases in evaluation, represent different challenges for RBIR. The first database, Corel, is extracted from Corel photo galleries (Wang 2004) covering a wide range of semantic categories of natural scenes with artificial objects. The dataset is partitioned into 15 categories—each category is repre-sented by 100 images, for a total of 1500 images. The second database is the VisTex database (Massachusetts Institute of Technology 2005) divided into 19 categories, between 3 and 20 images each. The same visual features as discussed in Section 11.4 are used here.

13.4 Performance Evaluation

The retrieval precision of the proposed method incorporating the Earth Mover image sim-ilarity measure and the firefly algorithm-based relevance feedback mechanism is evalu-ated through comparison with the GA-based method (Chan 1999) and the local similarity pattern method (Stejic et al. 2003b) as both compared methods use the optimization tech-nique. The GA-based methods make use of globally extracted image features, and the image similarity is expressed as a weighted average of the related feature similarities that interactively deduce the relative weight of each compared feature. The local similarity pattern method is based on a region-based image similarity model, and it employs an integer-valued GA to deduce the assignment of feature combinations to the image regions. Figures 13.1 and 13.2 depict the average precision rates for Corel and VisTex image data-bases, respectively. From the experimental results, it is inferred that the LSP method has better performance than the GA-based method, as the LSP method is a region-based one. The proposed method consistently outperforms the compared method as the GA does not directly use the information about relevant and irrelevant images (i.e., their features), which makes it less responsive to the user's discrepancy during the relevance feedback process.

Thus, the experiment on Corel and VisTex image databases compared with baselines shows the proposed RBIR based on a Gaussian firefly algorithm has a higher average precision for different image categories. In the next part, we explore the possibility of

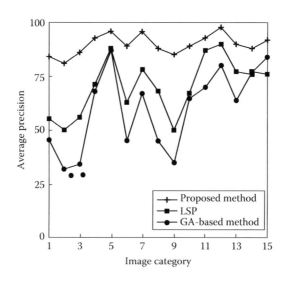

FIGURE 13.1
Average precision rate when different categories of a Corel image database are employed.

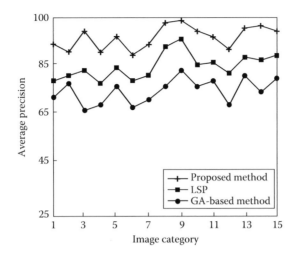

FIGURE 13.2
Average precision rate when different categories of VisTex image database are employed.

embedding the RF process such as support vector machine (SVM) into a stochastic optimization engine called a Gaussian firefly algorithm in an RBIR system, which appropriately determines the parameter of a SVM using the Gaussian firefly algorithm in addition to enhancing the ability to capture a user's perception of image content on retrieving desired images from a large database. In that way the issue of a long iteration problem and stagnation in local optima in RF is overcome. The hybridization of the proposed method eliminates the demerits of the stand-alone algorithms on one side while still keeping hold of all the advantages on the other side.

14

An Evolutionary Approach for Optimizing Region-Based Image Retrieval Using Support Vector Machine

In order to enhance the ability to capture a user's perception of image content on retrieving desired images from a large database and to suitably influence the parameters of a support vector machine (SVM) based on regional representation, in this chapter the SVM learning process is integrated into a Gaussian firefly algorithm as a relevance feedback approach in region-based image retrieval.

The problem of image retrieval is formulated as a problem of optimization and is worked out by using SVM and the Gaussian firefly algorithm (FA). The user is within the loop, and his or her interaction with the system is utilized as an iterative supervision of the classification. The user's feedback drives a SVM learning process and also the progress of the firefly swarm agent based on regional representation, in order to minimize the fitness function that takes into account the characteristics of irrelevant and relevant images, as points of repulsion and attraction. SVM learning automatically updates the weights of preferences for relevant images based on both relevant and irrelevant feedback images based on regional representation. The firefly algorithm is adopted as a search strategy that identifies the optimal feature subset and also explores the solution space efficiently.

Thus, the proposed hybrid work requires less user interaction to retrieve the relevant images present in the database according to the query image by enhancing the degrading performance of the SVM classifier with the assistance of one of the recently developed firefly algorithms in addition to enhancing the ability to capture a user's perception of image content on retrieving desired images from a large database.

The optimization of the SVM classifier using a FA in a region-based image retrieval (RBIR) has faster convergence speed than the SVM and FA and also since the firefly algorithm is used in relevance feedback, only the top fireflies are used for comparison with database images, which reduces its computational complexity.

The firefly optimizer guides the swarm agents to proceed toward the cluster of relevant images in the exploration of the search space based on a user's feedback. This research study has a focused approach to increase the performance by optimizing the region feature with the firefly algorithm. The system overcomes the semantic gap through optimized iterative learning and also provides a better exploration of solution space.

14.1 Region-Based Image Retrieval

An increasing number of applications necessitate sophisticated image search facilities. The most prominent ones are medical imagery, remote sensing, Internet, news, and media. Conventionally, these applications mostly deploy keyword-based search operations.

Newer searches moreover integrate content descriptors derived from the pixel data of the images into their retrieval algorithms. Often, one refers to this approach as content-based image retrieval (CBIR). RBIR is a promising extension of the classical CBIR: rather than deploying global features over the complete content, RBIR systems divide an image into a number of homogenous regions and excerpt local features for each region. Apart from the traditional similarity search, RBIR delivers novel query types, most prominently, the search for images containing related parts of a reference image, for example, "find pictures of this brown dog in an arbitrary environment." Penetrating with a different reference region is a simple extension of CBIR.

Searching absorbed images based on visual properties or contents of images is a challenging problem, and it established much attention from researchers in the last 20 years. The gap among low-level visual features and high-level semantic understanding of images, which is also known as the semantic gap problem, is the bottleneck to additional improvement of the performance of a content-based image retrieval system. In order to resolve this semantic gap problem, one of the most prevalent approaches in recent years is to change the focus from the global content description of images into the local content description by regions (region-based image retrieval) or even the objects in images (object-based image retrieval). Although much study in region-based image retrieval has previously been done, there are still three key problems that need to be undertaken properly: local region-based features, similarity measures, and relevance feedback built on regions.

1. *The local features problem*: In RBIR, local features, rather than global features of the whole image used in CBIR work, are extracted from segmented regions and used to signify images. However, region segmentation, which is based on low-level features of images, is often inconsistent on images of the same scene captured at different times. It may also carry little semantic meaning of objects therein. The local features extracted from regions barely reflect the high-level semantic understanding of the images. Likewise, after region segmentation, the choice of representation for local features is another factor that affects the retrieval performance.

2. *The similarity measure problem*: The similarity measure is used to select which regions in images are related to the target region in the query in RBIR. Henceforward, choosing a good similarity measure is essential for good retrieval performance in CBIR.

3. *The relevance feedback problem:* In image retrieval, as in text retrieval, relevance feedback is the greatest prevalent way to acquire feedback on the retrieved images from users for performance development. The approach is to ask users to mark relevant and/or irrelevant retrieved images after each round of image retrieval. Information composed from the returned images is utilized to further improve retrieval performance in the next round. Although relevance feedback has previously been extensively exploited in many CBIR studies and is reported to realize promising results, incorporating the method into RBIR research is a still challenging problem. The effort is that returned relevant images in a feedback round contain not only relevant regions, but likewise unrelated regions compared with target regions in a query. These unrelated regions may complicate the RBIR system and the intention of users, thus degenerating subsequent retrieval performance.

14.2 Behavior of Fireflies

The firefly algorithm is one of the latest artificial intelligence algorithms developed. Inspired by the flashing of fireflies, it gets its inspiration from nature, like many of the other metaheuristic algorithms. The social aspect of fireflies provides an efficient means of traversing a search space, and avoiding any local optima. There are around two thousand firefly types, and most fireflies produce little and rhythmic flashes. The pattern of flashes is often distinctive for a particular species. The blinking light is produced by a process of bioluminescence, and the true functions of such signaling systems are still debated. However, two essential functions of such flashes are to invite mating partners (communication) and to attract probable prey.

Metaheuristic algorithms form a significant part of modern global optimization algorithms, computational intelligence, and soft computing. These algorithms are generally nature inspired with multiple interacting agents. A subsection of metaheuristics is often stated as swarm intelligence (SI)-based algorithms, and these SI-based algorithms have been established by mimicking the SI features of biological agents such as birds, fish, humans, and others. For instance, particle swarm optimization (PSO) was based on the swarming behaviors of birds and fish, while the firefly algorithm was based on the flashing pattern of tropical fireflies and the cuckoo search algorithm was enthused by the brood parasitism of some cuckoo species.

In the last two decades, more than a dozen new algorithms such as PSO, differential evolution, bat algorithm, firefly algorithm, and cuckoo search have been performed, and they have exposed great potential in solving tough engineering optimization problems. Amid these new algorithms, it has been revealed that the firefly algorithm is very well organized in dealing with multimodal, global optimization problems.

14.3 Why Is the Firefly Algorithm So Efficient?

As the works about the firefly algorithm develop and new alternatives have emerged, all pointed out the firefly algorithm can overtake several other algorithms. Now we may ask logically, "Why is it so efficient?" To respond to this query, let us briefly study the firefly algorithm itself. FA is swarm intelligence based, so it has the related advantages that other swarm intelligence-based algorithms have. In fact, a simple investigation of parameters suggests that some PSO alternatives such as enhanced PSO are a special case of firefly algorithm when $\yen = 0$. Nevertheless, FA has two main advantages over other algorithms: automatic subdivision and the capability of dealing with multimodality. First, FA is based on attraction, and attractiveness decreases with distance. This leads to the fact that the entire population can automatically subdivide into subgroups, and each group can swarm around each mode or local optimum. Amid all these modes, the finest global solution can be found. Second, this subdivision permits the fireflies to be able to find all optima simultaneously if the population scope is sufficiently higher than the number of modes. Arithmetically, $1/\sqrt{\yen}$ controls the average distance of a group of fireflies that can be seen by adjacent groups. Therefore, a whole population can subdivide into subgroups with a given, average distance. In the exciting case when $\yen = 0$, the whole population will not subdivide. This automatic subdivision capability makes it particularly suitable for highly nonlinear, multimodal optimization problems.

In addition, the parameters in FA can be tuned to control the randomness as iterations proceed, so that convergence can also be sped up by tuning these parameters. These above advantages make it flexible enough to deal with continuous problems, clustering and classifications, and combinatorial optimization as well.

14.4 Machine Learning

Machine learning and relevance feedback methods have been offered to learn and to refine query concepts. The problem is that most traditional methods necessitate a large number of training instances, and they need seeding a query with "good" instances. Inappropriately, in many real scenarios, a learning algorithm must work with an insufficiency of training data and an inadequate amount of training time.

The ensemble methods such as bagging, arcing, and boosting have been proposed to develop learning accuracy for decision trees and neural networks. These ensemble schemes enjoy success in improving classification accuracy through bias or alteration reduction, but they do not help to decrease the number of samples and time required to learn a query concept. In fact, maximum ensemble schemes essentially increase learning time because they introduce learning redundancy in order to increase prediction accuracy.

To decrease the number of essential samples, researchers have led numerous studies of active learning for classification. Active learning can be modeled properly as follows: Given a dataset S consisting of an unlabeled subset U and a labeled subset X, an active learner L has two components: f and s. The f component is a classifier that is trained on the present set of labeled data X. The next component s is the sampling function that, given a current labeled set X, selects which subset u in U to select to query the user. The active learner precedes a new f after each round of relevance feedback. The sampling techniques active by the active learner regulate the selection of the next batch of unlabeled instances to be labeled by the user.

The query by committee (QBC) algorithm is an illustrative active learning scheme. QBC practices a distribution over all possible classifiers and efforts greedily to reduce the entropy of this distribution. This general purpose algorithm has been pragmatic in a number of domains using classifiers for which specifying and sampling classifiers from a distribution is natural. Probabilistic models such as the Naive Bayes classifier deliver interpretable results and principled ways to incorporate prior knowledge.

However, they classically do not achieve as well as discriminative approaches such as SVMs, especially when the amount of training data is negligible. For image retrieval where a query concept is typically nonlinear, our MEGA and SVM Active with kernel mapping deliver more flexible and exact concept modeling. For image retrieval, the PicHunter system uses Bayesian prediction to infer the goal image, based upon the user's input. Arithmetically, the aim of PicHunter is to find a single goal point in the feature space (e.g., a particular flower image), whereas our goal is to hunt down all points that match a query concept. Note that the points matching a target concept can be distributed all over the feature space. To find these points speedily with few hints, our learning algorithms must deal with many intimidating challenges.

14.5 Support Vector Machines

The SVMs are supervised learning models with associated learning algorithms that investigate data used for classification and regression analysis. Given a set of training instances, each marked as fitting to one or the other of two types, an SVM training algorithm forms a model that allocates new instances to one category or the other, making it a nonprobabilistic binary linear classifier. An SVM model is a representation of the instances as points in space, mapped so that the examples of the distinct categories are separated by a clear gap that is as wide as possible. New instances are then mapped into that same space and predicted to belong to a category based on which side of the gap they fall. In addition to performing linear classification, SVMs can professionally perform a nonlinear classification using what is called the kernel trick, implicitly mapping their inputs into high-dimensional feature spaces. When data are not labeled, supervised learning is not conceivable, and an unsupervised learning method is essential, which attempts to find natural clustering of the data to groups, and then maps new data to these formed groups. The clustering algorithm that delivers a development to the SVMs is called support vector clustering.

14.6 Optimization of SVM by PSO

The PSO-SVM system for classification, initially aims at optimizing the accuracy of the SVM classifier by detecting the subset of best informative features and estimating the best values for regularization of kernel parameters for the SVM model. In order to achieve this a PSO-based optimized framework is used. A PSO-SVM algorithm combines two machine learning methods by optimizing the parameters of SVM using PSO. PSO starts with n-randomly selected particles and searches for the optimal particle iteratively.

Each particle is an m-dimensional vector and represents a candidate solution. The SVM classifier is constructed for each candidate solution to calculate its performance through the cross-validation method. The PSO algorithm guides the selection of potential subsets that lead to the best prediction accuracy. The algorithm uses the fit particles to contribute to the next generation of n-candidate particles. Thus, on average, every successive population of candidate particles fits better than its predecessor. This process stays until the performance of SVM converges.

The PSO is used to discover optimal feature subsets by discovering the best feature combinations as they fly within the problem space from the handled datasets. The procedure describing the proposed PSO-SVM approach is as follows:

1. Initializing PSO with population size, inertia weight, and generations without improvement
2. Evaluating the fitness of each particle
3. Comparing the fitness values and determining local best and global best particles
4. Updating the velocity and position of each particle until the value of the fitness function converges

5. After converging, feeding the global best particle in the swarm to the SVM classifier for training

6. Training the SVM classifier

The PSO-SVM takes the benefit of minimum structural risk of SVM and the quick global optimizing capability of PSO. The application of the algorithm of optimization by particulate swarm, like any evolutionary algorithm, is prejudiced by factors such as the criterion of stop, the structure of particle, and the objective function:

- *Criterion of stop*: The criterion of stop can be an iteration count attached to the precondition, a value of function objectifies reached or a movement of the particles closer to zero.

- *Structure of the particles*: A particle *I* will contain a vector representing two values (a value for the coefficient of regularization *C* and a value for the parameter of core RBF "sigma") such as the position $x_{ij} = (x_{i1}, x_{i2})$.

- *The objective function*: The purpose of the function objectifies will be to reduce the error of generalization to the minimum.

14.6.1 SVM-Based RF

As an essential machine learning technology, SVM has not only solid theoretical foundations but also brilliant experimental successes. SVM has also been introduced into CBIR as a dominant relevance feedback (RF) tool, and it performs honestly well in the systems that use global representations. Assuming the RF information, usually two kinds of learning could be done in order to improve the performance. First estimate the distribution of the target images, and second learn a boundary that splits the target images from the rest. A kernel-based one-class SVM as density estimator for positive instances was revealed to outperform the whitening transform-based linear/quadratic technique. For the latter, the typical form of SVM as a binary classifier is suitable. A SVM captures the query notion by unraveling the relevant images from the irrelevant images with a hyperplane in a projected space.

When SVM is used as a classifier in RF, there are two display approaches. One approach is to display the most-positive (MP) images and use them as the training samples. The MP images are selected as the ones farthest from the boundary on the optimistic side, plus those nearest from the boundary on the negative side if necessary. The fundamental assumption is that the users are greedy and annoyed and thus expect the finest possible retrieval results after each feedback. It is also the approach adopted by most early relevance feedback systems. However, if we assume the users are supportive, another approach is more appropriate. In this approach, both the MP images and the most-informative (MI) images are shown. Additional user feedback, if any, will only be achieved on those MI images, while the MP images are shown as the final results. By taking benefit of the duality between the feature space and the parameter space, they exposed that the points near the boundary can approximately achieve this goal. Therefore, the points near the boundary are used to approximate the MI points.

Query-point movement (QPM) method: Enthused by the QPM process, a novel relevance feedback approach to region-based image retrieval is offered. The basic notion is that every region could be helpful in retrieval. Based on this assumption, all the regions of both initial query and positive examples are assembled into a pseudo image, which is used as the optimal query at the next iteration of the retrieval and feedback process. The significance of the regions of optimal query is standardized such that the sum of them is equal to 1. During the standardization, regions of those newly added positive examples, which reflect the user's latest query refinement of positive examples, which reflect the user's latest query refinement more precisely, are emphasized by giving them more importance. As more positive instances are available, the number of regions in the optimal queries grows rapidly. Since the time required to calculate image similarity is proportional to the number of regions in the query, the retrieval speed will slow down gradually. To eliminate this, regions similar in the feature space are combined into larger ones together via clustering. This process is related to region merging in an overseg-mented image.

14.7 Optimization Using a Stochastic Firefly Algorithm

The characteristics analysis of optimization using a stochastic firefly algorithm is carried out as we discussed in Section 13.2. The process ends when the user is satisfied with the retrieved results. Thus based on swarm intelligence, the firefly algorithm finds the global optima of the objective function by investigating the foraging behavior of fireflies.

14.8 Image Databases

Employ subsets from two various image databases in evaluation, representing dissimilar challenges for RBIR.

14.8.1 COIL Database

The Columbia Object Image Library (COIL) database comprises 100 diverse objects, seen from 72 different view angles, divided by 5-degree rotations. Consequently, the database contains 7200 color images. Seemingly, images have been resampled so that the larger of the two dimensions fits the image size. Consequently, the apparent size of an object may change considerably between the two images.

Preprocessing comprises the following stage:

1. Gray-level conversion
2. Subsampling

In object recognition, the luminance delivers enough information to be able to differentiate two different objects. Thus, the initial stage of our preprocessing is a gray-level conversion.

The novel resolution of the images is 128×128 pixels. Since such accurateness is not needed, the images are subsampled, henceforth providing a gain in training and classification speed. The resolution is decreased to 32×32 pixels by averaging 4×4 pixel patches.

14.8.2 The Corel Database

The Corel database is expected for image classification. It comprises a set of photos divided into about 200 groups, each with 100 images. The dataset is partitioned into categories, including butterfly, buildings, hills, flowers, earth, sky, trees, boats, birds, statue, horses, and elephants, etc., and each category is signified by 250 images, for a total of 2500 images.

14.9 Baselines

Four relevance feedback methods—PSO + SVM in RBIR, GA + SVM in RBIR, SVM in RBIR (Jing et al. 2004), and QPM in RBIR (Jing et al. 2004)—are compared with the proposed method. The firefly algorithm is compared with PSO and GA for region-based image retrieval along with SVM because these two methods are in the same class of population-based optimization techniques. We selected the third one as SVM in region-based image retrieval as it is based on machine learning techniques. For the fourth, we selected the QPM to demonstrate the consequence of irrelevant images in machine learning techniques. Except for the QPM, all three comparable methods make use of relevant and irrelevant images.

14.9.1 The Proposed SVM: FA Approach

In the proposed method, an innovative method is offered that incorporates SVM and the firefly algorithm in relevance feedback for region-based image retrieval. Primarily, each image of the database is segmented into regions by clustering the pixel types. The feature mechanisms are then calculated from segmented regions. The process is online for query image and offline for database image. When the user inputs a query image, it is segmented and the features are extracted from each region. Then the distance between the input image and all database images are measured based on Earth Mover's distance criteria.

The M_{FB} nearest images are then presented, and the first feedback from the user is requested. The user describes the feedback images as similar and dissimilar in binary by mapping one for similar and zero for dissimilar images. The similar and dissimilar images are progressively inhabited across iterations. There are two iterations in this system. They are support vector machine learning and firefly swarm updating. These two processes exploit the information collected from the user, who is iteratively concerned with the process of image search. Initially the weights of the features are set to one. Based on the two classified image subsets, support vector machine learning automatically generates preference weights for relevant images as well as utilizes the information from the irrelevant images, thereby achieving the user's mental expectation, and then the firefly optimization algorithm updates its swarm constantly to converge into the image clusters that contain the best solution. Ultimately, the system calculates the new ranking with the updated weights based on the Earth Mover's distance, and then the user is again faced with the M_{FB} nearest images for collecting the latest feedback until the convergence; the process is repeatedly iterated.

14.10 Discussion

The average execution period of our experiment is based on every RF iteration for all three databases (Corel, Caltech, and Pascal) and for all the evaluated RF approaches used. The execution time refers to the average time necessary for each RF approach to be skilled to the user's needs and to select images to be shown on each iteration. The execution time of the proposed method and comparison methods is influenced by the parameter choice and also by the number of images marked as relevant and irrelevant by the user on each iteration. In the firefly algorithm, only the distance is essential for the movement, whereas in PSO each particle will move a distance according to its personal best and the global best, and the GA-based retrieval method is significantly slower than PSO and FA, as it does not directly use the information about the relevant and irrelevant images, which makes it less receptive to the user's discrepancy during the relevance feedback process. Also when combining SVM with evolutionary algorithm, its computational complexity decreases. Thus, the experiments on integrated SVM and the Gaussian firefly algorithm in RBIR with the subset of Corel and Caltech database images shows that the retrieval performance yields higher average precision and recall when compared to existing approaches like PSO, GA, SVM, and QPM. The higher the precision-recall curves, the better is the performance.

The common retrieval performance study precision and the recall are used as the investigation of the search results. Precision P is marked as the ratio of the number of retrieved relevant images r to the total number of images n—that is, $P = r/n$. Precision P points to the accuracy and time of the retrieval. Recall R is defined as the ratio of the number of relevant images retrieved r to the total number m of relevant images in the entire database—that is, $R = r/m$. Recall R indicates the robustness of the retrieval performance. For each query, the precision of the retrieval at each level of the recall is obtained.

The analysis of the proposed system is done by giving input as Corel database images from which the relevant images are quickly retrieved with accuracy.

Accuracy: It is the degree to which the result of a measurement, calculation, or specification conforms to the correct value (true). The proposed system gives 95% accuracy.

$$Accuracy = \frac{(TP + TN)}{(TP + TN + FP + FN)}$$

where

- TP (True Positive) = Correctly Identified
- FP (False Positive) = Incorrectly Identified
- TN (True Negative) = Correctly Rejected
- FN (False Negative) = Incorrectly Rejected

Sensitivity: This is a true positive rate (TPR). It measures the propagation of actual positives which are correctly recognized. The TPR is 65%.

$$Sensitivity = \frac{TP}{(TP + FN)}$$

14.10.1 Comparison of FA with PSO and GA

Numerous studies show that PSO algorithms can outperform genetic algorithms (GAs) and other conventional algorithms for solving many optimization problems. This is moderately due to the fact that the broadcasting ability of the current best estimates gives better and quicker convergence toward the optimality. A general framework for evaluating statistical performance of evolutionary algorithms has been deliberated in detail by Shilane et al. Now we will compare the firefly algorithms with PSO and GAs for several standard test functions.

For GAs, we have used the standard version with no exclusiveness with a mutation probability of $pm = 0.05$ and a crossover probability of 0.95. For the PSO, we have also used the standard version with the learning parameters $\alpha = \beta = ¥ = 2$ without the inertia correction. We have used various population sizes from $n = 15$ to 200, and found that for most problems, it is sufficient to use $n = 15$ to 50. Therefore, we have used a fixed population size of $n = 40$ in all of our simulations for comparison. After implementing these algorithms using MATLAB®, we have carried out extensive simulations and each algorithm has been run at least 100 times so as to carry out meaningful statistical analysis. The algorithms stop when the variations of function values are less than a given tolerance $\epsilon \leq 10^{-5}$. The numbers are in the following format: average number of evaluations (success rate), so 3752 ± 725 (99%) means that the average number (mean) of function evaluations is 3752 with a standard deviation of 725. The success rate of finding the global optima for this algorithm is 99%. All of the results obtained throughout this work show that the FA performs well compared to others. In the benchmark functions, we have seen the FA achieves better results than the PSO, and does so in a small fraction of the time. The emission source localization proves quite the challenge, and the FA actually outperforms the PSO in noisy situations and appears as the superior algorithm when it comes to problems with many local optima. And when time is of the essence, the FA returns results extremely fast.

15

Optimization of Sparse Dictionary Model for Multimodal Image Summarization Using Firefly Algorithm*

With massive growth in the number of image sharing sites and social networks, image summarization is evolving as a competent task for traversing a large number of images. Despite the fact that the majority of available summarization methods utilize only visual features for image representation, recent studies have ascertained the advantages of taking tag information into account. The overlying facts persuade us to look to textual content for image summarization based on a sparse dictionary model rather than mere image content. Sparse representation involves approximation of an input signal with a linear combination of a few dictionary atoms (Wright and Yang 2009) and has grabbed the attention of various researchers while being successfully utilized in robust face recognition, visual tracking (Mei and Ling 2011), and transient acoustic signal classification (Zhang et al. 2012). Joint sparse representation has bestowed a substantial improvement of performance in a variety of multitask learning applications including target classification, biometric recognitions, and multiview face recognition (Zhang et al. 2012) when compared to several other proposed sparsity constraints (priors). However, the performance of joint sparse representation declines with a large set of training samples like sparse representation, though results obtained were noteworthy (Yuan et al. 2012). This limitation becomes even worse with multiple training matrices, which makes the solution more complex. Therefore, Shafiee (2014a,b) suggested integrating dictionary learning in joint sparse representation to circumvent this problem and illustrated improved results on face recognition.

These facts motivate us to consider leveraging dictionary learning for the joint sparse representation model to construct the summary and to represent the image. Specifically, the image summarization problem is reformulated into a dictionary learning problem by choosing the bases that can be sparsely united to signify the original image and attain a minimum global reconstruction error, such as mean square error (MSE), which is described to be a NP-hard problem.

Existing sparse coding and dictionary learning techniques such as principal component analysis (PCA), method of optimal direction (MOD) (Engan et al. 1999), and K-singular value decomposition (K-SVD) (Aharon et al. 2005) utilize machine learning techniques to acquire more condensed representations and results in local optimum. As a consequence, the current work has adopted the firefly algorithm for dictionary learning to achieve a global optimum with a high probability by diminishing the optimization function while undergoing adequate search steps.

Thus in our work, the problem of image summarization is formulated as the issue of dictionary learning under multimodality, sparsity, and diversity constrictions, and the firefly algorithm is adopted for dictionary learning to achieve global optimum with a high

* Source of publication: http://www.ripublication.com/Volume/ijaerv10n55spl.htm. Original material available in *International Journal of Applied Engineering Research*, 10(55), 1896–1901, January 2015.

probability by diminishing the optimization function while undergoing adequate search steps. Three noteworthy contributions of this work include

- Proposal of a novel method based on the multimodal sparse dictionary learning model for image summarization under sparsity and diversity constrictions
- Development of a global optimization algorithm named the firefly algorithm to obtain the solution of the optimization problem for multimodal image collection summarization, thereby evading the local optimum and establishing a superior reconstruction phenomenon with the global optimum
- Determination of the superiority of the proposed model over the state-of-the-art strategies as apparent from the experimental results

The methodology of this section is explained as follows. The main task of image summarization is to identify a small subset of images that signify both the visual features and the associated text. Hence, automatic image summarization involves optimization such that the images that best represent are chosen, which can reconstruct the original images in large size. The optimization function described in the proposed model is a NP-hard problem, and the firefly algorithm is adopted to attain a minimum global reconstruction error, such as MSE, during each iteration. The initial dictionary is chosen by randomly selecting k bases from an original image set Y. Each firefly (image) is assessed to resolve the objective function value. The firefly having a minimum objective function or fitness value is considered to be the best firefly. The smaller the fitness values, the better is the reconstruction ability. Whenever a set of candidate dictionaries is selected by the firefly algorithm, a set of coefficients for minimizing the optimization function has to be calculated using sparse coding. The dictionary and the coefficients are then updated simultaneously. Then, we go to another iterative basis selection stage, which strictly reduces the reconstruction function until convergence. The basis is updated iteratively in this stage, and the reconstruction function strictly decreases for each iteration. Then a new residue maximally approximating the current residue is identified. The coefficient matrix is then calculated using sparse coding after the update of all the K bases, and the update process is repeated until convergence. The details of the proposed system are described as follows.

15.1 Image Representation

In this section, a bag-of-words (BoW) approach has been followed to signify image content, which is one of the widely used representations in text mining and information retrieval. The summarization problem will very well utilize the BoW model as it attempts to generalize the primary visual features appearing in a collection. This work makes use of a mutual scheme for demonstrating both visual and textual data as multimodal images are dealt with. In particular, the visual features are displayed using a bag-of-features approach in which the scale invariant feature transform (SIFT) descriptor has been selected (Sivic and Zisserman 2003) as the feature to create BoW model since the SIFT descriptor has a broader usage. Each image is broken into nonoverlapping blocks of 8 * 8 pixels and for each block the SIFT descriptor is calculated. Then, a codebook of 1000 block is constructed by means of the k-means algorithm with the aid of an image training set. Last, a histogram is constructed with the manifestations of visual patterns appearing in the image. Visual data are processed to construct a matrix, which is referred to as $Y_v \in I^{l*n}$, where l is the number of visual features, and n is the number of images in the collection.

Correspondingly, a matrix of text descriptions is built denoted by $Y_t \in I^{m*n}$ with m being the number of text features and n the number of images in the collection. The matrix of text descriptions is built by constructing a vector with the frequencies of each index term for all text descriptions in a vector space model (Baeza-Yates et al. 1999). Inverse document frequency (*idf*) weighting can further be applied to make this matrix even better and to bring out the significance of words along the corpus. However, the resultant matrix still satisfies the non-negativity condition for our summarization approach.

This work comprises the construction of a multimodal matrix $Y = [\gamma Y_v^T (1-\gamma) Y_t^T]^T$ with $\gamma \in [0,1]$ a weighting parameter that leverages the comparative prominence of the two data modalities. We set $\gamma = 0.5$ in our experiments (to assign equal importance to visual and text data), unless otherwise stated. Then, the matrix $Y \in I^{(l+m)*n}$ or $Y = [Y_1, Y_2]$ comprises dual data modalities, which are visual features and textual features, autonomously built from diverse sources and directly joined to yield a single multimodal vector for denoting words, referred to as feature-level fusion. A similar model utilizing SVD, in which visual and textual features are aligned to create a multimodal latent semantic representation, was proposed by Hare et al. (2006).

15.2 Problem Formulation

Identification of a subset of images that signify both the visual features and the associated text information is the main task involved in general summarization (Jing et al. 2007). Hence, automatic image summarization involves optimization such that the images that best represent are chosen which can reconstruct the original images in large size (Yang 2008). When $Y \in I^{(l+m)*n}$ or $Y \in I^{p*n}$ is defined as the original images in large size, where p is the dimension of the image and $S \in I^{(l+m)*k}$ or $S \in I^{p*k}$ is described as the summary out of the given image set Y, where k is the size of the dictionary, automatic image summarization is to define the summary S such that it minimizes the global reconstruction error in L^2-norm:

$$\min_S \| Y - f(S) \|_2^2 \qquad (15.1)$$

where Y is the given image set, $\| \cdot \|2$ is the l^2 norm operator, and $f(S)$ is the reconstruction function. Thus, in order to govern image summarization, a multimodal semantic representation is made and the reconstruction function $f(\cdot)$ is chosen to evaluate the scope of each image in the original image set Y_i to be rebuilt by the most representative images in the summary S_i by minimizing the global reconstruction error by Equation 15.1. This facilitates the direct assessment of summarization performance by the respective value of the reconstruction function. The reconstruction function $f(\cdot)$ is defined as a linear regression model that applies the summary S_i to sparsely rebuild each image in the original set Y. The sparsity implies the participation of only nonzero elements of the bases in the reconstruction of images. Positive or zero weights are assigned based on the presence or absence of a visual pattern in an image. Hence, the additive property of the BoW model is evidence that negative weight for a vector is impractical. Consequently, only non-negative sparse coefficients should be employed on the dictionary, and the sparse matrix is described as $W \in I^{k*n}$. Hence, it becomes inevitable to apply the sparsity constraint to the objective function for assuring the involvement of only specific bases in reconstruction of the original image as only limited information is contained in the visual content of the image. This explains the selection of only bases with nonzero coefficients for rebuilding images in the original image set. An analytical solution is sought in the proposed work for automatic image summarization using L^1-norm (Donoho and Elad 2003):

$$I : \min_{W} \sum_{i} \| y_i - Sx_i \|_2^2 + \lambda \sum_{i} \| x_i \|_1$$
$$\forall i \in [1 \ldots N], \quad x_i \geq 0$$

(15.2)

where Y_i are the data items from the original image collection, S is the summary, x_i is the non-negative weight for the corresponding S, λ is the sparsity regularizing parameter, and $\|\cdot\|_1$ is the l^1 norm operator. In the meantime, the bases should be different; each basis should be specific for a particular type of major visual pattern, and all the bases should vary from one another. Hence, the objective function for dictionary learning should take account of the diversity restraint. On addition of the diversity constraint, Equation 15.2 is rewritten as follows:

$$\min_{S,W} \sum_{i} \| y_i - Sx_i \|_2^2 + \lambda \sum_{i} \| x_i \|_0 + \beta \, Div(S)$$

(15.3)

where $\|\cdot\|_0$ is the l^0 norm operator, and $Div(S)$ is the diversity of summary. A different summary will be produced for each of the weights β and a varied summary of the collection will thus be viewed. We set optimized diversity weight $\beta = 0.05$. The diversity (quality of the bases collection) of the summary can be demonstrated as an aggregation of the mutual distances between the pair of images. The minimum of the pair-wise distances of the summary images is used as the diversity of summary (pair-wise distances mean can also be selected as diversity of summary):

$$Div(S) = \min_{P_x, P_y \in S, x \neq y} Dist(P_x, P_y)$$

(15.4)

where P_x and P_y are the mean values of variable x and y, respectively. Thus, Equation 15.3 shows the reformulation of the automatic image summarization problem as the optimization problem, the optimization will be mutual with respect to the summary S (a small set of most representative images) and the non-negative coefficient matrix $W = [w_1^T, \ldots, w_n^T]^T, w_1 \in I^{1*k}$.

The reconstruction model (for automatic image summarization) proposed in this work is akin to non-negative matrix factorization, which studies the significant objects or chief constituents of an image set. The K-SVD algorithm is flexible and performs jointly with any sparse coding algorithms. The sparse coefficient matrix for multimodality under non-negative limitation is learnt to fit in the K-SVD algorithm in the proposed context.

The dictionary update process uses a firefly algorithm to learn the dictionary and then bases are updated iteratively ensuring the SVD decomposition process. Then, each basis in the dictionary will be assigned to its adjacent neighbor in the original image set, and the final summarization is generated.

The two varied aspects of design of sparse coding and traditional models of dictionary learning are (1) the coefficients should be non-negative and (2) the dictionary S is chosen from a cluster of certain candidates (original images) Y rather than their combinations.

15.3 Optimization of Dictionary Learning

The optimization problem described in Equation 15.3 is a NP-hard problem, and almost all of the existing algorithms are inescapable to fall into the traps of the local optimums. On the other hand, the firefly algorithm is a metaheuristic algorithm, appropriate for solving the global optimization problem by locating the global optimum of a particular function in a large search space. The search criteria in FA follow the fireflies swarm behavior (Yang 2008) and have three idealized rules.

FA searches the neighborhood space for all the feasible candidates (original images and their associated text) during each iteration as the final results are largely dependent on initial inputs and efficiently escape from falling into traps of local optimums as it brings in local attractions and automatic regrouping. The attraction among fireflies will be local or global depending on the light intensity and absorbing coefficient, which decrease with the distance between them. Moreover, the fireflies can subdivide into a few subgroups because affinity toward neighbors is greater than that of distant ones; thus swarming of subgroups in a local fashion is anticipated. If sufficient search is done, the aforementioned advantage makes FA specifically apt for providing a multimodal global optimum with a high probability, thereby eliminating the local traps. The light intensity and the attractiveness of each firefly are calculated to initialize the stochastic optimization.

Each firefly is assessed to resolve the objective function value. The firefly having minimum objective function or fitness value is considered to be the best firefly. The smaller the fitness values, the better is the reconstruction ability. The objective function value of each firefly is correlated with the light intensity of the respective firefly. The brightness I of a firefly corresponds to its fitness value $f(x)$, which is from Equation 15.3:

$$I_n = f(x_n) = \min_{S,W} \sum_i \| y_i - Sx_i \|_2^2 + \lambda \sum_i \| x_i \|_0 + \beta \, Div(S) \tag{15.5}$$

A firefly with less brightness is attracted and driven to a firefly with more brightness. The initial basis (dictionary) is selected by random choice of k bases from Y. Each basis is then iteratively updated by searching from its neighborhood for attractiveness. The attractiveness of the firefly is evaluated as described by

$$\beta(r) = \beta_0 e^{(-\gamma r_{nS}^2)} \tag{15.6}$$

where β_0 is the attractiveness with distance $r = 0$, and γ refers to the light absorption coefficient. Firefly attractiveness depends on the light intensity of adjacent fireflies. The distance between each pair of fireflies is given using cosine similarity as

$$r_{nk} = \| Y_n - S_k \| \quad n = 1, \ldots, N, \ k = 1, \ldots, K \tag{15.7}$$

The attractiveness for each firefly is determined. Then, the movement of the firefly is evaluated by Equation 15.8 based on the attractiveness of the firefly:

$$x_n(g+1) = x_n(g) + \beta_0 e^{(-\gamma r_{ns}^2)}(x_S - x_n) + \alpha\varepsilon_n \tag{15.8}$$

The first term in Equation 15.8 represents the current location of a firefly, the second term stands for attractiveness, and the third denotes randomization with a vector of random variable ε_n derived from the Gaussian distribution and $\alpha \in [0,1]$. The present best solution can be obtained by ranking the N fireflies depending on their movement. Random search in an adjacent basis will be conducted for each new basis in terms of attractiveness. These steps are reiterated until the fulfillment of termination criteria. The updating of each of these K bases is in parallel as per the above strategy. A total number of *HigScor* dictionaries are chosen in this stage and can be filtered by the movement of fireflies as provided in Equation 15.8. The accepted dictionaries generate a candidate set and are applied as the input for the next iteration.

15.4 Sparse Coding

Whenever a set of candidate dictionaries is selected, calculate a set of coefficients for minimizing the optimization function. Equation 15.2 is similar to the non-negative sparse coding and non-negative matrix factorization so the optimization problem can be solved by the multiplicative algorithm (Hoyer 2002). The objective function is non-increasing as per the rule of update:

$$W^{t+1} = W^t .*(S^T Y)./(S^T S W^t + \lambda 1) \tag{15.9}$$

where $.*$ and $./$ represent element-wise multiplication and division, respectively. Elements of S are always non-negative as each element is multiplied with a non-negative factor. The iteration of the update rule is guaranteed to achieve the global minimum until the initial values of S are all chosen to be strictly positive ($1/k$ in this case). The dictionary and the coefficients are updated simultaneously.

In real time, the present optimal combination is always stored as (W_{opti}, S_{opti}), which maintains $I (W_{opti}, S_{opti})$ in the current minimum. The firefly algorithm process terminates the maximum number of iterations reached or when the S_{opti} is not being updated for *MaxRepRej* (number of maximum repeated rejection) times of iterations. Then, we go to another iterative basis selection stage, which strictly reduces the reconstruction function until convergence.

15.5 Iterative Dictionary Selection Stage

The basis is updated iteratively in this stage, and the reconstruction function strictly decreases for each iteration. For instance, when the basis b_j is updated for those i whose corresponding coefficient s_{ij} is nonzero, all other $k-1$ bases are fixed, and the residue is calculated as below:

$$E_i = \sum \left| y_i - \sum_{q \neq j} s_q x_{iq} \right|^2 \tag{15.10}$$

Then a new residue maximally approximating the current residue is identified, and it is equivalent to

$$s_j^* = argmin \langle \sum E_i, s_j^* \rangle \tag{15.11}$$

which implies s_j^* is the closest point to the center of all the nonzero E_i. Then we ensure whether s_j^* decreases the objective function or not. The coefficient matrix is then calculated after the update of all the K bases using the method presented in the sparse coding stage by Equation 15.9, and the update process is repeated from Equations 15.5 through 15.8 until convergence. The purpose of this stage is to guarantee the convergence of the proposed algorithm to some points.

15.6 Performance Analysis

This section presents the experimental setup and evaluation results of the algorithm used. We have formulated the proposed algorithm such that it can be used to obtain the objective performance when compared to the other three baseline algorithms, namely, affinity ranking (AR) (Jiang et al. 2005), folding (van Leuken et al. 2009), and absorbed random walk (ARW) algorithm (Wang et al. 2011). The efficiency of the summary is revealed by its capability to reconstruct each individual image in the dataset or the original image set. The proposed method is objectively evaluated using the reconstruction potential in terms of MSE. In this formulation, the reconstruction error is termed to determine the "representativeness" of the images and tags. The non-zero elements of visual and text data matrices characterize the summary images that regulate the selection of images. It is hypothesized that the images with descriptive image content should also contain distinctive tags.

15.6.1 Experiment Setup

The *UW* (University of Washington 2011) collection created at the University of Washington contains 1109 images prearranged in 20 classes such as Arbogreens, Australia, Barcelona, and so on. It exhibits a greater degree of visual and textual similarity among candidates of the same class. In this collection, there is a high degree of visual and textual homogeneity among the images of the same class. The smallest class contains 22 images, while the biggest contains 255 images. The average class size is 55. A set of corresponding keywords represents each image. The annotation in total comprises 6383 words, among which 352 are unique. Each image can be best represented by 6 words on average with the maximum being 22 and minimum being 1. For the experiments, 110 images were chosen as query images. The quantity of images chosen from each class was comparative to its size.

15.6.2 Experimental Specification

Interest points are extracted and their SIFT descriptors are calculated for visual image representation. We have built a universal codebook (dictionary) containing 1000 visual words where the k-means algorithm is evaluated on 10 million interest points as given for codebook learning. The image representation (1000-dimensional histogram of code words) is acquired by computing all the interest points in the images into the code word dictionary. It is observed that a 1000-dimensional codebook can generate the best depictions of the images.

The text description is built by constructing a vector with the frequencies of each index term for all text descriptions. The *idf* weighting can further be applied to make this matrix even better and to bring out the significance of words along the corpus.

The optimal parameters for firefly are light absorption coefficient (γ) = 1, attractiveness (β_0) = 1, number of iterations (I) = 40, *MaxRepRej* = 20, *HigScor* = 40.

15.6.3 Baseline Algorithms

Affinity ranking (AR) (Jiang et al. 2005): This method is a re-ranking method for Web search results, by optimizing diversity and coverage metrics. The two metrics are determined from a directed link graph, known as an affinity graph, which models the organization of a set of documents based on the disproportionate content matches between each pair of documents.

Folding (van Leuken et al. 2009): Images having larger probabilities being higher in ranking are selected as representatives, and clusters are created around them in a linear pass. However, this method does not promise centralization of the cluster representatives.

The ARW algorithm (Wang et al. 2011): This changes the chosen items to the absorbing state by fixing the transition probability to 0 (from the present item to other items), and 1 when it turns to itself. The item with the greatest expected number of visits in the present iteration is chosen.

Compare the proposed algorithm with all other baseline algorithms for their reconstruction abilities under the multimodality, sparsity, and diversity constrictions as provided in Equation 15.3, specifically, in terms of MSE. A smaller MSE value denotes better reconstruction ability.

15.6.4 Mean Square Error Performance

Determine the MSE value for the proposed and baseline algorithms on 20 classes as reported in Table 15.1. It is perceived that our proposed algorithm is the best performer in terms of reconstruction ability on 20 classes. The improvement resides in two aspects: (1) the proposed approach considers multimodality, sparsity, and diversity constrictions, whereas the baseline algorithms do not have whole consideration for a good summary; and (2) the firefly algorithm is adopted to attain the global optimum, whereas the baseline algorithms look for local optimum. The convergence of the firefly algorithm avoids local

TABLE 15.1

Mean Square Error Comparison of Proposed Algorithm with Three Other Baseline
Algorithms in Terms of Reconstruction Error for 20 Classes from UW Image Collection
with Equal Summary Size of 12

	Affinity Ranking (Jiang et al. 2005)	Folding (van Leuken et al. 2009)	Absorbed Random Walk (Wang et al. 2011)	Proposed Approach
Arbogreens	0.138	0.127	0.123	0.108
Australia	0.165	0.144	0.137	0.109
Barcelona	0.146	0.130	0.125	0.104
Cambridge	0.142	0.129	0.125	0.108
Campus infall	0.158	0.137	0.132	0.106
Cannon beach	0.161	0.152	0.149	0.137
Cherries	0.153	0.145	0.142	0.131
Columbia gorge	0.169	0.159	0.155	0.136
Football	0.143	0.136	0.133	0.123
Green lake	0.160	0.147	0.143	0.126
Green land	0.171	0.155	0.149	0.127
Indonesia	0.163	0.147	0.142	0.121
Iran	0.145	0.128	0.122	0.099
Italy	0.149	0.142	0.139	0.129
Japan	0.144	0.125	0.118	0.092
Leafless trees	0.199	0.177	0.170	0.139
Sanjuans	0.148	0.134	0.129	0.110
Spring flowers	0.190	0.169	0.162	0.134
Swiss mountains	0.170	0.156	0.151	0.132
Yellow stone	0.146	0.133	0.129	0.112
Average	0.158	0.144	0.139	0.119

optima and restricts the basis update stage to a limited number of steps. Thus, the experiment on UW image collection shows that the proposed multimodal image summarization system has lesser MSE when compared with baseline algorithms, and thus it has better reconstruction capability.

Assessments of the proposed image retrieval system in terms of average precision and recall have been made.

Section V

Algorithmic Solutions to the Problems in Advanced IR Concepts

16

A Dynamic Feature Selection Method for Document Ranking with Relevance Feedback Approach[*]

16.1 Overview

This chapter covers advanced information retrieval (IR) concepts and provides the algorithmic solutions to the problems in conventional IR systems (i.e., document ranking, web page recommendations, facet generation, duplication detection in e-rule making, and predicting user satisfaction in Q&A communities).

An important issue that often confronts data miners in practice is the problem of having too many features. Simply put, not all features measured are likely necessary for accurate ranking, and including them in the IR model may in fact lead to a worse model than if they were removed. Feature is necessary either because it is computationally infeasible to use all available features, or because of problems of estimation when limited data samples (but many of features) are present. The latter problem is a curse of dimensionality. Feature selection (Roberto Ruiz et al. 2004) is important for a number of reasons. First, it provides a general, robust way of building models when there is little *a priori* knowledge about the types of features important for a given task. By using a feature selection algorithm, the model designer can focus less on building the best model and can instead focus on designing good features. Second, feature selection can reduce the number of noisy or redundant features in a large feature set. Such features may reduce training efficiency and may result in a model that has a number of nonidentifiable parameters. Nonidentifiable parameters are those that cannot be reasonably estimated given the training data. This often results from having redundant or highly correlated features. Feature selection helps overcome the problems associated with nonidentifiable parameters. Finally, feature selection can provide insights into the important features for a given task. Select the order by inspecting the features; we can often learn what characteristics of a given task are the most important or the most exploitable.

16.2 Feature Selection Procedures

Feature selectors are algorithms applied to the data before the data reach the document ranking program. Figure 16.1 describes the architecture of the feature selection procedure. A typical feature selection process consists of four basic steps, namely, subset

[*] Source of publication: https://doaj.org/toc/2229-6956/1/1; http://ictactjournals.in/ArticleDetails.aspx?id=84. Original material available from *ICTACT Journal on Soft Computing*, 1(1), 1–8, July 2010.

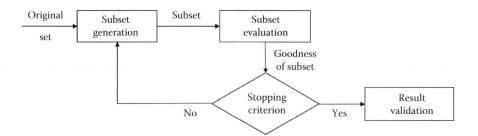

FIGURE 16.1
Architecture for feature selection.

generation, subset evaluation, stopping criterion, and result validation. Subset generation is a search procedure that produces candidate feature subsets for evaluation based on a certain search strategy. Evaluate each candidate subset and compare it with the previous best one according to a certain evaluation criterion. If the new subset turns out better, it replaces the previous best subset. Repeat the process of subset generation and evaluation until it satisfies a given stopping criterion. Then the selected best subset is usually validated by prior knowledge or different tests via synthetic and/or real-world datasets.

The method introduced in this section differs from the existing methodologies, especially in that it uses an efficient feature selector 0/1 knapsack-based heuristic with generalization and relevance feedback approach to determine the usefulness of features and evaluates its effectiveness with three common approaches such as Markov random field (MRF) model, correlation coefficient, and count difference.

The first methodology is the MRF model that is a graphical undirected model that provides a compact and flexible way of modeling joint distributions over a query $Q = q_1 \dots q_n$ and a document D. The second methodology, the most familiar measure of dependence between two quantities, is the Pearson product-moment correlation coefficient, or "Pearson's correlation." Correlation-based feature selection (Hall 2000) (CFS) uses a search algorithm along with a function to evaluate the merits of feature subsets.

The third methodology is count difference (Fang and Zhai 2006), which is the difference between the relative document frequencies of a feature for both relevant and irrelevant classes. This method favors features whose document frequencies fall into a mid-range. Last, but most importantly, the proposed approach uses, an efficient and dynamic feature selector 0/1 knapsack (Ho et al. 2004) based heuristic with generalization and a relevance feedback approach. The knapsack problem is a problem in combinatorial optimization: Given a set of items, each with a weight and a value, determine the number of each item to include in a collection so that the total weight is less than a given limit and the total value is as large as possible. Here the fall-out ratio is the weight, and the information gain is the value for the consideration of feature selection. The features extracted from the knapsack are the initial seeds for the generalization module. Employ association rule induction to capture feature co-occurrence patterns. Construct the generalized features by applying these rules. Essentially, rules preserve implicit semantic relationships between features. Finally, rank the retrieved features by normalized discount cumulative gain (NDCG) (Xiubo Geng et al. 2007) and then rank the documents by the sophisticated ranking function Okapi BM25 model. The expectation maximization (EM) algorithm is for relevance feedback (Matthew Lease 2008), and the documents are again ranked by the Okapi BM25 model.

16.2.1 Markov Random Field (MRF) Model for Feature Selection

An MRF is a graph G and a set of non-negative potential functions over the cliques in G. The nodes in the graph represent the random variables, and the edges define the independent semantics of the distribution. The MRF (Metzler and Croft 2005) satisfies the Markov property, which states that a node is independent of all of its non-neighboring nodes given observed values for its neighbors. Each feature is represented using a 3-tuple of the form (dependence model type, clique set type, weighting function) (Metzler 2007). In this work, the focus is on three dependence model types. The three types are full independence (FI), sequential dependence (SD), and full dependence (FD). The second entry in the tuple, the clique set type, describes the set of cliques within the graph that the feature was applied to. The set of cliques available for this model are single terms, ordered terms, and unordered terms. Finally, the third entry in the tuple is the weighting function, which describes how the feature values are computed. Let M_t denote the model learned after iteration t. Denote the features by f, and the weight (parameter) associated with feature f is λ_f. The candidate set of features is denoted by F. The algorithm begins with an empty model (i.e., $M_0 = \{\}$). Then, temporarily add a feature f to the model. Then hold all weights except λ_f fixed and find the setting for λ_f that maximizes the augmented model. The feature f is defined as maximum utility obtained during training. Repeat this process for every $f \in F$, resulting in a utility being computed for every feature in the candidate pool. The feature with the maximum utility is then added to the model and removed from F. The entire process is then repeated until either some fixed number of features has been added to the model or until the change in utility between consecutive iterations drops below some threshold. But this algorithm is guaranteed to find the local maximum for SCORE (M).

Under this parameterization, rank the documents in descending order according to $P(D|Q)$, which is rank equivalent to

$$P(D|Q) = \sum_{C \in C(G)} \lambda_c f_c(c) \qquad (16.1)$$

where $C(G)$ is the set of cliques in G, and λ_c is the weight (parameter) associated with clique c. The automatic feature selection algorithm associates new feature functions and weights (parameters) with cliques in G, which results in new $\lambda_f(\cdot)$ components being added to the ranking function.

Drawbacks: The algorithm used in this method is guaranteed only to find local maxima. The model has very high computational cost as it gets feedback about features from the model. Every feature is evaluated and selected using mean average precision, so time and complexity are high.

16.2.2 Correlation-Based Feature Selection

Correlation-based feature selection uses a search algorithm along with a function to evaluate the merit of feature subsets. Good feature subsets contain features highly correlated (predictive of) with the class, yet uncorrelated with (not predictive of) each other:

$$G_s = \frac{k\overline{rc_i}}{\sqrt{k + k(kk - 1)\overline{r_{ii}}}} \qquad (16.2)$$

where k is the number of features in the subset; r_{ci} is the mean feature correlation (Houle and Grira 2007) with the class; and $r_{ii'}$ is the average feature intercorrelation. The heuristic goodness measure should filter out irrelevant and redundant features as they will be poor predictors of the class. If X and Y are discrete random variables with respective ranges R_x and R_y, Equations 16.3 and 16.4 give the entropy of Y before and after observing X:

$$H(Y) = -\sum_{y \in R_y} p(y)\log(p(y)) \tag{16.3}$$

$$H\left(\frac{Y}{X}\right) = -\sum_{x \in R_x} p(x) \sum_{y \in R_y} p\left(\frac{y}{x}\right)\log\left(p\left(\frac{y}{x}\right)\right) \tag{16.4}$$

Equation 16.4 gives a measure of correlation or dependency of Y on X. This measure is sometimes called the *uncertainty coefficient* of Y:

$$C(Y|X) = \frac{H(Y) - H(Y/X)}{H(Y)} \tag{16.5}$$

This measure lies between 0 and 1. A value of 0 indicates that X and Y have no association; the value 1 indicates that knowledge of X completely predicts Y.

Drawbacks: The correlation coefficient measures linear relationships between X and Y, and for any relationship to exist, any change in X has to have a constant proportional change in Y. If the relationship is not linear, then the result is inaccurate. In addition to this, the correlation is meaningless if it is about categorical data, such as hair color or gender.

16.2.3 Count Difference-Based Feature Selection

Term discrimination tries to measure the ability of a feature for distinguishing one document from the others in a collection. Related to this concept, a new feature selection method is called count difference (CD) (Fang and Zhai 2006), which is based on the difference between the relative document frequencies of a feature for both relevant and irrelevant classes. Given a feature, the relative document frequency is the ratio of the document frequency of a feature for one class over the average document frequency for the same class:

$$\text{relative } DF(t,y) = at/a \tag{16.6}$$

$$\text{relative } DF(t,y1) = bt/\bar{b} \tag{16.7}$$

Here a and b denote the average document frequencies for the relevant and irrelevant classes and are computed as follows:

$$\bar{b} = \frac{1}{M}\sum_{t=1}^{M} b_t \quad \bar{a} = \frac{1}{M}\sum_{t=1}^{M} a_t \tag{16.8}$$

M is the number of original features before the selection process. With the relative document frequencies, the count difference score of a feature is the difference between its two relative document frequencies:

$$CD(t) = \left[\frac{a_t}{\bar{a}} - \frac{b_t}{\bar{b}} \right]^2 \tag{16.9}$$

The count difference tends to favor features whose relative document frequencies for one class are higher than those for the other class.

16.3 Proposed Approach for Feature Selection

This section presents a new methodology for enhancing existing IR systems with the goodness of the features. This begins with the n-gram architecture, and then focuses on its core, the feature selection module. An n-gram is n-items in any given sequence. In computational linguistics n-gram models are most commonly used in predicting words (in word level n-gram) or predicting characters (in character level n-gram) for the purposes of various applications. To analyze the efficiency of this methodology, use the online medical information database. Normally n-grams of length two or three are most useful for feature selection. Using gram lengths more than three reduces the feature selection performance.

Feature selection with dynamic 0/1 knapsack: Greedy approach and dynamic programming are the two ways to solve optimization problems. Most of the problems have been solved by both greedy and dynamic programming (Horowitz et al. 2007). But it is more difficult to determine whether a greedy algorithm always produces an optimal solution. But in the case of dynamic programming, we need only to determine whether the principle of optimality applies. We show the principle of optimality by solving the 0/1 knapsack by dynamic programming. This is for optimization problems, where we want to find the "best way" of doing something. This often produces a polynomial time for finding the optimal solution when brute force enumeration of possibilities would be exponential.

Pseudo code is as follows:

Dynamic 0/1 knapsack (n, W, $v1$, ... , v_n, w_1, ... , w_n)
1. for w from 0 to W, set V[0, w] = 0
2. for k from 1 to n
3. set V[k, 0] = 0
4. for w from 1 to W
5. if $w_k > w$
6. then set V[k, w] = V[k − 1, w]
7. else if V[k − 1, w] > v_k + V[k − 1, w − w_k]
8. then set V[k, w] = V[k − 1, w]
9. else set V[k, w] = v_k + V[k − 1, w − w_k]

Given: A set of features $F = \{f_1, f_2, ..., f_n\}$ of n features where each f_i has information gain (IG) value v_i and fall-out as weight w_i.

Required: To choose a subset O of F such that the total weight (fall-out) of the items chosen does not exceed W and the sum of the values v_i of items in O is maximal.

A feature's discriminatory power is a useful gauge of its goodness and is commonly ascertained using the IG score as follows:

$$\text{IG}(X,Y) = \sum_{x \in 0,1 y \in 0,1} \sum P(X = x, Y = y) \cdot \log_2 \frac{P(X = x, Y = y)}{P(X = x) \cdot P(Y = y)} \qquad (16.10)$$

Fall-out is the ratio of the retrieved nonrelevant documents, and the total number of non-relevant documents in the collection is

$$\text{fall-out} = \frac{|\{\text{non-relevant documents}\} \cap \{\text{retrieved documents}\}|}{|\{\text{non-relevant documents}\}|} \qquad (16.11)$$

Suppose the optimal solution for F and W is a subset O in which f_k is the highest numbered item.

Then $O\text{-}\{f_k\}$ is an optimal solution for $F_{k-1} = \{f_1, ..., f_{k-1}\}$ and total weight $W\text{-}w_k$. And the *value* of the global solution O is v_k plus the value of the subproblem solution.

Given a target weight w and a set $F_k = \{f_1, ..., f_k\}$, imagine examining all the subsets of F_k whose total weight is $\in w$. Some of these subsets might have bigger total values than others. Let $V[k, w]$ be the biggest total value of such a subset of F_k. Now we give a recursive definition of $V[k, w]$:

V[k, w] = 0 if either k = 0 or w = 0, otherwise
V[k, w] = if $w_k > w$ then V[k – 1, w]
else max{V[k – 1, w], v_k + V[k – 1, w – w_k] }.

The recursive definition of $V[k, w]$ says that the value of a solution for stage F_k and target weight w either includes item f_k, in which case it is v_k plus a subproblem solution for F_{k-1} and total weight $w - w_k$, or does not include f_k, in which case it is just a subproblem solution for F_{k-1} and the same weight w.

16.3.1 Feature Generalization with Association Rule Induction

Extract the features from the 0/1 knapsack algorithm, which are the initial seeds for the association rule algorithm (Wiratunga et al. 2004). It generates rules of the form $H \leftarrow B$, where the rule body B is a conjunction of items, and the rule head H is a single item. Discover the association rules in two stages. First APRIORI identifies sets of items that frequently co-occur—that is, above a given minimum threshold. It then generates rules from these item sets ensuring frequency and accuracy are above minimum thresholds. This means that rules are used to predict the head feature presence given that all the features in the body are present in the document. This means that a case satisfying the body even when the head feature is absent will not be considered.

16.3.2 Ranking

NDCG is designed for measuring ranking inaccuracies when there are multiple levels of relevance judgment. For features for which the several retrieved documents are less than n, NDCG is only calculated for the retrieved documents. In evaluation, NDCG is further averaged over all features. Compute NDCG using Equation 16.15.

16.3.2.1 Document Ranking Using BM25 Weighting Function

Finally rank the documents by the BM25 weighting function and presented by the following equation:

$$f_r, BM25(q_i, D) = \frac{(k1+1)tf_{w,D}}{k1(1-b)+b\left(\frac{|D|}{|D|_{avg}}\right)+tf_{w,D}} \log \frac{N-df_w+0.5}{df_w+0.5}$$

(16.12)

where $tf_{w,D}$ is the number of times the word w matches in document D, df_w is the total number of documents that have at least one match for word w, $|D|$ is the length of document D, $|D|_{avg}$ is the average document length, N is the number of documents in the collection, and b is the weighting function hyperparameter.

16.3.2.2 Expectation Maximization for Relevance Feedback

Personalization in full text retrieval or full text filtering implies re-weighing of the query terms based on some explicit or implicit feedback from the user. Relevance feedback (Tao and Zhai 2006) inputs the user's judgments on previously retrieved documents to build a personalized query or user profile. A standard procedure for estimating probabilities of unknown parameters from incomplete data is the expectation maximization algorithm (EM-algorithm). The iterate algorithm maximizes the query probability $t_1, t_2, \ldots, t_n$ given R relevant documents $d_1, d_2, \ldots, d_R$. The resulting EM-algorithm is defined as follows:

$$\text{E-step: } ri' = \sum_{j=1}^{R} \frac{\lambda_i(p)P((T_i = t_i)|D_j = d_j)}{(1-\lambda_i(p))(P(T_i = t_i)+\lambda_i(p)P((T_i = t_i)|D_j = d_j))}$$

(16.13)

$$\text{M-step: } \lambda_i^{(p+1)} = \frac{ri'}{R}$$

(16.14)

The expectation step calculates the expected documents in which t_i is important. The maximization step simply involves a maximum likelihood estimate. In the EM-algorithm, initialize the relevance weights to some initial value, for example, $\lambda l_i^{(0)} = 0.5$, and then iterate through the E-step and M-step until the value of λ_i does not change significantly (p denotes the iteration number). λ_i is an unknown parameter, denoting the probability that the term on position i in the query is important. So, for $\lambda_i = 0$ the term is definitely unimportant, where for $\lambda_i = 1$ the term is definitely important. Based on these new features the documents are re-ranked again by the BM25 weighting function.

16.4 Empirical Results and Discussion

16.4.1 Dataset Used for Feature Selection

The dataset used in the experiment is the OHSUMED data, used in many experiments in information retrieval, including the TREC-9 filtering track. The OHSUMED test collection is a set of 348,566 references from MEDLINE, the online medical information database, consisting of titles and/or abstracts from 270 medical journals over a period 1987, developed by Hersh et al. at the Oregon Health Sciences University.

16.4.2 *n*-Gram Generation

The training text of size is 12,363 features constructed by evenly combining text blocks from the OHSUMED data corpus. Comprehensive *n*-gram statistics were automatically generated and stored for training text. Establish the experimental conditions by bi-grams with the training texts.

16.4.3 Evaluation

Feature selection and generalization techniques enable organizing and ranking the documents. The features retrieval performance using test set accuracy is to compare the above algorithms with the proposed method. The dynamic 0/1 knapsack algorithm is for initially selecting the features, which differs from greedy approaches that have been used by the other algorithms. This is because of a recursive approach that involves breaking a global problem down into more local subproblems and assumes an *optimal substructure*. There is a simple way to combine optimal solutions of subproblems to get an optimal global solution. The feature selection on its own has not improved accuracy and ranking, but feature selection combined with generalization is significantly better than all other algorithms. Here the relevance feedback algorithm is introduced for feedback documents identification that shows improved performance compared to the other methods.

Table 16.1 describes the evaluation metrics, and their corresponding equations are to evaluate the proposed system performance with other systems. Table 16.2 summarizes the

TABLE 16.1

Evaluation Metrics

Features	Description	Equation
Mean average precision (MAP)	The average of precisions computed at the points of each of the relevant documents in the ranked sequence	$\text{Avep} = \dfrac{\sum_{r=1}^{N}(P(r)Xrel(r))}{\text{number of relevant documents}}$ where r is the rank, N the number of retrieved documents, $rel()$ a binary function on the relevance of a given rank, and $P()$ precision at a given cut-off rank.
Normalized discount cumulative gain (NDCG)	Designed for measuring ranking accuracies when there are multiple levels of relevance judgment	$N(n) = Z_n \displaystyle\sum_{j=1}^{n} \dfrac{2^{R(j)}-1}{\log(1+j)}$　　(16.15) where n denotes position, $R(j)$ denotes score for rank j, and Z_n is a normalization factor to guarantee that a perfect ranking NDCG at position n equals 1.
Kendall tau distance	A metric that counts the number of pair-wise disagreements between two lists	$K(\tau_1,\tau_2) = \displaystyle\sum_{\{i,j\}\in P} \overline{K}_{i,j}(\tau_1,\tau_2)$ where K is Kendall tau distance, values i and j are orders of elements τ_1 and τ_2, and P is the set of unordered pairs of distinct elements.

TABLE 16.2

Performance Evaluation of Feature Selection Techniques

Methods	Normalized Discount Cumulative Gain	Mean Average Precision	Kendall Tau Distance
Markov random field	0.8406	0.7195	0.9560
Correlation	0.8346	0.6286	0.9425
Count difference	0.8222	0.6251	0.9192
Proposed	0.8464	0.7413	0.9685

relative performance results achieved on the test set, by the existing feature selection systems and the proposed dynamic selection system evaluated with mean average precision, normalized discount cumulative gain, and Kendall tau distance as evaluation metrics. Feature selection significantly improves MRF performance on three metrics compared to correlation and count difference methods.

As the tau distances become larger, then the selected features become more distinct, and a higher NDCG value indicates smaller loss. Similarly, the higher are the mean average precision values, the higher is the retrieved performance. Count difference has low mean average precision (MAP), NDCG, and Kendall tau distance values when compared to correlation. This is due to the following reasons: the high degree of feature interaction and some of the relevant features in isolation are not distinguished from the irrelevant ones.

Count difference focuses both on the relative relevant document frequency and relative irrelevant document frequency of the features and not on the similarity between the features while selecting them. If the feature's relevant document frequency is higher than the irrelevant document frequency, then that feature presents more relevant documents than irrelevant. This means that the feature is present in both classes, leading to feature diversion. Since some of the features selected are present in both the classes, the order of the documents does not suit much for ranking, which leads to low MAP (62.51%) and NDCG (82.22%) values than the other three methods. Moreover the features selected are not distinct. The proposed method has drastically reduced and removed irrelevant attributes in the dataset. Thus, the proposed approach produces the maximum MAP, NDCG, and Kendall tau values and performs better than the other existing methods.

In Table 16.3 the results of feature selection for MRF and proposed are more successful. Record the significant improvement on 9 and 11 features. Interestingly, improvement is on feature selectors with a higher number of features. Record significant degradation on a smaller number of features. It turns out the feature selectors that are unable to learn the concepts and accuracy cannot be achieved. The feature subsets chosen for correlation are more or less the same as those chosen for count difference.

TABLE 16.3

Statistics of Feature Selection

Features	Markov Random Field	Correlation	Count Difference	Proposed
3	0.5666	0.5731	0.5121	0.5556
7	0.6298	0.5946	0.5501	0.6623
9	0.6724	0.5972	0.5623	0.6739
11	0.6985	0.5987	0.5873	0.7088
13	0.7195	0.6286	0.6251	0.7413

TABLE 16.4

Statistics of Feedback Documents

Feedback Docs	Mean Average Precision
3	0.5556
5	0.6287
7	0.6379
9	0.7736
11	0.8009

Table 16.4 presents official test set results of 3–11, submitted feedback documents for the proposed method and calculated corresponding MAP values on the dataset. Feedback avoids the risk of bringing unwanted terms into the ranking model. Important terms from feedback documents have the potential to attract and retrieve more relevant documents. Use NDCG to evaluate the selected features, which results in features that are capable of ranking the relevant documents at the top from which the feedback documents (i.e., relevant to user) are chosen. Again from these user's judged documents, select the features using expectation maximization, which focuses mainly on term frequency. So when the number of feedback documents increases, the system selects the term having higher term frequency in EM. The results demonstrate a steady improvement in retrieval accuracy across MAP metrics with growing amounts of feedback. The MAP improvement is moving to five feedback documents—that is, a large amount of feedback (7.31% over three feedback documents).

Regarding MAP, it would seem topic drift caused by feedback is to hurt performance, though this loss diminishes as greater feedback reduces drift. However, observe a very different trend on MAP. This difference in trends is simply a by-product of differences between how feedback documents are selected for development and for test sets. Because official evaluation only included top-ranked documents in pooling, assessment biases in favor of easier topics for which many relevant documents would be seen appear early in the ranked list.

Table 16.5 presents the proposed method performance difference with and without considering the feedback documents and features. It is clear that the MAP is always higher for the proposed system with feedback because of the expectation maximization relevance feedback approach, the best optimization algorithm. The relative performance increase on more features is somewhat better for MAP. Selecting features from user-judged (i.e., feedback) documents and ranking again the test documents with these features will be more relevant. The order of relevancy suits more the BM25 ranking which leads to higher MAP values than ranking without considering the feedback documents. The working hypothesis of the experimental results improves document ranking EM relevance feedback algorithm by taking the number of occurrences of terms in documents into account.

Figure 16.2 shows the MAP values achieved by all four feature selection methods on the test set, and proves that the proposed approach outperforms other methods. All

TABLE 16.5

Feature Selection Method with/without Feedback

Methods	Feedback	Without Feedback
Proposed	0.7413	0.7013

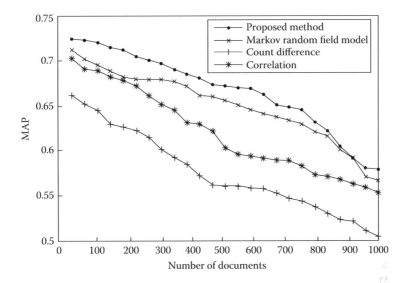

FIGURE 16.2
MAP versus number of documents.

four methods show decrements in the MAP value with the increment in the number of documents.

The reasons are as follows: all four methods such as correlation coefficient, count difference, MRF, and the proposed method present the relevant documents at the top, which results in large MAP values. If the number of documents is less in number, MAP emphasizes ranking relevant documents higher. Then when the number of documents continues to increase, the number of relevant documents remains the same, and relevant document positions do not change, which leads to low MAP values as MAP is the average precision computed at the point of the relevant documents in the ranked sequence. Moreover, an increase in the number of documents might result in more irrelevant documents than relevant ones, which thereby decreases the MAP value.

17

TDCCREC: An Efficient and Scalable Web-Based Recommendation System[*]

A Web recommenders system (WRS) is a Web-based interactive software agent. A WRS attempts to predict user preferences from user data and/or user access data for facilitating and personalizing user's experience by providing them with recommendation lists of suggested items. The recommended items could be products, such as books, movies, and music CDs, or online resources, such as web pages or online activities (*Path Prediction*).

With the explosive growth of knowledge available on the World Wide Web, which lacks an integrated structure or schema, it becomes much more difficult for users to access relevant information efficiently. Recommenders systems are a solution to information overload. The kind of broad-based recommenders (Shen et al. 2005) systems where we just match a set of users with other people, in general, are useful in situations where people have differing tastes and to find like-minded users. Different people like different styles, so we might want to use it for that. In general it is better for recognizing things where taste matters. Recommendation systems can play the role of a "peer reviewer" to continuously check changes and suggest quality improvement measures. Two main features are offered: detecting and highlighting areas that are error prone, and recommending patterns to increase the work product quality. Thus, recommenders systems provide many benefits to the users.

17.1 Recommendation Methodologies

Learning automata algorithms for web page recommendations are on the user's navigational behavior in a website to discover usage patterns that will generate recommendations for new users with similar profiles (Kleinberg 1999). This method is purely on the usage of previous user sessions, and it does not consider those pages content (Mobasher et al. 2000a). The connectivity feature of a Web graph plays an important role in the process of recommendation. The main drawback of a learning automata (LA)-based recommenders algorithm is that recommendation set computation is time consuming and limits the algorithm's performance.

Weighted association (WA) rule mining is when each web page has a weight based on the frequency of visits and duration spent on those web pages. Association rule mining is an important model in data mining. Many mining algorithms discover all web page associations (or rules) in the data that satisfy the user-specified minimum support and confidence constraints. Weights associated with web pages solve the question of importance of web pages (Borodin et al. 2005). The challenge of using weights in the iterative process is generating large frequent item sets. These item sets are for recommending the web pages.

[*] Source of publication: https://doaj.org/toc/2229-6956/1/2; ictactjournals.in/paper/ijsc2_page_70_77.pdf. Original material available in *ICTACT Journal on Soft Computing*, 1(2), 70–77, October 2010.

The problem with WA is that the process of matching a current user's session with all the generated rules requires a lot of time.

Content-based recommendation (Mobasher et al. 2000a) is one of the methods of recommending web pages. Here web pages are represented as *n*-grams that compare the frequency of *n*-gram occurrence present in the current user profile and in the user's history (Balabanovic and Shoham 1997). Hence this method takes into account the web pages content and is not based only on the usage. Systems that recommend web pages to the user based on web page description and a profile of the user's interests are content-based systems (Mooney and Roy 2000). Lack of diversity is one of the limitations in content-based approaches.

Collaborative filtering (CF) (Hofman and Puzicha 1999) technique, the basic idea is to offer web page recommendations or predictions based on the opinions of other like-minded users. The opinions of users are obtained explicitly from the users or by using some implicit measures (Deshpande and Karypis 2004). CF (Hofman and Puzicha 1999), the prevalent recommendation approach, has been successfully used to find users characterized as "similar" according to their logged history of prior transactions. However, limited CF applicability is due to the sparse problem, which refers to a situation in which the recommendations are only on previously rated web pages.

By considering these methods and taking advantage of both content and CF, and to improve the efficiency of the above-mentioned methods, propose a new system that provides the trustworthiness of websites and fact confidence. This system is mainly concerned with analyzing Web usage logs, discovering similar web pages from the Web logs, and making recommendations based on the extracted *n*-grams. Feed the pages with highest similarity (Erk 2007) to a truth finder process that finds the trustworthiness of those web pages and the fact confidence present in them. CF (Hofman and Puzicha 1999) is commercially the most successful approach for the generation of a recommendation set.

17.1.1 Learning Automata (LA)

Learning automata is one of the methodologies for recommending web pages. This algorithm includes a finite number of actions performed in a random environment, when a specific action is taken, the environment provides a random response that is either favorable or unfavorable (Kleinberg 1999). The objective in the design of the *learning automaton* is to find how the choice of the action at any stage is guided by past actions and responses.

Transition probability matrix: The initial step is to build a graph using the websites present in the user logs with vertices and edges. Let $G = (V, E)$, where V represents the web pages and E represents the links between them from the page x to y (Thathachar and Harita Bhaskar 1987). Then compute a transition matrix P using

$$P_{ij} = \begin{cases} \dfrac{1}{\deg(x_i)} & \text{if}: (x_i \rightarrow y_j) \in E \\ 0 : \text{otherwise} \end{cases} \tag{17.1}$$

Path probabilities: Compute the path probabilities for the transactions of the user as follows:

$$P_r(p_1 \rightarrow p_2 \rightarrow p_3 \ldots \rightarrow = p_k) X \prod_{i=2}^{k} \Pr\left(\frac{p_i}{p_{i-m}} \ldots p_{i-1} \right) \tag{17.2}$$

where $P_r(\bullet \rightarrow \bullet)$ represents the transition probability value, and $P_r()$ represents $q(j)/(\Sigma_{j\in V} q(j))$ the page rank determined by who visits the page i, and V is the set of learning automata. Finally present the pages with high probability values to the current user.

Drawbacks: The LA suffers from a serious drawback that the system considers only the usage—that is, the previous user's Web logs. It will not consider the particular web page content. These systems are mainly concerned with analyzing Web usage logs, discovering patterns from this data, and making recommendations based on the extracted knowledge. Unlike traditional personalization techniques, LA mainly recommend a set (referred to as the recommendation set) of items of interest to the user base, their decisions on user ratings on different items, or other explicit feedback provided by the user. In LA in fact, if two consecutive recommended page sets are too different, then the user may consider the system as unstable and will not pay any more attention to it after a while.

17.1.2 Weighted Association Rule

In this approach each web page p has assigned a weight measure for approximating the degree of interest of a web page to the user (Borodin et al. 2005). The general assumption is that high-frequency web pages are of high interest to the user.

$$\text{Frequency}(p) = \frac{\text{Number of Visits}(p)}{\sum_{p\in\text{Visited Pages}}(\text{Number of Visits}(p))} \tag{17.3}$$

$$\text{Duration}(p) = \frac{\text{Total Duration}(p)\text{Length}(p)}{\max_{p\in\text{Visited Pages}}(\text{Total}(\text{Duration}(p)/\text{Length}(p)))} \tag{17.4}$$

$$\text{Weight}(p) = \text{Frequency}(p) * \text{Duration}(p) \tag{17.5}$$

After finding the weight for each page according to Equation 17.5, compute the following to recommend the web pages (Fellbaum 1998).

Calculate the weight of each item set X present in a transaction t using Equation 17.6 and weights associated with pages present in a transaction $w(t_k)$ and computed using Equation 17.7:

$$w(x,t) = \begin{cases} \min(w(p_1, p_2, \ldots, p_n)) X \subseteq t \\ 0 \quad X \nsubseteq t \end{cases} \tag{17.6}$$

$$w(t_k) = \frac{\sum_{i=1}^{|t_k|} w(p_i)}{|t_k|} \tag{17.7}$$

where $w(p_i)$ is the weight of web page i, and $(p_1, p_2\ldots p_n)$ are web pages in the transaction; t_k is the set of transactions in the entire user session. Calculate the weighted support count and confidence of each item set in a transaction using Equations 17.8 and 17.9 (Mobasher et al. 2000a,b), where w_i is mean weight of web pages, $w(X, t_i)$ is the weight of an item set, and $w(t_k)$ is the weight of transactions. Apply APRIORI algorithm for finding the frequent item sets:

$$wsp(X) = \frac{\sum_{t_i \in T} w(t_i) * w(X, t_i)}{\overline{w} * \sum_{k=1}^{|t|} w(t_k)} \tag{17.8}$$

$$wconf(X \Rightarrow Y) = \frac{wsp(X \cup Y)}{wsp(X)} \tag{17.9}$$

For those item sets generated using APRIORI algorithm, find the item confidence. $wsp(X)$ is item set weighted support, where X and Y are the item sets. The recommendation of a web page needs two parameters, namely, similarity (Erk 2007) and recommendation score:

$$\text{Dissimilarity}(S, r_L) = \sum_{i:r_{Li}>0} \left[\frac{2 * (w(s_i) - w(r_{Li}))}{w(s_i) + w(r_{Li})} \right]^2 \tag{17.10}$$

$$\text{MathScore}(S, r_L) = 1 - \frac{1}{4} \sqrt{\frac{\text{Dissimilarity}(S, r_{Li})}{\sum_{i:r_{Li}>0} 1}} \tag{17.11}$$

$$w_i = \begin{cases} \text{weight}(p_i, r_{Li}), & \text{if} : p_i \in r_L \\ 0 : \text{otherwise} \end{cases} \tag{17.12}$$

where $w(r_{Li})$ is the left-hand side of weighted association rule $r_L = (w_1, w_2 \ldots w_m)$, and $w(s_i)$ is nothing but significance weight—that is, if a user has visited the page p_i in a session, then 1, $s_i = 0$ otherwise (Deshpande and Karypis 2004):

$$\text{Rec}(S, X \Rightarrow p) = \text{MatchScore}(S, X) * wconf(X \Rightarrow p) \tag{17.13}$$

As a result, present the web pages with high Rec value to the active user by calculating the needed parameters using Equations 17.10 and 17.11.

Drawbacks: In the association rule mining area, most of the research efforts are first to improve the algorithmic performance and second to reduce the output set by allowing the possibility to express constraints on the desired results. It simply divides pages into interesting and uninteresting groups, and neglects the difference in the degrees of interest. One of the main drawbacks of association rule algorithms is that the used algorithms have too many parameters. The obtained rules are also too many, most of them noninteresting and with low comprehensibility. This method assumes a fixed weight for each item while in the context of web usage mining; a page might have different importance in different sessions. The process of matching a current users' session with all the generated rules requires a lot of time.

17.1.3 Content-Based Recommendation

In order to provide recommendations, we need to generate *n*-grams for the current user and the user history. An *n*-gram is a subsequence of *n* items from a given sequence (Cavnar

1994). It is a type of probabilistic model for predicting the next item in such a sequence (Mooney and Roy 2000). If two strings of real text have a similar vector representation, then they are likely similar.

After generating n-grams (Ding 1999), cosine similarity, which is a measure of similarity between the user history and the active user profile, is determined by finding the cosine of the angle between them:

$$\text{Similarity} = \cos(\varphi) = \frac{L \cdot M}{\|L\| \|M\|} \tag{17.14}$$

where
  L and M are usually term weights, where $w_i = tf_i * \log(n/df_i)$.
  tf = number of occurrences of the tf_i (n-gram) in that web page.
  n = total number of web pages.
  df_i = number of web pages in which tf_i(n-gram) appears at least once. Web pages are recommended with top n similar values to the active user.

Drawbacks: The main limitation of content-based filtering is the lack of diversity in the recommendations. User studies have shown that users find online recommenders most useful when they recommend unexpected items, highlighting the fact that overspecialization by content-based filtering systems is a serious drawback. Common approaches to dealing with this problem of overspecialization include explicitly injecting diversity into the recommendation set.

17.1.4 Collaborative Filtering-Based Recommendation

Collaborative filtering is a method of making automatic predictions (filtering) about the interests of a user by collecting taste information from similar-minded users (collaborating). Through this method of filtering, user groups use and test the web page and provide ratings or vote as a feedback that is relevant to the item and the class in which it falls.

Initially find similar users, that is, nearest neighboring users (Anand and Mobasher 2005). Two users are similar-minded users if they have at least two commonly rated web pages (Balabanovic and Shoham 1997). Compute the similarity between them by Pearson correlation coefficient using

$$P_{a,u} = \frac{\sum_{i=1}^{m} (v_{a,i} - \overline{v_a}) \times (v_{u,i} - \overline{v_u})}{\sqrt{\sum_{i=1}^{m} (v_{a,i} - \overline{v_a})^2 \times \sum_{i=1}^{m} (v_{u,i} - \overline{v_u})^2}} \tag{17.15}$$

where $v_{a,i}$ is ratings for item i by active user a; $v_{u,i}$ is the ratings for item i by user in history u; v_a is the mean ratings by active user a; v_u is the mean ratings by user in history u; and m is the total number of items. Then consider n users who have highest similarity with active users as neighbors. Using the neighbors calculate the predictions as shown:

$$p_{a,i} = \overline{v_a} + \frac{\sum_{u=1}^{n} (v_{u,i} - \overline{v_u}) \times p_{a,u}}{\sum_{u=1}^{n} p_{a,u}} \tag{17.16}$$

These predictions are to predict web pages for the active user. The web pages with the highest vote calculated using Equation 17.16 are presented to the user.

Drawbacks: One of the main characteristics in collaborative filtering, compared to content-based filtering, is that the method knows nothing about the item's true content or what they are about. This means that they only rely on preference values, such as ratings, to generate the recommendations. This means that performance of penetration of each item is highly dependent on other user's ratings and might introduce averaging effects. The averaging effect causes the overall most popular items to be recommended more often, which means that they will be consumed and rated more frequently as a result.

Two other issues are generally well known and often associated with collaborative filtering: the first-rater problem and cold-start problem. The first-rater problem is by new items in the system that understandably has not yet received any ratings from any users. The system is unable to generate semantic interconnections to these items and therefore is never recommended. Similarly, the cold-start problem is by new users in the system, which have not submitted any ratings. Without any information about the user, the system is not able to guess the user's preferences and generate recommendations until a few items have been rated.

17.2 Proposed Approach: Truth Discovery-Based Content and Collaborative Recommender System (TDCCREC)

Lots of information retrieved by search engines can be conflicting and of varying quality (from low to high quality), therefore, a new approach is introduced, which includes methodologies like collaborative filtering, content-based filtering, and incorporation of a truth finder to judge the trustworthiness of the web page and confidence of the facts present in the web pages that the system recommends. Figure 17.1 describes the architecture of the proposed recommenders system.

This consists of two main categories:

Category A: If the current users' profile exists (collaborative filtering)

    Step 1: Filter out web pages from the user logs using the Pearson correlation coefficient.

    Step 2: Find the nearest neighbors.

    Step 3: Present the web pages with the highest prediction values to the active user.

Category B: If the current users' profile does not exist, then (content-based recommendation with truth finder)

    Step 1: Generate *n*-grams (tri-grams) from both the current user and the history.

    Step 2: Find cosine similarity between current and previous user pages.

    Step 3: Apply a truth finder algorithm for those pages with high similarity.

Truth finder: The ultimate aim here is to find two parameters: confidence of facts and trustworthiness of websites. We have to find the two parameters only for those websites with greater similarity values (Resnik 1995). Facts are the properties that describe a

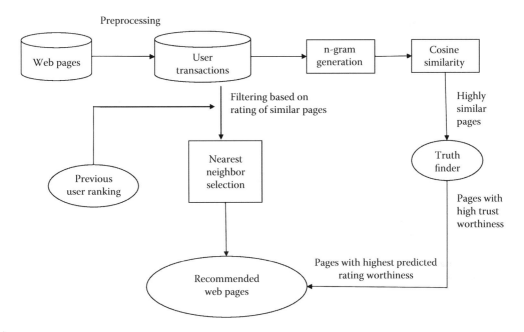

FIGURE 17.1
Architecture of the recommender system.

particular object. For example, the objects are book, movie, music, web page, and so on. This section considers admission dates of DePaul University website as an object.

Most people rely on small trusted groups of contacts to get their news and information, but when these arrive from some source outside their trusted circle, it is much harder to tell whether certain information is true or not. Users may be tempted to distrust things that use a lot of adjectives, adverbs, and loaded terms. And certainly users are suspicious. But sometimes people just write that way; it does not mean they are lying. The main thing is to find the facts—that is, objects—and just ignore the appearances. Measure the trust in any object by willingness of visitors to interact with it in some way. When the object is a web page, it is not just looking at the page, but believing the information presented, or acting on it. Trust cannot be totally rational, because it can never be based on enough experience. If a website is trying to convince us to believe one thing but actually talks about another thing, then the website is not trustworthy.

Trustworthiness of websites $tw(ws)$ is the prospected or expected confidence of facts $s(f)$ given by website ws:

$$tw(ws) = \frac{\sum_{f \in F(ws)} s(f)}{|F(ws)|} \tag{17.17}$$

where $F(ws)$ is the set of facts given by ws, and $tw(ws)$ is the trustworthiness of the website w. Many people may have seen the same source and reported on it themselves. They may have described it differently. We may never know exactly what was said, but if people on different sides of the same issue agree on what was said, then it is more likely to be true.

Confidence of facts $s(f)$ is the probability of fact f to be accurate according to the best of our wisdom.

Case 1: If an object has only one fact, then $s(f)$ is

$$s(f) = 1 - \prod_{w \in W(f)} 1 - tw(ws) \qquad (17.18)$$

Case 2: If an object has different facts f_1 and f_2, then $s(f)$ will be

$$s(f) = \frac{1}{1 + e^{-\gamma \sigma^*(f)}} \qquad (17.19)$$

where $W(f)$ is the set of facts provided by the website ws, and γ is the dampening factor (0.3 here), and ρ is the weight of objects. In order to facilitate the computation, the trustworthiness score of the website represents w as

$$\tau(ws) = -\ln(1 - 1 - t(ws)) \qquad (17.20)$$

$\tau(ws)$ is the trustworthiness score of the website ws. As this score increases, the trustworthiness of websites also increases. Equation 17.21 shows the confidence score $\sigma(f)$ of a fact f, where $\sigma^*(f)$ is the adjusted confidence score and *base_sim* is assumed as a constant value of some threshold level:

$$\sigma(f) = -\ln(1 - s(f)) \qquad (17.21)$$

$$\sigma^*(f) = \sigma(f) + p \cdot \sum_{\sigma(f') = \sigma(f)} \sigma(f') \cdot imp(f' \to f) \qquad (17.22)$$

$$imp(f_1 \to f_2) sim(f_1 = f_2) - base\_sim \qquad (17.23)$$

Algorithm (Truth Finder)

INPUT: The set of websites W, the set of facts F, and links between the web pages
OUTPUT: Website trustworthiness and fact confidence.
Calculate matrices A and B (using Equations 17.24 and 17.25).
For each $ws \in W$
$tw(ws) \leftarrow t_0$
$\tau(ws) \leftarrow -\ln(1 - t(ws))$
Repeat
$\vec{\sigma^*} \leftarrow B\vec{\tau}$
Compute $\vec{s}$ from $\vec{\sigma^*}$
$\vec{tw'} \leftarrow \vec{tw}$
$\vec{tw} \leftarrow A\vec{s}$

Compute $\vec{\tau}$ from $\vec{t}$ until cosine similarity of $\vec{tw}$ and $\vec{tw'}$ is greater than $1 - \delta$, where δ is maximum difference between two iterations and it is set as 0.001%.

Calculations and recommendation schema for the above algorithm: To implement the algorithm, we consider the above-mentioned equations such as trustworthiness of websites, trustworthiness score, confidence of facts, and confidence scores as vectors—that is, Equations 17.18 through 17.23.

$$\vec{t} = (t(ws_1)...,t(ws_M))^T \quad \vec{\tau} = (\tau(ws_1)...,\tau(ws_M))^T$$
$$\vec{\sigma^*} = (\sigma^*(f_1)...,\sigma^*(f_N))^T \quad \vec{s} = (s(f_1)...,s(f_N))^T$$

$$\vec{tw} \leftarrow \overline{As}\vec{\sigma^*} \leftarrow B\vec{\tau}$$

where A is an $m \times n$ matrix, m is the number of websites, and n is number of facts and is an $n \times m$ matrix, which is a transpose of the A matrix:

$$A_{ij} = \begin{cases} 1/|F(ws_i)|, & \text{if}: f_j \in F(ws_i), \\ 0: \text{otherwise} \\ 1, \text{if}: ws_i \text{ provides } f_j \end{cases} \tag{17.24}$$

$$B_{ij} = p \cdot imp(f_k \to f_i), \quad \text{if}: w_i \text{ provides } f_k \text{ and } o(f_k) = o(f_j)$$
$$0: \text{otherwise} \tag{17.25}$$

$o(f)$ is an object that the fact is about. Both A and B are sparse matrices. Compute the website trustworthiness and fact confidence conveniently with matrix operations. The above procedure is very different from Authority-Hub analysis. It involves nonlinear transformations and thus cannot be computed using eigenvector computation. Authority-Hub analysis defines the authority scores and hub scores as the sum of each other. On the other hand, a truth finder studies the probabilities of websites being correct and facts being true, which cannot be defined as simple summations because the probability is often computed in nonlinear ways. That is why a truth finder algorithm requires iterative computation to achieve convergence. Stop the algorithm until the last two iterations have same values. The proposed work presents the websites with high trustworthiness value to the active user.

17.3 Empirical Results and Discussion

Datasets: The dataset has the preprocessed and filtered data from the main DePaul CTI Web server (http://www.cs.depaul.edu). The data are on a random sample of users visiting this site for a 2-week period during April 2002. The original (unfiltered) data contained a total of 20,950 sessions from 5446 users. The filtered data files were produced by filtering low support page views, and eliminating sessions of size 1. The filtered data contain 13,745 sessions and 683 page views.

Evaluation Metrics: The increasing number of web pages retrieved when a query has been posed is an irritating issue for the users when situations arise as to which page is to be viewed first. These pages have to be indexed in different environments, particularly on the Internet. There is a lack of scalability of a single centralized index leading to the use of distributed information retrieval systems to effectively search for and locate the required information with ease. This section discusses the entire system performance using metrics like precision, coverage, freshness, similarity, and weight of the retrieved web pages.

Precision: This is the fraction of the documents retrieved that are relevant to the user's information need.

$$\text{Precision} = \frac{|\{\text{Relevant web pages}\} \cap \{\text{Retrieved web pages}\}|}{\{\text{Retrieved web pages}\}} \quad (17.26)$$

Coverage: This is the fraction of the documents relevant to the query and successfully retrieved:

$$\text{Coverage} = \frac{|\{\text{Relevant web pages}\} \cap \{\text{Retrieved web pages}\}|}{\{\text{Relevant web pages}\}} \quad (17.27)$$

Similarity: This is one of the metrics used for evaluating the performance of the proposed system. Many measures of similarities are available. Consider cosine similarity between web pages and processes using Equation 17.14.

Mean absolute deviation: The MAD (mean absolute deviation or mean deviation) represents the measurements of the average of the absolute deviations of data points from their mean. Literally, recommendations deviate from true user-specified values and are computed by

$$\text{MAD} = \sum_{i=1}^{N} \frac{|X_i - \bar{X}|}{N} \quad (17.28)$$

where X_i is the observed values, $\bar{X}$ is the average, and N is the number of values.

Support: This is the percentage of sessions in which the page view occurs.

Transaction weight: This is a weighting measure calculated from web logs to extract the interest of web pages for the visitor. Compute this by Equation 17.7.

Apply the above algorithms on a standard dataset and experiments show that the proposed recommender system performs better than the other algorithms, and at the same time, the proposed system is less complex with respect to memory usage and computational cost. Table 17.1 proves that the supplemented evaluation metrics are high for the

TABLE 17.1

Performance Evaluation of Web Page Recommender Systems

Method	Similarity	Mean Absolute Deviation	Transaction Weight	Support (%)
LA	0.5081	0.68	0.6123	55.62
WA	0.5123	0.63	0.6379	59.21
CF	0.8171	0.48	0.8354	70.45
Content based	0.8314	0.43	0.8566	72.90
Content and usage	0.7850	0.52	0.7992	69.34
Usage and CF based	0.7581	0.55	0.7867	67.11
Content and CF based	0.8423	0.4	0.8662	75.23
Proposed system	0.8598	0.3	0.8711	78.05

proposed system. Use metrics like mean absolute deviation, similarity, transaction weight of retrieved web pages, and support. The mean absolute deviation here shows that the proposed system works well. Lower MAD values indicate that the recommendation system predicts good recommendations. The MAD values are more—that is, around 60% and above for LA and WA systems. This is because both methods gave importance only for the usage patterns, while this is somewhat low for content-based and CF systems, as their recommendation is on content of the web pages and ratings.

As far as the metric similarity is concerned, LA provides only 50% similarity due to the reason that it analyzes the previous user logs from the extracted knowledge. While comparing with LA, WA has somewhat better results, because it focuses on duration, frequency, and interest of web pages additionally. The combined form of the content-based and the CF-based methods has a preferable similarity of about 84%. Infer from Table 17.1 that the proposed system can perform recommendations significantly, as it gains higher similarity than the other conventional methods.

Also TDCCREC gains higher transaction weight with parameters that are nothing but the frequency and duration. It seems natural to assume that web pages with higher frequency are of strong interest to the user. Support, which is one of the evaluation metrics, indicates that the proposed system has a better quantity of support count than the other methods. As said earlier, the TDCCREC system has lesser deviation (MAD) with increase in similarity, transaction weight, and support.

When content is considered as the important parameter in the proposed framework, it outperforms the other methods. But in spite of combining the content and usage methods, incorporate an efficient algorithm called the truth finder that gives support and increases the efficiency of the proposed work. Conduct a detailed comparative evaluation on different combined methods and recommendation techniques that affect the prediction accuracy of the proposed recommender. Considering Figures 17.2 and 17.3, we can see that the precision decreases when we increase the coverage, as expected. It shows that precision is

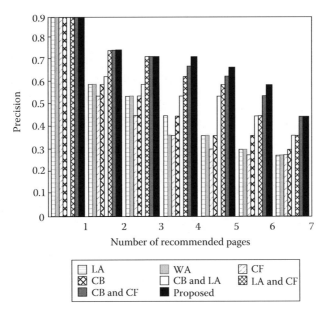

FIGURE 17.2
Comparison of proposed algorithm precision with other existing methods.

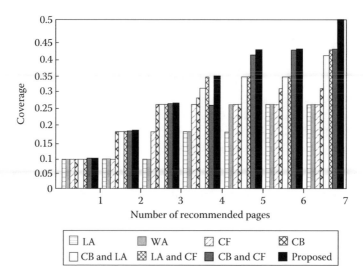

FIGURE 17.3
Comparison of proposed algorithm coverage with other existing methods.

inversely proportional to the coverage. As a result, some websites, for example, those with high link density, may favor a recommender system with high precision, while some others may favor a system with high coverage. The reason for learning automata to gain lowest precision is that it recommends web pages merely based only on the usage (Ishikawa et al. 2002). Nevertheless, it does not take the web page content into account. It can be concluded that the proposed approach is capable of making Web recommendations more accurately and efficiently against the conventional methods.

18

An Automatic Facet Generation Framework for Document Retrieval[*]

Traditionally, information retrieval systems return a ranked list of query results based on the similarity between the user's query and the documents. Unfortunately, returned results are often redundant. Users may need to reformulate their search to find the specific topic they are interested in. This active searching process leads to inefficiencies, especially in cases where queries or information needs are ambiguous. Thus, this leads to continuously reformulating the search query to discover all the facets of the event. Finding a list of facets that documents collection covers is an important problem in information retrieval. Use facets to describe or summarize the collection, or to cluster the collection. Facets provide a short and informative description of the documents used for quickly browsing and finding related documents.

The method introduced in this section differs from previous traditional methodologies and evaluates its effectiveness with three common approaches such as baseline, greedy, and feedback language models. A baseline facet identification system has four main parts: a preprocessor, a (standard) document retrieval system, a (standard) clustering package, and a labeler. The greedy method (Peng 2007) is for topic detection that automatically identifies the different facets of an event. It uses point-wise Kullback–Leibler (KL) divergence (Probst et al. 2007) along with the Jaccard coefficient to build a topic graph that represents the community structure of the different facets. Formulate the problem as a weighted set cover problem with dynamically varying weights. The algorithm is domain independent and generates a representative set of informative and discriminative phrases that cover the entire event. In feedback language models, with term-based feedback (Spink 1994), a user *directly* judges the relevance of individual terms without interaction with feedback documents, taking full control of the query expansion (Allan 1995) process. A cluster-based method is used for selecting terms to present the user for judgment, as well as effective algorithms such as combination of term and cluster feedback for constructing refined query language models from user term feedback. These approaches are to bring significant improvement in retrieval accuracy over a nonfeedback baseline, and achieve comparable performance to relevance feedback. They are helpful even when there are no relevant documents in the top.

In the proposed automatic facet generation framework (AFGF), the effort is made to fully automate the faceted interfaces construction, which is an *unsupervised* approach for extracting useful facets from a text collection. This technique relies on Word Net (Fellbaum 1998) hypernyms and on a Jaccard coefficient to assign new keywords to facets. The proposed method differs from the supervised learning technique that has some limitations. First, since the supervised learning technique relied on the facets that could be identified, it was, by definition, limited to the facets that appeared in the training set. Second, while the algorithm generated high-quality facets of keyword-annotated objects, the respective hierarchy's quality built on top of text documents was comparatively low.

[*] Source of publication: doi:10.1109/ACE.2010.63; http://dl.acm.org/citation.cfm?id=1844789. Original material available in *ACE '10 Proceedings of the 2010 International Conference on Advances in Computer Engineering*, pp. 110–114, Washington, DC: IEEE Computer Society, 2010.

18.1 Baseline Approach

The baseline facet identification (Fujimura et al. 2006) system has a preprocessor, a (standard) document retrieval system, a (standard) clustering package, and a labeler. A standard text preprocessing is performed, which includes stemming and stop-word removal, recognizing index phrases and named entities (NE). Use the standard information retrieval system for document retrieval. The baseline method uses a bag-of-words approach, where all phrases in the documents are features for clustering. Use an efficient stemmer to reduce the words to their stems (and conflate, e.g., singular and plural forms), which has the additional advantage of feature reduction. To further reduce the number of features, prune rare terms and stop-words and finally remove them. The feature set that remains after stemming and stop-word removal is the baseline feature set. In this approach, labels prediction for phrases is unclear because of the overused words feature set. These labels are often numbers or single letters and are due to the noisy nature of text collection. With clusters as input, the labeler produces a ranked list of candidate labels with a confidence score for each cluster. Choose the highest scoring label (per cluster) as the cluster label. Then duplicate detection is performed. If one of the cluster labels is also a label for another cluster, retain the label with the highest confidence. If a system removes a label, then add a new candidate label. This continues until no duplicates are left.

18.1.1 Drawbacks

- The labels prediction for phrases is unclear because of the overused words feature set.
- These labels are often numbers or single letters due to the noisy nature of text collection.
- This method also has a tendency to select stop-words as labels.
- It gives more importance to the terms that had higher term frequency and ignores other conceptually important terms.
- It provides poor precision compared to other methods.

18.2 Greedy Algorithm

Greedy algorithms are simple and straightforward. They are used to solve optimization problems. But it is more difficult to determine whether a greedy algorithm always produces an optimal solution. It computes a cost for each key phrase interactively and selects the key phrase with the highest cost. Generate the key phrases from the retrieved document set by text preprocessing. The cost of a key phrase should be such that a phrase with very high coverage is not chosen, and at the same time no words with very low document frequency are chosen since a very small collection of documents cannot judge a topic.

Figure 18.1 describes the pseudo-code for the greedy algorithm (Peng 2007). Form a general cost function from a linear combination of the three cost components, namely, relative document size $f_1(w_i)$, redundancy penalty $f_2(w_i)$, and subtopic redundancy memory effect $R(w_i)$. Provide two parameters α and β to represent the trade-off between coverage,

---

Algorithm Greedy algorithm for weighted set-cover

Input: Graph $G = (W,D,E)$, N: number of documents to cover

1. Output: Set of discriminative phrases for different topics
2. $W = \{w_1, w_2, w_n\}$
3. $W_{chosen} = \Phi$ & num_docs_covered = 0
4. While num_docs_covered < N
5.   do for $w_i \in W$
6.   do cost(w_i) = $\alpha \times f_1(w_i) + \beta \times f_2(w_i) + (1 - (\alpha + \beta)) \times R(w_i)$
7. $W_{selected}$ = argmax$_w$ cost(W_i)
8.   for $w_i \in W$
9.   do $R(w_i) = R(w_i) + J(W_{selected}, w_i)$
10.   num_docs_covered = num_docs_covered + adj($W_{selected}$)
11. $W_{chosen} = W_{chosen} \{W_{selected}\}$
12. $W = W - \{W_{selected}\}$
13. $D = D - $ adj(selected)
14. Return W_{chosen}

FIGURE 18.1
A greedy set-cover algorithm for detecting subtopics.

cohesiveness, and intersection; J ($w_{selected}, w_i$) is the Jaccard similarity coefficient between the selected word $w_{selected}$ with the remaining words; $G = (W,D,E)$ is the undirected graph, where W is the set of candidate phrases generated by the first step and D is the entire set of documents, E is the set of edges between W and D where there is an edge between a phrase and a document if the document has the phrase; and $|adj(w_{selected})|$ is the document frequency of the word. Note that the algorithm recomputes the costs several times. This is because the cost of a key phrase may change due to a change in any of the three components. After selecting a key phrase, it might make another key phrase redundant, which is covering the same content. This makes the problem a dynamic weighted set cover problem. Hence, the performance guarantees associated with the greedy algorithm for the weighted set cover problem do not hold true for the dynamic version.

18.2.1 Drawbacks

- It is more difficult to determine whether a greedy algorithm always produces an optimal solution.
- It is often hard to figure out when being greedy works.
- Solutions to the subproblems do not have to be known at each stage; instead a "greedy" choice can be made of what looks best for the moment.
- A disadvantage of the greedy algorithm is that it needs to compute minimum cost flow $k (k + 1)/2$ times.

18.3 Feedback Language Model

The feedback language model considers a more direct way to involve a user in query model improvement. The idea is to present a (reasonable) number of individual terms to the user and ask him or her to judge the relevance of each term or directly specify their probabilities in the query model. Presenting proper terms selection to the user for judgment is crucial to the success of the feedback language model (Allan 1995). It is important to carefully select presentation terms to maximize expected gain from user feedback—that is, those that can potentially reveal most evidence of the user's information need. It considers the top N documents from an initial retrieval using the original query from the source of feedback terms; it then presents all terms as candidates to the user. These documents serve as pseudo-feedback, because they provide a much richer context than the original query (usually very short), while the user is not asked to judge their relevance. Most of the time, the presentation list may not include all the important terms.

Feedback language models such as term feedback, cluster feedback, and term cluster feedback are explained in Section 10.3.

18.4 Proposed Method: Automatic Facet Generation Framework (AFGF)

In this section a proposed approach is for facet generation on the documents collection and examines several methods and evaluates on the OHSUMED dataset from a TREC-9 filtering track.

The proposed method contribution on facet generation focuses on

- Generating informative and unambiguous facets
- Constructing facets that cover the larger part of the text collection
- Exploring facets with minimum overlapping
- Building the facet hierarchies and finding the associated facets

Pruning the facet with point-wise KL divergence: The point-wise KL divergence (Probst et al. 2007) score δ_w is computed for each bigram w in the retrieved documents, which gives the relative importance of the bigram in the retrieved document set compared to the generic corpus. The point-wise KL divergence score of the bigram w is

$$\delta_w(p \parallel q) = p(w) \log \frac{p(w)}{q(w)} \tag{18.1}$$

where $p(w)$ is the probability distribution of bigram w in the retrieved document set, and $q(w)$ is the probability distribution of bigram w in the generic corpus. Now eliminate bigrams whose δ_w is less than a threshold θ. Based on the word overlapping of bigrams, perform clustering. Consider the terms from each cluster that have more overlapping with other elements as represented by the Jaccard similarity coefficient.

Identify the similarity between the phrases using the Jaccard similarity coefficient: Compute the pair-wise Jaccard coefficient between the target and every other key phrase. The pair-wise coefficient vector provides information on how much overlap there is between a key phrase and every other key phrase. Phrases with a high average Jaccard coefficient are general facets that cover the entire cluster. The Jaccard similarity coefficient is as follows:

$$J(A, B) = \frac{|A \cap B|}{|A \cup B|} \tag{18.2}$$

where $J(A,B)$ is the Jaccard similarity value between the key phrases A and B. The average Jaccard similarity f_1 is

$$f_1 = \frac{\sum_{w_j \in W - w_i} J(W_i, W_j)}{|W| - 1} \tag{18.3}$$

where W is the set of key phrases in the cluster.

Finding associated facets using Word Net: For each facet discovered, identify the semantically related words with the help of Word Net (Vossen 2001). Figure 18.2a and b represents the core tree construction by using paths derived from unambiguous terms (facet). A term is unambiguous if it meets at least one of two conditions:

- The term has only one sense within Word Net.
- (Optional) The term matches one of the preselected Word Net domains.

The next step is to add the paths for the remaining facets that are ambiguous according to Word Net (Fellbaum 1998) and presented in Figure 18.2c. When confronted with a facet that has multiple possible IS-A paths corresponding to multiple senses, the system favors the more common path over other alternatives.

Two rules are used for compressing the tree:

- Starting from the leaves, recursively eliminate a parent that has fewer than k children, unless the parent is the root or has an item count larger than $0.1 \times$ (maximum term distribution).

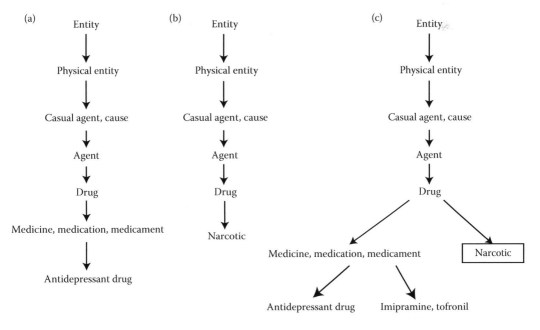

FIGURE 18.2
(a,b,c) Merging hypernym paths.

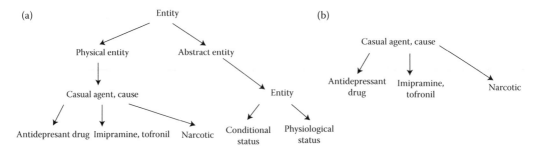

FIGURE 18.3
(a,b) Eliminating top levels.

- Eliminate a child whose name appears within the parent's name, unless the child contains a Word Net domain name.

The last step is to create a set of facet subhierarchies. The goal is to create a moderate set of facets, each of which has moderate depth and breadth at each level, in order to enhance the navigability of the categories. To eliminate the top levels in an automated fashion, for the tree roots in the Word Net noun database, manually cut the top t levels as represented in Figure 18.3a and b. Then, for resulting trees, recursively test if its root has more than n children. If it does, then consider the elements in the tree as a facet set; otherwise, delete the current root and algorithm tests to see if each new root has n children. Those subtrees that do not meet the criterion are omitted from the final set of facets.

18.5 Empirical Results and Discussion

This section describes the experimental setup and presents an overview of various method's performance. Then the effects of varying the facets in the above algorithms are discussed. The approach is proposed, and its relation to retrieval performance with baseline approach, greedy algorithm, and feedback language models are analyzed. Finally, the Fleiss kappa score of the proposed approach is compared with various methodologies and proved that it has a particular advantage. The dataset used in the experiment is the OHSUMED (Hersh et al. 1994) data, used in many experiments in information retrieval, including the TREC-9 filtering track. Table 18.1 shows the performance of various algorithms as several facets range from 3 to 11. The proposed performance is more susceptible to a higher number of facets than that of others. For example, at 9 facets the mean average precision (MAP) of the proposed is 81.3%, while the numbers for baseline, greedy, and language feedback models (TFB, CFB, and TCFB) are 71.9%, 74%, 75.1%, 78%, and 77.4%, respectively. We conjecture the reason that baseline performance heavily depends on overused terms that are chosen for query expansion, is that the greedy algorithm needs only an estimate of feasible solutions to work. The feedback language model produces the results that are closer to the greedy. Also, several facets seem to produce a more accurate set of documents than a less number, which is natural, as for several facets, it is easier to get into the situation to make topic diversification useful. Overall, the proposed approach is

TABLE 18.1

MAP, Recall, and F-Score for the Six Methodologies

Facet	Metric	Baseline	Term Feedback	Cluster Feedback	Term-Cluster Feedback	Greedy	Proposed
Facet @3	MAP	0.467	0.531	0.540	0.561	0.550	0.580
	Recall	0.732	0.741	0.748	0.760	0.732	0.782
	F	0.572	0.619	0.627	0.646	0.628	0.666
Facet @5	MAP	0.497	0.555	0.563	0.578	0.568	0.631
	Recall	0.692	0.710	0.702	0.721	0.716	0.751
	F	0.579	0.623	0.624	0.642	0.634	0.682
Facet @7	MAP	0.597	0.609	0.632	0.693	0.653	0.745
	Recall	0.591	0.646	0.686	0.698	0.680	0.691
	F	0.594	0.629	0.657	0.694	0.666	0.717
Facet @9	MAP	0.719	0.740	0.751	0.780	0.774	0.813
	Recall	0.523	0.551	0.591	0.632	0.612	0.652
	F	0.602	0.632	0.662	0.698	0.684	0.724
Facet @11	MAP	0.777	0.850	0.855	0.883	0.878	0.910
	Recall	0.491	0.510	0.561	0.586	0.571	0.611
	F	0.610	0.640	0.678	0.710	0.692	0.731

TABLE 18.2

Fleiss' Kappa Scores for the Six Methodologies

	Baseline	Term Feedback	Cluster Feedback	Term-Cluster Feedback	Greedy	Proposed
Fleiss Score	0.6063	0.6410	0.6601	0.6889	0.6780	0.7283

able to perform reasonably well in terms of accuracy, coverage, and F-measure, even when the facets are small. The F-score reaches its best value at 1 and worst score at 0.

Fleiss' kappa measure: Fleiss' kappa is a statistical measure for assessing agreement reliability between a fixed numbers of raters when assigning categorical ratings to several items or classifying items. It can be interpreted as expressing the extent to which the observed amount of agreement among raters exceeds what would be expected if all raters made their ratings completely randomly. It is important to note that where Cohen's kappa assumes the same two raters have rated a set of items, Fleis's kappa specifically assumes that although there are a fixed number of raters (e.g., three), different items are rated by different individuals. That is, Item 1 is rated by Raters A, B, and C; but Item 2 could be rated by Raters D, E, and F. This measure calculates the degree of agreement in classification over that which would be expected by chance and is scored as a number between 0 and 1. Use Fleis's kappa only with binary or nominal-scale ratings. The set of experiments explores the agreement between human assessors. In Table 18.2, measure the agreements using Fleis's kappa score. The human assessors have very high interhuman agreement for the proposed approach. The term feedback approach showed fair agreement among the raters. For the baseline method both evaluators had a large amount of disagreement on what they considered facets.

19

ASPDD: An Efficient and Scalable Framework for Duplication Detection[*]

Information is increasingly accessible on the Web. The performance and scalability of the Web engines face considerable problems due to the enormous amount of Web data. Internet expansion has resulted in problems for search engines because flooded search results are of less relevance to users. The Web has duplicate documents and mirrored Web documents in abundance. Apart from these the Web has a lot of near duplicates and partial duplicates; for the duplicates, type identification is a vital issue.

Owing to the high rate of duplication in Web documents, the need for detection of duplicated and nearly duplicated documents is high in diverse applications like crawling, ranking, clustering, archiving, and caching. The performance and scalability of duplicate document detection algorithms are affected by the huge amount of duplicate documents. Near duplicates possess minute differences and so are not regarded as exact duplicates. Typographical errors, mirrored or plagiarized documents, multiple representations of the same physical object, spam emails generated from the same template, and the like are some of the chief causes for near duplicate documents. Such near duplicates contain similar content and vary only in minimal areas like adding or deleting some contents.

Identification of duplicate documents by their content is becoming increasingly important in enterprise environments. Examples of the performance issues with respect to enterprise environments include the following:

1. To ensure data consistency (i.e., everyone works off the same document)
2. To remove clutter (confusion)
3. To save data storage space
4. To comply with regulations and to protect a company from unnecessary liability

19.1 Duplication Detection Techniques

To detect the near duplicates of form letters, use some duplicate document detection techniques. These techniques are generally partitioned into three main categories: overlapping, non-overlapping, and similarity measure techniques. Overlap methods use a sliding window. Basically, the window is shifted by a word and a word sequence in the window or its hash value is handled as a chunk. That is, methods based on the sliding window are *overlap methods* in that the adjacent windows overlap each other. Generally, overlap methods generate many chunks, but show good performance. However, since processing a

[*] Source of publication: doi:10.1109/ACE.2010.61; dl.acm.org/citation.cfm?id=1844798. Original material available in *ACE '10 Proceedings of the 2010 International Conference on Advances in Computer Engineering*, pp. 153–157. Washington, DC: IEEE Computer Society, 2010.

large number of chunks as fingerprints (Schleimer et al. 2003) can be too expensive, chunk selection techniques have been introduced. Full fingerprint, digital syntactic clustering (DSC), IIT (or) I-Match, 0 mod p, winnowing, and K-gram are some of the overlap methods. These methods use shingling techniques that take a set of contiguous terms (or shingles) of documents and compare the number of matching shingles. The comparison of document subsets allows the used algorithms to calculate the percentage of overlap between the documents. This type of approach relies on hash values for each document subsection and filters those hash values to reduce the number of comparisons. In the shingling approach, subdocuments instead of full documents are compared; thus, each document produces many potential duplicates. Returning many potential matches requires vast user involvement to sort out potential duplicates, diluting the potential usefulness of the approach. A main idea of nonoverlap methods is splitting text into a few meaningful text segments such as phrases or sentences instead of generating many subsequences of words.

Thus, sliding windows are not used, and accordingly, there is no overlap between chunks. We refer to a process of splitting text segments as *breaking*. A word position where a break occurs is a *breakpoint*. The third approach that computes document-to-document similarity measures (Metzler and Croft 2005) is similar to document clustering work in that it uses similarity computations to group potentially duplicate documents. Compare all pairs of documents, compare each document to every other document, and calculate a similarity measure. A document-to-document similarity comparison approach is thus computationally prohibitive given the theoretical $O(d^2)$ runtime, where d is the number of documents. Word-overlap and Jaccard are the similarity-based methods. The challenging task of duplicate detection is the focus of this section's described effort. Partition the problem into four dimensions: the duplication is symmetry, neighbor, partial, and asymmetry replica:

1. If two documents are almost identical, one is a photocopy or a fax of the other, say, they are *symmetric replica*.
2. If two documents have identical textual content, but in this case, add a short passage of text to another document. A typical example is observed in blogs—that is, copying the entire text of a news article and appending a short comment about the article. They are *neighbor replica*.
3. In this case, a whole document is a partial text of a new document. These are typically shown in cases where a news article is composed of several small news articles or where a document quotes interviews from other short news articles. They are *partial replica*.
4. If two documents do not share any significant content—that is, they have a distinct set of features—they are *asymmetry replica*.

The proposed algorithm, called All Pairs Shortest Path based Duplicate Detection (ASPDD), categorizes documents based on distance between term collection statistics. The results show that ASPDD is more accurate than the shingling algorithms. Furthermore, it has been proved that ASPDD categorizes each document into at most one duplicate set. Hence, this increases accuracy and usability. Other approaches place potentially duplicate documents in multiple clusters. Hence, it is harder for a user to detect the actual duplicates. Finally, the sets of duplicates that the proposed detect are usually "tighter" than shingling and similarity measures (Metzler and Croft 2005). We need an "exact match" for the terms on letters and email generated by endangered and threatened wildlife and plants; however, unlike other approaches, the proposed method has identified nonexact duplicates like neighbor and partial replica.

19.1.1 Prior Work

This section discusses and evaluates eight distinct classes of algorithms for finding duplicates on the letter forms. Each algorithm produced a list of duplication categories, each category representing a possible duplication relationship. Duplication relationship validity is judged in terms of precision, recall, and F-measure in an efficient way. This occurs by fetching a subset of letters, emails from endangered and threatened wildlife and plants, and it is tested to see if the other letter or email had text with highly similar content.

19.1.1.1 Similarity Measures

Word-overlap approach: The first technique is a simple word overlap measure and is quite competitive when compared to more elaborate retrieval methods:

$$sim(q,r)_{\text{overlap}} \equiv \frac{q \cap r}{|q|} \tag{19.1}$$

where $|q \cap r|$ is the number of words that appear in q and r. We note that this measure is nonsymmetrical, which ensures that $sim(q,r)_{\text{overlap}} = 1$ if $q \subset r$. This property is useful in the case of long retrieved sentences that contain the query q. Also $sim(q,r)_{\text{overlap}}$ does not account for word order, which makes it more flexible than a strict duplicate matching.

The Jaccard measure: The Jaccard measure (Metzler et al. 2005b) and the following two measures (i.e., the dice measure and the overlap measure) are all based on the vector-space model. The document representations are the same with the cosine measure, and the word weights are all based on $tf \times idf$ calculation. The three measures differ from the cosine measure in that they normalize the inner product of two document vectors in different ways. Here, a and b are two documents, and $w_{a,t}$ is the word count of t in a:

$$sim_{\text{jaccard}}(a,b) = \frac{\sum_{t \in a \cap b} (w_{a,t} \times w_{b,t})}{\sum_{t \in a} w_{a,t}^2 + \sum_{t \in b} w_{b,t}^2 - \sum_{t \in a \cap b} (w_{a,t} \times w_{b,t})} \tag{19.2}$$

19.1.1.2 Shingling Techniques

Full fingerprinting (full): Select every substring of size s in the documents and hashed ($s = 3$ in the experiments). Select every hash value (NIST 1995) and store the document ID as a <hash-value, document id> tuple. Duplicate detection is performed by (1) sorting the list of tuples; (2) for any hash-value that also appears in the reference copy, turning this hash-value's flag to 1, keeping the document ID information to create another kind of tuple <document id, flag = 1>; and (3) counting the hash-values with flag = 1 for every document, and getting <document id, count>. The count is the number of overlap fingerprints between a document and the reference copy. If the overlap is above 80%, the document is considered as a (near) duplicate.

Digital syntactic clustering (DSC): Performed in the same way as described in full fingerprinting except that every five overlapping substrings of size s in the documents are selected and hashed. Then s is set to three again. If the count of the overlap fingerprints in a document to form a letter is above 80%, it is a (near) duplicate.

IIT(I-Match): Select N words with the highest *idf* values in a document, $(N = 30)$. Ignore the five words with the highest *idf*s, because they might be mistakes such as misspellings. Generate a single fingerprint for each document. Perform the duplicate detection by sorting all <fingerprint, document id> tuples. Those agreeing with the fingerprint of the form letter are selected as the (near) duplicates.

0 mod p: Instead of using all the chunks generated by the sliding window, 0 mod p tries to select some of them as fingerprints. A random selection of chunks would reduce the number, but we cannot predict which chunks would be selected. If different chunks are selected each time, then determine two documents as different even when they are identical. All chunk selection methods have to satisfy the property that the same chunks are selected for identical documents. 0 mod p selects only chunks such that $C(D, i)$ mod p $\equiv 0$, When two documents are identical, chunks in the documents are the same. Assuming that the chunk values are uniformly distributed, the expected number of selected chunks—that is, the number of fingerprints of document D—is given by

$$M_{0\ mod\ p} = M_{K\text{-gram}} - \frac{(D)}{p} \tag{19.3}$$

That is, 0 *mod p* can reduce the number of the fingerprints by a factor p. This method may, however, not represent the document accurately. For example, although the upper of two documents are identical, the lower halves are different. In the worst case, if chunks in either the upper halves or the lower halves are selected, then the detection algorithms would falsely determine the reuse relationship.

K-gram: K-gram is the simplest technique of the overlap methods. It uses all the chunks generated from each sliding window as fingerprints. Thus, the number of the fingerprints of document D is computed as $L(D) - K + 1$, where $L(D)$ is the term count of document D. As K-gram uses all chunks, it generally shows good performance. However, it might be infeasible in big collections because of too many fingerprints.

Winnowing: Winnowing is another selection method based on K-gram. Winnowing adopts another fixed size window—that is, a winnowing window over the chunks generated by the original window—and it selects a chunk whose value is the minimum in each winnowing window. If there is more than one minimum value in the winnowing window, then the rightmost minimum value in the window is selected. Schleimer et al. (2003) showed that winnowing performs better than 0 mod p in practice. Further, they showed that the expected number of fingerprints has a lower bound as $(2/w + 1)M_{K\text{-gram}(D)}$, where w is the size of winnowing window.

19.1.2 Proposed Approach (ASPDD)

Partition the problem along four dimensions: the duplication includes symmetry, neighbor, partial, and asymmetry replica explained in a previous section. The focus of the proposed method is mainly on duplicate document detection from the public comments submitted through email and through Web forms. In order to identify the duplicate documents, the proposed approach employs the topical similarity detection and content similarity detection techniques. In topical similarity detection, analyze the document through its attributes such as subject, the receiver, timestamp, address block, signature block, docket identification number, and footer block. In the proposed approach, the subjects in the emails are for identifying topical similarity.

Dice measure (topical similarity identification): For identifying the topical similarity, the dice measure employs the *tf*idf* calculation. Identify the similarity between the topics by setting the threshold range $Sim(a,b) > 95\%$, the two topics are similar. This measure identifies the replica of the public comments obtained through mails. This measure greatly reduces the duplicate documents and identifies the almost identical duplicates;

$$sim_{Dice(a,b)} = \frac{2 \times \sum_{i \in a \cap b} (w_{a,t} \times w_{b,t})}{\sum_{t \in a} w_{a,t}^2 + \sum_{t \in b} w_{b,t}^2} \tag{19.4}$$

where a,b are documents and $w_{a,t}$ is the word count of the term t in document a.

The problem: This section presents a new methodology for enhancing existing duplication detection Systems with the goodness of the All Pairs Shortest Path Algorithm. The greedy approach and dynamic programming are the two ways to solve optimization problems. Most of the problems are solved by both greedy and dynamic programming. But it is more difficult to determine whether a greedy algorithm always produces an optimal solution. But in the case of dynamic programming we need only to determine whether the principle of optimality applies. We show the principle of optimality by solving the All Pairs Shortest Path algorithm (Horowitz et al. 2007) by dynamic programming. This algorithm employs maximal distance replacement value to identify the exact duplicates between the documents and helps to identify the transitive closure property. Based on the distance between the vertices, the documents are categorized and summarized as symmetry, neighbor, partial, and asymmetry according to the range of values. For any random documents d_a, d_b, and d_c, the transitive closures of the three types of constraints are below. $d_a = d_b$ and $d_b = d_c \Rightarrow d_a = d_c$. This algorithm finds the shortest path from a source vertex s to a target vertex t in a directed graph. As it turns out, the best algorithms for this problem actually find the shortest path from s to every possible target (or from every possible source to t) by constructing a shortest path tree. In the All Pairs Shortest Path problem, the idea is to find the shortest path from every possible source to every possible destination. Specifically, for every pair of vertices u and v, we need to compute the following information:

1. $dist(u,v)$ is the length of the shortest path (if any) from u to v;
2. $pred(u,v)$ is the second-to-last vertex (if any) on the shortest path (if any) from u to v.

For example, for any vertex v, we have $dist(v,v) = 0$ and $pred(v,v) = $ NULL. If the shortest path from u to v is only one edge long, then $dist(u,v) = w(u \rightarrow v)$ and $pred(u,v) = u$. If there is no shortest path from u to v—either because there is no path at all, or because there is a negative cycle—then $dist(u,v) = \infty$ and $pred(v,v) = $ NULL. The output of the shortest path algorithms will be a pair of $V \times V$ arrays encoding all V^2 distances and predecessors. There is a completely different solution to the All Pairs Shortest Path problem that uses dynamic programming instead of a single-source algorithm. For dynamic programming algorithms, we first need to come up with a recursive formulation of the problem. In other words, to find the shortest path from u to v, try all possible predecessors x, compute the shortest path from u to x, and then add the last edge $u \rightarrow v$. To avoid this circular dependency, we need an additional parameter that decreases at each recursion, eventually

```
DYNAMIC PROGRAMMING ASPDD (V,E,w):

for all vertices u ∈ V

for all vertices v ∈ V if u = v

                    dist [u,v,0] ← 0

        else

                    dist [u,v,0] ← ∞

    for k=1 to V − 1

        for all vertices u ∈ V

            for all vertices v ∈ V dist [u,v,k] ← ∞

                for all vertices x ∈ V

dist [u,v,k] ← min { dist [u,v,k], dist [u,x,k − 1] + w(x → v)}
```

FIGURE 19.1
Pseudo code for ASPDD.

reaching zero at the base case. One possibility is to include the number of edges in the shortest path as this third magic parameter. So let's define dist(u,v,k) to be the length of the shortest path from u to v that uses at most k edges. Since we know that the shortest path between any two vertices has at most $V − 1$ vertices, to compute dist($u,v,V − 1$). Figure 19.1 describes the pseudo-code for ASPDD.

19.2 Empirical Results and Discussion

Adopt an ASPDD technique: U.S. Fish and Wildlife Service which has 282,992 comments from the source FWS-Wolf (RIN: 1018.AU53) of size 622 MB. Analyze the degree of duplication of letters and emails by duplication-detection algorithms and evaluate in terms of precision, recall, and F-measure. In Table 19.1, the 0 mod p algorithm performs the worst, with an average precision of 0.8135 at partial replica detection. The word overlap and Jaccard algorithms produce better results with average precisions of 0.9164 and 0.9059 at neighbor replica.

It is difficult to show theoretically how many changes the fingerprinting techniques (Schleimer et al. 2003) are tolerant of because input signal values are almost randomly mapped to by hashing (NIST 1995). That is, while a minor change, for example, a change from "product" to "products" might cause a big change of the hash value of the word, a word replacement might be coincidentally mapped to the same value. Nevertheless, a single word change tends to change a few high-frequency components, and we can ignore the high-frequency components by the formatting scheme. Two other techniques DSC and I-Match are not as effective as full fingerprinting and ASPDD. In general, DSC outperforms I-Match. I-Match is very sensitive to both "block added" and "block deleted," "minor change" editing patterns. When the changed words are critical—that is, appearing

TABLE 19.1

Performance Evaluation of Duplication Detection Algorithms

Type of Duplica-tion	Metrics	Word Over-lap	Jaccard Mea-sure	Full Finger-print	DSC	I-Match	0 Mod p	K-gram	Win-nowing	Pro-posed
Symmetric replica	AP	0.9164	0.9059	0.8803	0.8770	0.8344	0.8135	0.8836	0.8204	0.9461
	AR	0.8102	0.8063	0.7863	0.7754	0.7631	0.7461	0.7984	0.7528	0.826
	F	0.8597	0.8528	0.8305	0.8230	0.7959	0.7781	0.8385	0.7849	0.8819
Neighbor replica	AP	0.9597	0.9481	0.929	0.9166	0.8981	0.8261	0.9318	0.8361	0.9660
	AR	0.8221	0.8254	0.8162	0.8132	0.7963	0.7629	0.8231	0.7631	0.8312
	F	0.8852	0.8824	0.8689	0.8615	0.8440	0.7557	0.8740	0.7978	0.8935
Partial replica	AP	0.8981	0.888	0.8634	0.8519	0.8391	0.8021	0.879	0.8180	0.9233
	AR	0.7962	0.7738	0.7632	0.7422	0.7362	0.6984	0.7591	0.7366	0.8128
	F	0.8441	0.208	0.8125	0.7928	0.7841	0.7457	0.8146	0.7751	0.8645
Asymmet-ric replica	AP	0.9432	0.9339	0.9100	0.8997	0.8796	0.879	0.9264	0.8838	0.9624
	AR	0.8361	0.8062	0.7973	0.7832	0.7632	0.7384	0.7956	0.7466	0.8831
	F	0.8863	0.8649	0.8512	0.8374	0.824	0.8025	0.8558	0.8078	0.9208

in the fingerprint that I-Match selected—the algorithm fails to detect the near-duplicates. In general, I-Match produces fairly low precision and recall.

A modified version of Cohen's kappa (Gwet Kappa 2002), interhuman agreement, measures effectiveness relatively. Cohen's kappa is a more common choice, but it suffers from bias and a prevalence problem when agreement between assessors is high but skewed to a few categories, as is common in public comment datasets. Equation 19.5 corrects this flaw:

$$\text{Modified}_{\text{Kappa}} = \frac{p(A) - p(E)}{1 - p(E)} \tag{19.5}$$

where $p(A)$ is the observed agreement between two assessments x and y; a is the number of pairs in the same groups in both x and y; b is the number of pairs in the same groups in x but different in y; c is the number of pairs in the different groups in x but the same in y; and d is the number of pairs in the different groups in both x and y. Calculate $p(A)$ as $(a + d)/m$, where $m = a + b + c + d$. $p(E)$ is the agreement expected by chance and calculated as $p(E) = 2P(1 - P)$, where $P = ((a + b) + (a + c))/2m$. In Table 19.2, measure the agreements using kappa score. The human assessors have very high interhuman agreement for the proposed approach. The word overlap and Jaccard measure showed fair agreement among the raters. For the 0 mod p method, both evaluators had much disagreement on what they considered duplicates.

TABLE 19.2

Cohen's Kappa Score for Duplication Detection Techniques

Method	Word Overlap	Jaccard Measure	Full Fingerprint	DSC	I-Match	0 Mod p	Winnowing	K-Gram	Proposed
Kappa Score	0.9297	0.9185	0.8955	0.8857	0.8645	0.8295	0.8385	0.8972	0.9492

TABLE 19.3

Average Precision of Duplication Detection Techniques by Varying Shingles

Methods	5 Shingles	10 Shingles	15 Shingles	20 Shingles	25 Shingles
Word overlap	0.9064	0.9192	0.9286	0.9328	0.9369
Jaccard measure	0.8920	0.8962	0.9081	0.9105	0.9165
Full fingerprint	0.8812	0.8864	0.8893	0.8910	0.8966
DSC	0.8218	0.8324	0.8419	0.8594	0.8667
I-Match	0.8011	0.8089	0.8194	0.8260	0.8321
0 mod p	0.714	0.7778	0.7862	0.7992	0.8120
Winnowing	0.7014	0.7096	0.8074	0.8166	0.8215
K-gram	0.8847	0.8864	0.8981	0.9030	0.9061
All Pairs Shortest Path based Duplicate Detection	0.9063	0.9181	0.9348	0.9403	0.9496

TABLE 19.4

Average Precision of Duplication Detection Techniques at Different Precision Levels

Methods	Precision @ 5	Precision @ 10	Precision @ 15	Precision @ 20
Word overlap	0.9511	0.9386	0.9200	0.9086
Jaccard measure	0.9481	0.9361	0.9021	0.8699
Full fingerprint	0.932	0.9185	0.8876	0.8552
DSC	0.9288	0.9065	0.8686	0.8491
I-Match	0.9162	0.9045	0.8591	0.8289
0 mod p	0.8992	0.8854	0.8334	0.7954
Winnowing	0.9057	0.8981	0.8461	0.8066
K-gram	0.9387	0.9261	0.8992	0.8601
All Pairs Shortest Path based Duplicate Detection	0.9621	0.9485	0.9301	0.9187

Table 19.3 shows the performance of various algorithms as the number of shingles ranges from 5 to 25. Table 19.4 shows the performance of various algorithms at different precision levels ranging from 5 to 25. We find that the performance of ASPDD is more susceptible to a higher number of duplicates than that of others. For example, at 15 shingles, the average precision of ASPDD is 93.62%, while the numbers for word overlap, Jaccard, and full fingerprint are 92.86%, 90.81%, and 88.93%. We conjecture the reason that while a minor change, the fingerprint might cause a big change of the hash value of the word. Also, the more shingles there are seems to indicate that a more accurate set of results may be detected, but a larger number of text collections seems to provide more coverage than accuracy. Overall, the proposed approach is able to perform reasonably well in terms of accuracy and coverage than others.

20

Improvisation of Seeker Satisfaction in Yahoo! Community Question Answering Using Automatic Ranking, Abstract Generation, and History Updation*

The process of posting and obtaining answers to a question is an important phenomenon in community question answering (CQA) (Agichtein et al. 2008). A user posts a question by selecting a category, and then enters the question subject (title) and, optionally, details (description). For conciseness, QA (Liu and Agichitein 2008a) will refer to this user as the asker for the context of the question, even though the same user is likely to also answer other questions (Lin and Demner-Fushman 2006) or participate in other roles for other questions. To prevent abuse, the community's rules typically forbid the asker from answering his or her own questions or voting on answers.

After a short delay (which may include checking for abuse, and other processing) the question appears in the respective category list of open questions, normally listed from the most recent down. At that point, other users can answer the question, vote on other user's answers, or comment on the question (e.g., to ask for clarification or provide other, nonanswer feedback), or provide various metadata for the question. At that point, consider the question as closed by the asker and no new answers will be accepted. QA believes that in such cases, the asker is likely satisfied with at least one of the responses, usually the one he or she chooses as the best answer. But in many cases the asker never closes the answer personally, and instead, after some fixed period, the question is closed automatically.

In this case, voters may choose the "best" answer, or by some others. So, while the best answer chosen automatically is of high quality, it is unknown if the asker's information need was satisfied. There are many reasons why the asker never closed a question by choosing a best answer. Based on the exploration we believe that the main reasons are as follows:

1. The user loses interest in the information.
2. None of the answers are satisfactory.
3. The duration is too long.

The QA community has "failed" to provide satisfactory answers on time and "lost" the asker's interest. Question answering communities are an important application by itself, and they provide unprecedented opportunity to study feedback from the asker. Furthermore, asker satisfaction plays a crucial role in the growth or decay of a question answering community.

If the asker is satisfied with any of the answers, he or she can choose it as *best*, and provide feedback ranging from assigning *stars* or rating for the best answer, and possibly textual feedback.

* Source of publication: https://doaj.org/toc/2229-6956; ictactjournals.in/paper/ijsc7_page_152_162.pdf. Original material available in *ICTACT Journal on Soft Computing*, 1(3), 152–162, January 2011.

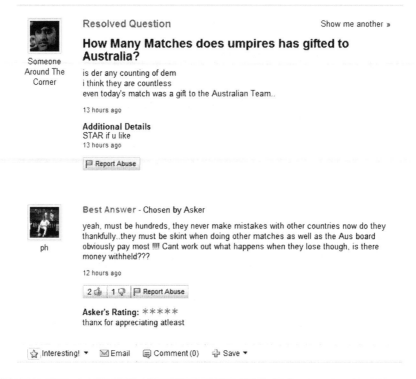

FIGURE 20.1
Example of "satisfied" question thread.

QA believes that in such cases, the asker is likely *satisfied* with at least one of the responses, usually the one he or she chooses as the best answer. Figure 20.1 shows an example of such a "satisfactory" interaction. If many of the askers in CQA (Liu and Agichtein 2008a,b) are not satisfied with their experience, they will not post new questions and will rely on other means of finding information, which creates asker satisfaction problems.

20.1 The Asker Satisfaction Problem

While the true reasons are not known, for simplicity, to contrast with the "satisfied" outcome above, we consider this outcome as "unsatisfied." Figure 20.2 shows an example of such an interaction.

20.2 Community Question Answering Problems

The analysis of distinction between possibly satisfied and completely unsatisfied, or dissection of the case where the asker is not satisfied is not attempted. Now the proposed problem is formally stated in four different angles.

FIGURE 20.2
Example of "unsatisfied" question thread.

Answer justify problem: The asker may receive more answers for each question. Now the asker intended to read all answers and select one suitable answer for his or her question. Here the problem is that the asker may not know which answer he has to choose.

To overcome this problem, explore the automatic ranking system to provide the rank for answers.

Answer understanding problem: How does the asker identify the objective of each answer?

To avoid this problem, abstract generation is used to provide a summary of answers and is often used to help the reader quickly ascertain the answer's purpose. When used, an abstract always appears at the beginning of all displayed answers, acting as the point of entry.

Asker taste changes: One important problem is to determine what an asker wants. What form of answer does the asker expect? It is crucial to determine what the user is thinking.

History updation using distributed learning automata is the best solution to this problem. It is used to remember the information about the previous behavior of the asker who has selected an answer in the past history to show relevant answers from the learned behavior and is updated in the asker's history.

Time-consuming problem: To read all retrieved answers, the asker needs more time. Does the time factor affect the asker satisfaction?

> Compute the time duration by how long the asker views the displayed answers, and use this to predict whether the asker is satisfied or unsatisfied.

20.3 Methodologies

Automatic ranking based on generalization method: The objective of applying learned association rules (Agrawal et al. 1995; Lin et al. 2000) is to improve QA comparison by providing a more generalized representation. Good generalization (Pietra et al. 1997) will have the desired effect of bringing QA that are semantically related closer to each other than they previously would have been due to being incorrectly treated as being further apart. Association rules (Lin et al. 2000) are able to capture implicit relationships that exist between features of QA. When applying these rules, they have the effect of squashing these features and are viewed as feature generalization.

Initially extract the most important features using the Markov random field (MRF) (Metzler and Croft 2005) model. These features are as the initial seeds for generalization (Pietra et al. 1997). Then employ the association rule (Agrawal et al. 1995; Lin et al. 2000) to capture feature co-occurrence patterns.

It generates rules of the form $H \rightarrow B$, where the body B is a feature from answers, and the head H is a feature from a question. This means that rules are used to predict the head feature given that all the features in the questions are present in the answer. This excludes a rule satisfying the body, when the head feature is absent.

The idea of feature generalization (Pietra et al. 1997) can be combined with feature selection to form a structured representation for ranking.

Feature generalization (Pietra et al. 1997) helps tone down ambiguities that exist in free text by capturing semantic relationships and incorporating these in the query representation. This enables a better comparison of features in QA.

An interesting observation is that with feature selection and generalization, a more effective ranking can be achieved even with a relatively small set of features. Finally the retrieved features are used for ranking answers. This is attractive because smaller vocabularies can effectively be used to build concise indices that are understandable and easier to interpret.

Abstract generation: With the rapid growth of online information, there is a growing need for tools that help in finding, filtering, and managing the high dimensional data. Automated text categorization (Leopold and Kindermann 2002) is a supervised learning task, defined as assigning category labels to answers based on likelihood suggested by a training set of answers.

Real-world applications of text categorization (Leopold and Kindermann 2002) often require a system to deal with tens of thousands of categories defined over a large taxonomy. Since building these text classifiers by hand is time-consuming and costly, automated text categorization has gained importance over the years.

Develop an automatic abstract generation (Sumita et al. 2007) system for answers based on rhetorical structure extraction. The system first extracts the rhetorical structure, the compound of the rhetorical relations between sentences in answers, and then cuts out less important parts in the extracted structure to generate an abstract (Sumita et al. 2007) of the desired length.

Abstract generation is, like machine translation, one of the ultimate goals of natural language processing. This is a suitable application of the extracted rhetorical structure. This section describes the abstract generation system based on it.

Rhetorical structure: Rhetorical structure represents relations between various chunks of answers in the body of each question. Represent the rhetorical structure in terms of connective expressions and its relations. There are 40 categories of rhetorical relations and exemplified in Figure 20.3.

Relations	Expressions
Confident<co>	I can
Example <eg>	For example
Recommend <rd>	Try this
Reason <re>	Because
Assumption <as>	I think
Plus <pl>	And
Specialization <sp>	Almost, most, always
Serial <sr>	Thus
Summarization <su>	After all, finally
Extension <ex>	This is, there
Suggestion <sg>	You can
Explanation <en>	So
Advice <ad>	You need, you would
Capture <ca>	Take
Appreciate <ap>	Good question
Next <ne>	Then
Simple <si>	Just, easy
Rare <ra>	Some time
Condition <cn>	If you
Negative <po>	But, I don't, not sure
Must <mu>	You should
Expectation <en>	Hope this
Trust <tr>	I believe
Starting <st>	First of all
Doubt <dt>	May be
Accurate <ac>	Yes, no
Positive <po>	Why not?
Request <rq>	Please
Repeat <rt>	Again
Utilize <ut>	Use this
Direction <di>	Here is
While <wi>	Since
Memorize <me>	Remember
Question <qu>	Can you, ate you
Same <sa>	Sound like
Opinion <op>	Statement
Verify <ve>	Ask
Apology <ay>	Sorry, excuse
Wishes <wi>	All the best, welcome, best wishes, Good luck

FIGURE 20.3
Example of rhetorical relations.

TABLE 20.1

Relative Importance of Rhetorical Relations

Relation Type	Relation	Important Node
Right nucleus	Experience, negative, example, serial, direction, confident, specialization	Right node
Left nucleus	Especially, reason, accurate, appropriate, simple, rare, assumption, explanation, doubt, request, apology, utilize, opinion	Left node
Both nuclei	Plus, extension, question, capture, appreciate, next, repeat, many, condition, since, ask, same, starting, wishes, memorize, trust, positive, recommend, expectation, advice, summarization	Both nodes

The rhetorical relation of a sentence is the relationship to the preceding part of the text, extracted by the connective expression in the sentence.

The rhetorical structure represents logical relations between sentences or block of sentences of each answer. Linguistic clues, such as connectives, anaphoric expressions, and idiomatic expressions, in the answers are to determine the relationship between the sentences.

In the sentence evaluation stage, the system calculates each sentence importance in the original text on the relative importance of rhetorical relations. Table 20.1 shows the categorization of three types. For the relations categorized into right nucleus, the right node is more important, from the point of view of abstract generation (Sumita et al. 2007), than the left node. In the case of the left nucleus relations, the situation is opposite. And both nodes of the both-nucleus relations are equivalent in their importance. Figure 20.4 shows a sample question and answer and the rhetorical structure.

History updation by using learning automata (LA): Based on the asker's past history (already selected answer for his or her previous question), the taste of the asker is updated, and we can predict what kind of answer the asker will choose for his or her current question.

Learning automata (Thathachar and Harita Bhaskar 1987) are adaptive decision-making devices operating on unknown random environments. The automata (Beigy and Meybodi 2002) approach to learning involves an optimal action determination from a set of allowable actions. An automaton is regarded as an abstract object that has a finite number of possible actions. Apply this action to a random environment used by automata (Beigy and Meybodi 2002) in further action selection. By continuing this process, the automata learn to select the best grade action. The learning algorithm (Thathachar and Harita Bhaskar 1987) is used by automata to determine the next action from the response of the environment.

The proposed algorithm takes advantage of usage data and link information to recommend answers to the asker based on learned patterns. For that, it uses the rewarding and penalizing schema of actions that updates the action's probabilities in each step based on a learning algorithm. The rewarding factor for history updation is shown in Equation 20.1:

$$a = w + \lambda. \tag{20.1}$$

where w is a constant, and λ is obtained by this intuition. Classify the asker's tastes into six categories (definition, open-ended answer, close-ended answer, link, opinion, and summary) from the format of the answers selected.

If a user goes from taste i to taste j and there is no link between these tastes, then the value of λ is constant; otherwise it is zero.

If there is a cycle in a user's navigation path, the actions in the cycle indicate the change of taste of the asker over a time or penalize the asker's dissatisfaction from the previous

Question: does McDonald's veg Burger in India contain egg?

Answer 1: Nope, In India Its purely veg, I had taken one of my close associate who is purely veg and I discussed it with the Delhi shop and the manager confirmed and even wanted to give in writing. Made Indian food is my FAVVVV. I would be all over the street eating all the home cooked food out there I live USA and there's mD's on every block. Thus the Rhetorical structure for answer I can be represented by a binary tree

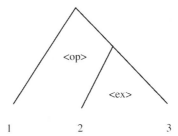

This structure can also be represented as follows,

[[1<ex>2]<op>3]]

Answer 2: No, way it's a guaranteed company <co>

Answer 3: I think yes. But can ask the manager of McDonald's, Good Luck.

[[1<ad>2]<wi>3]]

Finally the abstract from all the answers will be,

"I had taken one of my close associate who is purely veg and I discussed it with the Delhi shop and the manager confirmed and even wanted to give in writing- No, way it's a guaranteed company- you can ask the manager of McDonald's."

FIGURE 20.4
Abstract generation using rhetorical structure.

tastes. The penalized task increases with cycle length. So, calculate parameter *b*, which is the penalization factor, from Equation 20.2:

$$b = (\text{steps in cycle containing } k \text{ and } l) * \beta \tag{20.2}$$

where β is a constant factor. The penalization factor has a direct relation with the length of cycle traversed by the asker.

These navigational patterns are then used to generate recommendations based on the asker's current status. Present answers in a recommendation list according to their importance and similarities, which is in turn computed based on usage information.

Duration: Time spent by the asker for viewing a page that contains answers as very important pieces of information in measuring the asker's interest on the page and is defined in Equation 20.3:

$$\text{Total duration of the page} = \frac{\text{Duration}}{\text{Number of answers}} \quad (20.3)$$

Based on the time spent by the asker on the particular page and number of received answers, calculate the time for each answer taken by the asker, and predict whether the asker is satisfied or not for a given question.

There are many reasons why the asker never closed a question by choosing a best answer and closing a question with voting. Based on the exploration, we believe that the main reasons are as follows:

1. Closing a question within a minimum span of time and may not have interest in voting
2. Closing a question within a minimum span of time with voting
3. Never closing a question because the asker loses interest in the information
4. Never closing a question because none of the answers are satisfactory

In Option 1 the true reasons are not known for closing a question without voting. The asker might have read the best answer in the answer collection but not had interest in voting. At this juncture, calculate time duration and decide the automatic ranking. The answers for questions that are not voted on can also be rated using the automated ranking function, which will be helpful for future askers.

20.4 Experimental Setup

This section presents the experimental evaluation of asker satisfaction phenomenon over the Yahoo! Answers (Liu and Agichtein 2008a). The proposed approach has addressed the concrete areas of question answering community portals by automatic ranking, history updation, abstract generation, and duration-based problems. These areas tend to have significant interest among the askers, and the proposed methodologies are outperforming, predicting (Agichtein et al. 2006), and presenting best results to the asker's point of view. Also evaluate the proposed method solutions by human and system judgment called the kappa score (Cicchetti and Feinstein 1990), which is efficient in providing the correct score toward answer relevancy.

This section describes the baselines and proposed specific methods for predicting asker satisfaction. In other words, "truth" labels are on the rating subsequently given to the best answer by the asker. It is usually more valuable to correctly predict whether a user is satisfied (e.g., to notify a user of success). This section describes the experimental setting, datasets, and metrics for producing results.

Evaluation metrics: Three variants of standard information retrieval metrics, such as precision, recall, and *F*-measure, are used to examine the effectiveness of Yahoo! Answers (Liu and Agichitein 2008a) for answering questions: in experiments compute the metrics using relevance judgments given by the user and the system. In an automatic ranking system, compute the results by evaluating the answers for each question thread in decreasing order (top-ranked answers for the question). This models a "naive" searcher that examines results in order. To determine whether the results given by the system are producing sufficient information for a human to consistently gain knowledge from the answers according to this goal framework, a specialized score called kappa (Cicchetti and Feinstein 1990) is used.

Precision: This is the fraction of the predicted *satisfied* asker information needs that are rated satisfactory by the asker. It can also be defined as the fraction of the retrieved answers that are relevant. Precision at *K* for a given query is the mean fraction of relevant answers ranked in the top *K* results; the higher the precision, the better is the performance. The score is 0 if none of the top *K* results contain a relevant answer. The problem of this metric is that the relevant answer's position within the top *K* is irrelevant, while it measures overall potential satisfaction with the top *K* results. Here the "best answers" tagged by the Yahoo! Answers (Liu and Agichitein 2008a) website are considered as the ground truth for the experiments.

Recall: This is the fraction of all rated *satisfied* questions that were correctly identified by the system. It can also be defined as the fraction of the relevant answers that has been retrieved. This is to separate high-quality content from the rest of the contents and evaluate the quality of the overall answer set. If more answers are retrieved, recall increases while precision usually decreases. Then, a proper evaluation has to produce precision/recall values at given points in the rank. This provides an incremental view of the retrieval performance measures. Analyze the answer set from the top answers and compute precision-recall values to find each relevant answer.

F-measure: The weighted harmonic mean of precision and recall is called the traditional *F*-measure. It is on van Rijsbergen's effectiveness measure $E = 1 - (1/(\alpha/P + (1 - \alpha)/R))$. Their relationship is $F\beta = 1\ E$, where $\alpha = 1/(\beta 2 + 1)$.

Datasets: The data for this study come from the resolved questions of Yahoo! QA service log, having different requirements on the questions associated with "games," "food and drinks," "education and reference," "computer and Internet," "travel," social culture," "family," and "news and events." This system created a pool of 3568 QA Pairs drawn over 50 categories as a training dataset among 5000 queries. Associate a question in the QA pool with a minimum of 5 answers and maximum of 20 answers. In order for large-scale evaluation of interactive question answering, practical, encapsulated user-system interactions in the Yahoo! QA community are in HTML pages called interaction forms, similar to clarification forms that focused on arbitrary interface controls that could appear on an HTML form—thumbs up, thumbs down, report abuse, sliding bar, stars for level of interest, and comments.

Methods compared: This section describes the study of ranking the answers and details of ranking algorithms. *Vector-space model* (or term vector model) is an algebraic model for representing answers (and any objects, in general) as vectors (Mitchell 2008) of identifiers, such as, for example, index terms. It is in information filtering, information retrieval, indexing, and relevancy rankings.

Represent questions and answers vectors (Mitchell 2008):

$$a_i = (W_{ij}, W_{2j,...,} W_{tj})$$

$$q = (W_{1,q}, W_{2,q,...}, W_{t,q})$$ (20.4)

Each dimension corresponds to a separate term. If a term occurs in the answer, its value in the vector is nonzero. Several different ways of computing these values, also known as (term) weights, have been developed. One of the best-known schemes is *tf-iaf* (Salton and Buckley 1988) weighting vector (Mitchell 2008) operations used to compare answers with queries.

Relevancy rankings of answers in a keyword search are calculated, using the assumptions of answer similarity theory (Resnik 1995; Erk 2007), by comparing the angle deviation between each answer vector and original query vector where the query is represented as the same kind of vector as the answers.

Use cosine similarity (Resnik 1995; Erk 2007) between answer a and calculate query q using

$$\text{sim}(a_j, q) = \frac{a_j \cdot q}{\|a_j\|\|q\|} = \frac{\sum_{i=1}^{t} w_{i,j} * w_{i,q}}{\sqrt{\sum_{i=1}^{t} w_{i,j}^2} * \sqrt{\sum_{i=1}^{t} w_{i,q}^2}}$$ (20.5)

where a_j is the *j*th answer for the query q; $w_{i,j}$ is the weight of the *i*th term in the answer j; and $w_{i,q}$ is the weight of the *i*th term in the query q. A cosine value is zero if the question and answer are orthogonal and have no match (i.e., the question term does not exist in the answer being considered).

Indri method: This returns a ranked list of answers containing the important term and its term frequency:

$$H(p, q) = H(p) + D_{KL}(p \| q)$$ (20.6)

Here $H(p)$ is an entropy and Indri (Strohman et al. 2005) handles ranking via *KL*-divergence/cross-entropy for each answer:

$$H(P) = \sum_{i=1}^{n} p(x) \log p(x)$$ (20.7)

$$D_{KL}(p \| q) \equiv \sum_{i} p(x) \log \frac{p(x)}{q(x)}$$ (20.8)

where $P(x)$ is the probability of selecting an answer for the given query, and q is answers collection. The lower the *KL*-divergence value, the more similar are two distributions P and Q.

Lucene ranking: In the Lucene ranking algorithm, it is found that the participants of QA community benefited from a search experience where good answers were called out and bad ones were downplayed or filtered out. And this is with the absolute threshold through careful normalization (Singhal et al. 1996) (of a much more complex scoring mechanism). The sole purpose of the normalization is to set the score of the highest-scoring result. Once this score is set, determine all the other scores since the ratios of their scores to that of the top-scoring result do not change. But this normalization (Singhal et al. 1996) would not change the ranking order or the ratios among scores in a single result set from what they are now. It uses the term frequency and inverse answer frequency to calculate the score for each answer. The scores are intrinsically between 0 and 1. The top score will always be 1.0 assuming that the entire query phrase matches (while the other results have arbitrary fractional scores based on the *tf-iaf* ratios) with the answers. The top score would be 1.0 or 0.5 depending on whether one or two terms matched. The rank of each answer is obtained using

$$score\_a = sum\_t((tf\_q * iaf\_t) / norm\_q) * ((tf\_a * iaf\_t) / norm\_a\_t)) \tag{20.9}$$

where:

score_a = score for answer *a*
sum_t = sum for all terms *t* in answer
tf_q = the square root of the frequency of *t* in the question
tf_a = the square root of the frequency of *t* in answer
iaf_t = log (*numans/ansFreq_t* + 1) + 1.0
numans = number of answers in index
ansFreq_t = number of answers containing *t*
norm_q = sqrt(*sum_t*((*tf_q* * *iaf_t*)^2))
norm_a_t = square root of number of terms in *a* in the same field as *t*

Mutual information (MI): Mutual information is a quantity that measures the mutual dependence of two terms in the question for the given answers.

Formally the mutual information (Sari and Adriani 2008) of two terms *X* and *Y* is defined as

$$I(X;Y) = \sum_{y \in Y} \sum_{x \in X} p(x,y) \log \frac{p(x,y)}{p_1(x)p_2(y)} \tag{20.10}$$

where *X* and *Y* are the selected terms from the question; *p(x, y)* is the joint probability distribution of *X* and *Y*; and *p(x)*, *P(y)* are the marginal probability distribution of *X* and *Y*.

Instinctively, mutual information (Sari and Adriani 2008) measures the information that *X* and *Y* share. It measures how much, knowing one of these variables reduces uncertainty about the other. For example, if *X* and *Y* are independent, then knowing *X* does not give any information about *Y*, and vice versa, so their mutual information is zero. At the other extreme, if *X* and *Y* are identical then share all information conveyed by *X* with *Y*, knowing *X* determines the value of *Y*, and vice versa. As a result, in the case of identity the mutual information is the same as the uncertainty contained in *Y* (or *X*) alone, namely, the entropy of *Y* (or *X*: clearly if *X* and *Y* are identical they have equal entropy).

Mutual information (Sari and Adriani 2008) quantifies the dependence between the joint distribution of *X* and *Y* and what the joint distribution would be if *X* and *Y* were independent. It is a measure of dependence in the following sense: *I(X; Y)* = 0 if and only if *X* and *Y* are independent random variables, then *p(x, y)* = *p(x) p(y)*, described by Equation 20.11:

$$\log \frac{p(x,y)}{p(x)p(y)} = \log 1 = 0 \tag{20.11}$$

Moreover, mutual information is non-negative (i.e., $I(X; Y) \geq 0$) and symmetric (i.e., $I(X; Y) = I(Y; X)$).

*Weight calculation method (tf * iaf):* The *tf-iaf* (Salton and Buckley 1988) weight (term frequency-inverse answer frequency) is a statistical measure used to evaluate how important a word is to an answer in an answers collection. The importance increases proportionally to the number of times a word appears in the answer but is offset by the frequency of the word in the collections. Compute one of the simplest ranking functions by summing the *tf-iaf* for each query term; many more sophisticated ranking functions are variants of this simple model:

$$\text{Weight}(w) = tf * iaf \tag{20.12}$$

The term frequency (*tf*) in the given answer is simply the number of times a given term appears in that answer. This frequency is usually normalized to prevent a bias toward longer answers (which may have a higher term count regardless of the actual importance of that term in the answer) to give the importance of the term t_i within the particular answer a_j. Thus we have the term frequency as

$$tf_{i,j} = \frac{n_{i,j}}{\sum_k n_{k,j}} \tag{20.13}$$

where $n_{i,j}$ is the number of occurrences of the considered term (t_i) in answer a_j, and the denominator is the number of occurrences of all terms in answer a_j. The inverse answer frequency is a measure of the general importance of the term (obtained by dividing the total number of answers by the number of answers containing the term, and then taking the logarithm of that quotient):

$$iaf = \log \frac{|a|}{|\{a: t_i \in a\}|} \tag{20.14}$$

$|a|$ is the total number of answers in the corpus, and $\{a: t_i \in a\}$ is a number of answers where the term t_i appears (that is $n_{i,j} \neq 0$). If the term is not in the corpus, this will lead to a division-by-zero. It is common to use $1 + |\{a: t_i \in a\}|$.

A high weight in *tf-iaf* (Salton and Buckley 1988) is by a high term frequency (in the given answer) and a low answer frequency of the term in the collection of answers; the weights hence tend to filter out common terms. The *tf-iaf* value for a term will always be greater than or equal to zero.

Markov random field (MRF): MRF ranks the answer in response to a query that focuses on textual features (Metzler 2007) defined over query/answer pairs. Thus, the input is a query/answer pair, and the output is a real value. The MRF (Metzler and Croft 2005) model generalizes various dependence models and is defined by

$$P(A/Q) = \sum_{c \in C(G)} \lambda_c f(c) \tag{20.15}$$

where $P(A/Q)$ is the probability of choosing the answer A for the given query Q. λ_c is *iaf* (inverse answer frequency), and $f_c(c)$ is a feature value (Metzler 2007) from answers calculated using (best match) BM 25.

Okapi BM25 is a ranking function used by MRF to rank answers according to their relevance to a given search question. BM25 is a bag of words that ranks a set of answers based on the query terms appearing in each answer, regardless of the inter-relationship between the query terms within an answer. It is not a single function, but actually is a whole family of scoring functions, with slightly different components and parameters. One of the most prominent instantiations of the function is as follows.

Given a query Q, containing keywords $q_1, \ldots, q_n$, the BM25 score of an answer is

$$f_r, \mathrm{BM25}(q_i, a) = \frac{(k_1 + 1) tf_w, a}{k_{1(1-b)} + b \dfrac{|a|}{|a|_{\mathrm{avg}}} + tf_w, a} \log \frac{N - af_w + 0.5}{af_w + 0.5} \tag{20.16}$$

$f(q_i, a)$-q_i is a term frequency in the answer a, $|a|$ is the length of the answer a in words, (tf_w, a) is the number of times the term w matches in answer a, and $|a|_{\mathrm{avg}}$ is the average answer length in words. Here k_1 and b are free parameters, usually chosen as $k_1 = 2.0$ and $b = 0.75$, N is the total number of answers, and af_w is the total number of answers that have at least one match for the term w.

20.5 Empirical Results and Discussion

Now the focus is on the analysis of asker's satisfaction prediction (Liu and Agichitein 2008a,b) in CQA. The number of newly posted questions and answers over a period remains steady, but satisfaction level varies inherently with respect to asker's mentality. If the askers are continuously posting questions but not selecting answers, that introduces a complicated situation for future users to select answers without any background knowledge. Experimental results show that the level of asker satisfaction is excellent for the proposed method. This implies that instead of the best feature selection method (BM25), MRF slightly improves the performance and generates a good precision of 0.889. Also an algorithm (Indri method) shows that just by posting the questions, the proposed methods satisfy and encourage the Yahoo! participants to select the best answer (highly correlate with asker's question) for the asker's question.

The results of satisfaction prediction level by the proposed methods are shown. From the collected Yahoo! Answers (Liu and Agichitein 2008a) snapshots, consider 70% of data as a training set and the rest for testing.

Automatic ranking, abstract generation, and history updation are the contributions to the CQA (Agichtein et al. 2008), which are not available in any of the CQA portals and prove that the highest precision and recall levels are attained with the above contributions. Table 20.2 reports the results. The first set of experiments investigates the answers obtained from different ranking algorithms. Algorithms that use a bag-of-words approach such as vector-space model (Mitchell 2008), Lucene, and weight calculation are producing fair results compared to others. Interestingly the proposed method called "generalization" produces a higher precision of 0.9223 than other ranking methods. Adding Strohman et al. (2005) generates a lower precision value of 0.8029 that uses cross-entropy. The ranking algorithm's performances are similar. The next set of experiments focuses on abstract generation and history updation by computing precision and recall measures. Both methods outperform with precisions 0.9178 and 0.9058.

TABLE 20.2

Precision, Recall, and *F*-Measure for Ranking Algorithms, Abstract Generation, and History Updation

Type	Method	Precision	Recall	*F*-Measure
	Generalization method	0.9223	0.8730	0.8972
	Vector-space model	0.851	0.771	0.809
	Indri method	0.8029	0.7134	0.756
Ranking methods	Markov random field	0.889	0.800	0.842
	Weight calculation method	0.8432	0.749	0.793
	Lucene ranking	0.8376	0.7615	0.798
	Mutual information	0.9201	0.8630	0.891
Abstract generation	Rhetorical structure	0.9056	0.7813	0.844
History updation	Learning automata	0.9178	0.824	0.869

Figure 20.5 demonstrates the satisfaction prediction accuracy for various methodologies and highlights the generalization method (Pietra et al. 1997) for ranking answers to improve the performance of the Yahoo! Answers community. The proposed methods have established promising preliminary results on asker satisfaction even with relatively simple models. An algorithm with *tf* and *iaf* (vector-space model [Mitchell 2008], weight calculation method, and Lucene algorithm) achieves moreover the same precision value.

Summarization of answers: Human judgment often has wide variance on what is considered a "good" summary (Cohen 1987), which means that making the evaluation process automatic is particularly difficult. Manual evaluation can be used, but this is both time and labor intensive as it requires humans to read not only the summaries (Cohen 1987) but also the source answers. Other issues are those concerning coherence and coverage.

The metric used here is the kappa score (Cicchetti and Feinstein 1990) in which the abstract generation (Sumita et al. 2007) system submits the results to the human experts who evaluate them. The proposed system generates summaries (Cohen 1987) automatically and compares them with the human-generated summaries (Lehnert 1980). High overlap between the two summaries indicates a high level of shared concepts between them. The generated abstracts were evaluated for key sentence coverage. In Table 20.3,

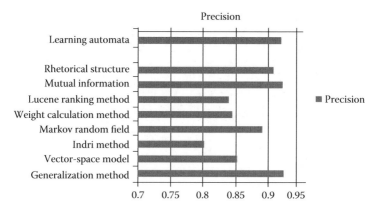

FIGURE 20.5
Method's satisfaction prediction accuracy.

TABLE 20.3

Key Sentence Coverage of the Abstract

Material	Number of Answer	Word Count	Abstract Word Count	Length Ratio	Cover Ratio Key Sentence	Most Important Sentence
Q 1	5	19	8	0.421	0.429	0.75
Q 2	7	23	11	0.478	0.429	0.50
Q 3	6	29	13	0.448	0.571	0.75
Q 4	11	37	14	0.378	0.571	0.75
Q 5	8	58	21	0.362	0.714	0.75
Q 6	14	60	29	0.483	0.714	1
Q 7	13	67	32	0.478	0.857	1
Q 8	16	74	35	0.473	0.714	0.75
Q 9	10	85	41	0.482	0.857	1
Q 10	14	93	43	0.462	0.857	1
Q 11	17	102	49	0.480	0.714	1
Q 12	19	114	52	0.456	0.571	0.75
Q 13	20	138	54	0.391	0.714	0.75
Q 14	18	152	70	0.461	0.857	1
Q 15	21	161	73	0.453	0.857	1

select samples of 15 questions from food and drink, sports, and home and garden categories present short answers of six or seven sentences. Seven subjects (experience, example, confident, negative, serial, direction, and specialization) judged the key sentences, and the first four judged the most important key sentence of each answer. As for Questions 9 and 10, the average correspondence rates of the key sentence and the most important key sentence among the subjects are 86% and 100%.

The key sentence coverage increases with the abstract (Sumita et al. 2007) word count. The reason is the less word count answers contain only less rhetorical expressions. That is, they provide less linguistic clues and the system cannot extract the rhetorical structure exactly. The average length ratio (abstract/original) reduced to 36.2% (Question 5) to make the length of the abstract shorter.

Human judgment: To complement the asker ratings, human judgments were obtained from users of Yahoo! Answers (Liu and Agichitein 2008a). Here Cohen's kappa score (Cicchetti and Feinstein 1990) is to evaluate human judgment.

Table 20.4 shows the kappa score (Cicchetti and Feinstein 1990) for various methodologies.

TABLE 20.4

Human Judgments

	Ranking Algorithms								
Type	Vector Space	Markov Random Field	Lucene	Weight	Indri	Mutual	Generalization	Abstract Generation	History Updation
Kappa score	0.8743	0.8853	0.8413	0.8659	0.8292	0.9049	0.9267	0.9218	0.9289

Surprisingly, the proposed methods abstract generation, history updation, and automatic ranking using generalization (Pietra et al. 1997) are highly correlated with but not exceeding the human judgments, because it is very difficult to predict what the user thinks in his or her mind, and the tastes of humans continuously change based on environmental factors.

Section VI

Findings and Summary

21

Findings and Summary of Text Information Retrieval Chapters

21.1 Findings and Summary

This chapter presents the important conclusions of various information retrieval (IR) model formulations and the investigations reported in the previous chapters. They are summarized below:

1. The retrieval problem formalized with clustering to reduce the solution space and time complexity, as well as the difficulties in traditional retrieval methods. Here, the scalability of various algorithms is tested on datasets collected from TREC and PubMed repository, which varied from 250 to 1000 documents. The TABU annealing approach is developed, which appears to be the method of choice for finding higher-quality solutions and guaranteeing asymptotic convergence (fast rate of convergence) toward the global optimum. This is obtained by randomly perturbing a very simple selection scheme of simulated annealing (SA). The main idea is limiting the search space by SA. Then the partitions (clusters) are given as the initial seeds to TABU. The TABU search algorithm is able to skip the local optimum and continue the search. TABU search heuristics start from an initial solution, and at each step such a move to a neighboring solution is chosen to hopefully improve the objective criterion value.

2. Dimensionality reduction using latent semantic indexing allows for concept-based IR, which throws light on the solution for synonymy and polysemy problems. The particle swarm optimization (PSO)+K-means algorithm combines the capability of globalized searching of the PSO algorithm and the fast convergence of the K-means algorithm. Hence, the proposed approach avoids the drawback of both algorithms. The datasets are taken from the TREC (2006) dataset, a collection of proceedings from Text Retrieval conference; PubMed dataset (2004) contains documents from medical publications and 7-Sectors dataset, a collection of web pages from various domains. Better precision and recall rates for searching a very large set of documents from a corpus are provided by SA. Since the documents are reduced dimensionally and clustered before retrieval, the accuracy of retrieval is increased.

3. The hybrid Harmony-TABU algorithm produces better solutions with high quality considering precision, recall, and mean average precision quality measures than Harmony and TABU alone. The results of the hybridized methods are the initial seeds for the relevance feedback approaches. The dataset used here is OHSUMED,

a bibliographical document collection, developed by Hersh et al. at the Oregon Health Sciences University. There are 16,140 query-document pairs. Here we use term feedback for interactive IR in the language modeling approach. The best-performing algorithm has been found to be term-cluster feedback (TCFB), which benefits from the combination of directly observed term evidence with term feedback (TFB) and indirectly learned cluster relevance with cluster feedback (CFB).

4. A novel feature selection technique is presented, which is a combined form of dynamic feature selection algorithm and association rules. It uses normalized discount cumulative gain (NDCG), which is a popular metric to measure the usefulness of the ranking algorithm based on relevance feedback. It also incorporates the relevance feedback concept using expectation maximization methodology that suits most for the BM25 ranking algorithm. Thus the results obtained from the experiments show that the feature selection technique using the 0/1 knapsack algorithm can efficiently provide a solution and improve the performance of IR as well as or better than other feature selection systems.

5. A new framework is proposed which integrates content-based recommendation, collaborative filtering techniques, and truth finder. One of the major obstacles for recommendation systems is lack of trustworthiness of websites. The proposed framework is designed in such a way to deal with problems associated with them and to enhance the performance of existing approaches for web page recommendations. The dataset used here contains the preprocessed and filtered data from the main DePaul CTI Web server. The data are based on a random sample of users visiting this site for a 2-week period during April 2002. The original (unfiltered) data contained a total of 20,950 sessions from 5446 users. The filtered data files were produced by filtering low support page views, and eliminating sessions of size 1. The filtered data contain 13,745 sessions and 683 page views. This proposed framework provides reasonable accuracy in predictions in the face of high data sparsely.

6. A new algorithm is presented based on the identification of generalized facets using Word Net for finding subtopics in a corpus. The point-wise KL divergence metric is used to decide query expansion terms as the term relevance measure. The average pair-wise Jaccard coefficient is calculated by finding the coefficient for every pair of subtopics in the collection and averaging this value, and this is a measure of the redundancy. The algorithm performs very well in practice compared to the baseline standard, greedy, and language feedback models.

7. Finding duplication on the text collection is an IR problem of interest to the search engine and Web caching communities. Here different classes of algorithms are evaluated for duplication detection, namely, (1) similarity-based approaches such as Word Overlap and Jaccard measure; (2) shingling techniques like full finger-printing, DSC, I-Match, 0 mod p, winnowing, and K-gram; and (3) ASPDD, the dynamic proposed approach that compares duplication of letters and emails from public comments. These were evaluated on a collection of 82,992 comments from the source FWS-Wolf (RIN: 1018.AU53) of size 622 MB. The similarity-based algorithms; K-gram shingling, and ASPDD are the best algorithms. The experimental results conclude that all the approaches except the above are limited in terms of accuracy and recall. ASPDD achieves a higher precision, recall, and *F*-measure considering public comments.

8. Seeker satisfaction prediction in Yahoo! Answers is described. This work has introduced and formalized automatic ranking algorithm, abstract generation, and history updation to improve asker satisfaction. Also the results on satisfaction prediction demonstrate significant accuracy improvements using "generalization" ranking methodology, "rhetorical structure," and "learning automata" technique. The proposed techniques work well with crucial problems like answer understanding, answer justifying, and asker's taste changes over a time period. Thus this work outlines a promising area in the general field of modeling user intent, expectations, and satisfaction, and can potentially result in practical improvements to the effectiveness and design of question answering communities.

21.2 Future Directions

This book can be extended by incorporating the following suggestions:

1. Selection of top-ranked documents must be made carefully, so that all are relevant.
2. Investigation is required for Word Net for hypernym path generation for the coverage of subtopics in the text collection.
3. An answer may be fully relevant to the question according to the ranking system, but not to the asker's point of view, because the system cannot fully predict what the asker really wants, and it cannot understand in what context the user expects the answer.
4. The gist prepared by rhetorical structure may not be preferred by some users, and in such cases they may use replicated answers.

22

Findings and Summary of Image Retrieval and Assessment of Image Mining Systems Chapters

This chapter presents an evaluation of the proposed image mining systems via average precision-recall curves of proposed image retrieval systems for Pascal database, average precision of top-ranked results after the ninth feedback for the Corel database, average recall of top-ranked results after the ninth feedback for the Corel database, average precision of proposed methods for different semantic classes for the Pascal database, average recall of proposed methods for different semantic classes for the Pascal database, average precision of top-ranked results after the ninth feedback for information retrieval (IR) with summarization and IR without summarization for the Pascal database, average execution time of proposed methods (in seconds), and performance analysis of top retrieval results obtained with the proposed image retrieval systems.

22.1 Experimental Setup

The feature components are computed from segmented regions of the whole image, whereas for content-based image retrieval systems, features are computed from whole images. As usual, the feature computation process is online for query image and offline for database image. The feature components of database images are stored in a database for runtime access. The visual signature of each image is composed of four different feature vectors. They are 32-bin color histogram, 9-bin color moment, 8-bin edge direction histogram, and 18-wavelet texture energy values. To be a fair comparison, all the systems use the same visual signature. To compare the query image and database images, weighted Euclidean distance is applied for a content-based image retrieval system and Earth Mover distance for a region-based image retrieval system.

For each image database in our experiments, we simulated the presence of users by using each image as an initial query point. For a query image, 10 iterations of user-and-system interaction were carried out. At each iteration, the system examined the top 18 images, apart from those positive examples labeled in previous iterations. Images from the same (different) category of the query image were considered as relevant (irrelevant) images.

To show the comparison of these approaches in our evaluation, we have employed the Pascal database which is extracted from the VOC2007 dataset (Everingham and Gool 2010). A subset of 2500 images is partitioned into 23 classes which have different numbers of images, varying from 72 to 446 subimages each. Subsets from Corel photo galleries (Wang 2004) are also employed, which covers a wide range of semantic categories of natural scenes with artificial objects. The dataset is partitioned into 25 categories, with each category represented by 100 images, for a total of 2500 images.

The swarm of fireflies is randomly initialized in the solution space. The same firefly parameter settings used previously are utilized here, which include number of fireflies

$(F) = 18$, light absorption coefficient $(\gamma) = 1$, attractiveness $(\beta_0) = 1$, and number of generations $(I) = 110$. All the experiments were run on a 1.83 GHz Intel machine, and the performance has been measured based on a JAVA implementation.

22.2 Results and Discussions

Average precision, average recall, F-measure, true positive, and false positive are used to evaluate the performance of RF algorithms. The average precision refers to the percentage of relevant images in top retrieved images and is calculated as the average precision values of all the queries to evaluate the effectiveness of the algorithm. The average recall shows the fraction of the related images that are successfully retrieved and is defined as the percentage of retrieved images among all relevant images in the dataset. F-measure refers to the harmonic mean of precision and recall, true positive refers to the number of images correctly retrieved as belonging to the class of query image, and false positive refers to the number of images incorrectly retrieved as belonging to the class of query image.

The performance of the system is usually measured based on the degree of retrieval accuracy. In CBIR, precision-recall is the prevalent method used to calculate the retrieval accuracy. Precision and recall have been used as a performance measure to compute the effectiveness of the proposed approach. Precision is the ratio of the number of retrieved relevant images to the total number of retrieved images, and recall is defined as the ratio of the number of retrieved relevant images to the total number of relevant images in the whole database. A perfect precision score of 1.0 implies that every result retrieved is relevant (but yields no information about whether all relevant documents were retrieved), whereas a perfect recall score of 1.0 implies that all relevant documents were retrieved by the search (but does not show how many irrelevant documents were also retrieved).

To enhance the number of retrieved relevant images (and the recall), the number of returned images needs to be increased. Hence, both precision and recall must be high. Every so often, an inverse relationship exists between precision and recall, where it is possible to increase one while the other gets reduced. For instance, a search engine can improve its recall by retrieving more documents, while increasing the number of irrelevant documents retrieved and thereby decreasing precision. Consequently, the precision-recall curve is made use of to display this relation and to characterize the performance of content-based image retrieval (CBIR).

Precision and recall scores are not viewed separately. As an alternative, either values for one measure are compared for a fixed level of the other measure (e.g., precision at a recall level of 0.80) or both are combined into a single measure, such as a precision-recall graph. A precision-recall pair endows the best results when the nature of the database is familiar and has been used successfully in previous research. For every query, the precision of the retrieval at every level of the recall is obtained. Corel archives usually perform better, especially for some image classes commonly utilized in the literature. The PASCAL database imposes more challenges than the Corel database.

22.3 Findings 1: Average Precision-Recall Curves of Proposed Image Retrieval Systems for Pascal Database

The average precision-recall curves more than 600 randomly chosen images from various semantic classes in the database were recorded as queries to compare the efficacy of the four variant approaches, and each query provided the top 18 images from the database. The precision of retrieval was analyzed for each query image according to the relevance of the semantic meaning between the query and the retrieved images. The precision of retrieval at each level of the recall was attained by slowly increasing the number of retrieved images. The average of 10,800 retrieval results was computed to provide the final precision-recall curve of each approach for the Pascal database, and it is illustrated in Figure 22.1. All precision and recall values were assessed by finding the average of five consecutive runs for every query image, enabled by the stochastic nature of a firefly-based algorithm. The performance of the image retrieval system seems better with a higher precision-recall curve.

From Figure 22.1, it could be interpreted that the system of the firefly algorithm (FA) and support vector machine (SVM) in region-based image retrieval (RBIR) has better average precision values over various recall levels. The average precision is at the maximum of 96% at a recall level of 0.1 but declines to a precision value of 0.28 at a recall level of 1.0. For instance, for an average recall value of 20%, the average precision value is 91% (i.e., if the user desires to obtain 20% of the relevant images from the database, 91% of the retrieved images will be relevant and 9% of them will be irrelevant). Precision values decrease with an increase in the recall levels as expected for a good retrieval system.

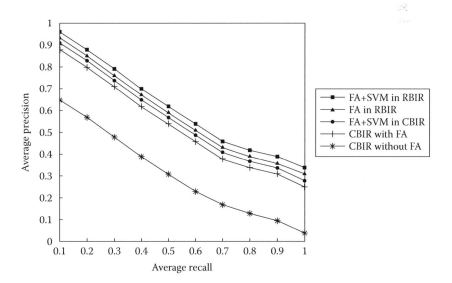

FIGURE 22.1
Average precision-recall curves of proposed image retrieval systems for Pascal database.

22.4 Findings 2: Average Precision and Average Recall of Proposed Methods for Different Semantic Classes

From the precision-recall curves of Figure 22.1, and from the graph of average precision and average recall for different semantic classes as depicted in Figures 22.2 and 22.3, respectively, it is observed that the FA and SVM in an RBIR system outperforms all other approaches proving that the advantage of having both, signifying the images at the region level after the segmentation process and doing a classification step in the feedback-based learning process. The precision-recall curve of FA in an RBIR system is higher than the approach of FA and SVM contribution in a CBIR system and firefly algorithm-based CBIR system. This shows the significance of a region-based system over the global feature-based system. From Figure 22.1, it is also noticed that the precision-recall curve of FA and SVM

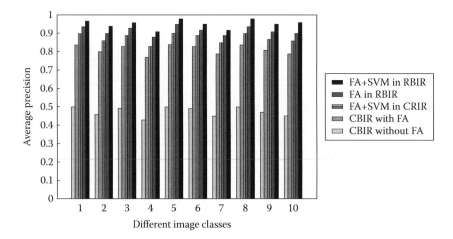

FIGURE 22.2
Average precision of proposed methods for different semantic classes for Corel database.

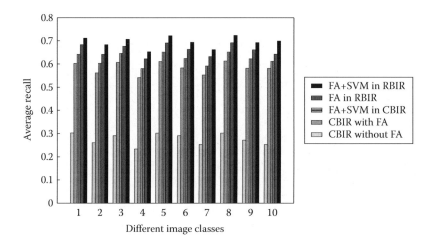

FIGURE 22.3
Average recall of proposed methods for different semantic classes for Corel database.

in a CBIR system outperforms FA in a CBIR system, showing the importance of the classification step in the relevance feedback-based learning process.

Tables 22.1 through 22.5 show the average performance of FA+SVM in RBIR, FA in RBIR, FA+SVM in CBIR, CBIR with FA, and CBIR without FA for different categories of Corel database.

TABLE 22.1

Average Performance of FA+SVM in RBIR for Categories of Corel Database

Categories	Precision (%)	Recall (%)	*F*-Measure (%)	TP (%)	FP (%)
Butterfly	97.35	71.12	82.19306	97.35	2.65
Buildings	94.32	68.14	79.12058	94.32	5.68
Hills	96.21	70.52	81.38582	96.21	3.79
Flowers	91.41	65.11	76.05041	91.41	8.59
Earth	98.25	72.12	83.18119	98.25	1.75
Sky	95.34	69.25	80.22717	95.34	4.66
Tree	92.42	66.31	77.21754	92.42	7.58
Boat	98.24	72.12	83.17761	98.24	1.76
Bird	95.31	69.01	80.0553	95.31	4.69
Statue	96.23	70.12	81.12591	96.23	3.77

TABLE 22.2

Average Performance of FA in RBIR for Categories of Corel Database

Categories	Precision (%)	Recall (%)	*F*-Measure (%)	TP (%)	FP (%)
Butterfly	94.21	68.13	79.07512	94.21	5.79
Buildings	90.31	64.11	74.98736	90.31	9.69
Hills	93.24	67.52	78.32253	93.24	6.76
Flowers	88.42	62.11	72.96574	88.42	11.58
Earth	95.31	69.12	80.12926	95.31	4.69
Sky	92.24	66.25	77.11401	92.24	7.76
Tree	89.21	63.15	73.95132	89.21	10.79
Boat	94.25	69.23	79.82539	94.25	5.75
Bird	91.23	66.01	76.59746	91.23	8.77
Statue	90.15	64.01	74.8638	90.15	9.85

TABLE 22.3

Average Performance of FA+SVM in CBIR for Categories of Corel Database

Categories	Precision (%)	Recall (%)	*F*-Measure (%)	TP (%)	FP (%)
Butterfly	90.15	64.12	74.93898	90.15	9.85
Buildings	86.23	60.14	70.85977	86.23	13.77
Hills	89.25	64.53	74.90314	89.25	10.75
Flowers	83.21	58.12	68.43791	83.21	16.79
Earth	90.24	65.12	75.64919	90.24	9.76
Sky	89.31	62.25	73.36431	89.31	10.69
Tree	85.42	59.13	69.88426	85.42	14.58
Boat	90.21	65.21	75.69932	90.21	9.79
Bird	87.23	62.01	72.48904	87.23	12.77
Statue	86.12	61.24	71.57965	86.12	13.88

TABLE 22.4

Average Performance of CBIR with FA for Categories of Corel Database

Categories	Precision (%)	Recall (%)	*F*-Measure (%)	TP (%)	FP (%)
Butterfly	84.12	60.14	70.13693	84.12	15.88
Buildings	80.23	56.11	66.03646	80.23	19.77
Hills	83.21	60.52	70.07402	83.21	16.79
Flowers	77.42	54.13	63.71333	77.42	22.58
Earth	84.31	61.12	70.86608	84.31	15.69
Sky	83.24	58.25	68.53813	83.24	16.76
Tree	83.21	55.13	66.32019	83.21	16.79
Boat	83.25	62.13	71.1559	83.25	16.75
Bird	83.23	58.01	68.36834	83.23	16.77
Statue	83.15	58.14	68.43147	83.15	16.85

TABLE 22.5

Average Performance of CBIR without FA for Categories of Corel Database

Categories	Precision (%)	Recall (%)	*F*-Measure (%)	TP (%)	FP (%)
Butterfly	50.12	30.21	37.69763	50.12	49.88
Buildings	46.23	26.01	33.29021	46.23	53.77
Hills	49.25	29.13	36.60762	49.25	50.75
Flowers	43.21	23.13	30.13106	43.21	56.79
Earth	50.24	30.21	37.73152	50.24	49.76
Sky	49.31	29.12	36.61627	49.31	50.69
Tree	45.42	25.13	32.35732	45.42	54.58
Boat	50.31	30.32	37.83701	50.31	49.69
Bird	47.23	27.45	34.7205	47.23	52.77
Statue	45.12	25.21	32.3468	45.12	54.88

22.5 Findings 3: Average Precision and Average Recall of Top-Ranked Results after the Ninth Feedback for Corel Database

As can be perceived from Figure 22.4, the average precision values are high for a small number of retrieved images, and as the number of retrieved images increases, the average precision values decrease, demonstrating that the system gives a better ranking for the retrieved images. This is because the precision values are based on the ratio of the number of retrieved relevant images to the total number of retrieved images; accordingly, as the number of retrieved images increases, precision starts to decrease naturally.

As can be perceived from Figure 22.5, the average recall values are small for a small number of retrieved images, and as the number of retrieved image increases the average recall values increase, demonstrating that the system gives a better ranking for the retrieved images. This is because the recall values are based on the ratio of the number of retrieved relevant images to the total number of relevant images in the whole database; accordingly, as the number of retrieved images increases, the relevant retrieved image is also increasing naturally.

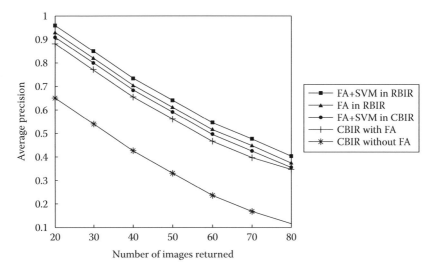

FIGURE 22.4
Average precision of top-ranked results after the ninth feedback for Pascal database.

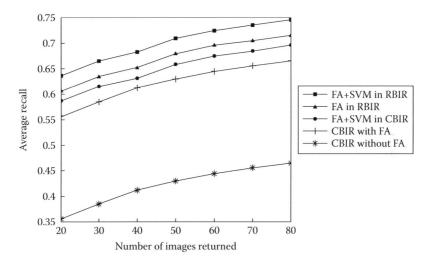

FIGURE 22.5
Average recall of top-ranked results after the ninth feedback for Pascal database.

22.6 Findings 4: Average Precision of Top-Ranked Results after the Ninth Feedback for IR with Summarization and IR without Summarization

To examine the efficiency of our summarization scheme, we measure the retrieval time and average precision of our proposed work with and without summarization schemes. The results are revealed in Table 22.6 and Figure 22.6, respectively. IR denotes image retrieval. The automatic image summarization task is viewed as an optimization problem, for example, choosing a subset of the most representative images that can best rebuild the

TABLE 22.6

Average Execution Time of Proposed Methods (in Seconds)

	CBIR+FA without RF	CBIR+FA with RF	CBIR+ SVM+FA without RF	CBIR+ SVM+FA with RF	RBIR+FA without RF	RBIR+ FA with RF	RBIR+ SVM+FA without RF	RBIR+ SVM+FA with RF	Image Retrieval with Summarization
Time	0.3407	0.0287	1.3387	1.0267	1.05	0.738	2.048	1.736	0.736

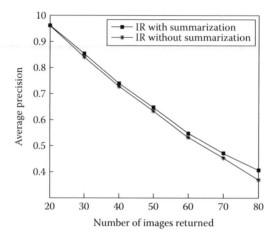

FIGURE 22.6
Average precision of top-ranked results after the ninth feedback for IR with summarization and IR without summarization for Pascal database.

real image set in large size. If the automatic image summarization is done before the image retrieval process, the performance is improved. Also it reduces the execution time of the image retrieval process.

22.7 Findings 5: Average Execution Time of Proposed Methods

Table 22.6 shows the average execution time of our experiments for each iteration. The execution time refers to the average time required by each RF approach to be trained by the user (or the time taken to retrieve relevant image) and to select images to be shown on each iteration. The execution time of the proposed approach and comparison methods is influenced by the parameter choice and also the number of images marked as relevant and irrelevant by the user on each iteration. From Table 22.6, it is inferred that SVM+FA in RBIR have higher execution times that can be overcome by applying image summarization before the retrieval process.

From the precision-recall curves of Figure 22.1, and from the graph of average precision and average recall for different semantic classes as depicted in Figures 22.2 and 22.3, respectively, it is noticed that the precision-recall curve of FA and SVM in the CBIR system outperforms FA in the CBIR system, showing the importance of the classification step in the relevance feedback-based learning process, but its average execution time increases by 0.998 seconds. The precision-recall curve of FA in the RBIR system is higher than the approach of FA and SVM contribution in the CBIR system and firefly algorithm-based CBIR system and also the average execution time decreases by 0.2887 seconds. This shows the significance of the region-based system compared to the global feature-based system. From Figures 22.1 through 22.3, it is also observed that the FA and SVM in the RBIR system outperform all other approaches, proving the advantage of having both, signifying the images at the region level after the segmentation process and doing the classification step in the feedback-based learning process, but its average execution time increases by 0.998 seconds. This higher execution time can be overcome by applying image summarization before the retrieval process, and thus its execution time decreases to 0.736.

22.8 Findings 6: Performance Analysis of Top Retrieval Results Obtained with the Proposed Image Retrieval Systems

To further explain the difference between the proposed systems in responding to a sample query image, we show in Figures 22.7b through 22.10 the top 10 retrieval results of the proposed image retrieval systems responding to given query images from the bus class in the Corel database. The query image has a distinct object of a large area, which is a bus with less area and color contrast from the background.

From Figures 22.7b through 22.10 we can notice that Figure 22.7b gives good results as an FA and SVM in an RBIR system. It represents images at the object level by the segmentation process in addition to doing a classification step of SVM while optimizing the image retrieval process. Thus, the top 10 retrieval results of the query image bus contain all the images of the bus as well as those from the same class. Thus, the retrieval accuracy of the retrieved result is 10/10 = 100%.

(a)

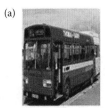

(b)

FIGURE 22.7
(a) Query image. (b) Top 10 retrieval results for FA+SVM in RBIR system.

FIGURE 22.8
Top 10 retrieval result for FA in RBIR system.

From Figure 22.8, one can notice that nine images are from the bus category, but one is not from the class of bus, so the system is able to capture the distinct object of the bus but not classify it well. So the retrieval result of Figure 22.8 is 9/10 = 90%. From Figure 22.9, one can notice that eight images are from the bus category, but two are not from the class of bus. This is due to the system being based on a global feature-based system; it cannot capture the distinct object well, even though it has a classification step in the relevance feedback process. So the retrieval result of Figure 22.9 is 8/10 = 80%. From Figure 22.10, one can notice that seven images are from the bus category, but three images are not from the class of bus, so the system does not capture the distinct object of buses and does not classify the class of bus well. This is due to the global feature-based system, and it does not have a classification step in the relevance feedback process. So the retrieval result of Figure 22.10 is 7/10 = 70%.

FIGURE 22.9
Top 10 retrieval result for FA+SVM in CBIR system.

FIGURE 22.10
Top 10 retrieval result for FA in CBIR system.

22.9 Summary

Seeing that the optimization research studies have promoted the prevalent expansion in information retrieval, in this book, four different approaches have been developed based on a Gaussian firefly algorithm in the relevance feedback loop of an image retrieval system for optimizing the image retrieval process. The proposed approaches improved the image retrieval performance by scaling down the semantic gap. Also the increased explosion of images has been managed by developing a multimodal image summarization system that constructed a summary by organizing the large sets of image collections. This enabled the users to get an overview of the interesting information in the image collections without scanning through the entire database.

In the first approach, the image retrieval problem has been formulated as an optimization problem by exploiting a nature-inspired algorithm called a firefly algorithm in a content-based image retrieval system, which dynamically reflected the user's intention in the retrieval process by optimizing the objective function. The experiment on Corel and Caltech database images compared with particle swarm optimization (PSO) and genetic algorithm (GA) showed that the proposed image retrieval system based on the firefly algorithm has a better average precision curve as the number of images returned increases and the computation time is minimal.

Next, SVM learning has been embedded with the Gaussian firefly algorithm in the relevance feedback process of a content-based image retrieval system as an optimization model that enhanced the retrieval precision of an image retrieval system. The parameters of the SVM are suitably influenced by the Gaussian firefly algorithm, and consequently, the number of relevant or positive feedback images increases such that it tunes the feedback learning process and provides better results. The proposed system outperformed the comparable baseline algorithms for all iterations, and as the iterations increased, the average precision also increased. The precision-recall curve showed improvement as the number of iterations increases. Also, this system showed a higher precision-recall curve than the image retrieval system based on a firefly algorithm, as it suitably influences the parameters of the SVM, which increased the workability of the learning process in addition to optimizing the image retrieval process.

Then the Gaussian firefly algorithm was integrated into a region-based image retrieval system that attempted to conquer the shortage of global feature-based search by signifying images at the region level. The region-level signification is intended to be close to the observation of the human visual system; thus, it improved the capability of capturing in addition to signifying the focus of the user's acuity of image content on retrieving desired images from a large database such that it boosted the performance of an image retrieval process. The experiment on Corel and Vistex image database compared with baselines showed that the proposed RBIR based on a Gaussian firefly algorithm has a higher average precision for different image categories. Also, as this system is represented at the regional level when optimizing the image retrieval process, it showed a higher average precision-recall curve than the proposed content-based image retrieval systems based on the firefly algorithm and integrated SVM and Gaussian firefly algorithm.

Next, in the relevance feedback loop of an RBIR system, SVM has been integrated with the Gaussian firefly algorithm. The proposed system worked out the problem of SVM by suitably influencing the parameters of SVM as well as signifying the focus of the user's acuity of image content on retrieving desired images from a large database by signifying the images at the region level. The experiments with the subset of Corel and Caltech database images showed that the retrieval performance yielded higher average precision and recall value when compared to the existing methods, like PSO, GA, SVM, and query point movement. Also, it has faster convergence speed than the comparative methods. This system has better average precision-recall curves than all the proposed image retrieval systems in this book, as it tunes the learning process by suitably influencing the parameters of SVM in addition to representing images at the region level while optimizing the image retrieval process.

Finally, the image summarization task has been formulated as an optimization problem by employing the firefly algorithm for a multimodal image summarization system in order to manage today's image explosion. The proposed system has been treated as the issue of dictionary learning for a joint sparse representation model that attempted to select a small set of the best representative images to assist interactive exploration and navigation of large-scale image collections. The efficiency of the summary is revealed by its capability to reconstruct each individual image in the dataset or the original image set. The experiment on the UW image collection showed that the proposed multimodal image summarization system has lesser MSE when compared with baseline algorithms, and thus it has better reconstruction capability. The image retrieval performance after the image summarization process has better average precision and less computation time than image retrieval without image summarization. The improvement resided in two aspects: (1) the proposed approach considered multimodality, sparsity, and diversity constrictions, whereas the baseline algorithms do not have such consideration for a good summary; and (2) the adopted firefly algorithm attained a global optimum solution, whereas the baseline algorithms look for local optimum solutions. Assessment of various experiments showed the advantages of the proposed system.

22.10 Future Scope

The following can be addressed in the future:

- The user's profile may be incorporated into the proposed approach to improve the quality of retrieval.

- The proposed work may be tried with other optimization algorithms such as a social spider algorithm, cuckoo search, bat algorithm, harmony search, flower algorithm, and so on.
- The automatic image summarization system may incorporate context data like location and orientation along with visual and textual content to construct a summary.

Appendix: Abbreviations, Acronyms and Symbols

Abbreviations and Acronyms

ADDC	Average distance of documents to the cluster centroid
AFGF	Automatic facet generation framework
AR	Affinity ranking
ARW	Absorbed random walk
ASPDD	All pairs shortest path based duplicate detection
BoW	Bag of word
BP	Basis pursuit
CBIR	Content-based image retrieval
CD	Count difference
CF	Collaborative filtering
CFB	Cluster feedback
CFS	Correlation-based feature selection
CQA	Community question answering
CR	Cross-over
CS	Cohesion separation
DE	Differential evolution
DETS	DE with TS
EAs	Evolutionary algorithms
EMD	Earth Mover's distance
FCA	Formal concept analysis
FCT	Frequent co-occurring term
FD	Full dependence
FI	Full independence
FOCUSS	Focal underdetermined system solver
GA	Genetic algorithm
GP	Genetic programming
HBM	Hierarchical bisecting medoids
HM	Harmony memory
HMCR	Harmony memory considering rate
HMS	Harmony memory size
HS	Harmony search
HSV	Hue saturation value
IDF	Inverse document frequency

IGA	Interactive genetic algorithm
IQE	Interactive query expansion
IR	Information retrieval
IRM	Integrated region matching
KL	Kullback–Leibler divergence
KS	Keyword search
KSA	K-means with SA
K-SVD	K-singular value decomposition
KTS	K-means with TS
LA	Learning automata
LAP	Local aggregation pattern
LSI	Latent semantic indexing
LSP	Local similarity pattern
MAP	Mean average precision
MEDLINE	Medical line
MI	Mutual information
MOD	Method of optimal direction
MP	Matching pursuit
MRF	Markov random field
MSE	Mean square error
NDCG	Normalized discount cumulative gain
NE	Named entities
NP	Nondeterministic polynomial
OMP	Orthogonal matching pursuit
OPF	Optimum path forest
PAR	Pitch-adjusting rate
PCA	Principle component analysis
PSO	Particle swarm optimization
PubMed	Medical publications
QA	Question answering
QPM	Query point movement
RBF	Radial basis function
RBIR	Region-based image retrieval
RF	Relevance feedback
RFSP	Region and feature saliency pattern
RGB	Red, green, blue
SA	Simulated annealing
SD	Sequential dependence
SIFT	Scale invariant feature transform
SOM	Self-organizing features maps
SVD	Singular value decomposition
SVM	Support vector machine
TABU	Tabulated search
TCFB	Term cluster feedback

TDCCREC	Truth discovery-based content and collaborative recommender system
TFB	Term feedback
TREC	Text retrieval conference
TS	TABU search
UW	University of Washington
VSM	Vector space model
WA	Weighted association
WRS	Web recommender system
WSP	Weighted support

Symbols

c_1, c_2	Acceleration coefficients
$*(f)$	Adjusted confidence score
$r_{ii'}$	Average feature intercorrelation
$Cent_i$	Centroid
$Chrom_{fit}$	Chromosome fitness
c_i	Cluster
V	Concept document matrix
$S(f)$	Confidence of facts
(f)	Confidence score
COS	Cosine similarity between two vectors
$c(w; q)$	Count of w in q
Pgd	Current optimal value of the dimension "d" of the swarm
x_{id}	Current value of the dimension "d" of the dividual "i"
V	Current velocity
v_{id}	Current velocity of the dimension "d" of the individual "i"
Xr2-Xr3	Difference vector
$d(X_i, X_j)$	Distance metric between two documents X_i and X_j
d_k	Document vector
.	Dot product of two vectors
E_j	Entropy
$H(Y)$	Entropy of Y
e	Exponential
W	Inertia weight factor
IG	Information gain
iaf	Inverse answer frequency
IDF_i	Inverse document frequency
F_1	Jaccard similarity
$J(w_{selected}, w_i)$	Jaccard similarity coefficient between the selected word $w_{selected}$ with the remaining words

$X_j(i)$	*j*th pattern belonging to the *i*th cluster
w	KL divergence score
X	Location
iaf_t	Log (numans/ansFreq_t+1) + 1.0
rci	Mean feature correlation
M_t	Model learned after iteration t
‖	Modulus of vector
V_i	Mutant vector
$N(i)$	Neighborhood of a solution i
ansFreq_t	Number of answers containing t
numans	Number of answers in index
K	Number of cluster centroids
N_c	Number of clusters
n_i	Number of document vectors
Pid	Optimal value of the dimension "d" of the individual "i" so far
q	Original query model
Fresh(p_i)	Page freshness
Pr ()	Page rank
$P_{a,u}$	Pearson correlation coefficient
b	Penalizing factor
$P(w)$	Probability distribution of bigram w in retrieved document set
$Q(w)$	Probability distribution of bigram w in the generic corpus
pij	Probability that document i belongs to cluster j
$|q|$	Query length
F	Relevancy function
a	Rewarding factor
score_a	Score for answer a
C(G)	Set of cliques
F(ws)	Set of facts given by websites w
$sim(a_j, q)$	Similarity between the answer and the query
S	Singular matrix
S_0	Solution (partition)
$N(i,k)$	Some recently visited solutions are removed from $N(i)$
norm_q	sqrt(sum_t((tf_q*iaf_t)^2))
norm_a_t	Square root of number of terms in a in the same field as t
sum_t	Sum for all terms t in answer
T	TABU list
X_i	Target vector
$T0$	Temperature
(t)	Temperature reduction function
tf_i	Term frequency for the term i
U	Term-concept matrix
A	Term-document matrix
$M(i)$	The set of moves that can be applied to i in order to obtain a new solution j

tf_q	The square root of the frequency of t in the question
w_{ij}	The weight of the jth document for the ith cluster
F_2	This measure is calculated where recall weights twice as much as precision
$F0.5$	This measure is computed if precision weights twice as much as recall
$Pr()$	Transition probability value
$tw(ws)$	Trustworthiness of websites
(ws)	Trustworthiness score
i	Unigram language model
q'	Updated query model
f	Weight associated with the feature f
Wconf	Weighted confidence
Wsp(X)	Weighted support of item set X
A	Word-by-document matrix in a lower dimensional space
$\geq$	Greater than or equal to
$\leq$	Less than or equal to
$\sum$	Sum of terms
c_p^{ch}	Color histogram
c_p^{cm}	Color moments
c_p^{edh}	Edge direction histogram
c_p^{wt}	Texture wavelet feature values
M_{ch}	Dimension of color histogram
M_{cm}	Dimension of color moments
M_{edh}	Dimension of edge direction histogram
M_{wt}	Dimension of texture wavelet feature values
D	Dimension of feature vector
C_p	pth image feature vector
C_S	Stored database images
C_Q	Query image
M_{FB}	Number of feedback images
$WMSE$	Weighted mean square error
w_r^k	Vector of weights
k	Iteration number
M_{DB}	Number of database images
A_n	Swarm of agents
$\phi^k(A_n)$	Weighted cost function
C_r^k	Relevant image subsets
C_i^k	Irrelevant image subsets
R_{rel}^k	Kth relevant images
R_{irr}^k	Kth irrelevant images
$Dist(.)$	Distance computations
x_n	Solution for a firefly n
$f(x)$	Fitness value
I_n	Brightness of nth firefly

$\beta(r)$	Attractiveness function
r_{ns}^k	Distance between the nth and an arbitrarily chosen Sth feature vector
β_0	Attractiveness with distance $r = 0$
γ	Light absorption coefficient
ε_n	Being drawn from the Gaussian distribution
$N_{P(Q)}$	Number of retrieved relevant images
$N_{R(Q)}$	Total number of retrieved images for a given query Q
$N_{T(Q)}$	Total number of relevant images available in the database for a given query Q
F	Number of fireflies
I	Number of generations
C_f	Retrieved feedback images
$y_f = 1$	Relevant image
$y_f = 0$	Irrelevant image
R	Set of collective retrievals or number of support vectors
α_f	Lagrange multipliers
Z	Parameter Z controls the separation error
$K_R(C_f, C_g)$	Radial basis function kernel or generalized Gaussian kernel
b	Biases
$iter_{max}$	Maximum iteration number
$iter$	Present iteration number
W_{iter}	Coefficient to enhance the algorithm performance
m	Nonlinear coefficient
p	Normal Gaussian distribution
μ	Mean
σ	Variance
$U(x, z)$	Random number between 0 and 1
$x_n(t+1)$	New firefly position
P_{avg}	Average precision
R_{avg}	Average recall
C	An image
c_n	nth region features
w_n	nth region weight
c_{qi}	ith region feature of the input query image
c_{sj}	jth region feature of the desired database image
w_{qi}	ith region weights of query image
w_{sj}	jth region weights of database image
t_{qi}	ith region size of input query image
t_{sj}	jth region size of desired image
t_{qv}	Total regions in an image
$EMD(C_Q, C_S)$	Earth Mover's distance between query image and database images
d_{ij}	Ground distance between the region of query image and database image
N	Dimension of features

h_{ij}	Best possible flow between the region of query image and database image
$F(C)$	Score for each database image C
Y_v	Matrix of visual data
l	Number of visual features
n	Number of images in the collection
Y_t	Matrix of text descriptions
m	Number of text features
Y	Multimodal matrix
γ	Weighting parameter
S	Summary of the given image set Y
$f(S)$	Reconstruction function
$W \in I^{k \times n}$	Non-negative sparse coefficients
$Div(S)$	Diversity of summary
$Dist(P_x, P_y)$	Pair-wise distances
K	Number of images in the summary
$MaxRepRej$	Number of maximum repeated rejection
E_i	Residue

Bibliography

Abd-Alsabour, N. and M. Randall 2010. Feature selection for classification using an Ant Colony system. *E-Science Workshops. Sixth IEEE International Conference*, Brisbane, Queensland, Australia, December 7–10. pp. 86–91. New York, NY: IEEE.

Acid, S., L. M. De Campo, J. M. Fernández-Luna, and J. F. Huete. 2003. An information retrieval model based on simple Bayesian networks. *International Journal on Intelligent Systems*, 251–265.

Agichtein, E., E. Brill, S. Dumais, and R. Ragno. 2006. Learning user interaction models for predicting web search result preferences. *Proceedings of the ACM Conference on Research and Development on Information Retrieval (SIGIR)*, Seattle, WA, pp. 3–10. New York, NY: ACM.

Agichtein, E., C. Castillo, D. Donato, A. Gionis, and G. Mishne. 2008. Finding high quality content in social media with an application to community-based question answering. *Proc. of WSDM*, Palo Alto, CA, pp. 183–194. ISBN: 978-1-59593-927-2.

Agrawal, R., H. Mannila, R. Srikant, H. Toivonen, and A. Verkamo. 1995. Fast discovery of association rules. In *Advances in Knowledge Discovery and Data Mining*. AAAI/MIT, pp. 307–327.

Aharon, M., M. Elad, and A. Bruckstein, 2005. K.-SVD: Design of dictionary for sparse representation. *Proceedings of SPARS*, Rennes, France, pp. 9–12.

Aizawa, A. 2003. An information-theoretic perspective of tf - idf measures. *Journal on Information Processing and Management*, 39(1), 45–65.

Alijla, B. O., L. C. Peng, A. T. Khader, and M. A. Al-Betar. 2013. Intelligent water drops algorithm for rough set feature selection. *Fifth Asian Conference on Intelligent Information and Database Systems*. Kuala Lumpur, Malaysia: Springer-Verlag, pp. 356–365.

Allan, J. 1995. Relevance feedback with too much data. *Proc. 18th Annual International ACM SIGIR Conf. on Research and Development in Information Retrieval*, Seattle, WA, pp. 337–343. ISBN: 0-89791-714-6.

Alvarez, S. A. and C. Ruiz. 2000. Collaborative recommendation via adaptive association rule mining. *Proc. of the International Workshop on Web Mining for E-Commerce*, Boston, MA, pp. 35–41.

Amati, G. and C. J. V. Rijsbergen. 2002. Probabilistic models of information retrieval based on measuring the divergence from randomness. *ACM Transactions on Information Systems*, 20(4), 357–389.

Amati, G., C. Carpineto, and G. Romano. 2001. FUB at TREC 10 web track: A probabilistic framework for topic relevance term weighting. *Proceedings of the Tenth Text Retrieval Conference (TREC-10)*. NIST Special Publication 500-250, Gaithersburg, MD.

Anand, S. S. and B. Mobasher. 2005. *Intelligent Techniques in Web Personalization*. Lecture Notes in Artificial Intelligence, Vol. 3. Berlin, Germany: Springer-Verlag, pp. 1–3.

Anderberg, M. R. 1973. *Cluster Analysis for Applications*. New York: Academic Press.

Arevalillo-Herraez, M., F. H. Ferri, and S. Moreno-Picot. 2011. Distance-based relevance feedback using a hybrid interactive genetic algorithm for image retrieval. *Applied Soft Computing*, 11(2), 1782–1791.

Azad, S. K. and S. K. Azad. 2011. Optimum design of structures using an improved firefly algorithm. *International Journal of Optimization in Civil Engineering*, 1(2), 327–340.

Azzopardi, L., M. Girolami, and C. Van Rijsbergen. 2004. Topic based language models for ad hoc information retrieval, in neural networks. *IEEE International Joint Conference on Neural Networks*, July 25–29, pp. 3281–3286. New York, NY: IEEE.

Back, T. H. and H. P. Schwefel. 1993. An overview of evolutionary algorithms for parameter optimization. *Journal on Computation*, 1(1), 1–23.

Baeza-Yates, R. A. and B. Ribeiro-Neto. 1999. *Modern Information Retrieval*. USA: Addison-Wesley Longman Publishing Co.

Balabanovic, M. and Y. Shoham. 1997. Fab: Content-based collaborative recommendation. *Comm. ACM*, 40(3), 66–72.

Banati, H. and M. Bajaj. 2011. Firefly based feature selection approach. *Int. Journal of Computer Chaos Science Issues*, 8(2), 473–480.

Basu, B. and K. Mahanti. 2011. Firefly and artificial bees colony algorithm for synthesis of scanned and broadside linear array antenna. *Progress in Electromagnetic Research B.*, 32, 169–190.

Batch, J. R., C. Fuller, A. Gupta, A. Hampapur, B. Horowitz, R. Humphery, R. Jain, and C. F. Shu. 1996. The virage image search engine: An open framework for image management. *Proceedings of SPIE Storage and Retrieval for Image and Video Databases IV*, Vol. 2670, San Jose, CA,. pp. 76–87. Bellingham, WA: SPIE.

Batlle, E. and C. Cano. 2000. Automatic segmentation using competitive hidden Markov models. http://ciir.cs.umass.edu/music2000/posters/batlle.pdf

Battiato, S., G. Farinella, G. Gallo, and D. Ravi. 2010. Exploiting textons distributions on spatial hierarchy for scene classification. *Journal of Image and Video Processing*, 2010(7), 1–13.

Beel, 2009. *Collaborative Computing: Networking. Applications and Work Sharing*. Washington.

Beigy, H. and M. R. Meybodi. 2002. A new distributed learning automaton based algorithm for solving stochastic shortest path problem. *Proc. of the Sixth International Joint Conference on Information Science*, Durham, pp. 339–343.

Belkin, N. C., D. Cool, and Kelly. 2001. Iterative design and evaluation support for query reformulation in interactive information retrieval. *Journal on Information Processing and Management*, 37(3), 403–434.

Ben Schafer, J., D. Frankowski, J. Herlocker, and S. Sen. 2007. Collaborative filtering recommender systems. *Lecture Notes in Computer Science*, 4321, 291–324.

Bendersky, M. and W. B. Croft, 2009. Finding text reuse on the web. *Proc. Second ACM International Conference on Web Search and Data Mining*, pp. 262–271.

Benitez, B., M. Beigi, and S. F. Chang. 1998. Using relevance feedback in content-based image meta search. *IEEE Internet Computing*, 2, 59–69.

Bernstein, Y. and J. Zobel. 2006. Accurate discovery of co-derivative documents via duplicate text detection. *Information Systems*, 31, 595–609.

Binitha, S. and S. Sathya. 2012. A survey of bio inspired optimization algorithms. *International Journal of Soft Computing and Engineering*, 2(2), 137–151.

Black, J. A., Jr., G. Fahmy, and S. Panchanathan. 2002. A method for evaluating the performance of content-based image retrieval systems. *Proceedings-Fifth IEEE Southwest Symposium on Image Analysis and Interpretation*, IEEE Computer Society, Los Alamitos, pp. 96–100.

Borodin, A., G. O. Roberts, J. S. Rosenthal, and P. Tsaparas. 2005. Link analysis ranking: Algorithms, theory and experiments. *ACM Trans. Internet Technology*, 5(1), 231–297.

Bosch, A., X. Munoz, and R. Marti. 2007. Which is the best way to organize/classify images by content. *Image and Vision Computing*, 25(6), 778–791.

Bouma, G., J. Mur, G. Van Noord, L. Van Der Plas, and J. Tiedemann. 2005b. Question answering for Dutch using dependency relations. *Proceedings of the CLEF2005 Workshop*, Vienna, Austria.

Britannica Concise Encyclopaedia, https://www.britannica.com/topic/information-system, Publisher: Encyclopædia Britannica, inc.

Brodatz, P. 1966. *Textures: A Photographic Album for Artists and Designers*. New York: Dover Publications.

Broder, A., R. Kumar, F. Maghoul, P. Raghavan, S. Rajagopalan, R. Stata, A. Tomkins, and J. Wiener. 2000. Graph structure in the Web, pp. 309–320.

Broilo, M. and F. G. B. De Natale. 2010. A stochastic approach to image retrieval using relevance feedback and particle swarm optimization. *IEEE Transaction on Multimedia*, 12(4), 267–277.

Bruza, P. D. 1993. *Stratified information disclosure: A synthesis between hypermedia and information retrieval*. Ph.D. thesis, Katholieke University Nijmegen, Netherlands.

Bruza P. D. and T. W. C. Huibers 1992. Investigating aboutness axioms using information fields. *SIGIR Conference on Research and Development in Information Retrieval*, pp. 112–121.

Burges, C. J. C. 1998. A tutorial on support vector machines for pattern recognition. *Data Mining and Knowledge Discovery*, 2(2), 121–167.

Cagnina, L. C., S. C. Esquivel, and C. A. Coello Coello. 2008. Solving engineering optimization problems with the simple constrained particle swarm optimizer. *Informatica Ljubljana*, 32(3), 319–326.

Cai, J. and Fei Song. 2008. Maximum entropy modeling with feature selection for text categorization. *Lecture Notes in Computer Science*, 4993, 549–554. Berlin/Heidelberg: Springer.

Calado, P., E. Moura, and I. Silva. 2003. Local versus global link information in the web. *ACM Transactions on Information Systems*, 21(1), 1–22.

Callan, J. P., W. B. Croft, and S. M. Harding. 1992. The INQUERY retrieval system. *Third International Conference on Database and Expert Systems Applications*, Vienna, Austria, pp. 78–83.

Caltech. http://www.vision.caltech.edu/Image_Datasets/Caltech101

Calvin, N. 1958. The Theory of Digital Handling of Non-numerical Information and its Implications to Machine Economics. Cited in Fairthorne.

Carpineto, C. and G. Romano. 1993. Galois: An order-theoretic approach to conceptual clustering. *International Conference on Machine Learning*, Amherst, MA, pp. 33–40.

Carson, M., S. Thomas, J. M. Belongie, and J. Malik. 1999. Blobworld: A system for region-based image indexing and retrieval. *Proceedings of the Int. Conf. Visual Information Systems*, Berlin, Heidelberg, pp. 509–516.

Carterette, B., V. Pavlu, E. J. Kanoulas, A. Aslam, and J. Allan. 2008. Evaluation over thousands of queries. *SIGIR*, pp. 651–658.

Catledge, L. J. and Pitkow. 1995. Characterizing browsing strategies in the World Wide Web. *Journal on Computer Networks and ISDN Systems*, 27(6), 1065–1073.

Cavnar, W. B. 1994. Using an n-gram-based document representation with a vector processing retrieval model. *TREC*, pp. 269–278.

Cerny, V. and S. E. Dreyfus. 1985. Thermo dynamical approach to the traveling salesman problem: An efficient simulation algorithm. *Journal of Optimization Theory and Applications*, 45.

Chaiyaratana, N. and A. M. S. Zalzala. 1997. Recent developments in evolutionary and genetic algorithms: Theory and applications. *Genetic Algorithms in Engineering Systems: Innovation and Applications*, pp. 270–277.

Chan. 1999. Weight assignment in dissimilarity function for Chinese cursive script character image retrieval using genetic algorithm. *Workshop Information Retrieval with Asian Languages*, Taipei, Taiwan, pp. 55–62.

Chandramouli, K. 2007. Particle swarm optimization and self-organizing maps based image classifier. *Workshop Semantic Media Adaptation and Personalization*, Uxbridge, UK, pp. 225–228.

Chandramouli, K. and E. Izquierdo. 2006. Image classification using self organising feature maps and particle swarm optimization. *Proceedings of the 7th Int. Workshop Image Analysis for Multimedia Interactive Services WIAMIS06*, Hyatt Regency Incheon, Korea, pp. 313–316.

Chandramouli, K. and E. Izquierdo. 2008. Image retrieval using particle swarm optimization. In: *Ser. Advances in Semantic Media Adaptation and Personalization*. Boca Raton, FL: CRC. Chapter 14, pp. 297–318.

Chandramouli, K., T. Kliegr, J. Nemrava, V. Svatek, and E. Izquierdo. 2008. Query refinement and user relevance feedback for contextualized image retrieval. *Proceedings of the 5th International Conference on Visual Information Engineering*, Xian China, China, pp. 453–458.

Chang, T. and C. C. Jay Kuo. 1993. Texture analysis and classification with tree structured wavelet transform. *IEEE Transaction on Image Processing*, 2(4), 429–441.

Chapelle, O., D. Metzler, Y. Zhang, and P. Grinspan. 2009. *Expected Reciprocal Rank for Graded Relevance*. Hong Kong, China: CIKM, pp. 621–630.

Chatterjee, A., G. K. Mahanti, and A. Chatterjee. 2012. Design of a fully digital controlled reconfigurable switched beam conconcentric ring array antenna using firefly and particle swarm optimization algorithm. *Progress in Electromagnetic Research B*, 36, 113–131.

Chen, D., J. M. Odobez, and H. Bourlard. 2004. Text detection and recognition in images and videos. *Journal of Pattern Recognition*, 595–609.

Chen, J. Y., C. A. Bouman, and J. C. Dalton. 2000. Hierarchical browsing and search of large image databases. *IEEE Transactions on Image Processing*, 9(3), 442–455.

Chen, S. S., D. L. Donoho, and M. A. Saunders. 2001. Atomic decomposition by basis pursuit. *SIAM Rev.*, 43(1), 129–159.

Chen, Y. 2001. One-class SVM for learning in image retrieval. *International Conference on Image Processing*, Thessaloniki, Greece, pp. 815–818.

Chiang, C. C., M. H. Hsieh, Y. P. Hung, and G. C. Lee. 2005. Region filtering using color and texture features for image retrieval. *Proceedings of the Fourth ACM Conference on Image and Video Retrieval Singapore*, pp. 487–496.

Chiaramella, Y. and J. P. Chevallet. 1992. About retrieval models and logic. *The Computer Journal*, 35(3), 279–290.

Chiaramella, Y., P. Mulhem, and F. Fourel. 1996. *A model for multimedia information retrieval*. Technical report, FERMI ESPRIT BRA 8134, University of Glasgow.

Cho, S. B. 2002. Towards creative evolutionary systems with interactive genetic algorithm. *Appl. Intell.*, 16(2), 129–138.

Cicchetti, D. V. and A. R. Feinstein. 1990. High agreement but low kappa: II. 43, 551–558.

Clarke, C. L. A., N. Craswell, and H. Voorhees. 2013. Overview of the TREC 2012 web track. *The Twenty-First Text REtrieval Conference, NIST*, Gaithersburg, MD. SP 500-298, pp. 1–8.

Clarke, C. L., N. Craswell, and E. M. Voorhees. 2011. Overview of the TREC 2011 web track. *20th Text REtrieval Conference*, Gaithersburg, MD, pp. 1–9.

Clarke, C. L., V. Craswell Nick, and M. Ellen. 2012. Overview of the TREC 2012 web track. *The Twenty-First Text REtrieval Conference*, Gaithersburg, MD, 2012.

Cohen, R. 1987. Analyzing the structure of argumentative discourse. *Computational Linguistics*, 13, 11–24.

Cohon, J. L. 1978. *Multiobjective Programming and Planning*. New York: Academic Press.

Cook, D. J. and B. L. Holder. 2000. Graph-based data mining, *IEEE Intelligent Systems*, 15(2), 32–41.

Crestani, F., L. M. de Campos, J. M. Fernandez-Luna, and J. F. Huete. 2003a. A multi-layered Bayesian network model for structured document retrieval. *Lecture Notes in Computer Science*, 2711, 74–86.

Crestani, F., L. M. de Campos, J. M. Fernandez-Luna, and J. F. Huete. 2003b. Ranking structured documents using utility theory in the Bayesian network retrieval model, In: Nascimento M.A., de Moura E.S., Oliveira A.L. (eds), *String Processing and Information Retrieval, SPIRE*, pp. 168–182.

Cristopher, D. 2009. Stanford University. http://nlp.stanford.edu/IR-book/newslides.html.

Crucianu, M., J. P. Tarel, and M. Ferecatu. 2005. A comparison of user strategies in image retrieval with relevance feedback. *Proc. of the 7th International Workshop on Audio-Visual Content and Information Visualization in Digital Libraries (AVIVDiLib'05)*, Cortona, Italy, pp. 121–130.

Csurka, G., C. R. Dance, L. Fan, J. Willamowski, and C. Bray. 2004. Visual categorization with bags of key points. *Workshop on Statistical Learning in Computer Vision, ECCV*, Prague, Czech Republic, pp. 1–22.

Cui, P. 2007. A tighter analysis of set cover greedy algorithm for test set. *ESCAPE*, pp. 24–35. DOI: 10.1007/978-3-540-74450-4_3.

Cui, X. and T. E. Potok. 2005. Document clustering using particle swarm optimization. *IEEE Swarm Intelligence Symposium*, Pasadena, California, pp. 185–191. DOI: 10.1109/SIS.2005.1501621.

Cui, X. and T. E. Potok. 2005. Document clustering analysis based on hybrid PSO+K-means algorithm. *Journal of Computer Sciences (Special Issue)*. 27–33. ISSN 1549-3636. Science Publications.

Cutting, D. R., J. O. Pedersen, D. R. Karger, and J. W. Tukey. 1992. Scatter/gather: A cluster-based approach to browsing large document collections. *Proc. ACM SIGIR. Copenhagen*, pp. 318–329.

Dakka, W., R. Dayal, and P. Ipeirotis. 2006. Automatic discovery of useful facet terms. *Proc. of the ACM SIGIR 2006 Workshop on Faceted Search*, Washington.

Das-Neves, F. 2001. *A tri-valued belief network model for information retrieval*. Technical Report TR-01-25. Computer Science Department. Virginia Polytechnic Institute and State University.

Datta, R., D. Joshi, J. Li, and J. Z. Wang. 2008. Image retrieval: Ideas, influences, and trends of the new age. *ACM Computer Survey*, 40(2), 1–60. Article 5.

Davis, G., S. Mallat, and M. Avellaneda. 1997. Adaptive greedy approximations. *Journal of Constructive Approximation*, 13, 57–98.

Davis, J. and M. Goadrich. 2006. The relationship between precision-recall and ROC curves. *Proc. 23rd International Conf. on Machine Learning*, Pittsburgh, pp. 233–240. ISBN: 1-59593-383-2.

Deerwester, S. C., S. T. Dumais, G. W. Furnas, T. K. Landauer, and R. A. Harshman. 1990. Indexing by latent semantic analysis. *Journal of the American Society of Information Science*, 41(6), 391–407.

Deng, D. 2007. Content-based image collection summarization and comparison using self-organizing maps. *Pattern Recognition*, 40(2), 718–727.

Deng, Y. and B. Manjunath. 2001. Unsupervised segmentation of color -texture regions in images and video. *IEEE Transaction on Pattern Analysis and Machine Intelligence*, 23(8), 800–810.

Deselaers, T., D. Keysers, and H. Ney. 2008. Features for image retrieval: An experimental comparison. *Information Retrieval*, 11(2), 77–107.

Deshpande, M. and G. Karypis. 2004. Item-based top-n recommendation algorithms. *ACM Transaction on Information Systems*, 22(1), 143–177. Springer-Verlag.

Digalakis, J. G. and K. G. Margaritis. 2002. An experimental study of benchmarking functions for genetic algorithms. *International Journal of Computer Mathematics*, 9(4), 403–416.

Ding, C. H. Q. 1999. Similarity-based probability model for latent semantic indexing. *Proc. Twenty-Second Annual International ACM/SIGIR Conf. on Research and Development in Information Retrieval*, Berkeley, CA, pp. 59–65.

Ding, Y., G. G. Chowdhury, S. Foo, and W. Qian. 2000. Bibliometric information retrieval system (BIRS): A web search interface utilizing bibliometric research results. *Journal of the American Society for Information Science*, 51(13), 1190–1204.

Doan, A., J. Madhavan, P. Domingos, and A. Halevy. 2002. Learning to map between ontologies on the semantic web. *11th International Conference on World Wide Web*, pp. 662–673.

Donoho, D. and M. Elad. 2003. Optimally sparse representation in general non orthogonal dictionaries via l1 minimization. *Proceedings of the National Academy of Science USA*, 100(5), 2197–2202.

Doyle, L. B. 1975. *Information Retrieval and Processing*. Los Angeles, CA: Melville.

Duygulu, P., K. Barnard, J. F. G. De Freitas, and D. A. Forsyth. 2002. Object recognition as machine translation: Learning a lexicon for a fixed image vocabulary. *Proceedings of the 7th European Conference on Computer Vision Copenhagen. Denmark*, pp. 349–354.

Eberhart, R. C. and Y. Shi. 2001. Particle swarm optimization: Developments, applications and resources. *Proceedings of the Congress Evolutionary Computation*, Seoul, South Korea, Vol. 1, 81–86.

Engan, K., S. Aase, and J. Husoy. 1999. Method of optimal directions for frame design. *Proceedings of the IEEE International Conference on Acoustics, Speech, and Signal Processing*, March 15–19, Vol. 5, pp. 2443–2446. Washington, DC: IEEE Computer Society.

Erk, K. 2007. A simple similarity-based model for selection preferences. *Proc. of ACL*, Prague, Czech Republic, pp. 216–223.

Everingham, H. 2007. *The Pascal VOC Challenge 2007 Development Kit*. University of Leeds.

Everingham, M. and L. V. Gool. 2010. The pascal visual object classes challenge. http://pascallin.ecs. soton.ac.uk/challenges/VOC/voc2010/index.html

Everitt, B. 1980. *Cluster Analysis*. New York: Halsted Press.

Falco, I., A. D. Cioppa, and E. Tarantino. 2007. Facing classification problems with particle swarm optimization. *Applied Soft Computing*, 7(3), 652–658.

Falkenauer, E. 1998. *Genetic Algorithms and Grouping Problems*. New York: John Wiley & Sons, Inc. ISBN: 0471971502

Faloutsos, C., R. Barber, M. Flickner, J. Hafner, W. Niblack, D. Petkovic, and W. Equitz. 1994. Efficient and effective querying by image content. *Journal of Intelligent Information Systems*, 3, 231–262.

Fan, W., E. A. Fox, P. Pathak, and H. Wu. 2004. The effects of fitness functions on genetic programming-based ranking discovery for web search. *J. Am Soc Inf. Sci. Technol.*, 55(7), 628–636.

Fang, H. and C. Zhai. 2006. Semantic term matching in axiomatic approaches to information retrieval. *Proc. 29th Ann. Intl. ACM SIGIR Conf. on Research and Development in Information Retrieval*, Seattle, WA, pp. 115–122.

Farahani, ShM, A. A. Abshouri, B. Nasiri, and M. R. Meybodi. 2011. A Gaussian firefly algorithm. *International Journal of Machine Learning and Computing*, 1(5), 448–453.

Faria, F. F., A. Velosa, H. M. Almeida, E. Valle, R. S. Torres, and M. A. Goncalves. 2010. Learning to rank for content-based image retrieval. *Conference on Multimedia Information Retrieval*, Philadelphia, PA, pp. 285–294.

Feder, J. 1997. Towards image content based retrieval for World Wide Web. *J. Adv. Imaging*, 11(1), 26–29.

Fei-Fei, L., R. Fergus, and P. Perona. 2006. One-shot learning of object categories. *IEEE Transactions on Pattern Recognition and Machine Intelligence*, 28(4), 594–611.

Fellbaum, C. 1998. *WordNet: An Electronic Lexical Database*. Cambridge, MA: MIT Press.

Ferreira, C., J. Santos, R. S. Torres, M. Goncalves, R. Rezende, and W. Fan. 2011. Relevance feedback based on genetic programming for image retrieval. *Pattern Recognition Letter*, 32(1), 27–37.

Ferrucci, D. and A. Lally. 2004. UIMA: An architecture approach to unstructured information processing in a corporate research environment. *Journal on Natural Language Engineering*, 10(3–4), 327–348.

Fister, I., I. Fister Jr., X.-S. Yang, and J. Brest. 2013. A comprehensive review of Firefly Algorithms. *Swarm and Evolutionary Computation*, 13, 34–46.

Flickner, M., H. Sawhney, W. Niblack, J. Ashley, Q. Huang, B. Dom, M. Gorkani. et al. 1995. Query by image and video content: The QBIC system. *IEEE Computer*, 28(9), 23–32.

Fonseca, C. M. and P. J. Fleming. 1993. Genetic algorithms for multi-objective optimisation: Formulation, discussion and generalisation. *5th International Conference on Genetic Algorithms*, San Francisco, CA, pp. 416–423.

Foote, J. 1999. An overview of audio information retrieval. *Journal Multimedia System Special Issue on Audio and Multimedia*, 7(1), 2–10.

Forsati, R. and M. R. Meybodi. 2010. Effective page recommendation algorithms based on distributed learning automata and weighted association rules. *An International Journal of Expert Systems with Applications*, 37(2), 1316–1330.

Forsati, R. and M. Mahdavi. 2010. Web text mining using harmony search. *Studies in Computational Intelligence*, 270, 51–64.

Foth, K. and W. Menzel. 2006. Hybrid parsing: Using probabilistic models as predictors for a symbolic parser. *Proceedings of the 21st International Conference on Computational Linguistics and 44th Annual Meeting of the Association for Computational Linguistics*, Sydney, Australia, pp. 321–327.

Frakes, B. W. and R. Baeza-Yates. 1992. *Information Retrieval Data Structures and Algorithms*. Upper Saddle River, NJ: Prentice-Hall. ISBN: 0-13-463837-9.

Fuchs, J. J. 2004. On sparse representations in arbitrary redundant bases. *IEEE Transaction on Inference Theory*, 50, 1341–1344.

Fujimura, K. O., H. Toda, T. Inoue, N. Hiroshima, R. Kataoka, and M. Sugizaki. 2006. A multi-faceted blog search engine. *Proc. 3rd Annual WWE*, Edinburgh.

Fuhr, N. 1992. Probabilistic models in information retrieval. *The Computer Journal*, 35(3).

Gan, C. K. and R. W. Donaldson. 1988. Adaptive silence deletion for speech storage and voicemail application. *IEEE Transactions on Acoustics, Speech, and Signal Processing*, 36(6), 924–927.

Gandomi, A. H., X. S. Yang, and A. H. Alavi. 2013. Cuckoo search algorithm: A meta-heuristic approach to solve structural optimization problems. *Engineering with Computers*, 29, 17–35.

Geem, Z. W., C. Tseng, and Y. Park. 2005. Harmony search for generalized orienteering problem: Best touring in China Springer. *Lecture Notes Computer Science*, 3412, 741–750.

Gendreau, M. 2002. Recent advances in Tabu search in essays and surveys in metaheuristics. In: *Handbook of Metaheuristics*. International Series in Operations Research and Management Science, Vol. 15, pp. 369–377.

Gendreau, M., J. Potvin, and G. Laporte. 2002. Meta heuristics for the capacitated VRP. In: Toth, P. and Vigo, D. eds. *The Vehicle Routing Problem, SIAM Monographs on Discrete Mathematics and Applications*. Philadelphia: Society of Industrial and Applied Mathematics SIAM, Chapter 6, pp. 129–154.

Geng, X., T.-Y. Liu, T. Qin, and H. Li. 2007. Feature selection for ranking. *Proc. 30th Annual International Conference on Research and Development in Information Retrieval*, Amsterdam, The Netherlands, pp. 407–414.

Gersho, A. 1992. *Vector Quantization and Signal Compression*. Boston, MA: Kluwer Academic Publishers.

Gevers, T. and A. Smeulders. 2000. Pictoseek: Combining color and shape invariant features for image retrieval. *IEEE Trans. Image Processing*, 9(1), 102–119.

Gevers, T. and H. Stokman. 2003. Classifying color edges in video into shadow geometry, highlight, or material transitions. *IEEE Transactions on Multimedia*, 5(2), 237–243.

Giacinto, G., F. Roli, and G. Fumera. 2001. Content-based image retrieval with adaptive query shifting. In: Petra, P. ed. *Machine Learning and Data Mining in Pattern Recognition*, Vol. LNAI 2123, pp. 337–346. Berlin, Germany: Springer-Verlag.

Giannakouris, G., V. Vassiliadis, and G. Dounias. 2010. Experimental study on a hybrid nature-inspired algorithm for financial portfolio optimization. *SETN 2010. Lecture Notes in Artificial Intelligence. LNAI*, 6040, 101–111.

Gies, D. and Y. Rahmat-Samii. 2003. Reconfigurable array design using parallel particle swarm optimization. *Proceedings of the IEEE International Symposium Antennas and Propagation*, June 22–27, pp. 177–180 New York, NY: IEEE.

Glover, F. 1986. Pubs/174—Future paths for integer programming TS, future paths for integer programming and links to artificial intelligence. *Computers and Operations Research*, 13(5), 533–549.

Glover, F. 1990. Tabu search, Part II. *ORSA Journal on Computing*, 2, 4–32.

Glover, F. and M. Laguna. 1997. Tabu search. *Journal of the Operational Research Society*, 50(1), 106–107.

Godin, R. and T. Chau. 1998. Incremental concept formation algorithms based on Galois lattices. *Journal on Computational Intelligence*, 11(2), 246–267.

Goldberg, D. E. 1989. *Genetic Algorithms in Search, Optimization, and Machine Learning*. USA: Addison-Wesley Publishing Company.

Goldberg, D. E. and Holland, J. H. Machine. 1989. Genetic algorithms in search. *Optimization and Machine Learning*, 3(2), 95–99.

Gonzales, R. and R. E. Woods. 2002. *Digital Image Processing*. New Jersey: Prentice-Hall.

Goodrum, A. 2000. Image information retrieval: An overview of current research. *Informing Science*, 3(2), 63–67.

Gopalan, N. P., K. Batri, and B. Siva Selvan. 2007. Adaptive selection of Top-m retrieval schemes for data fusion using Tabu search. *ICCIMA, International Conference on Computational Intelligence and Multimedia Applications ICCIMA 2007*, Sivakasi, Tamil Nadu, India, Vol. 1. pp. 136–138.

Griffin, G., Holub, A., and Perona, P. 2007. *Caltech-256 object category dataset*. Technical report. California Institute of Technology.

Guan, H. and S. Wada. 2002. Flexible color texture retrieval method using multiresolution mosaic for image classification. *Proceedings of the 6th International Conference on Signal Processing*, Beijing, China, Vol. 1. pp. 612–615.

Guan, J. and G. Qiu. 2007. Modeling user feedback using a hierarchical graphical model for interactive image retrieval. *Proceedings of the eighth Pacific Rim Conference on Multimedia Hong Kong. China*, pp. 18–29.

Guillaumin, M., J. Verbeek, and C. Schmid. 2010. Multimodal semi-supervised learning for image classification. *Proceedings of the IEEE Conference on Computer Vision and Pattern Recognition (CVPR)*, June 13–18, pp. 902–909. New York, NY: IEEE.

Gungor, Z. and A. Unler. 2007. K-harmonic means data clustering with simulated annealing heuristic. *Applied Mathematics and Computation*, 184(2), 199–209.

Guo, G., A. K. Jain, W. Ma, and H. Zhang. 2002. Learning similarity measure for natural image retrieval with relevance feedback. *IEEE Transaction on Neural Networks*, 12(4), 811–820.

Gupta, A. and R. Jain. 1997. Visual information retrieval. *Comm. Assoc. Comp. Mach.*, 40(5), 70–79.

Gwet Kappa, K. 2002. Statistic is not satisfactory for Assessing the Extent of Agreement between Raters. Statistical Methods for Inter-rater Reliability Assessment, No.1.

Haeghen, Y., J. Naeyaert, I. Lemahieu, and W. Philips. 2000. An imaging system with calibrated color image acquisition for use in dermatology. *IEEE Transaction on Medical Imaging*, 19(7), 722–730.

Hall, M. A. 2000. Correlation-based feature selection for discrete and numeric class machine learning. *Proc. 17th International Conf. on Machine Learning*, San Francisco, CA, pp. 359–366.

Han, J. and M. Kambr. 2006. *Data Mining Concepts and Techniques*. San Francisco: Morgan Kaufmann Publisher, pp. 71–73.

Hao, J.-K. and J. Pannier. 1998. Simulated annealing and Tabu search for constraint solving. *Fifth International Symposium on Artificial Intelligence and Mathematics Fort Lauderdale*, Florida.

Hare, J., P. Lewis, P. Enser, and C. Sandom. 2006. A linear-algebraic technique with an application in semantic image retrieval. *Lecture Notes in Computer Science*, 4071, 31–40.

Harman, D. and D. Hiemstra. 2008. Saving and accessing the old information retrieval literature, pp. 16–21.

Hearst, M. 1997. TextTiling: Segmenting text into multi-paragraph subtopic passages. *Journal on Computational Linguistics*, 23(1), 33–64.

Hersh, W., C. Buckley, T. J. Leone, and D. H. Hickman. 1994. OHSUMED: An interactive retrieval evaluation and new large text collection for research. *SIGIR*, pp. 192–201.

Hiemstra, D. 2001. *Using Language Models for Information Retrieval*. PhD dissertation, University of Twente, Enschede, The Netherlands.

Hitchcock, F. L. 1941. The distribution of a product from several sources to numerous localities. *J. Math. Phys.*, 20, 224–230.

Ho, S.-Y, J.-H. Chen, and M.-H. Huang. 2004. Inheritable genetic algorithm for Biobjective 0/1 combinatorial optimization problems and its applications. *Systems, Man and Cybernetics. Part B*, 34, 609–620.

Hofmann, T. 1999. Probabilistic latent semantic indexing. *Proc. Twenty-Second Annual International SIGIR Conf. on Research and Development in Information Retrieval*, Berkeley, CA: International Computer Science Institute, and UC Berkeley: EECS Department, CS Division, pp. 50–57. ISBN: 1-58113-096-1.

Hofmann, T. and Puzicha, J. 1999. Latent class models for collaborative filtering. *Proc. Sixteenth International Joint Conf. Artificial Intelligence*, Stockholm, Sweden, pp. 688–693.

Hoi, C., C. Chan, K. Huang, M. R. Lyu, and I. King. 2004. Biased support vector machine for relevance feedback in image retrieval. *Proceedings of the International Joint Conference on Neural Networks IJCNN04*, Budapest, Hungary, pp. 3189–3194.

Hoi, C. H. and M. R. Lyu. 2004. Group-based relevance feedback with support vector machine ensembles. *Proc. 17th Intl Conf. Pattern Recognition*, Cambridge, UK, Vol. 3. pp. 874–877.

Holland, J. H. 1973. Genetic algorithms and the optimal allocations of trials. *SIAM, Journal of Computing*, 2(2), 88–105.

Hong, P., Q. Tian, and T. S. Huang. 2000. Incorporate support vector machines to content-based image retrieval with relevant feedback. *Proceedings of the IEEE Intl Conference on Image Processing*, Vancouver, BC, Canada, Vol. 3. pp. 750–753.

Horng, M. H. 2012. Vector quantization using the firefly algorithm for image compression. *Expert Systems with Applications*, 39, 1078–1091.

Horng, M. H. and R. J. Liou. 2011. Multilevel minimum cross entropy threshold selection based on the firefly algorithm. *Expert Systems with Applications*, 38, 14805–14811.

Horng, M. H., Y. X. Lee, M. C. Lee, and R. J. Liou. 2012. Firefly metaheuristic algorithm for training the radial basis function network for data classification and disease diagnosis. In: Parpinelli, R. and Lopes, H. S. eds. *Theory and New Applications of Swarm Intelligence*. Chapter 7, pp. 115–132. ISBN 978-953-51-0364-6.

Horowitz, E., S. Sahni, and S. Rajasekaran. 2007. *Computer Algorithms/C++*. Universities Press.

Houle, M. E. and N. Grira. 2007. A correlation-based model for unsupervised feature selection. *Proc. 16th ACM SIGIR Conf. on Information and Knowledge Management*, Barcelona, Spain, pp. 897–900.

Hoyer, P. 2002. Non-negative sparse coding. *Neural Networks for Signal Processing XII (Proc. IEEE Workshop on Neural Networks for Signal Processing)*, Martigny, Switzerland, pp. 557–565.

Hsu, C. W., C. C. Chang, and C. J. Lin. 2003. *A Practical Guide to Support Vector Classification*. Technical report. Department of Computer Science. National Taiwan University.

Hu, X., Y. Shi, and R. Eberhart. 2004. Recent advances in particle swarm. *Proceedings of the 2004 Congress on Evolutionary Computation, CEC2004*. Portland. OR, pp. 90–97.

Huang, T. S., C. K. Dagli, S. Rajaram, E. Y. Chang, M. I. Mandel, G. E. Poliner, and D. P. W. Ellis. 2008. Active learning for interactive multimedia retrieval. *Proceedings on IEEE*, Piscataway, NJ, 96(4), 648–667.

Huang, T. S., S. Mehrotra, and K. Ramachandran. 1996. Multimedia analysis and retrieval system MARS project. *Proceedings of the 33rd Annual Clinic on Library Application of Data Processing – Digital Image Access and Retrieval*, University of Illinois at Urbana-Champaign, pp. 1–15.

Huang, Y. P., T. W. Chang, and F. E. Sandnes. 2005. Improving image retrieval efficiency using a fuzzy inference model and genetic algorithm. *Conference of the North American Fuzzy Information Processing Society - NAFIPS*, Detroit, MI, pp. 361–366.

Huibers, T. 1996. *Formalising Intelligent Information Retrieval Agents*. England: Manchester Metropolitan University, pp. 125–143.

Hurst, W. and G. Gotz. 2004. Interface issues for interactive navigation and browsing of recorded lectures and presentations. *Proceedings of World Conference on Educational Multimedia, Hypermedia & Telecommunications (ED-MEDIA 04)*. *AACE*, Lugano, Switzerland, pp. 4464–4469.

Ilhan, I. and G. Tezel. 2013. A genetic algorithm–support vector machine method with parameter optimization for selecting the tag SNPs. *Journal of Biomedical Informatics*, 46, 328–340.

Ishikawa, H., T. Nakajima, T. Mizuhara, S. Yokoyama, J. Nakayama, M. Ohta, and K. Katayama. 2002. An intelligent web recommendation system: A web usage mining approach. *ISMIS*, pp. 342–350.

Jaimes, A. L., C. A. Coello, and D. Chakraborty. 2008. Objective reduction using a feature selection technique. *Proc. 10th Annual Conf. on Genetic and Evolutionary Computation*, Atlanta, GA, pp. 673–680.

Jain, K. and B. Yu. 2004. Automatic text localization in images and video frames. *Pattern Recognition*, 31(12), 2055–2076.

Jansen, B. J. 2010. The seventeen theoretical constructs of information searching and information retrieval. *Journal of the American Society for Information Science and Technology*, 61(8), 1517–1534.

Jardine, N. and C. J. van Rijsbergen. 1971. The use of hierarchic clustering in information retrieval, pp. 217–240.

Jeon, J., V. Lavrenko, and R. Manmatha. 2003. Automatic image annotation and retrieval using cross-media relevance models. *ACM SIGIR 2003*, pp. 119–126.

Jeon, J., W. Croft, and J. Lee. 2005. Finding similar questions in large question and answer archives. *Proc of the 14th ACM International Conference on Information and Knowledge Management CIKM*, Bremen, Germany, pp. 84–90.

Jiang, W., K. L. Chan, M. Li, and H. J. Zhang. 2005. Mapping low-level features to high-level semantic concepts in region-based image retrieval. *Proceedings of the IEEE Conference on Computer Vision and Pattern Recognition*, San Diego, CA, Vol. 2. pp. 244–249.

Jijkoun, V. and M. de Rijke. 2005. Retrieving answers from frequently asked questions pages on the web. *CIKM 05: Proc of the 14th ACM International Conference on Information and Knowledge Management*, Bremen, Germany, pp. 76–83.

Jing, F., M. Li, H. J. Zhang, and B. Zhang. 2003. Support vector machines for region-based image retrieval. *Proceedings of the IEEE Int. Conf. Multimedia and Expo*, Baltimore, MD, Vol. 2, pp. 21–24.

Jing, F., M. Li, H. J. Zhang, and B. Zhang. 2004. Region-based relevance feedback in image retrieval. *IEEE Transaction on Circuits and Systems for Video Technology*, 14(5), 672–681.

Jing, Y., S. Baluja, and H. Rowley. 2007. Canonical image selection from the web. *ACM International Conference on Image and Video Retrieval*, Amsterdam, The Netherlands, pp. 280–287.

Joachims, T. 1997. *Text categorization with support vector machines*. Technical report, LS VIII Number 23, University of Dortmund.

Jones, K. and S. P. Willet. 1997. *Readings in Information Retrieval*. Los Altos: Morgan Kaufmann.

Kaasten, S., S. Greenberg and C. Edwards. 2002. How people recognize previously seen WWW pages from titles, URLs and thumbnails, pp. 247–265.

Kao, Y. and K. Cheng. 2006. *An ACO-Based Clustering Algorithm*, Vol. 4150. Berlin: Springer, pp. 340–347.

Karaboga, D. and C. Ozturk. 2010. A novel cluster approach: Artificial Bee Colony ABC algorithm. *Applied Soft Computing*, 11(1), 652–657.

Kawahara, T., M. Hasegawa, K. Shitaoka, T. Kitade, and H. Nanjo. 2004. Automatic indexing of lecture presentations using unsupervised learning of presumed discourse markers. *IEEE Transactions on Speech and Audio Processing*, 12(4), 409–419

Kazem, A., E. Sharifi, F. K. Hussain, M. Saberi, and O. K. Hussain. 2013. Support vector regression with chaos-based firefly algorithm for stock market price forecasting. *Applied Soft Computing*, 13(2), 947–958.

Keerthi, S. S. and C. J. Lin. 2003. Asymptotic behaviors of support vector machines with Gaussian kernel. *Neural Computation*, 15(7), 1667–1689.

Kelly, D. 2009. Methods for evaluating interactive information retrieval systems with users. *Journal on Foundations and Trends in Information Retrieval*, 3(1–2), 1–224.

Kennedy, J. and D. C. Washington. 2000. Stereotyping: Improving particle swarm performance with cluster analysis. *Evolutionary Computation*, 2, 1507–1512.

Kennedy, J. and R. C. Eberhart. 1995. Particle swarm optimization. *Proceeding of the IEEE Conf. Neural Networks IV*, Piscataway, NJ, Vol. 4, pp. 1942–1948.

Kennedy, J. and R. Eberhart. 1997. Discrete binary version of the particle swarm algorithm. *Proceedings of the 1997 IEEE International Conference on Systems. Man and Cybernetics. Part 1 of 5*, Orlando, FL, pp. 4104–4108.

Kennedy, J. and R. Eberhart. 2011. Particle swarm optimization. *IEEE International Conference on Neural Networks*, Perth, Australia. ISBN 978-0-387-30768-8, pp. 760–766.

Kennedy, J., R. C. Eberhart, and Y. Shi. 2001. *Swarm Intelligence*. San Francisco: Morgan Kaufmann Publishers.

Kennedy, L. S. and M. Naaman. 2008. *Generating Diverse and Representative Image Search Results for Landmarks*. New York: World Wide Web.

Kerfi, M. L. and D. Ziou. 2004. Image retrieval based on feature weighing and relevance feedback. *Proceedings of the IEEE Int. Conf. Image Processing ICIP2004*, Singapore, Vol. 1, pp. 689–692.

Khadwilard, A., S. Chansombat, T. Thepphakorn, P. Thapatsuwan, W. Chainate, and P. Pongcharoen. 2011. *Investigation of Firefly Algorithm Parameter Setting for Solving Job Shop Scheduling Problems*. Operation Research Network in Thailand, pp. 89–97.

Kim, D. H., J. W. Song, J. H. Lee, and B. G. Choi. 2007. Support vector machine learning for region-based image retrieval with relevance feedback. *ETRI Journal*, 29(5), 700–702.

Kirkpatrick, S., C. D. Gelatt, Jr and M. P. Vecchi. 1983. Optimization by simulated annealing, Science. *New Series*, 220-4598, 671–680.

Kleinberg, J. M. 1999. Authoritative sources in a hyperlinked environment. *Journal of ACM*, 46(5), 604–632.

Ko, B. and H. Byun. 2002. Integrated region-based image retrieval using regions spatial relationships. *Proceedings of the IEEE International Conference on Pattern Recognition ICPR*, Quebec, Canada, Vol. 1. pp. 196–199.

Ko, B. C., S. Y. Kwak, and H. Byun. 2004. SVM-based salient regions extraction method for image retrieval. *Proceedings of the 17th IEEE International Conference on Pattern Recognition*, Cambridge, UK, Vol. 2. pp. 977–980.

Kompatsiaris, I., E. Triantafillou, and M. G. Strintzis. 2001. Region based color image indexing and retrieval. *Proc. IEEE ICIP*. Thessaloniki, Greece.

Korfhage, R. R. 1997. *Information Storage and Retrieval*. New York: John Wiley & Sons. Inc. ISBN: 0-471-14338-3.

Koskela, M., J. Laaksonen, and E. Oja. 2004. Entropy-based measures for clustering and SOM topology preservation applied to content-based image indexing and retrieval. *Proc. 17th International Conf. on Pattern Recognition ICPR04. IEEE Computer Society*, Washington, DC, pp. 1051–4651.

Krause, A. and V. Cevher. 2010. Sub modular dictionary selection for sparse representation. *Proceedings of the International Conference on Machine Learning, ICML*, Haifa, Israel, pp. 567–574.

Kuhn, A. S. and Ducasse. 2007. Semantic clustering: Identifying topics in source code. *International Conference on Information and Software Technology*, pp. 230–243.

Kulturel Konak, S., A. E. Smith, and B. A. Norman. 2006. Multi-objective tabu search using a multinomial probability mass function. *European Journal of Operational Research*, 169(3), 918–931.

Laaksonen, J., M. Koskela, and E. Oja. 1999. Picsom: Self-organizing maps for content-based image retrieval. *Proceedings of the Intl Joint Conf. Neural Networks*, Washington, DC, Vol. 4. pp. 2470–2473.

Lai, C. C. and Y. C. Chen. 2011. An adaptive approach for color image retrieval. *Proceedings of the IEEE 3rd International Conference on Communication Software and Networks ICCSN*, Xi'an, China, pp. 137–140.

Lai, C. C. and Y. C. Chen. 2011a. A user-oriented image retrieval system based on interactive genetic algorithm. *IEEE Trans on Instrumentation and Measurement*, 60(10), 3318–3325.

Latha, K. 2010. Rhetorical based music-inspired optimization algorithm: Harmony-Tabu for document retrieval using relevance feedback. *Conference on Recent Trends in Engineering*, Trivandrum, India, Vol. 3, pp. 6–10.

Latha, K., B. Bhargavi, C. Dharani, and R. Rajaram. 2010. A dynamic feature selection method for document ranking with relevance feedback approach. *ICTACT Journal on Soft Computing (An International Publication of ICT Academy of Tamil Nadu), A Consortium of Government of India, Government of Tamil Nadu and CII*, 1(1), 1–8, ISSN: 0976-6561.

Latha, K., B. Rajmohan, and R. Rajaram. 2010a. ASPDD: An efficient and scalable framework for duplication detection. *International Conference on Advances in Computer Engineering*, Bangalore, India, Vol. 1, pp. 153–157.

Latha, K., K. Rathna Veni, and R. Rajaram. 2010b. AFGF: An automatic facet generation framework for document Retrieval. *International Conference on Advances in Computer Engineering*, Bangalore, India, Vol. 1. pp. 110–114.

Latha, K. and R. Manivelu. 2010. Music inspired optimization algorithm: Harmony Tabu for document retrieval using relevance feedback approach. *International Conference on Recent Trends in Business Administration and Information Processing*, Trivandrum, India.

Latha, K. and R. Manivelu. 2010. Rhetorical based music-inspired optimization algorithm: Harmony-Tabu for document retrieval using relevance feedback. *International Joint Journal Conferences in Engineering 2010*, Finland: Academy Publishers, also available in Digital Library resources including IEE INSPEC, EI (Compendex), Thomson ISI (ISTP).

Latha, K. and R. Rajaram. 2008. An efficient LSI based information retrieval framework using particle swarm optimization and simulated annealing approach. *16th International Conference on Advanced Computing and Communication*, Chennai, India, December 14–17, pp. 94–101. New York, NY: IEEE.

Latha, K. and R. Rajaram. 2009. TABU annealing: An efficient and scalable strategy for document retrieval. *International Journal of Intelligent Information and Database Systems*, 3(3), 326–337. DOI: 10.1504/IJIIDS.2009.027690.

Latha, K., S. Vigneshbabu, and R. Rajaram. 2009. DETS: A meta heuristic approach for document retrieval. *International Journal of Knowledge Engineering and Soft Data Paradigms*, 1(2), 139–150. Also available in ACM Digital Library. DOI: 10.1504/IJKESDP.2009.022720.

Latha, K. and T. Kanimozhi. 2013. A meta-heuristic optimization approach for content based image retrieval using relevance feedback method. *Lecture Notes in Engineering and Computer Science. Proceedings of The World Congress on Engineering*, London, UK, pp. 775–780.

Latha, K. and T. Kanimozhi. 2013. An Approach for content based image retrieval using Gaussian Firefly Algorithm CCIS 375, pp. 213–218.

Latha, K. and T. Kanimozhi. 2013. Stochastic firefly for image optimization. *IEEE International Conference on Communication and Signal Processing*, pp. 592–596.

Latha, K. and T. Kanimozhi. 2014. An evolutionary approach for optimizing content ased image retrieval using support vector machine. *Proceedings of the 3rd International conference on Computer Engineering and Mathematical Sciences*, Langkawi, Malaysia, pp. 544–554.

Latha, K. and T. Kanimozhi. 2014. An integrated approach to region based image retrieval using firefly algorithm and support vector machine. *International Conference on Neuro Computing*, Nanning, China, Vol. 151, no. 3. Impact Factor 2.202. pp. 1099–1111.

Latha, K. and T. Kanimozhi. 2014. Evaluation of light inspired optimization algorithm-based image retrieval. *Applied Mechanics and Materials Journal*, 7, 64–72, 529–536.

Latha, K. and T. Kanimozhi. 2015. Optimization of sparse dictionary model for multimodal image summarization using firefly algorithm. *Proceedings of the International Conference on Advances in Applied Engineering & Technology*, Ramanathapuram, India, pp. 1–7.

Latha, K., and T. Kanimozhi. 2015. Optimization of sparse dictionary model for multimodal image summarization using firefly algorithm. *International Journal of Applied Engineering Research*, 10(55), 1896–1901.

Lavrenko, V. and W. B. Croft. 2001. Relevance-based language models. *SIGIR'01*, September 9–12, 2001, New Orleans, Louisiana.

Lehnert, W. 1980. Narrative text summarization. *Proc. of AAAI*, Stanford University, Stanford, CA, pp. 337–339.

Leopold, E. and J. Kindermann. 2002. Text categorization with support vector machines. How to represent texts in input space? *Machine Learning*, 46, 423–444.

Lew, M., N. Sebe, C. Djeraba, and R. Jain. 2006. Content-based multimedia information retrieval: State of the art and challenges. *ACM Transactions on Multimedia Computing, Communications and Applications*, 2(1), 1–19.

Lewicki, M. S. and B. A. Olshausen. 1999. A probabilistic framework for the adaptation and comparison of image codes. *J. Opt. Soc. Amer. A: Opt., Image Sci. Vision*, 16(7), 1587–1601.

Lewicki, M. S. and T. J. Sejnowski. 2000. Learning over complete representations. *MIT Press Journals on Neural Comp.*, 12(2), 337–365.

Li, J., J. Z. Wang, and G. Wiederhold. 2000. IRM: Integrated region matching for image retrieval. *International Conference on ACM Multimedia*, Marina del Rey, CA, pp. 147–156.

Li, J., N. Allinson, D. Tao, and X. Li. 2006. Multi training support vector machine for image retrieval. *IEEE Transaction on Image Process*, 15(11), 3597–3601.

Li, J. and O. Zaiane. 2004. Combining usage content and structure data to improve web site recommendation. *International Conference on E-commerce and Web Technologies*, Zaragoza, Spain, pp. 305–315.

Lianze, M. A., L. Lin, and M. Gen. 2011. A PSO-SVM approach for image retrieval and clustering. *41st International Conference on Computers & Industrial Engineering*, Los Angeles, CA, pp. 629–634.

Lin, J. and D. Demner-fushman. 2006. Methods for automatically evaluating answers to complex questions. *Information Retrieval*, 9(5), 565–587.

Ling, X., M. Qiaozhu, C. X. Zhai, and B. R. Schatz. 2008. Mining multi-faceted overviews of arbitrary topics in a text collection. *Proc. of the 15th ACM SIGKDD International Conference on Knowledge Discovery and Data Mining KDD08*, Las Vegas, NV, pp. 497–505.

Liu, D. and H. Qi. 2009. K-harmonic means data clustering with differential evolution. *BioMedical Information Engineering, FBIE 2009. International Conference on Future*, Sanya, China, pp. 369–372.

Liu, H. B., Y. Y. Tang, J. Meng and Y. Ji. 2004. Neural networks learning using VBEST model particle swarm optimization. *Proceedings of the 3rd Internal Conference on Machine Learning and Cybernetics*, Shanghai, China, pp. 3157–3159.

Liu, T. Y. 2009. Learning to rank for information retrieval. *Foundations Trends Information Retrieval*, 3(3), 225–231.

Liu, Y. and E. Agichitein. 2008a. You've got answers: Towards personalized models for predicting success in community question answering. *Proceedings of the 46th Annual Meeting of the Association for Computational Linguistics ACL*, Columbus, OH, June 16–17, pp. 97–100. Stroudsburg, PA: Association for Computational Linguistics.

Liu, Y. and E. Agichtein. 2008b. On the evolution of the yahoo! answers qa community. *Proc. of the 31st Annual International ACM SIGIR Conference on Research and Development in Information Retrieval SIGIR*, Singapore, pp. 737–738.

Liu, Y., X. Chen, C. Zhang, and A. Sprague. 2006. An interactive region-based image clustering and retrieval platform. *Proceedings of the IEEE International Conference on Multimedia and Expo*, Toronto, Canada, pp. 929–932.

Long, F., H. Zhang, H. Dagan, and D. Feng. 2003. *Fundamentals of Content Based Image Retrieval*. Berlin Heidelberg, New York: Springer-Verlag, pp. 1–26.

Lope, Z., C. López-Pujalte, V. P. Guerrero-Bote, and F. de Moya-Anegon. 2003a. Genetic algorithms in relevance feedback a second test and new contributions. *International Conference on Information Process Management*, 39(5), 669–687.

Lope, Z., C. López-Pujalte, V. P. Guerrero-Bote, and F. de Moya-Anegon. 2002. A test of genetic algorithms in relevance feedback. *Conference on Information Process Management*, Tarrytown, NY, Vol. 38, no. 6, pp. 793–805.

Lope, Z., C. López-Pujalte, V. P. Guerrero-Bote, and F. de Moya-Anegon. 2003b. Order-based fitness functions for genetic algorithms applied to relevance feedback. *Journal on Information Science*, 54(2), 152–160.

Lowe, D. 2004. Distinctive image features from scale invariant key points. *International Journal of Computer Vision*, 60, 91–110.

Lu, K. and D. Walfram. 2012. Measuring author research relatedness: A comparison of word based, topic-based and author co-citation approaches. *Journal of the Association for Information Science and Technology*, 63(10), 1973–1986.

Lu, Y., C. Hu, X. Zhu, H. Zhang, and Q. Yang. 2000. A unified framework for semantics and feature based relevance feedback in image retrieval systems. *ACM International Conference on Multimedia*, Marina del Rey, CA, pp. 31–37.

Lytinen, S. L. and N. Tomuro. 2002. The use of question types to Match Questions in FAQ Finder. *Proc. of the AAAI Spring Symposium on Mining Answers from Texts and Knowledge Bases*, Palo Alto, CA, pp. 46–53.

Ma, W. Y. and B. S. Manjunath. 1997. Netra: A toolbox for navigating large image databases. *Proceedings of the IEEE International Conference on Image Processing*, Santa Barbara, CA, Vol. 1. pp. 568–571.

Ma, W. Y. and B. S. Manjunath. 2000. Edge flow: A technique for boundary detection and image segmentation. *IEEE Transactions on Image Processing*, 9(8), 1375–1388.

MacArthur, S., E. C. Brodley, and Chi-Ren Shyu. 2000. Relevance feedback decision trees in content-based image retrieval. *Proceedings of the IEEE Workshop on Content-Based Access of Image and Video Libraries*, Hilton Head Island, SC.

Mahale, R. A. and S. D. Chavan. 2012. A survey: Evolutionary and swarm based bio-inspired optimization algorithms. *International Journal of Scientific and Research Publications*, 2(12), 1–6.

Mahdavi, M., M. Fesanghari, and E. Damangir. 2007. An improved harmony search algorithm for solving optimization problems. *Conference on Applied Mathematics and Computation*. Elsevier, Vol. 188, no. 2, pp. 1567–1579. Berlin, Heidelberg: Springer.

Mallat, S. and Z. Zhang. 1993. Matching pursuit with time-frequency dictionaries. *IEEE Transactions on Signal Processing*, 41(12), 3397–3415.

Manchanda, P., S. Gupta, and K. K. Bhatia. 2012. On the automated classification of web pages using artificial neural network. *IOSR Journal of Computer Engineering (IOSRJCE)*, 4(1), 20–25.

Manjunath, B. S. and W. Y. Ma. 1996. Texture features for Browsing and retrieval of image data. *IEEE Transactions on Pattern Analysis and Machine Intelligence*, 18(8), 837–842.

Manjunath, B. S. and W. Y. Ma. 1995. *Texture Features for Browsing and Retrieval of Image Data*. Technical Report 95-06. Univ. of California at Santa Barbara.

Manning, C. and D. Raghavan. 2008. *Introduction to Information Retrieval*. Cambridge, England: Cambridge University Press.

Marcus, A., A. Sergeyev, V. Rajlich, and J. I. Maletic. 2010. An information retrieval approach to concept location in source code. *Proceedings of the 11th working Conference on Reverse Engineering*, Beverly, MA.

Maron, E. and Melvin. 2008. An historical note on the origins of probabilistic indexing. *Journal on Information Processing and Management*, 44(2), 971–972.

Massachusetts Institute of Technology. 2005. Media Laboratory, Vistex database. http://vismod. media.mit.edu

Matthew Lease. 2008. Incorporating relevance and Psuedo-relevance feedback in the Markov random field model. *Proc. 17th Text Retrieval Conf. TREC*, Gaithersburg, MD. Volume Special Publication, pp. 500–277.

McCarthy, J. 1968. *Semantic Information Processing*. Cambridge, MA: MIT Press.

McCarthy, J. 1987. Generality in artificial intelligence. *Magazine on Communications of the ACM*, 30(12), 1030–1035.

McKenzie, B. and A. Cockburn. 2001. An empirical analysis of web page revisitation.

Mei, X. and H. Ling. 2011. Robust visual tracking and vehicle classification via sparse representation. *IEEE Transaction Pattern Analytics Mathematical Intelligence*, 33(11), 2259–2272.

Meilhac, C. 1999. Relevance feedback and category search in image databases. *IEEE International Conference on Multimedia Computing and Systems*, Florence, Italy, pp. 512–517.

Messai, N., M. D. Devignes, and A. Napoli. 2006. An FCA-based algorithm for information retrieval. *Fourth International Conference on Concept Lattices and Their Applications*, Tunis, Tunisia, pp. 1–7.

Metropolis, N., A. W. Rosenbluth, M. N. Rosenbluth, A. H. Teller, and E. Teller. 1953. Equation of state calculations by fast computing machines. *Journal of Chemical Physics*, 21, 1087–1092.

Metzer, D. A. 2007. Automatic feature selection in the markov random field model for information retrieval. *Proc. of the Sixteenth ACM Conference on Information and Knowledge Management*, Lisbon, Portugal, November 6–10, pp. 253–262. New York, NY: ACM.

Metzler, D. and W. B. Croft. 2005. A Markov random field model for term dependencies. *Proc. 28th Ann. Intl. ACM SIGIR Conf. on Research and Development in Information Retrieval*, Salvador, Brazil, August 15–19, pp. 472–479. New York, NY: ACM.

Metzler, D., Y. Bernstein, W. B. Croft, A. Moffat, and J. Zobel. 2005. Similarity measures for tracking information flow. *Proc. CIKM*, Bremen, Germany, pp. 517–524. ISBN: 1-59593-140-6.

Mitchell, M. L. 2008. Vector-based models of semantic composition. *Proc. of ACL*, Columbus, OH, pp. 236–244.

Mobasher, B., H. Dai, T. Luo, Y. Sun, and J. Zhu. 2000a. Integrating web usage and content mining for more effective personalization. *Proc. First International Conf. on Electronic Commerce and Web Technologies*. Springer-Verlag, Berlin, Germany, pp. 165–176.

Mobasher, B., R. Cooley, and J. Srivastava. 2000b. Automatic personalization based on web usage mining. *Comm. ACM*, 43(8), 142–151.

Moghaddam, H., T. Khajoie, and A. Rouhi. 2003. A new algorithm for image indexing and retrieval using wavelet correlogram. *Proceedings of the International Conference on Image Processing*, Barcelona, Spain, Vol. 3. pp. 497–500.

Mooers, C. E. 1950. Coding, information retrieval, and the rapid selector. *American Documentation*, 1(4), 225–229.

Mooney, R. J. and L. Roy. 2000. Content-based book recommending using learning for text categorization. *Proc. of the Fifth ACM Conf. on Digital Libraries*, San Antonio, TX, pp. 195–204. ISBN: 1-58113-231-X.

Morana, M., E. Ardizzone, M. L. A. Cascia, and F. Vella. 2009. Clustering techniques for photo album management. *Journal of Electronic Imaging*, 18(4), 043014–043014-12.

Mutschke, P. and P. Mayr. 2015. Science Models for Search: A Study on Combining Scholarly Information Retrieval and Scientometrics, pp. 2323–2345.

Nandy, S., P. P. Sarkar, and A. Das. 2012. Analysis of nature-inspired firefly algorithm based backpropagation neural network training. *International Journal on Computer Applications*, 43(22), 8–16.

Nguyen, G. P. and M. Worring. 2005. Relevance feedback based saliency adaptation in CBIR. *ACM Multimedia Systems*, 10(6), 499–512.

NIST. 1995. *Secure Hash Standard*. Federal Information Processing Standards Publication.

Nobuhara, H. 2007. A lattice structure visualization by formal concept analysis and its application to huge image database. *Proceedings of the IEEE/ICME International Conference on Complex Medical Engineering*, Beijing, China, pp. 448–452.

Ogle, V. E. and M. Stonebraker. 1995. Chabot: Retrieval from a relational database of images. *IEEE Computational*, 28(9), 40–48.

Okayama, M., N. Oka, and K. Kameyama. 2008. Relevance optimization in image database using feature space preference mapping and particle swarm optimization. *International Conference on Neural Inf. Process*, Auckland, New Zealand, Vol. 4985, pp. 608–617.

Ouyang, A. and Y. Tan. 2002. A novel multi-scale spatial-color descriptor for content based image retrieval. *Proceedings of the 7th International Conference on Control, Automation, Robotics and Vision*, Singapore, Vol. 3, pp. 1204–1209.

Pappas, T. N. 1992. An adaptive clustering algorithm for image segmentation. *IEEE Transactions on Signal Processing*, 40(4), 901–914.

Parsopoulos, K. E. and M. N. Vrahatis. 2002. Recent approaches to global optimization problems through particle swarm optimization. *Natural Computing*, 1(2–3), 235–306.

Pedronette, D. and R. Torres. 2012. Exploiting contextual information for image re-ranking and rank aggregation. *International Journal of Multimedia Information Retrieval*, 1, 1–14.

Pentland, A., R. Picard, and S. Sclaroff. 1997. Photobook: Content based manipulation of image databases. *International Journal of Computer Vision*, 18(3), 233–254.

Pickard, R., C. Graszyk, S. Mann, J. Wachman, L. Pickard, and L. Campbell. 1995. *VisTex databases*. Technical report. MIT Media Laboratory.

Pietra, S. D., V. D. Pietra, and J. Lafferty. 1997. Inducing features of random fields. *IEEE Transactions on Pattern Analysis and Machine Intelligence*, 19(4), 380–393.

Pighetti, R., D. Pallez, and F. Precioso. 2012. Hybrid content based image retrieval combining multi-objective interactive genetic algorithm and SVM. *International Conference on Pattern Recognition (ICPR)*, Sukuba Science City, Japan, Vol. 11, no. 15, pp. 2849–2852.

Ponte, J. M. and W. B. Croft. 1998. A language modeling approach to information retrieval. *Proceedings of the 21st Annual International ACM SIGIR Conference*, Melbourne, Australia, pp. 275–281.

Porkaew, K. and K. Chakrabarti. 1999. Query refinement for multimedia similarity retrieval in MARS. *Proceedings of the 7th ACM International Conference on Multimedia*, Orlando, FL, pp. 235–238.

Price, K. and R. Storn. 1995. *Differential evolution - a simple and efficient adaptive scheme for global optimization over continuous spaces*. Technical report. Berkley: International Computer Science Institute, pp. TR-95-012.

Price, K. and R. Storn. 1997. Differential evolution—A simple evolution strategy for fast optimization. *Dr. Dobb's Journal*, 22(4), p. 1824 and 78.

Price, K. V. 1999. *An Introduction to Differential Evolution, New Ideas in Optimization*. London: McGraw-Hill, pp. 79–108.

Priss, U. 2000. Lattice-based Information Retrieval, pp. 132–142.

Probst, K., R. Ghani, M. Krema, A. E. Fano, and Y. Liu. 2007. Semi-supervised learning of attribute value pairs from product descriptions. *IJCAI*. pp. 2838–2843.

PubMed Central Open Access Initiative 2004. https://www.ncbi.nlm.nih.gov/pmc/

Qi, X. and B. D. Davison. 2009. Web page classification: Features and algorithms. *ACM Computing. Survey*, 41(2), Article No. 12.

Qian, G., S. Sural, Y. Gu, and S. Pramanik. 2004. Similarity between Euclidean and cosine angle distance for nearest neighbour queries. *Proceedings of the ACM Symposium on Applied Computing*, Nicosia, Cyprus, Vol. 12, no. 22, pp. 1232–1237.

Qin, T., T. Y. Liu, J. Xu, and H. Li. 2010. LETOR: A benchmark collection for research on learning to rank for information retrieval. *International Conference on Information Retrieval*, Vol. 13, no. 4, pp. 346–374. Hingham, MA: Kluwer Academic Publishers.

Rahman, M. M., B. C. Desai, and P. Bhattacharya. 2006. A feature level fusion in similarity matching to content-based image retrieval. *9th International Conference on Information Fusion ICIF*, Florence, Italy, pp. 1–6.

Rahmat-Samii, Y. 2007. Modern antenna designs using nature inspired optimization techniques: Let Darwin and the bees help designing your multi band MIMO antennas. *IEEE Radio and Wireless Symposium, RWS*, Long Beach, CA, pp. 463–466.

Rampriya, B., K. Mahadevan, and S. Kannan. 2010. Unit commitment in deregulated power system using Lagrangian firefly algorithm. *IEEE International Conference on Communication Control and Computing Technologies (ICCCCT2010)*, Ramanathapuram, India, pp. 389–393.

Rao, B. D., K. Engan, S. F. Cotter, J. Palmer, and K. Kreutz-Delgado. 2003. Subset selection in noise based on diversity measure minimization. *IEEE Transaction on Signal Processing*, 51, 760–770.

Resnick, P. and H. R. Varian. 1997. Recommendation systems. *Comm. ACM*, 3, 56–58.

Resnik, P. 1995. Using information content to evaluate semantic similarity in taxonomy. *Proc. of IJCAI-95. Montreal*, Canada, pp. 448–453.

Ritchie, A., S. Robertson, and S. Teufel. 2008. Comparing citation contexts for information retrieval. *17th ACM Conference on Information and Knowledge Management*, pp. 213–222.

Robertson, S. 2008. On the history of evaluation in IR. *Journal of Information Science*, 34(4), 439–456.

Robertson, S.E. 1997. The probability ranking principle in IR, *Journal of Documentation*, 33(4), 294–304.

Robertson, S. E., C. J. Van Rijsbergen and M. F. Porter. 1980. Probabilistic models of indexing and searching. Presented at Research and development in information retrieval, Cambridge In: R. N. Oddy, S. E. Robertson, C. J. van Rijsbergen, and P. W. Williams (eds), Information retrieval research. Butterworths, 1981, pp. 35–56.

Rocchio Jr, J. J. 1971. *Relevance Feedback in Information Retrieval. The SMART Retrieval System: Experiments in Automatic Document Processing*. Englewood Cliffs: Prentice-Hall, pp. 313–323.

Roeva, O. 2012. Optimization of *E. coli* cultivation model parameters using firefly algorithm. *International Journal on Bio Automation*, 16, 23–32.

Rose, J., W. Klebsch, and J. Wolf. 1990. Temperature measurement and equilibrium dynamics of simulated annealing placement. *IEEE Transation on Computer-Aided Design of Integrated Circuits and Systems*, 9(3), 253–259.

Rosen-Zvi, M., T. Griffiths, M. Steyvers, and P. Smyth. 2004. The Author-topic Model for Authors and Documents, pp. 487–494.

Rubner, Y., C. Tomasi, and L. Guibas. 1998. A metric for distributions with applications to image databases. *Proceedings of the IEEE International Conference on Computer Vision*, Mumbai, India, pp. 59–66.

Rui, Y. and T. S. Huang. 1993. Relevance feedback: A power tool for interactive content-based image retrieval. *IEEE Transactions on Circuits and Systems for Video Technology*, 644–655.

Rui, Y., T. S. Huang, and S. Mehrotra. 1997. Content based image retrieval with relevance feedback in MARS. *Proceedings of International Conference on Image Processing*. Santa Barbara, CA, ISBN: 0-8186-8183-7.

Ruiz, R., J. S. Aguilar-Ruiz, and J. C. Riquelme. 2004. Wrapper for ranking feature selection. *Intelligent Data Engineering and Automated Learning-Lecture Notes*, 3177, 384–389.

Ruthven, I. 2003. Re-examining the potential effectiveness of interactive query expansion. *Proc. 26th Annual International ACM SIGIR Conf. on Research and Development in Information Retrieval*, Toronto, Canada, pp. 213–220. ISBN: 1-58113-646-3.

Salton, G. 1989. *Automatic Text Processing*. Boston, MA: Addison-Wesley.

Salton, G. and C. Buckley. 1988. *Term Weighting Approaches in Automatic Text Retrieval*. Information Processing and Management, pp. 513–523.

Salton, G. and M. McGill. 1983. *Introduction to Modern Information Retrieval*. McGraw-Hill Book Company.

Salton, G., A. Wong, and C. S. Yang. 1975. A vector space model for automatic indexing. *Journal on Communications of the ACM*, 18(11), 613–620.

Sami, M., N. El-Bendary, T. H. Kim, and A. E. Hassanien. 2012. *Using Particle Swarm Optimization for Image Regions Annotation. Future Generation Information Technology*, LNCS 7709. Heidelberg: Springer, pp. 241–250.

Sanderson, M. and W. B. Croft. 2012. The history of information retrieval research. *Proceedings of the IEEE International Conference*. Chicago, Vol. 100, no. 13, pp. 1444–1451.

Sankar Ganesh, S., K. Ramar, D. Manimegalai, and M. Sivakumar. 2012. Image retrieval using heuristic approach and genetic algorithm. *Journal of Computational Information Systems*, 8(4), 1563–1571.

Santos, J. A., A. T. Silva, R. S. Torres, A. X. Falcao, L. P. Malgalhaes, and R. A. C. Lamparelli. 2011. Interactive classification of remote sensing images by using optimum-path forest and genetic programming. *Lecture Notes in Computer Science*, 6855, 300–307.

Santos, J. A., C. Ferreira, and R. Torres. 2008. A genetic programming approach for relevance feedback in region-based image retrieval systems. *Brazilian Symposium on Computer Graphics and Image Processing*, pp. 155–162.

Saraç, E. and S. Ayse Ozel. 2013. Web page classification using firefly optimization. *IEEE International Symposium on Innovations in Intelligent Systems and Applications (INISTA)*, pp. 1–5.

Sari, S. and M. Adriani. 2008. Using mutual information technique in cross-language information retrieval. *Springer Link*, 5362, 276–284.

Schleimer, S., D. S. Wilkerson, and A. Aiken. 2003. Winnowing: Local algorithms for document fingerprinting. *Proc. ACM SIGMOD Intl. Conf. on Management of Data*, San Diego, CA, pp. 76–85.

Selim, S. Z. and M. A. Ismail. 1984. K-means type algorithms: A generalized convergence theorem and characterization of local optimality. *IEEE Transaction on Pattern Anal. Mach. Intell.*, 6, 81–87.

Senthilnath, J., S. N. Omkar, and V. Mani. 2011. Clustering using firefly algorithm: Performance study. *Swarm and Evolutionary Computation*, 1(3), 164–171.

Seo, K. K. 2007. Content-based image retrieval by combining genetic algorithm and support vector machine. *International Conference on Artificial Neural Network – ICANN.LNCS 4669*, Berlin, Heidelberg, pp. 537–545.

Shafiee, S., F. Kamangar, V. Athitsos, J. Huang, and L. S. Ghandehari. 2014a. Multimodal sparse representation classification with fisher discriminative sample reduction. *Proceedings of the IEEE International Conference on Image Processing (ICIP)*, Paris, France, pp. 5192–5196.

Shafiee, S., F. Kamangar, and L. Sh Ghandehari. 2014b. Cluster based multi-task sparse representation for efficient face recognition. *IEEE Southwest Symposium on Image Analysis and Interpretation*, pp. 125–128.

Shapiro, L. G. and G. C. Stockman. 2001. *Computer Vision*. New Jersey: Prentice-Hall, pp. 279–325.

Shareghi, E. and L. S. Hassanabadi. 2008. Text summarization with harmony search algorithm-based sentence extraction. *Proc. of the 5th International Conference on Soft Computing as Trans Disciplinary Science and Technology*, Cergy-Pontoise, France, pp. 226–231. ISBN: 978-1-60558-046-3, New York, NY:ACM.

Shen, X., B. Tan, and C. Zhai. 2005. Implicit user modeling for personalized search. *Proc. 14th ACM International Conf. on Information and Knowledge Management*, Bremen, Germany, pp. 824–831. ISBN: 1-59593-140-6.

Sheng, L., L. J. Hua, and L. Hui. 2007. Image retrieval technology of Multi-MPEG-7 features based on genetic algorithm. *Proceedings of the International Conference on Machine Learning and Cybernetics*, Hong Kong, China, Vol. 6, pp. 19–22.

Shi, J. and J. Malik. 2000. Normalized cuts and image segmentation. *IEEE Transactions on Pattern Analysis and Machine Intelligence*, 22(8), 888–905.

Shi, S., J. Z. Li, and L. Lin. 2007. Face image retrieval method based on improved IGA and SVM. *Proceedings of the ICIC, LNCS*, Qingdao, China, Vol. 4681, pp. 767–774.

Shi, Y. and R. Eberhart. 1998. Modified particle swarm optimizer. *Proceedings of the IEEE International Conference on Evolutionary Computation ICEC'98*, Anchorage, AK, pp. 69–73.

Shrivakumar, N. and H. Garcia-Molina. 1998. Finding near-replicas of documents on the Web. *Proc. Workshop on Web Databases WebDB 98*, Valencia, Spain, pp. 204–212.

Shulman, S. W. 2005. E-rulemaking: Issues in current research and practice. *International Journal of Public Administration*, 28, 621–641.

Shyu, M., S. C. Chen, M. Chen, C. Zhang, and K. Sarinnapakorn. 2003. Image database retrieval utilizing affinity relationships. *Proceedings of the 1st ACM International Workshop on Multimedia Databases*, New Orleans, LA, pp. 78–85.

Silva, A. T., J. A. Santos, A. X. Falcao, R. S. Torres, and L. P. Malgalhaes. 2012. Incorporating multiple distance spaces in optimum-path forest classification to improve feedback-based learning. *Computer Vision and Image Understanding*, 116(4), 510–523.

Silva, A. T., A. X. Falcao, and L. P. Magalhaes. 2010. A new CBIR approach based on relevance feedback and optimum path forest classification. *Journal of WSCG*, 18(1–3), 73–80.

Silva, S. F., M. A. Batista, and C. A. Z. Barcelos. 2007. Adaptive Image Retrieval through the use of a Genetic Algorithm. *International Conference on Tools with Artificial Intelligence—ICTAI*, Patras, Greece, Vol. 1, pp. 557–564.

Simon, I., N. Snavely, and S. Seitz. 2007. Scene summarization for online image collections. *Proceedings of the International Conference on Computer Vision ICCV*, Rio de Janeiro, Brazil, pp. 1–8.

Singhal, A., C. Buckley, and M. Mitra. 1996. Pivoted document length normalization. *Proc of the 19th Annual International ACM SIGIR Conference on Research and Development in Information Retrieval*, Zurich, Switzerland, pp. 21–29.

Singhal, A. 2001. Modern Information Retrieval: A Brief Overview, pp. 35–43.

Sinha, P. 2011. Summarization of archived and shared personal photo collections. *20th International World Wide Web Conference*, Hyderabad, India, pp. 421–425.

Sivic, J. and A. Zisserman. 2003. Video Google: A text retrieval approach to object matching in videos. *Proceedings of the Ninth IEEE International Conference on Computer Vision*, Nice, France, Vol. 2, pp. 1470–1477.

Smeulders, A. W. M., M. Worring, S. Santini, A. Gupta, and R. Jain. 2000. Content-based image retrieval at the end of the early years. *IEEE Transaction on Pattern Analytics Mathematical Intelligence*, 22(1), 1349–1380.

Smit, S. F. C. Jr. 1996. A fully automated content-based image query system. *Proc. ACM Multimedia Conference*, Boston, MA, pp. 87–98.

Smith, J. and S. Chang. 1996. Visualseek: A Fully Automated Content-Based Image Query System. *Proceedings of the 4th ACM International Conference on Multimedia Table of Contents.* Boston, MA, pp. 87–98.

Smith, J. R. and S. F. Chang. 1997. Querying by Color Region using the Visual SEEK Content Based Visual Query System. *Intelligent Multimedia Information Retrieval*, pp. 23–41.

Spink, A. 1994. Term relevance feedback and query expansion: Relation to design. *Proc. 17th Annual International ACM SIGIR Conf. on Research and Development in Information Retrieval*, Dublin, Ireland, pp. 81–90.

Spink, A., D. Wolfram, B. J. Major, and S. T. Jansen. 2001. Searching the web: The public and their queries. *Journal of the American Society for Information Science and Technology*, 52(3), 226–234.

Stejic, Z., Y. Takama, and K. Hirota. 2003. Relevance feedback based image retrieval interface incorporating region and feature saliency patterns as visualizable image similarity criteria. *IEEE Transactions on Industrial Electronics*, 50(5), 839–852.

Stejic, Z., Y. Takama, and K. Hirota. 2003a. Genetic algorithms for a family of image similarity models incorporated in the relevance feedback mechanism. *Appl. Soft Computing*, 2(4), 306–327.

Stejic, Z., Y. Takama, and K. Hirota. 2003b. Genetic algorithm-based relevance feedback for image retrieval using Local Similarity Patterns. *International Conference on Information Process Management*, Vol. 39, no. 1, pp. 1–23.

Stejic, Z., Y. Takama, and K. Hirota. 2005. Mathematical aggregation operators in image retrieval: Effect on retrieval performance and role in relevance feedback. *Signal Processing*, 85(2), 297–324.

Stejic, Z., Y. Takama, and K. Hirota. 2007. Variants of evolutionary learning for interactive image retrieval. *Soft Computing – SOCO*, 11(7), 669–678.

Stricker, M. A. and M. Orengo. 1995. Similarity of Color Images in Storage and Retrieval for Image and Video Databases (SPIE), pp. 381–392.

Strohman, T., D. Metzler, H. Turtle, and W. B. Croft. 2005. Indri: A language model-based search engine for complex queries. *Proc. of the International Conference on Intelligent Analysis*, McLean, VA.

Sudheer, C. H., S. K. Sohani, D. Kumar, A. Malik, B. R. Chahar, A. K. Nema, B. K. Panigrahi, and R. C. Dhiman. 2014. A Support Vector Machine-Firefly Algorithm based forecasting model to determine malaria transmission. *International Conference on Neuro Computing*, Amsterdam, The Netherlands, Vol. 129, pp. 279–288.

Sumita, K., S. Miike, K. Ono, and T. Chino. 2007. Automatic abstract generation based on document structure analysis and its evaluation as a document retrieval presentation function. *Journal of Systems and Computers in Japan*, 13, 32–43.

Susan Dumais, T. 1994. Latent semantic indexing LSI and TREC-2. In: Harman D. ed. *The 2nd Text Retrieval Conference TREC-2*, Gaithersburg, MD. National Institute of Standards and Technology Special Publication 500-215, pp. 105–116.

Swain, M. and D. Ballard. 1991. Color indexing. *International Journal of Computer Vision*, 7(1), 11–32.

Takagi, H., S. B. Cho, and T. Noda. 1999. Evaluation of an IGA-based image retrieval system using wavelet coefficients. *Proceedings of the IEEE International Conference on Fuzzy System*, Seoul, South Korea, Vol. 3, pp. 1775–1780.

Tan, P. N., M. Steinbach, and V. Kumar. 2005. Introduction to data mining book, Chapter 8. In: *Cluster Analysis: Basic Concepts and Algorithms*, 1st Ed. Pearson-Addison Wesley Higher Education Publishers, pp. 532–568.

Tang, B., X. Luo, M. I. Heywood, and M. Shepherd. 2004. *A Comparative Study of Dimension Reduction Techniques for Document Clustering. TR # CS-2004-14. Faculty of Computer Science*, Dalhousie University. DOI: 10.1109/IJCNN.2011.6033447.

Tao, T. and C. X. Zhai. 2006. Regularized estimation of mixture models for robust pseudo-relevance feedback. *Proc. 29th Annual International ACM SIGIR Conf. on Research and Development in Information Retrieval*, Seattle, WA, pp. 162–169.

Tao, D. and X. Tang. 2004. Nonparametric discriminant analysis in relevance feedback for content-based image retrieval. *Proc. IEEE Int'l Conf. Pattern Recognition*, Cambridge, UK, Vol. 2, pp. 1013–1016.

Tao, D. et al. 2007. Asymmetric bagging and random subspace for support vector machines-based relevance feedback in image retrieval. *IEEE Transaction on Pattern Analytics Machine Intelligence*, 28(7), 1088–1099.

Thathachar, M. A. L. and R. Harita Bhaskar. 1987. Learning automata with changing number of actions. *IEEE Transactions on Systems Man and Cybernetics*, 17(6), 1095–1100.

Tieu, K. and P. Viola. 2000. Boosting image retrieval. *Proceedings of the IEEE Conf. Computer Vision and Pattern Recognition*, Hilton Head Island, SC, Vol. 1, pp. 228–235.

Tong, S. and E. Chang. 2001. Support vector machine active leaning for image retrieval. *Proceedings of the 9th ACM Conference on Multimedia*, Ottawa, Canada, pp. 107–118.

Torres, R. S. et al. 2009. A genetic programming framework for content-based image retrieval. *Pattern Recognition*, 42(2), 283–292.

Toutanova, K. and D. Klein. 2013. Stanford Core NLP. http://nlp.stanford.edu/software/corenlp.html

The TREC. 2006. Information Technology Laboratory's (ITL) Retrieval Group of the Information Access Division and the Advanced Research and Development Activity of the U.S. Department of Defense. http://trec.nist.gov, 2006. http://trec.nist.gov/data/t9_filtering/oshu-trec.tar.gz

Tropp, J. A. 2004. Greed is good: Algorithmic results for sparse approximation. *IEEE Transaction on Inference Theory*, 50, 2231–2242.

Tseng, V. S., J. H. Su, B. W. Wang, and Y. M. Lin. 2007. Web image annotation by fusing visual features and textual information. *Proceedings of the 22nd ACM Symp. on Applied Computing*, Seoul, South Korea, pp. 1056–1060.

Tseng, V. S., J. H. Su, J. H. Huang, and C. J. Chen. 2008. Integrated mining of visual features, speech features and frequent patterns for semantic video annotation. *IEEE Transaction on Multimedia*, 10(2), 260–267.

Turpin, A. and F. Scholer. 2006. User performance versus precision measures for simple search tasks. *SIGIR Conference on Research and Development in Information Retrieval*, pp. 11–18.

University of Washington database. 2011. http://www.cs.washington.edu/research/imagedatabase/groundtruth

Van Leuken, R. H., L. Garcia, X. Olivares, and R. van Zwol. 2009. Visual diversification of image search results, pp. 341–350.

Vapnik, V. N. 1995. *The Nature of Statistical Learning Theory*. New York: Springer-Verlag.

Vapnik, V. N. 1998. *Statistical Learning Theory*. New York. ISBN: 978-0-471-03003-4.

Vasconcelos, N. and A. Lippman. 1999. Learning from user feedback in image retrieval systems. *Advances in Neural Information Processing Systems*, pp. 977–983.

Voorhees, E. and M. D. Harman. 2005. *TREC: Experiment and Evaluation in Information Retrieval*. Cambridge: MIT Press. ISBN: 0262220733.

Voorhees, E. M. 2007. TREC: Continuing information retrieval's tradition of experimentation. *Magazine on Communications of the ACM*, 50(11), 51–54.

Vossen, P. 2001. Extending, trimming and fussing word net for technical documents. *NAACL Workshop and Other Lexical Resources*, East Stroudsburg.

Wang, C. D. and M. Blei. 2011. Collaborative topic modeling for recommending scientific arti-
     cles. *17th ACM SIGKDD International on Conference on Knowledge Discovery and Data Mining*,
     pp. 448–456.
Wang, J. 2004. *Research Group, Corel Database*. Corel Corporation, Corel Gallery. http://wang.ist.psu.edu
Wang, J., J. Li, and G. Wiederhold. 2001. SIMPLIcity: Semantics-sensitive integrated matching for
     picture libraries. *IEEE Transaction on Pattern Analytics machine Intelligence*, 23(9), 947–963.
Wang, J., L. Jia, and X. Hua. 2011. Interactive browsing via diversified visual summarization for
     image search results. *Multimedia Systems*, 17(5), 379–391.
Wang, S. F., X. F. Wang, and J. Xue. 2005. An improved interactive genetic algorithm incorporating
     relevant feedback. *Proceedings of the International Conference Machine Learning and Cybernetics*,
     Guangzhou, China, Vol. 5. pp. 2996–3001.
Wei, X. W. and B. Croft. 2006. LDA-based document models for adhoc retrieval. *SIGIR Conference on
     Research and Development in Information*, pp. 178–185.
Wille, R. 1992. Concept lattices and conceptual knowledge systems. *Journal on Computer and
     Mathematics with Application*, 23(6–9), 493–515.
Wiratunga, N., I. Koychev, and S. Massie. 2004. Feature selection and generalisation for retrieval of
     textual cases. *Proc. 7th European Conference on Case-Based Reasoning*, Madrid, Spain: Springer,
     Vol. 3155, pp. 806–820.
Witten, I. H., F. Azuaje, and E. Frank. 2005. *Data Mining: Practical Machine Learning Tools and Techniques*.
     Morgan Kaufmann: San Francisco.
Wolfram, D. 2003. *Applied Informetrics for Information Retrieval Research*. Libraries Unlimited.
Wright, J., A. Y. Yang, A. Ganesh, S. S. Sastry, and Y. Ma. 2009. Robust face recognition via sparse
     representation. *IEEE Transactions on Pattern Analysis and Machine Intelligence*, 31(2), 210–227.
Wu, K., K. H. Yap, and L. P. Chau. 2006. Region-based image retrieval using radial basis function net-
     work. *Proceedings of the IEEE International Conference on Multimedia and Expo*, Toronto, Canada,
     pp. 1777–1780.
Wu, Y. and A. Zhang. 2002. A feature re-weighing approach for relevance feedback in image retrieval.
     Proceedings of the IEEE Int. Conf. Image Processing (ICIP2002), Rochester, NY, Vol. 2. pp. 581–584.
Wu, Y., Q. Tian, and T. S. Huang. 2000. Discriminant-EM algorithm with application to image
     retrieval. *Proceedings of the IEEE Conference Computer Vision and Pattern Recognition*, Hilton
     Head Island, SC, Vol. 1. pp. 222–227.
Wu, Z. and M. Palmer. 1994. Verb semantics and lexical selection. *32nd Annual Meeting on Association
     for Computational Linguistics*, pp. 133–138.
Xu, J. and W. B. Croft. 2000. Improving the effectiveness of information retrieval systems with local
     context analysis. *ACM Transactions on Information Systems*, 18(1), 79–112.
Xue, B. 2012. Particle swarm optimization for feature selection in classification: A multi-objective
     approach. *IEEE Transactions on Cybernetics*, 43(6), 2168–2267.
Xue, B., M. Zhang, and W. N. Browne. 2013. Particle swarm optimization for feature selection in clas-
     sification: A multi-objective approach, IEEE Trans. *Cybern*, 43(6), 1656–1671.
Yang, C., J. Shen, J. Peng, and J. Fan. 2012. Image collection summarization via dictionary learning
     for sparse representation. *Pattern Recognition*, 46, 948–961.
Yang, X. S. 2008. *Nature-Inspired Metaheuristic Algorithms*. UK: Luniver Press.
Yang, X. S. 2009. Firefly algorithms for multimodal optimization. In: *Stochastic Algorithms Foundations
     and Applications*. Lecture Notes in Computer Sciences, Vol. 5792, pp. 169–178.
Yang, X. S. 2010. *Engineering Optimization: An Introduction with Metaheuristic Applications*. EBook,
     p. 347.
Yang, X. S. 2010. *Engineering Optimization: An Introduction with Metaheuristic Applications*. John Wiley
     and Sons, Inc, pp. 221–229.
Yang, X. S. 2010. Firefly algorithm stochastic test functions and design optimization. *International
     Journal Bio-Inspired Computation*, 2(2), 78–84.
Yang, X. S. 2011. Chaos-enhanced firefly algorithm with automatic parameter tuning. *International
     Journal on Swarm Intelligence Research*, 2(4), 1–11.

Yang, X. S. 2012. Swarm-based metaheuristic algorithms and no-free-lunch theorems. *International Conference on Theory and New Applications of Swarm Intelligence*, Brussels, Belgium, pp. 1–16.

Yang, X. S. 2013. Multi objective firefly algorithm for continuous optimization. *Engineering with Computers*, 29(2), 175–184.

Yazdani, M. and R. Meybodi. 2010. AFSA-LA A new model for optimization. *Proceedings of the 15th Annual CSI Computer Conference (CSICC'10)*, Tehran, Iran, pp. 1–8.

Yee, K. P., K. Swearingen, K. Li, and M. Hearst. 2003. Faceted metadata for image search and browsing, In Proc. *of SIGCHI Conference on Human Factors in Computing Systems, Florida*, pp. 401–408, ISBN: 1-58113-630-7.

Younsi, R. and W. Wang. 2004. *A New Artificial Immune System Algorithm for Clustering*, Vol. 3177. Berlin: Springer, pp. 58–64.

Yu, H., M. Li, H. Zhang, and J. Feng. 2002. Color texture moments for content-based image retrieval. *Proceedings of the International Conference on Image Processing*, Rochester, NY, Vol. 3. pp. 929–932.

Yuan, P., C. Ji, Y. Zhang, and Y. Wang. 2004. Optimal multicast routing in wireless ad hoc sensor networks. *Proceedings of the IEEE International Conference on Networking Sensing and Controls*, Taipei, Taiwan, Vol. 1. pp. 367–371.

Yuan, X. T., X. Liu, and S. Yan. 2012. Visual classification with multitask joint sparse representation. *IEEE Transactions on Image Processing (TIP)*, 21(10), 4349–4360.

Zaman, M. A. and M. A. Matin. 2012. Non-uniformly spaced linear antenna array design using firefly algorithm. *International Journal on Microwave Science and Technology*, 1–8.

Zhai, C. and J. Lafferty. 2001. Model-based Feedback in the Language Modeling approach to Information Retrieval. *Proc. Thirteenth International Conf. on Information and Knowledge Management*, pp. 403–410.

Zhai, C. and J. Lafferty. 2002. Two- stage language models for information retrieval. *SIGIR Conference on Research and Development in Information*, Atlanta, GA, pp. 49–56.

Zhang, B., H. Li, Y. Liu, L. Ji, W. Xi, W. Fan, Z. Chen, and W. Y. Ma. Improving web search results using affinity graph. *In: SIGIR*, pp. 504–511.

Zhang, C. and X. Chen. 2007. OCRS: An interactive object-based image clustering and retrieval system'. *Multimedia Tools and Applications - MTA*, 35(1), 71–89.

Zhang, D. and F. Nunamaker Jay. 2004. A natural language approach to content based video indexing and retrieval for interactive e-learning. *IEEE Transactions on Multimedia*, 6(3), 1520–9210.

Zhang, H., Y. Zhang, N. M. Nasrabadi, and T. S. Huang. 2012. Joint structured-sparsity-based classification for multiple-measurement transient acoustic signals. *IEEE Trans. Syst., Man, Cybern.*, 42(6), 1586–1598.

Zhang, L., F. Lin, and B. Zhang. 2011. Support vector machine learning for image retrieval. *Proceedings of the IEEE Conference on Image Processing*, Thessaloniki, Greece, pp. 721–724.

Zhang, X., B. L. Guo, G. Zhang, and Y. Yan. 2011. An image retrieval method based on r/KPSO. *Proceedings of the IEEE Second International Conference on Innovations in Bio-Inspired Computing and Applications*, Shenzhan, China, pp. 69–72.

Zhang, Y. and L. Wu. 2012. A Novel method for rigid image registration based on Firefly Algorithm. *International Journal of Research and Reviews in Soft and Intelligent Computing (IJRRSIC)*, 2(2), 141–146.

Zhang, Y. and L. Wu. 2012. *Rigid Image Registration by PSOSQP Algorithm Advances in Digital Multimedia*, Vol. 1. pp. 4–8.

Zhao, S., M. Zhou, and T. Liu. 2007. Learning question paraphrases for QA from Encarta Logs. *Proc of the 20th International Joint Conference on Artificial Intelligence*, Hyderabad, India, pp. 1795–1801.

Zhao, Y. and G. Karypis. 2004. Empirical and theoretical comparisons of selected criterion functions for document clustering. *Machine Learning*, 55(3), 311–331.

Zhou, X. and T. Huang. 2001. Small sample learning during multimedia retrieval using biasmap. *Proceedings of the IEEE International Conference on Computer Vision and Pattern Recognition*, Kauai, HI, Vol. 1. pp. 11–17.

Zhou, X. S. and T. S. Huang. 2003. Relevance feedback for image retrieval: A comprehensive review. *International Conference on Multimedia System*, Berlin, Heidelberg, Vol. 8. no. 6. pp. 536–544.

Index

A

Absorbed random walk, 167
Abstract generation, 123–124
Accuracy, 40–41
Answer justify problem, 215
Answer understanding problem, 215
Asker satisfaction Problem, 214
Asker taste, 215
ASPDD (All Pairs Shortest Path based Duplicate
    Detection), 206–207
Association Rule Mining, 185
Asymmetry Replica, 206
Automatic Facet Generation Framework
    (AFGF), 200–202
Automatic ranking based on generalization
    method, 216

B

Bag-of-features approach, 162–163
Bag-of-words approach, 198
Baseline Approach, 198
Binary Independence Retrieval, 32–33
Blog Search, 8
Boolean Model, 27
Breakeven Point, 45

C

Caltech database classes, 133
Case Based Reasoning, 48
CFB (Cluster Feedback), 120
Cohen's kappa, 211
Cohesion, 107
Collaborative Filtering (CF), 186
Community question answering, 213
Conceptual Search, 23–26
Content-Based Filtering, 81
Content Based Image Retrieval (CBIR), 62–63,
    69–73, 139, 235
Context search, 19–23
Conventional IR Systems, 173
Cooling schedule, 92
Corel image database, 131–132
Correlationcoefficient, 174
Cosine similarity, 28–29, 106
Crawler, 20
Cut segmentation algorithm, 144

D

Data retrieval, 12
Dice Coefficient, 29
Differential Evolution, 55
Digital Syntactic Clustering (DSC), 207–208
Dimensionality reduction, 101–103
Discrete Random Variables, 176
Document Ranking, 59–60
Document Retrieval, 65–66
Duplication Detection Techniques, 205–210
Dynamic programming, 177, 209–210

E

Evaluation Metrics, 221
Evolutionary Algorithms, 51–56, 125
Evolutionary computation, 49–50
Evolutionary Programming, 48–49
Evolutionary Search, 4–5
Expectation Maximization (EM) Algorithm, 174
Expert search, 6

F

F-measure, 41, 94, 221
Facet Generation, 83–84, 200
Fall out, 178
Feature Selection Approach, 66–67
Federated search, 8
Feedback Language Model, 199–200
Firefly algorithm, 51–52, 130–131, 147, 157
Fitness function, 92
Fleiss' kappa Measure, 203
Fowlkes–Mallows index, 41
Full Dependence (FD), 175
Full fingerprinting, 207
Full Independence (FI), 175

G

G-measure, 41–42
Gaussian distribution, 147
Gaussian firefly algorithm, 148–149, 246
Generalization Techniques, 180
Genetic Algorithms, 52–53, 55
Genetic programming, 53
Greedy Algorithm, 198–199

H

Harmony Search Algorithm (HSA), 113
Harmony Search (HS), 55, 113, 114–115
Harmony Memory Considering Rate
       (HMCR), 55
Harmony Memory initialization, 115
Harmony Memory(HM), 115
Harmony-TABU Algorithm, 116–117
Heterogeneous image databases, 147–148
Heuristics, 47–48
Heuristic Goodness Measure, 176
Human visual system, 143
Hybridization, 116
Hybrid PSO+K-Means Algorithm, 106

I

IIT(I-Match), 208
Image clusters, 144
Image database, 139
Image retrieval, 144–146, 235
Image Similarity Computation, 143
Image summarization, 75–80
Indexer, 20
Indri Method, 222
Information Extraction, 6, 12
Information filtering, 5
Information Retrieval, 11
Inverse document frequency, 30, 65, 77
Interactive Query Expansion (IQE), 118

J

Jaccard Measure, 207
Jaccard Similarity Co-efficient, 200

K

K-gram, 208
K-L divergence, 36
K-means algorithm, 93
K-means with Simulated Annealing
       (KSA), 94
K-means with TS (KTS), 94
KL Divergence, 197
Knapsack Problem, 174

L

Language Model, 33–38
Latent Semantic Indexing (LSI), 99, 101,
       113–114

Learning Automata (LA), 186–187, 218
Lemmatization, 14–15
Light absorption coefficient, 131
Linguistic methods, 24
Local Similarity Pattern (LSP), 143, 148
Lucene ranking, 222–223

M

Magnitude feedback, 16
Markov Random Field Model (MRF), 174,
       175, 224
Mean Average Precision, 45
Meta-heuristic algorithm, 52
Miss Rate, 43
Moment Correlation Coefficient, 174
MSE (Mean Square Error), 168–169
Multimodal image summarization,
       161–169
Multimodal vector, 163
Multinomial distributions model, 34–35
Multiplicative algorithm, 166
Music Information Retrieval, 7
Mutual Information (MI), 223

N

N-Gram Generation, 180
Navigational Behavior, 185
Non-Identifiable Parameters, 173
Non-Negative Potential Function, 175
Normalized Discount Cumulative Gain, 174,
       180, 232
NP-hard problem, 165

O

Okapi BM25, 225
Ontology Repository, 21
Ontology, 23–24
Optimization function, 162
Optimization Problems, 47–48
Optimal Substructure, 180
Optimized Iterative Learning Approach, 143

P

Partial Replica, 206
Pascal databases, 236–237
Particle Swarm Optimization (PSO) Algorithm,
       52, 99–111, 103–104, 153, 231
Path Probabilities, 186–187

Pearson's Correlation, 174
Phrase Detection, 14
Pitch Adjusting Rate (PAR), 55, 115
Polysemy, 19, 103
PR–Curves, 44
Precision, 39–40, 43–44, 194, 245
Prevalence, 42
Probabilistic Models, 31–33
Probabilistic Ranking Principle, 31–32

Q

Query expansion, 15, 82, 118–120
Query likelihood model, 35–36
Query point movement (QPM), 156–157
Query processing, 15

R

R-Precision, 44–45
Ranked Retrieval System, 39–43
Recall, 40, 43–44, 94, 159, 237–241
Recommender systems, 6
Reduce Training Efficiency, 173
Region and Feature Saliency Pattern
        (RFSP), 143
Region Based Image Retrieval, 63–64, 73–75,
        143–149, 151–152
Relevance feedback, 60–64, 118–120
Relevant and Irrelevant Classes, 176
Rewarding factor, 218
ROC Curve, 46

S

Sequential Dependence (SD), 175
Shannon entropy, 107
Shingling Techniques, 206, 207–208
Significant Degradation, 181
Similarity Measures, 28–29, 207
Simulated Annealing (SA), 54, 91–92, 99–111
Sparse coding algorithms, 79, 166
Sparse coefficient matrix, 164–165
Stochastic component, 143
Stochastic Firefly (SF) Algorithm, 127–129,
        137–139, 146–147, 157
Support Vector Machines (SVM), 155–157, 237

Synonymy, 61, 103
Symmetric Replica, 206

T

TABU Annealing Algorithm, 93–94
Tabulated Search, 56
TCFB (Term-cluster Feedback), 120
Term-frequency, 30, 65
Term relevance feedback, 16
Term weighting, 15, 64–65
Text clustering, 6
Text preprocessing, 100–101
Tf-idf, 30–31
TFB (Direct Term Feedback), 119–120
Transition Probability Matrix, 186
Translation Model, 36–37

U

Uncertainty Coefficient, 176
Unigram model, 34
Universal codebook, 168
Unranked Retrieval System, 39–43

V

Vector Model, 28–29
Vector space model, 28, 221
Visual Signature, 129

W

Web Based Recommendation System, 80–81,
        185–196
Web Page Classification, 81–83
Web Search, 4
Weighted Association (WA), 185, 187
Weight calculation Method, 224
Weighted Euclidean distance, 235
Winnowing, 208
Word-Net, 20, 197, 232
Word-Overlap Approach, 207

Z

0 mod p Method, 211